BODY POLITICS

POLITICS & CULTURE

Avery Gordon and Michael Ryan, *editors*

Politics and Culture is a serial publication that will publish material from a diverse number of disciplinary perspectives, from literature to law, from anthropology to political science, from cultural studies to sociology. The serial is concerned with the political significance of cultural forms and practices as well as with the cultural character of social institutions and political formations.

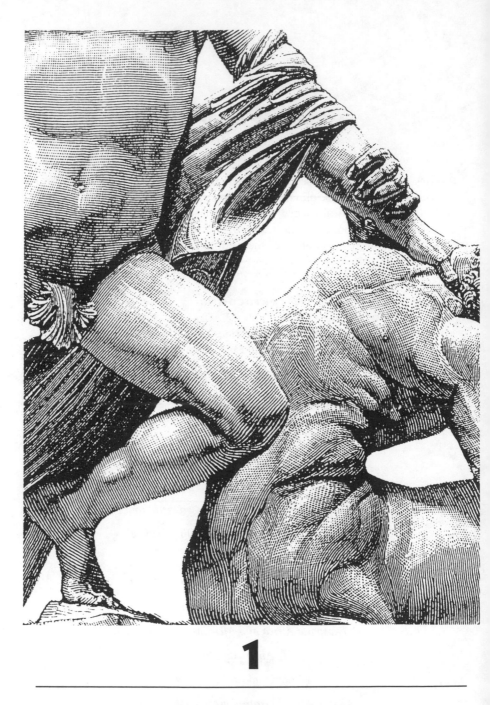

1

POLITICS AND CULTURE

BODY POLITICS

Disease, Desire, and the Family

edited by
MICHAEL RYAN &
AVERY GORDON

WESTVIEW PRESS

Boulder • San Francisco • Oxford

Politics and Culture 1

Copyright © 1994 by Westview Press, Inc., except Chapter 1 (© Henry Abelove) and Chapter 20 (© Michael Ryan)

Published in 1994 in the United States of America by Westview Press, Inc., 5500 Central Avenue, Boulder, Colorado 80301-2877, and in the United Kingdom by Westview Press, 36 Lonsdale Road, Summertown, Oxford OX2 7EW

Library of Congress Cataloging-in-Publication Data
Body politics : disease, desire, and the family / edited by Michael
    Ryan and Avery Gordon.
        p.   cm. — (Politics and culture ; 1)
    Includes index.
    ISBN 0-8133-1840-8 — ISBN 0-8133-1841-6 (pbk.)
    1. Politics and culture.   2. Sex role—Political aspects.   3. Mind
and body—Political aspects.   4. Emotions.   5. Postmodernism.
I. Ryan, Michael, 1951–   .   II. Gordon, Avery.   III. Series.
JA75.7.B63   1994
306.2—dc20   93-7934
                                                                                                         CIP

Printed and bound in the United States of America

∞   The paper used in this publication meets the requirements
      of the American National Standard for Permanence of Paper
      for Printed Library Materials Z39.48-1984.

10   9   8   7   6   5   4   3   2   1

To the memory of
Denise Carty-Bennia
Mary Jo Frug
Franticek Galan
Craig Owens

Contents

PART THREE
POLITICAL BODIES

PART FOUR
TORTURE, KNOWLEDGE, AND THE STATE

PART FIVE
ALTERNITIES

Introduction

MICHAEL RYAN

OUR CULTURE—our very white, very male, and very heterosexual culture—teaches us to ignore bodies. It does so because it fears the implications of attending to body politics.

The heterosexual white males who largely shape and run our world don't like bodies. They prefer the abstractions of moral mythography, which transform people and things like welfare mothers, communism, Saddam Hussein, gays and lesbians, homelessness, economic inequality, and the like into allegorical figures like "Evil," "Individual Responsibility," and "Political Correctness." Those people and things are thereby denied the complex modes of representation they deserve, modes that elude moral allegorization. Moral allegorization is especially difficult when one is connected bodily to the people and things one represents. Would we so easily have chanted mass slogans of patriotic hysteria if we were obliged to meet the parents and widows of the 150,000 men killed in Iraq? If we had to help dig their graves?

The heterosexual white males don't like the political complications that result when you think about people and things in terms of your own material connections to them or in terms of their own material connectedness to each other. Such connections run counter to the imperatives of their own psychosexual makeup, which disconnects out of a fear of relational loss, a horror of dirt, a desire for phallic control, a hysteria verging on violence that is the essence of the competition for power, and a perversion that over time becomes confused with an acceptable normality. That perversion of disconnectedness translates those imperatives into social rules and hierarchies that assure the power and survival of these men by sanitizing the world of its bodily character. The painful anguish of hunger and homelessness becomes the superiority of freedom to community; the mean-spirited subordination of one to another becomes the triumph of efficiency; and the violence of regimented inequality becomes the embodiment of rationality. Such reasonable disconnection banishes to the realm of sentimentality all those bodily emotions that might undo the rigorous reasons that serve as alibis for systemic murder. And these men do indeed tend to kill any-body that gets in the way of the abstract machinery, any-body who insists on the priority of bodies—of such things as hunger, homelessness, plague, and torture—to the hetero-male ideals of freedom, domesticity, efficiency, national security, and the like.

These men react so violently to the world of matter in part because they are afraid of the involuntary movements to which their own bodies are prone, movements of panic, hysteria, and excretion that are not subject to regimentation, to the policing that assures the dignity and the position of the great white male in relation to all the endangering margins—women, nonwhites, gays and lesbians, anticapitalists, and the like—that threaten his power and his identity. It's hard to know which came first—the abstraction from bodies that grounds the power of these men or the various domestic, national, cultural, and economic institutions that promote and enforce the process of abstraction on which they thrive. We may never know. But neither should we much care. We have a far more important matter to attend to: dismantling the world these men have built for themselves. This book is an effort in that direction.

The matters addressed in the following pages are ones preferably ignored or rendered abstract by big-boy culture—the plague of AIDS, the extermination of 150,000 young Iraqi men for the sake of proving George Bush's phallicity, the concentrationing of women in families, the radical contradiction of home-owning ideology and the social pathology of homelessness, the comic dysfunction-ality of drunks declaring war on drugs, the torture and mutilation of the body of dissent, the banal violence of chauvinist ethnic identity, and so on. … But we address as well the tremendous creative potential of all of us who labor that threatens to elude and undo the power of capital, the ultimate artifice of matter itself—the cyborg in all of us—that so frightens the big boys, and the threat of constitutional revision, the possibility that we might all—all of us this time—start over again from scratch and rewrite our world.

We assume that a first step in any revision of the world these men have created is to materialize oneself. Self-materialization desanitizes the abstractions of power. It leads necessarily to a sense of dispossession, an abandonment of the safe havens of abstraction. Lost most notably are control and distance, a sense of safe separation from the varieties of bodily pain, violence, and hysteria that are the causes and the consequences of hetero-male power.

To read with us requires that you disengage yourself from certain distancing procedures. You must agree to move and be moved, to depart from whatever place you now occupy and to undertake an emotional as much as an intellectual journey. Form a connection to certain kinds of bodily pain, from homelessness and alcoholism to torture and disappearance.

There are a lot of good ideas to be found here, but we would also like you to take away a sense that what you do with your own life and your own body matters as much as any good thinking you might encounter here. In addition to reflecting on what we have to say, we ask you to extend this book into the world, connect it with other physical realities and other material things. Other, if you will, body politics. The form of such extra-textual connection is necessarily active rather than simply cognitive. It can consist of donating money to AIDS research or giving a speech at a demonstration the next time the big boys murder in your name. And while doing whatever you do, let your mind explore the possibility that sometime, somewhere, a world might exist where you wouldn't have to. Then you will have entered the realm into which we wish to invite you.

Welcome to *Body Politics*.

PART ONE

DISEASE, WAR, & THE FAMILY

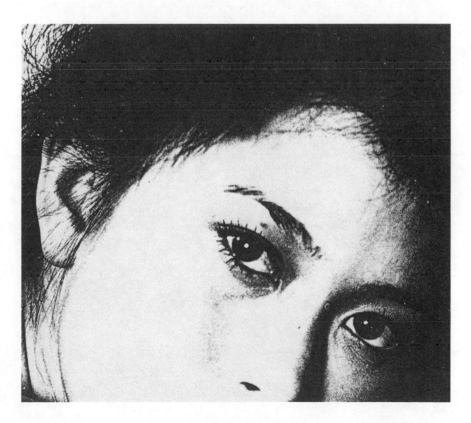

1

The Politics of the "Gay Plague": AIDS as a U.S. Ideology

HENRY ABELOVE

In memory of Jack Winkler

FROM THE FIRST notice of AIDS in the United States until now, about 55 percent to 60 percent of the cases diagnosed have been among gay men. Roughly the same percent of the deaths have been among gay men, and in the earliest years of the epidemic in the United States, the disease was commonly believed to be largely a liability of the gay male culture and of those unlucky enough to be transfused with blood from gay donors. "Gay plague," AIDS was often then called. We spoke that term or heard it spoken and maybe felt a shudder of fear and revulsion.

At present the proportion of gay men among those dying is said to be declining. But this decline is also said to be proceeding slowly. Some projections suggest that even in 1992, the majority of the annual AIDS fatalities in the United States will still be gay men. Nevertheless, the term "gay plague" isn't spoken or heard as often as it was a while back. So many news stories have lately appeared about the vulnerability of intravenous drug users to AIDS, about the prenatal infection of infants born to HIV sero-positive mothers, even about the gradually rising incidence of HIV transmission in heterosexual sex!

Just a few years ago, in the mid-1980s, in the era of the term "gay plague," the view usual among government functionaries, among people in the health-care industry, and maybe among American newspaper readers generally, had been that transmission in heterosexual sex was really likely only in Africa. Some American medical scientists had even developed a theory to rationalize this view. Call it the theory of the very, very bad African vagina. What they had argued was that vaginas, unlike assholes, were ordinarily far too strong to be penetrable by HIV. After all, vaginas were built tough, by nature, to accommodate a mighty thrusting dick

3

and childbirth, too. In Africa, however, the naturally strong vagina deteriorated. For venereal diseases of many kinds must of course be endemic there, and medical care must be scanty and inefficient. So African vaginas would be raw and chancred in consequence of repeated venereal infections that were uncured or incompletely cured and these vaginas would therefore be disastrously open to HIV. In the United States there were virtually no such deteriorated vaginas.[1]

This theory had been widely promulgated and accepted, and it has not yet been widely disavowed. But we hear less of it now than formerly, just as we hear less of the term "gay plague" and more talk emanating from almost everywhere about how AIDS ought to be a matter of concern for all Americans. Lesbians, to be sure, experience much difficulty in finding themselves inside that "all." As usual, they remain invisible. News stories or posters on HIV transmission virtually never discuss risk levels in lesbian sexual behaviors. But the discourse of prevention, though it tends importantly to except lesbians, is otherwise now rapidly universalizing, and those authoritative voices speaking to us, and through us, suggesting that HIV prefers to kill gay men and Africans, are now relatively muted.

What purpose does the new tendency to universalizing serve? Please note that it is just a tendency. Older notions still persist,[2] if less pervasively than before, and as I've just remarked, lesbians are hardly comprehended in the new and enlarged discourse of prevention. One purpose the tendency serves is to deflect attention from the actual deaths of an extraordinarily high number of gay male Americans, all of whom should have died hereafter. Another purpose is to obscure the extent to which American responses to AIDS have been, and still are, saliently conditioned by the epidemiological accident that the disease appeared here on a large-scale basis first and most noticeably among gay men. A third purpose is to reassert and reinforce both racism and conventional, regulative positions about sex and the family. I wish I could say that the most important purpose of all was to save lives. But the new, enlarged discourse of prevention does not give foremost place to the saving of lives. On the contrary, life is subordinate to the other purposes the discourse is meant to serve. I know of no recent U.S. news feature on AIDS prevention, no pronouncement by any official of any state government or of the federal government, no message from any health-care industry authority, any hospital, any physicians' organization, or any insurance company that has been primarily concerned with saving lives. Certainly government policy on prevention has not been primarily concerned with saving lives.

Another way of saying what I mean: If the earlier discourse, summarily describable as the discourse of the gay plague and the very, very bad African vagina, was meant to speak the conviction that those who had AIDS owed it to their loathesomeness, the new discourse is meant to speak a preference for returning the lesbian-gay community to oblivion (the men backgrounded or forgotten, the women made invisible) while reestablishing the primacy of the U.S. bourgeois white family.

I know that what I've just said, particularly by way of characterizing the new and enlarged discourse of prevention, will seem cryptic. I intend to try to clarify it, but I mustn't pretend that the work of communication will be easy. What I'm going to examine are voices that are inside of us as well as outside of us, voices that constitute us as well as regulate us. Trying to know anything about what's most familiar must produce a sense of strangeness, difficulty. It's like taking your pulse with your own finger.

Before I go on with my task of clarification, I want to pause and talk some about the quilt, or the Names Project, as it is also called, and, to borrow a couple of words of Milton's from his elegy, "somewhat loudly" recall those dead of AIDS. You may perhaps know that the quilt is a memorial of an unusual kind. It's made up of many, many separate panels, all the same size, six by three feet, the size of a grave, but each naming a different person, each sewn by that person's lovers, friends, relatives, each saying or picturing something evocative of that person's life. Anyone dead of AIDS can be memorialized there, but the names on the panels are overwhelmingly of gay men, partly because, as I've already said, a substantial majority of the fatalities in the United States have been gay men, partly because the quilt has been greatly favored by the lesbian-gay community almost from the moment the first several panels were sewn together.

But why is the quilt favored, and what does it represent anyway? Or perhaps we should ask why isn't the favored memorial something more usual—a statue in a park or a city square, a stained-glass window, a specially dedicated and newly established hospital, a laboratory or a lecture hall at a university? First of all, no public space, no park, no square could in a certain sense be *appropriate* as a site. For in the public domain we gay men and lesbians are unwelcome. In twenty-three of the fifty states our sexual behaviors are still criminalized. In some of these states the penalties stipulated in law for our sexual behaviors are very heavy and can amount to five years' imprisonment. Enforcement of the laws against us isn't of course uniformly stringent, and there are jurisdictions where there is no enforcement. Even in those jurisdictions, however, there is the potential of enforcement, and perhaps more to the point, we who live there or pass through must feel a kind of edgy awareness that in the still-official view of these states' governments, we become criminals whenever we act like ourselves. In forty-three states there is no specific protection for us in law if, on account of our sexual orientation, we are discriminated against in employment or housing or credit. Only in seven states, and in some cities in other states, is there specific legal protection for us from such discrimination. Even in those jurisdictions where we enjoy some protection, our entitlement is typically very qualified. Take Massachusetts, for instance. There the act that protects us against discrimination was lately passed after a seventeen-year-long struggle. It may yet be challenged in a referendum whose proponent says that the state's voters will cancel the act when they have the chance to do so.

He may be right; the voters of Irvine, California, cancelled their new lesbian-gay rights act in a recent referendum.

For now the Massachusetts act is binding, but as worded it takes from us perhaps as much as it allows us. What it says is that nothing in the act should be construed to mean that the state of Massachusetts "condones" homosexuality, as though to declare that our lives require but do not deserve condoning. The lesbian-gay rights bill that failed to pass the Connecticut legislature in 1987 contained the same qualification. The Connecticut bill's failure to pass was saddening and appalling. But since the bill included that qualification, passage would also have been saddening and appalling. (A similar bill did finally pass in Connecticut in 1991.) From the American commonweal we have been excluded, and our favored memorial to our losses cannot be easily in public space because we ourselves are not yet permitted to belong to the public, even *de jure,* even in law.

Nor would we be likely to favor a church- or synagogue-based memorial. In the view of those denominations to which the overwhelming majority of Americans committed to organized religion feel loyal, our sexual behaviors are simply sinful. In the view of some other, smaller denominations, our sexual behaviors are maybe almost acceptable, provided of course that each of us practices sex only in the context of an intimate, ongoing relationship with one other person, that is, in the context of a simulacrum of a heterosexual marriage as ideally conceived. This conditional almost-acceptance is about as much of a boon to us as the legislative refusal to condone. Both gestures are also in a certain sense alike. Both displace us, one to tell us of what we don't deserve, the other to tell us of what we might nearly deserve, if only we approached closer to the one great good.

Nor would we be any more likely to favor the financing of a hospital or medical laboratory as a memorial. The health-care industry in the United States has long been our antagonist. Until relatively recently, the doctors, for instance, regarded us all without exception as sick. We were sick just because we were lesbian or gay. Homosexuality was a disease in their official list of diseases. In 1973, as a result of intense, hostile pressure from us, the doctors dropped their commitment to the view that homosexuality was a disease. But in 1977 they added a new disease to their list of diseases. They called it "ego-dystonic homosexuality," or in simpler language, homosexuality that doesn't fit well with an individual's ego.[3] This disease, they assured us, was characteristic of only some gay people. They did not simultaneously add to their list another new disease called ego-dystonic heterosexuality, presumably because they imagined that heterosexuality always did, or always should, fit well with any human ego. "Ego-dystonic homosexuality" remains a diagnostic category, and it testifies to the continuing interest the doctors have in pathologizing us.

As for the colleges and universities, popular as they may be as recipients of memorial gifts, they would not do for our memorial. The level of bigotry against lesbians and gay men within the universities is breathtakingly high. Although very current personal testimonies to this bigotry can be easily gathered, the last survey research demonstrating it is now about a decade old. When the chairs of 640 U.S. sociology departments were questioned, some 63 percent said they would be reluctant to hire an openly gay scholar and 84 percent said they would be reluctant to hire an openly gay, activist scholar.[4] A decade may be a long time. Yet I know of no reason to suppose that a similar survey done tomorrow would yield results much different.

For the state we cannot be condoned or protected, and in many instances we are even criminalized. For the big churches we are always sinful, for some of the smaller churches, conditionally almost-acceptable if we try hard enough to pass. For the health-care industry we are intrinsically pathological, at least potentially, and for higher education we have long been an object of frank bigotry. These institutions all exclude us to protect yet another institution, the family.

To understand the Names Project, you must know all this. Otherwise you may miss the significance of its most salient feature, its removability. The project, like us, has no ongoing places of its own on American soil, no necessary connection anywhere to any major American institution. Nothing located or fixed could serve well as a memorial to our losses. The Names Project's other features may be more readily summed up. It's a quilt, something that gives warmth and comfort, because these are what we now need. It's a quilt because quilts traditionally were made by women and all of us in the lesbian-gay community are in a sense women. We gay men are socially gendered female, no matter how butch we may look, and lesbians are socially gendered female too, though perhaps less emphatically than the men. When anyone identifies performatively with the feminine, the gesture is called camp. The quilt is a production of camp, chastened by great sorrow. It's a quilt because quilts were traditionally a conjoining of many separate and very particular pieces. Our losses are like that, too. Each of them is distinctive, but they have a special weight and purport collectively. So many have died, particularly of the generation that came to maturity during the 1960s, that the proper term for these losses taken together may be, as Simon Watney says, "ethnocide." What the quilt figures is a destruction so extensive that it threatens the discontinuance of a whole culture.[5] Younger lesbians and gay men, as they wander around the quilt, may see no name that they recognize, but their sense of loss, however formless, is still acute. As they try to explain themselves and their pain, they often report that they feel as though they have missed out on everything; and that "everything" is typically understood to be the happy carefree sex of the 1970s. "Everything" probably does include that, but its crucial significance is different. What they mostly miss is an opportunity to learn their own culture. It isn't something they can learn from parents; it's rarely something they can learn at school; and from peers they can learn it in only very incomplete ways. The Names Project names those who ought to be present to transmit the culture to a younger generation but who are gone, destroyed. Since the loss is so importantly collective, each panel has been attached to the others, and all are united.

I shall describe just one part of a particular panel. Then I'll return to the new, enlarged, and universalizing discourse of prevention, which as I said before has among its several purposes the deflecting of attention from the actual deaths of a very large number of gay men. That's a purpose I have of course been deliberately opposing by my account of the Names Project. In so opposing, I have also been tacitly explaining, or trying to explain, what produces that purpose. For the oblivion these dead are now assigned is produced by the same phenomena that gave them nowhere to live, the same phenomena that allocated to them illness and early death in a measure so terrible and disproportionate. Jean Valentine referred to this particular panel at the start of her poem titled "X." Remarkably enough for what is, after all, a part of the Names Project, the panel includes no name. There are just these words: "I have decorated this banner to honor my brother. Our parents did not want his name used publicly."[6]

Removable, unsituateable in any one place or institution, comforting and camp, various but conjoined so as to figure a collective loss that amounts to ethnocide, the quilt is incidentally as telling an expression of American art as any in our times. It has of course no artist, no price, and it cannot be reproduced, though it can be temporarily divided, and it can and will be added to. It is also, in some part, written, as the panel I've just mentioned so poignantly testifies, by the same phenomena it struggles to reverse, the phenomena that want oblivion for the lesbian and gay community.

I proceed from the quilt to a political cartoon that was reproduced during the summer of 1989, and widely so, a cartoon signed by an artist named H. Payne and sold by the Scripps Howard/United Feature Syndicate to hundreds of American newspapers. I saw it first in the *Hartford Courant*, a newspaper in the big Times-Mirror chain, which in 1988 earned $331.9 million on revenues of $3.33 billion. Like the quilt, the cartoon offers itself as memorializing those dead of AIDS. But the cartoon also works as a warning, a warning that's now conventionally part of the new, enlarged, universalizing discourse of prevention. The cartoon takes the term "flower children" and the types to whom the term might be thought to belong and, killing them off, gives them flowers with a vengeance. I should explain that the term "flower children" comes originally from Pete Seeger's 1960s song "Where Have All the Flowers Gone?" When the song was first popular, C. Day Lewis argued that it was the contemporary inheritor of the lyric tradition in European poetry, and certainly the song engages that tradition.[7] The flowers that are gone, that are no longer available for mourning because too many men have been killed in too many wars now, and so too many flowers have had to be picked to honor them, are the flowers of elegies like Milton's, the flowers that he still had available to strew over Lycidas's hearse: amaranthus, primrose, violet, jessamine, woodbine, cowslips, daffidillies. Seeger sings: "Where have all the flowers gone / long time passing? / Where have all the flowers gone / long time ago? / Where have all the flowers gone? / Young girls have picked them every one. / Oh when will they

ever learn? / When will they ever learn?"* Those in the 1960s who agreed that
there were no flowers left for mourning, especially for mourning the people killed
in the war in Vietnam, were called "flower children." On the left in the cartoon,
three of them are pictured, probably at the Woodstock Festival, reclining together
on a blanket and enjoying themselves. The next frame changes reclining to re-
cumbency, in fact to death, which is presumably the proper consequence of nonproductive reclining. But these three deserve death or create it not just because
they are nonproductive. The man on the left has spoken for peace and so is responsible for the war refugees; the man on the right has smoked pot and so is responsible for death due to drug overdosing; the ungendered and not discernibly
lesbian, gay, or straight one in the middle has chosen "free love," instead of the
costly and constraining kind associated with marriage, and so is responsible for
AIDS deaths.

This cartoon repeats connections that already are firmly embossed in our
minds and so makes a kind of familiar sense, even though there may be nothing
in the cartoon that is really sensible. The responsibility for the terrible fate of the
war refugees of Southeast Asia may belong at least arguably to the war makers
rather than to the peace advocates. Death due to excess may be the fate of some
1960s-style dropouts who do pot, but I know of no evidence to show that such
death is more likely for them than for their opposites, the achievers who never
touch illegal drugs but who exceed differently, say by overeating, overworking,
and jet-setting, and so have coronaries, strokes, and crashes. "Free love" doesn't
make anybody vulnerable to AIDS, though unsafe sexual practices do. These,
however, may or may not be part of nonmarital sex. Similarly, marriage is no pro-
phylaxis against AIDS; HIV is, oddly enough, indifferent as to whether or not its
prospective human hosts wear wedding rings. Insofar as this cartoon is about
AIDS, and I think it is centrally about AIDS, it does nothing to help in the work of
universal prevention in which it seems to be engaged. On the contrary, the cartoon makes prevention less manageable, less doable. For what is necessary for
prevention is obfuscated here. But the cartoon does succeed in directing us toward productivity, support for war and empire, achievement, and marriage. If
any of these has dangers, the cartoon hides them. It also leads us to see the person
with AIDS (PWA) as someone responsible for her or his own death. This is a responsibility determined in a special way.

No woman who dies in bearing a legitimate child (bearing legitimate children
is her rightful vocation after all) is likely to be figured as responsible for her own
death, though it is the outcome of an avoidable sexual act. What determines responsibility isn't the fact that this PWA has performed an act that culminates
eventually in death. Other acts, even sexual acts, culminate eventually in death

---

*"Where have All the Flowers Gone?" by Pete Seeger. Copyright © by Fall River Music, Inc. (renewed).
All rights reserved. Used by permission.

FLOWER CHILDREN ·1969·

PEACE IN VIETNAM

FREE LOVE!

DRUGS MAN!

WOODSTOCK

FLOWER CHILDREN ·1989·

THE BOAT PEOPLE VIETNAM R.I.P.

AIDS VICTIM R.I.P.

DRUG OVERDOSE R.I.P.

Henry Payne reprinted by permission of United Feature Syndicate, Inc.

without becoming responsible for the death. It's rather the fact that the PWA's act was forbidden, forbidden by everything and all of us. That's what makes her or him responsible. While intimating this responsibility, the cartoon also renders the whole lesbian-gay community, its losses and its sufferings, absent.

I move from the press to the Roman Catholic church, whose local spokesmen, the U.S. bishops, have also joined in the new universalizing discourse of prevention. At their meeting in Baltimore in November 1989, the bishops fought back a text proposed for adoption by Bishop Austin Vaughan of New York, a text that suggested that AIDS might be a "direct punishment by God." This text really belonged to the now largely superseded discourse of the mid-1980s, what I've called the discourse of the gay plague and the very, very bad African vagina, and the defeat of the text isn't at all surprising. Instead of suggesting that AIDS might be a "direct punishment by God," the bishops devoted themselves to preaching up prevention, which they said could be accomplished by chastity until marriage and by monogamy within marriage. They also refused to allow the use of condoms in any circumstances. Other devices for safer sex, devices like dams, which lesbians sometimes use, the bishops apparently did not deign even to condemn. Lesbians are invisible to them. Condoms, they said, were not only bad for the soul, they were also "technically unreliable." For the latter reason as well as for the former, they were never to be recommended or permitted. The bishops' final statement, which included the remarks on condoms I've just quoted, passed 219 to 4.[8]

Suppose we were to ask the bishops, who say that condoms are "technically unreliable," just what is more likely to break, an American-made condom or an American-made marriage. *Consumer Reports* has tested condoms, and American society has been testing marriage for some time now. The question is in principle answerable. Or suppose we were to take a different tack, and ask the bishops why, since they condemn condoms on the chance one might possibly break, they do not also condemn auto seat belts and preventive auto maintenance, since they do not always suffice to protect us against traffic fatalities.

But there is no point in asking the bishops anything. What is in a way most distressing about their statement is its pretense that it is concerned with saving life. Nothing could be less concerned with saving life than the bishops' statement. If we wanted to save lives that might be otherwise lost on the road, we wouldn't condemn seat belts and preventive maintenance. If we wanted to save lives that might be otherwise lost to AIDS, we wouldn't condemn condoms, ignore dams, and oppose all safer-sex education. What the bishops really want to do is to reassert and reinforce the family, regardless of the cost in life. That cost is likely to be very high. In force and direction the statement is murderous. "Blind mouths" was the term Milton used for such clergymen as these bishops. But the same voices that speak them all too often speak us, and if the bishops are blind mouths, then so surely are we.

Take the next item, a statement on sex and AIDS in a pamphlet prepared by the staff of the Yale–New Haven Hospital.

Safe Sex and AIDS

AIDS is a sexually transmitted disease. You can get AIDS by having sex with anyone who has the HIV virus in their body.

People don't have to look sick to have the virus. Gay or bisexual men and both men and women who shoot drugs may have the virus. The more sex partners a person has or the more people he or she shares needles with, the more likely he or she is to have the virus. Here are some ways you can reduce your risk of picking up the AIDS virus:

1. Cut down the number of people you have sex with. It's dangerous to have sex with people you don't know.

2. If you are a man, wear a condom (rubber). If you are a woman make sure the man uses a rubber. Use a rubber during oral sex too. Don't swallow semen.

3. French kissing may be risky. Kissing on the lips without exchanging saliva is safe. You can kiss or touch your partners cheek, ears, neck, breast, and genitals as long as you don't exchange fluids and the man wears a rubber.

4. Do not make your partner or yourself bleed. Avoid contact with blood if the woman is menstruating (having a period).

5. Don't place your uncovered penis or finger in your partner's anus (rectum) or allow him to do this to you. Don't share vibrators, dildos or other sex stimulators.

6. Putting your tongue on your partner's private parts is dangerous.

The statement is very nearly as murderous as the bishops' is, but its force and direction may be harder for us to gauge. It may be rather closer to what we're accustomed to, to what speaks us habitually. First of all, the terms of sex are politely elevated (private parts, penis, rectum, semen, genitals) so that only persons with a certain kind of class-based language at their disposal will understand. All others will be shut out. Second, the vectors of illness are identified exclusively and quite astonishingly wrongly as "gay or bisexual men" and "men and women who shoot drugs," a phrase that is easily readable as coded to mean people of color. So the dangerous ones are gay, bi, or people of color. This position is an ordinary mix of homophobia and racism, nothing else. Third, the safer-sex advice given, insofar as any is given at all, is ludicrously distorted to favor marriage and family rather than life. What the statement presses toward is monogamy, which is what marriage or its simulacrum, the ongoing relationship of partners, is supposed to be about. "Cut down the number of people you have sex with," the statement says. "The more sex partners a person has," the worse, the statement suggests. But neither marriage nor an ongoing relationship necessarily provides protection against AIDS.

Unless you and your partner-to-be are both virginal (and how would you know that anyway?), or unless you have an already established partnership to which both of you have been faithful for at least twenty years (and how would you know *that* anyway?), the issue that matters most isn't your partnership. What matters most is the sort of sexual behaviors you practice. If the behaviors are safer, then the number of people with whom you do them is comparatively insignificant. If the behaviors aren't safe, then just one partner could be very risky. It may even be that AIDS-preventing sex is likelier with a succession of casual partners. As Cindy Patton has suggested, we may feel relaxed about refusing demands for unsafe practices when they come from a stranger but reluctant to refuse them when they come from a committed partner.[9] If her suggestion is right, then the statement's advice, "It's dangerous to have sex with people you don't know," advice which is in effect probably classist and racist, may actually need to be reversed.

In a relatively short space the statement manages a veritable blitzkrieg of prohibitions, including several that so far as I can judge from my reading of the clinical literature are unnecessary, such as the prohibition on wet kissing ("French kissing," as the statement calls it) and on some kinds of tonguing of the lower body. Nor need a man always wear a condom in sex, as the statement advises. He should certainly have one on if he is going to fuck, but that isn't by any means the only thing he may want to do, regardless of what the statement thinks. The advice carried by t-shirts sometimes seen in New York ("Men, wear a condom or beat it!") is probably more to the point. But the assumption that a man will want to fuck, along with the nervous prohibitions on nonrisky behaviors of the tongue, do make a pattern, even if it has nothing to do with AIDS prevention. The pattern is of the usual hierarchy of sexual behaviors culminating in fucking, and that is what the statement enforces.

Despite the blitzkrieg of prohibitions, one important bit of information is omitted. If a man is involved in the sex, and he is going to fuck either another man or a woman, then the safest practice is that he not only wear a condom but also pull out before coming. I should be inclined to call this omission sexist. But the indubitably sexist aspect to the statement is the almost total neglect of safer-sex information for women. They are told to "make sure" that the man wears a condom (the presence of a man is of course assumed, along with the woman's responsibility for him), but the women are told little else. It's as though the condomed dick were, as Scripture says, "the one thing needful." Nothing is told the women about what they could do with a dam or a cut-up condom or a condom on one of their fingers or on a vibrator or dildo. Nor are they advised about how to do alternative insemination safely. This is a procedure that is of interest to many women, but if done without certain kinds of care it can transmit HIV.

Moreover, the statement does little to help people find thrilling substitutes for the sexual behaviors that are now risky. But this kind of advice is crucial to what safer-sex education ought to be. If the statement were really interested in saving lives it would provide a little list of substitutes, if only to authorize its readers to do some fantasizing on their own. When I am helping with safer-sex education, I always mention j.o. parties (jill off/jack off group sex based on the rule "No sucking, no fucking"). This option pleases me because it images community rather than marriage, but it doesn't of course please everybody else present. What it does for everybody else present, unfailingly, I believe, is to sanction their thinking about what they might care to try that's safer but outside the rules as currently and so very riskily established.

To sum up on the Yale statement: It can't do much to prevent AIDS. It isn't primarily about that, whatever it may pretend. It's primarily about encouraging marriage or a simulacrum of marriage, which is virtually irrelevant to AIDS prevention. It's about enforcing racism, classism, homophobia, and sexism. It's about enforcing the usual hierarchy of sexual behaviors, culminating in fucking. It's about withholding safer-sex information that might be particularly hard for a man to accept. It's about silence on sexual options that may be subversive of the family but consistent with life. The statement doesn't much want to protect our lives. It wants to regulate us instead, whatever the cost in life, just as the statement of the bishops did. If the Yale–New Haven Hospital pamphlet allows condoms and the bishops don't, the difference is much less significant than might at first appear. Both statements are murderous, as is the press cartoon, as is so much of what we speak, or speaks us, on the subject of AIDS.

I do not want to omit all discussion of the way the new, enlarged, universalizing discourse of prevention encompasses nonsexual transmission, particularly in regard to the sharing of unsterile instruments. I shall comment briefly on one statement, which is at least suggestive.

The statement comes from the Report of the Surgeon-General of the United States on AIDS prevention. This report was mailed in 1988, purportedly to every household in the country. There are probably few government documents of any kind that have ever been so widely reproduced and so widely distributed over so short a time span as this one was.

The Problem of Drugs and AIDS

Today, in some cities, the sharing of drug needles and syringes by those who shoot drugs is the fastest growing way that the AIDS virus is being spread.

No one should shoot drugs. It can result in addiction, poor health, family disruption, emotional disturbances and death. Many drug users are addicted and need to enter a drug treatment program as quickly as possible.

In the meantime, these people must avoid AIDS by not sharing any of the equipment used to prepare and inject illegal drugs.

Sharing drug needles, even once, is an extremely easy way to be infected with the AIDS virus. Blood from an infected person can be trapped in the needle or syringe, and then injected directly into the bloodstream of the next person who uses the needle.

Other kinds of drugs, including alcohol, can also cause problems. Under their influence, your judgment becomes impaired. You could be exposed to the AIDS virus while doing things you wouldn't otherwise do.

Teenagers are at an age when trying different things is especially inviting. They must understand how serious the drug problem is and how to avoid it.

> Drugs are also one of the many ways in which prostitutes become infected. They may share needles themselves or have sex with people who do. They then can pass the AIDS virus to others.
>
> For information about drug abuse treatment programs, contact your physician, local public health agency or community AIDS or drug assistance group.

Please note that the sharing of unsterile instruments is not what the document primarily warns against. What it primarily warns against is the shooting up of illegal drugs. But for AIDS prevention, the issue is the sharing of unsterile instruments, particularly needles. These needles include the bad ones used in the shooting up of illegal drugs and the good ones used in acupuncture, ear-piercing, tattooing, and free cholesterol testing at supermarkets. HIV isn't known to have an ideological preference among these various kinds of needles. Because the statement really wants to condemn the shooting up of illegal drugs, it fails to provide information that may be important in AIDS prevention for the many Americans who happen to use needles that have no connection to illegal drugs.

But the statement also provides no real help for the many Americans who do use needles to take illegal drugs. It is important to see and understand that the statement deliberately withholds such help. It could tell the drug shooters how to sterilize their needles. All that sterilization requires is a little household bleach. You fill the needle with bleach three times, squirt it out after each filling, rinse the needle by filling it with tap water three times, then squirt it out after each filling. It's probably even better to boil the needles in a bleach–tap water solution, but the simpler and quicker procedure for sterilizing I've just described is likely to be effective in most instances. If there is no bleach handy, the drug-shooter may use rubbing alcohol or even wine instead. HIV is exceptionally fragile as viruses go and these other common substances would probably kill it, too. The statement says none of this, however, though it has long been well known, because it thinks that if drug-shooters will not stop shooting up, then they should not be protected from AIDS. The purpose is to condemn the shooting up of illegal drugs, not to prevent AIDS.

We should also be clear about how racist the statement is. It knows, or rather thinks it knows, that many of those who shoot up illegal drugs are people of color. It communicates this unspeakable knowledge clearly enough in its first sentence with the phrase "in some cities." What the statement seems to desire, what the government that wrote and distributed the statement seems to desire, is the deaths of those people of color and of all others who "share" blood with them. The statement and the state go a long way toward achieving that desire by withholding here the very information that could really be effectual in saving their lives. In a similar way, the government usually also withholds dams, condoms, and other safer-sex devices from prisoners, many of whom are people of color. In Connecticut about half of the prisoners are. There are very roughly 50,000 releases a year from Connecticut's prisons. Since many prisoners have sex in prison and since the state forbids them to use or even possess safer-sex devices while incarcerated, I cannot doubt that a high proportion of these prisoners, by the time they are released, are HIV sero-positive. If the statement really wants, as it says in its second paragraph, to discourage "family disruption," then the family it is keeping from disruption is white, and the way it is doing the job is by meaning to kill off people of color and their miscegenate friends.

These voices that speak the press, the bishops, the health-care industry, and the government are within us, too. They're peculiarly, almost salaciously intimate, and they speak us in some measure or another, all of us, myself of course included, when we try to broach the subject of AIDS. To appreciate the force and direction of these voices, which call incessantly for the sacrifice of so much life, we should "look homeward," at the family.

I don't intend on this occasion to try to explain historically why the white bourgeois family has come to be so dominative an institution and a discourse in the United States during the era that we sometimes call late capitalism. That is a topic for another occasion. I only want to indicate my conviction that there can hardly be in all of human history many versions of Moloch more bloodthirsty than this family is.

I said a moment ago that I knew that I too must be spoken in some measure by the voices that speak the new, enlarged, universalizing discourse of prevention. After all, I too am committed to prevention. I am particularly worried about the distinction that I and all other AIDS activists must make between unsafe and safer sex. Is this distinguishing really about life, or is it just a replay of an old drive to classify and therefore control and regulate in the realm of sex? Is it maybe potentially both?

These are questions that I cannot yet answer. What I do believe is that positioning ourselves to try to answer them, and therefore also to recognize the voices that speak us, is a task of crucial importance both for study and for politics. This task is the heart of what Nietzsche called "the gay science."

•   •   •

Postscript (February 1993): I wrote this essay in October and November of 1989. It belongs to that moment. Some of what the essay highlights is now gone. I understand, for instance, that the Yale–New Haven Hospital no longer distributes the pamphlet I quote and criticize. If I have agreed to publish the essay now, and with very little revision, that is because I think there may be some use in letting its views and arguments stand for the record.

NOTES

1. For an excellent account of our prejudicious and tendentious vision of AIDS in Africa, see Simon Watney, "African AIDS," *Differences* 1 (1989).

2. For an instance of the persistence of the older discourse in modified form, see Michael Fumento, *The Myth of Heterosexual AIDS* (New York: Basic Books, 1989).

3. Ronald Bayer, *Homosexuality and American Psychiatry: The Politics of Diagnosis* (New York: Basic Books, 1981), pp. 176–177.

4. John D'Emilio, "Not a Single Matter: Gay History and Gay Historians," *Journey of American History* 76, no. 2 (September 1989), p. 441.

5. I do not mean to deny that the AIDS emergency has been energizing for the lesbian-gay community. In response to the emergency, many new and valuable community institutions have been established. On this matter, see, for instance, Robert Padgug, "More Than the Story of a Virus: Gay History, Gay Communities, and AIDS," *Radical America* 21, nos. 2–3 (March-April 1987), pp. 38–39. Still, the measure of our loss is incalculable.

6. Michael Klein (ed.), *Poets for Life: Seventy-Six Poets Respond to AIDS* (New York: Crown, 1989), p. 222.

7. C. Day Lewis, *The Lyric Impulse* (Cambridge: Harvard University Press, 1965), p. 145.

8. *New York Times*, November 11, 1989, p. 10; *Hartford Courant*, November 11, 1989, p. 14.

9. Cindy Patton, "Resistance and the Erotic," *Radical America* 20, no. 6 (November-December 1986), p. 72.

2

Fatal Abstraction:
The Death and Sinister Afterlife
of the American Family

NANCY ARMSTRONG

I WANT TO CONSIDER what happened to the concept of "family" as it worked in concert with "war" in the so-called war on drugs in 1989 and then, in 1990–1991, in the war in the Gulf. I can neither claim specialized knowledge of this subject beyond that of a literary scholar and critic nor offer an adequately theorized description even on that level. But I do believe these particular terms have detached themselves from the whole order of people and events that they nevertheless claim to "represent." I think they have taken up what might well be a historically new relationship with one another, their power increasing exponentially in this sinister combination. I find the very methods that are supposed to expose the operations of discourse mysteriously incapable of dealing with such material. And I want to call attention to this fact. The problem, as I will describe it, lies not in "war." Most of us have contempt for its traditional meanings. Like military music, a "good," "just," or even "necessary" war tends to strike academics as a contradiction in terms. Indeed, institutional practices that smack of military discipline are usually met with suspicion (and likely to invite epithets comparing that institution with a police state). But "family" is another matter. The family still appears to provide the very refuge and antidote to a world dominated by the police and the military. It can be held up in opposition to the military's regulation and instrumentalization of human bodies even though the family has done much the same thing to people throughout modern history.

In *City of Women,* Christine Stansell provides a stark example of exactly how one class brought this abstraction to bear on another in the United States. Her study of working-class women in nineteenth-century New York shows that at the very time in our national history when the middle-class family was failing conspicuously to take care of working-class women with children, the family also served as the standard that defined those women as lacking, even vicious, and thus deserving of a sorry fate. "On their errands of mercy into the tenements," she explains, "evangelical men and women encountered patterns of womanly behavior and child rearing that clashed with their deepest-held beliefs. As genteel writers and ministers after 1820 articulated more clearly their own ideas about domesticity in the context of their disapproving encounters with the laboring poor," more and more people apparently took to visiting impoverished households in hopes of converting those women to the sexual practices of the relatively well-to-do.[1] The family thus offered the motive and instrument of "a class intervention" that drew women out of the workplace or, failing that, plunged them into a lower class.[2]

What must be seen as a kind of feminism grew up in opposition to this ideology during the 1860s and again in the early decades of the twentieth century. As the pressures of immigration and unstable supplies of male labor made it impossible for poor women to exist within a middle-class family structure, they survived, Stansell explains, "by becoming family heads and utilizing their children's labor, by depending on other women and by pressing their needs upon the municipality."[3] Their economic independence was always shaky and their political power slight. Nevertheless these women did "represent an important challenge to the gender system predicated on the control of daughters' labor and daughters' sexuality," a system that cannot be distinguished from the new brand of respectability that apparently drew reformers in droves into working-class homes. Thus the same domestic ideology that provided the means of upward mobility also arrogated to less fortunate working-class women the unfeminine qualities that members of the respectable class had rejected as beneath them. A feminism whose authority depended on maintaining the strictest gender differences was destined to suppress a feminism that arose from another class position, where a woman's authority depended on abolishing those same gender differences.[4] The success of the gendered ideal did not simply perpetuate the misogynist view of working-class women, however; it ultimately worked against the very women who sought to improve their positions by fulfilling that ideal. Twentieth-century feminism came to see the exclusion of women from the wage-labor system not as the source of social empowerment but as the cause of economic oppression.

Yet, despite our decisive turn against the gendered workplace, the family will continue to provide the means of political domination so long as feminism underestimates its capacity to live a double life.[5] As Michele Barrett has pointed out, "The family-household constitutes both the ideological ground on which gender difference and women's oppression are constructed, and the material relations in which men and women are differentially engaged in wage labour and the class structure."[6] Though they appear to be different versions of the same thing, the discursive construction of the family does not necessarily share the same fate as the social construction of the family. Indeed, as I intend to demonstrate, the discursive family has detached itself in some irrevocable way from the social. As a word, image, fiction, fantasy, or figure of speech, it gained in discursive power precisely when it was most obviously failing to meet the basic needs of poor and ethnic America.

If, as Stansell suggests, the respectable middle-class family began in the early nineteenth century as an evangelical fantasy and a means to upward mobility, then during the course of the century the fiction appeared to come true. Domestic ideology worked hand in glove with the sexual division of labor, as she explains, to serve the interests of one class of people at the expense of another. The slippage between the discursive and social operations of the family became unavoidably apparent only as American culture began to manifest all the signs and symptoms we associate with late capitalism. During the past twenty years or so, however, it has become all but impossible for even the most economically secure citizen to believe that the middle-class family provides an adequate means of distributing resources through working men to the rest of the population. At the same time, middle-class women have pressed with increasing effectiveness for equal access to the workplace. And yet the feminist rhetoric mounted on behalf of this effort has been equally concerned with maintaining the status of the home as a domestic sanctuary into which the government cannot intrude. Thus we have allowed a situation to develop in which a decisive improvement in day-care facilities for professional people coincides with the deterioration of food-stamp and school-lunch programs, elimination of subsidies for low-income housing, discontinuation of federally financed prenatal care for the poor and immunization programs for their children—the collapse, in other words, of that part of the tax-based welfare system specifically intended to compensate families for the loss of wage earners. It may be that by concentrating on discrimination in the workplace, feminism has done much to improve the lot of single professional women and for families in which both parents work. But no critique can begin to undo the effects of the gender system so long as it preserves the sanctuary of the home.[7]

Foucault affords a case in point. He has done perhaps more than any other historian to detach the modern family from nature and identify it with a specific bundle of discursive operations. He has done perhaps more than any other historian to tear down the wall between gendered spheres, allowing us to establish a causal relationship between the production of such a sexuality and the rise of the modern ruling class. The first volume of his *History of Sexuality* retells the story of what Raymond Williams calls "the long revolution" as a twofold process in which certain people with access to the printed word simultaneously produced the very thing they were worried about—namely, sexuality—and developed an intricate set of techniques for managing it that would eventually harden into the institutions most characteristic of industrialized nations. Thus Foucault equates the development of the modern Western nation state with a struggle that reorganized the entire culture into private and public and consolidated a class on the basis of the symbolic practices surrounding biological reproduction.[8] In so doing, Fou-

cault forces us to regard "the family" as a fact of culture and the means of producing an individuated and sexualized population peculiarly suited to an industrial-
izing world. He breaks "the family" in this sense away from nature and even from
the actual households that were supposed to distribute national resources from
an elite corps of working men to the rest of the population. But although he calls
attention to the family as a class- and culture-specific orchestration of discursive
effects, Foucault avoids all explicit mention of gender. And although he forces us
to grant the household that formed around the monogamous heterosexual couple
and their immediate offspring a place in modern history, he does not acknowledge the power that the family continues to exercise as a set of untheorized assumptions. Because he neglects the gendered and gendering operations of the
modern family, even Foucault allows gender to reattach itself to "actual" bodies.
His attempt to detach "sexuality" from anything remotely resembling nature ultimately falls under the spell of the family too.

The figure of Bentham's panopticon occupies the center of the central chapter
of *Discipline and Punish,* where its architecture provides a visual correlative for
Foucault's rational explanation of modern institutional power. Before he can spell
out this logic, however, Foucault uses another example, that of the city under
plague. Why, one is tempted to ask, must he conjure up this particular image?
What does it offer that is not present in the architectural plan of the modern
prison but must be there in order for the logic of his argument to unfold? The dis-
eased city provides the metaphorical ground on which discipline can take over
European culture and Foucault's thinking as well. Let us observe what first allows
its characteristic procedures to click into gear as a social rather than a military institution. In contrast with leprosy, which he characterizes as a disease requiring
the exclusion of diseased individuals, the plague calls for their containment and
surveillance. An adaptation of the military methods for regulating bodies, quarantine procedures first confine the populace to the space of the city. Next, the
space so defined is divided into successively smaller districts, each with its own set
of tasks and appropriate overseers, until everyone is fixed to a spot—within his or
her household. Then, Foucault writes,

> five or six days after the beginning of the quarantine, the process of purifying the
> houses one by one is begun. All the inhabitants are made to leave; in each room "the
> furniture and goods" are raised from the ground or suspended from the air; perfume
> is poured around the room; after carefully sealing the windows, doors and even the
> keyholes with wax, the perfume is set alight. Finally, the entire house is closed while
> the perfume is consumed; those who have carried out the work are searched, as they
> were on entry, "in the presence of the residents of the house to see that they did not
> have something on their persons as they left that they did not have on entering." Four
> hours later, the residents are allowed to re-enter their homes.[9]

Ritual purification amounts to reclassification at the most elementary cultural
level. The household seals the space occupied by the family unit, quite literally,

from the public space of the streets. This curiously superfluous description in-
stantly redefines the interior of the household as an enclosed world and the entire
city as an enormous cluster of such tiny private interiors connected systematically
by lines of information-power that anticipate the institutional procedures
crisscrossing the interior space of the panopticon.

Nowhere in *Discipline and Punish* does Foucault explicitly establish a relationship between what goes on inside the household (the practices associated with biological reproduction and the ordinary care of the body) and what goes on outside (the practices of surveillance, education, remediation, or, in a word, social
reproduction). It is as if the ritual purification of the household has a similar effect on his thinking. For this space remains prophylactically sealed off from modern institutional life, much as if politics stopped at the threshold, mysteriously incapable of penetrating the world of women. Yet the redefinition of the household
as a space in which the modern family could be inscribed is absolutely essential to
his historical argument. Discipline does not escape confinement to the military
institutions until it magically appears as the total regulation of bodies within the
household that will presumably remain even after the external quarantine procedures have been lifted. *Discipline and Punish* indeed reveals how the military notion of discipline escaped from the sphere to which it had been confined and began to organize both information and people (indeed, began to organize people
as information) at many locations within European culture. But while his book
establishes the vital link between the military and the prison, it does not explain
what it implies—the crucial role played by the family in effecting this historical
transformation.

To argue that "family" should be no more acceptable in our political vocabulary than "war" because the two cannot in fact be distinguished, let me turn first
to an example from contemporary journalism. A story entitled "In Cities, Poor
Families Are Dying of Crack" made the front page of the *New York Times* a year
ago (when the so-called "war on drugs" was still in its domestic phase). With two
exceptions, the article reduces the victims of crack—representing virtually millions of people in the United States—to no more than three family roles. Conspicuously lacking is any mention of race or class. However, there is no question that
the crack cocaine victims are poor and belong to an unspecified ethnic and/or racial minority. So what is accomplished by describing them in terms of their roles
in "the family"? Examples from the article provide the best answer.

It begins with the following statement, "Crack is rapidly accelerating the destruction of families in poor urban neighborhoods where mothers are becoming
increasingly addicted and children are selling the drug in greater numbers than
ever before."[10] The article proceeds to classify the "observed elements of family
breakdown" in the following manner:

1. Children are taking over as heads of their families, largely because of their in-
    comes from selling crack.

2. Young pregnant mothers are endangering their lives to get the drug, and in many cases, people describe mothers or brothers procuring sex for the young women in their families to raise money to buy it.
3. Teenage girls are abandoning their families and forming what social scientists say are new and violent gangs to sell or buy crack.
4. In some neighborhoods, female users outnumber male users for the first time. For years, it had been women, more often than not, who held poor families together.

After thus listing the wisdom to be garnered from the story that follows, the article offers six columns' worth of small domestic tragedies. The entire cast of characters consists of "mother," "baby," "boy," "girl," or "women." There are two violations of this generic rule—one a hideously scarred female addict named Sonya H. and the other a former addict named Larry Brown. Now in a treatment center, Larry is neither anonymous nor foreign. He has joined the world of ethnically assimilated people with last names—Dr. Peter Pinto, Dr. Phillip Bourgois, Dr. Richard Curtis, Dr. Terry Williams, Dr. Ansley Hamid, Dr. William Kornblum—from whom expert testimony has been solicited. According to the naming practices at work in the article, however, he is (like Sonya) marked as the anomalous case for doing so.

The result of all these family melodramas is a single melodrama in which "the family" becomes the victim of crack. It invites us to hold specific though nameless individuals responsible for destroying a highly abstract set of roles. It turns the war against drugs into a war against the women and children who are victims of drugs. In every statement just cited from the *New York Times,* the presence of an active verb translates an ostensible victim into an aggressor: "Children *take over* as heads of their families"; "Young pregnant mothers *endanger* their lives"; "Teenage girls are *abandon*ing their families"; but, worst of all, "female users are *outnumber*ing male users" (italics mine). How could women be committing the ultimate act of aggression simply by "outnumbering" men? In the words of the article, "it had been women, more often than not, who held poor families together." Because these women and children ceased to exist within the domestic model, the press seems to hold them, especially the women, responsible for the death of "the family." Boldly entitled "Use of Crack Is Said to Stifle the Instincts of Parenthood," another article argues, "The one thing crack addicts have in common … is utter disregard for their children." "'I've been working with female drug addicts and their children for 21 years, and I've never seen anything like it,'" reports Dr. Lorraine E. Hale, president of Hale House in Harlem, which cares for addicts' babies until homes can be found for them.[11]

It is important to remember that the very people most likely to indict women addicts would also be willing to admit that the traditional family is an exceptional case if not downright fiction for nonaddicts as well. Its failures provide the material for American talk shows and advice columns, the plots of our popular romances, the typical situations for situation comedies on television, the object of satire for such outrageously antisentimental shows as "The Simpsons" and "Married with Children," the staple of popular journalism surrounding politicians and TV evangelists, and the conceptual framework for accounts of domestic violence that regularly make front-page news in this country. These are but a few of the signs substantiating findings that indicate that less than 40 percent of our population has lived within a traditional household for the past two decades. Most recently, the number has fallen below 30 percent.[12] Furthermore, in view of statistics describing what happens to people who do live in nuclear families, one can hardly feel sorry for those who do not.[13] A recent study finds that 42 percent of the women murdered in the United States are killed by another member of their family, most often the husband. According to the American College of Obstetricians and Gynecologists, as many as 45 percent of battered women are assaulted while pregnant.[14] When someone has done violence to a woman, according to statistics offered by law enforcement agents and social scientists, the most likely suspects are those males most closely related to her. Indeed, it could be said that wife battering is one problem in the United States that seems ruthlessly democratic. The higher a family's income, the ore likely it is that a female member of that family will die at the hands of another family member—simply because she is less likely to die on the streets.[15] The statistics for child abuse are even more deplorable. Yet the *New York Times* article on the consequences of crack uses the lack of a traditional family structure to place crack victims outside the imaginary borders of American culture.

Nothing demonstrates that what I am calling "the family" has grown more powerful as it ceased to exist as a social fact perhaps so well as a recent encounter between William Bennett, former "czar" in the presidential "war on drugs" (a mixture of metaphors that is itself revealing), and twenty-five women residents of Women, Inc., a drug treatment center in Dorchester, Massachusetts. According to an article entitled "The Two William Bennetts" that appeared in the *New York Review of Books,* Bennett began the interview by insisting the women describe the life they lead inside Women, Inc.: "Pressed for details as to their life at the center, the women described their daily routine—taking showers in the morning, cooking breakfast, cleaning the center."[16] Although these details constituted the message that Bennett wanted to hear, they did not convey the message the women wanted to express. As author Michael Massing explains, "They had the chance to talk with the nation's top drug official and wanted to tell him about the things that had drawn them to drugs—child abuse, broken families, lack of opportunity." They asked for more adequate education and detoxification facilities that would allow others like them to become fit to work and to care for their children. In response to any claim that drugs required an economic solution, however, Bennett offered a classic tautology: Economic opportunity comes to those who work hard and take responsibility. Presumably, any impoverished women could "just say no" to dope and "yes" to bathing, and her standard of living would magically improve with the ritual self-purification of her body. Massing's account of the exchange between Bennett and the members of Women, Inc., shows the czar mobilizing much the same logic at work in "the city under plague" whenever the women tried to identify an economic source for their problems.

But how did the women respond to this inversion of their argument for financial support that would increase the detoxification center's capacity to help women reclaim their children? One woman evidently sensed that Bennett came to the interview with the conviction that the women he addressed were really the source of their own predicament. For she confronted him with the question, "Do you believe that people addicted to drugs or alcohol are *bad?*" After some hesitation, he replied that while certain addicts might not be able to control themselves, others do drugs "because they don't exercise responsibility" and because they "care more about themselves than their kids and other people." This insistence on defining and solving the problem of drugs at the personal level cost Bennett his authority with the women addicts. When a member of his entourage asked the group if they noticed any effects from the so-called war on drugs, the women greeted the question with spontaneous laughter. Then one spoke up in an effort to translate their personal problems back into an economic issue. "It's not drugs," she contended, "it's gangs. You got to create jobs for them."

In the end, however, the press restored the absolute disymmetry of the exchange between Bennett and the women of Women, Inc. His failure to convince them that the solution to their problems rested solely with themselves did not keep them from reporting his visit as a success. Rather than deal with the stubborn fact that drug dealing was an occupation—if not the only work available to some people, then certainly profitable work—Bennett left the detoxification center. He displayed his absolute power over the communication situation by leaving it at will and then using Women, Inc., as he had obviously intended to use it all along, namely, to demonstrate that these women polluted and must purify themselves. This is how he described the reformed addicts to the press waiting for him outside of Women, Inc.:

> I was struck by people talking about their day here—about getting up in the morning, coming downstairs, and cooking breakfast. People are learning about good habits. They're learning about punctuality, they're learning about neatness, they're learning about personal responsibility. That's a very old lesson, but somehow along the way we forgot it. Isn't it interesting that the way out of drug addiction is to relearn this lesson about personal responsibility?[17]

This statement implies that the war on drugs can be won by redeeming fallen women and resurrecting the family. By so confining the problem to a domestic framework, Bennett shifts the whole problem of addiction out of the domain of production (the failure to provide jobs for certain groups within this country) and into the domain of reproduction (and the immorality traditionally arrogated to working-class and ethnic women).

It is important to note that Bennett presumed to speak on behalf of the same people against whom he was waging this rhetorical war. This in itself secured his victory. There is a wrong note, something deeply insulting, about the locution, "I was struck by." If we examine more closely what exactly Bennett "was struck by," we find it was nothing else but the similarity between the orderliness of his own life and the daily behavior of women who find their way to a detoxification center. *They* wake up. *They* bathe. *They* eat breakfast. Apparently these are not things he expected such women to do, not if he was so "struck by" the fact they actually do them. But behind this incredulity, I would argue, lies a strategy as old as capitalism itself. One can see it at work in the descriptions of nineteenth-century Manchester and the reports on the condition of the working classes that began to proliferate in England during the 1830s, as well as in the reports based on nineteenth-century visits to the homes of working-class New York.[18] The "lesson" of his encounter with Women, Inc., is arguably so "old," as Bennett says, because it is so effective. By focusing on the bodies of women and the conduct of personal life, these reports not only pathologize the domestic practices of ethnic and economic subgroups but also prescribe gendered norms of behavior as the appropriate cure. In the summer of 1990, Bennett could resign his position as drug czar claiming he had "won" the war on drugs. Of course he had done nothing to change the conditions that brought about drug addiction, but he had dumped the problem squarely in the laps of those least capable of solving it, namely, poor and/or ethnic single mothers. By inviting Bennett to head the Republican National Committee (an offer he later refused), the Bush administration as much as admitted that such a purely discursive victory was the only victory he sought by waging this particular war.

It could be argued that the 1988 presidential election was a competition between George Bush and Michael Dukakis in which each claimed to speak on behalf of the family. Bush won in part because he made the same noises Bennett would soon be making—those of an embattled father defending the neighborhood from Spanish-speaking hoodlums who hook "American" children on drugs. The terms in which Bush represented the un-American way people live in most of Central and South America remind one of the way the government regards drug addicts within the United States—that is, as a source of pollution. (In retrospect one can see why it was probably a mistake for Dukakis to identify himself as an ethnic or to speak fluent Spanish on national TV.) The media saw no contradiction between Bush's threats of military aggression—nor even the actual invasion of Panama—and his election promise to lead "a kinder and gentler nation." Conspicuous among the first bits of information to come out of Panama after the U.S. invasion was a report that, before calling his wife, the deposed General Manuel Noriega called his mistress to let her know he was safe. Upon breaking into his headquarters, the officers who led that phase of the invasion reported that they found testimony to his filth—pornography, the trappings of "witchcraft" ceremonies, and fifty pounds of cocaine. Several weeks after Noriega had been incarcerated by U.S. drug enforcement authorities, the Pentagon admitted that what were believed to be bags of cocaine, upon further investigation, turned out to be the flour for making tamales.

This much of my essay was completed in July 1990, with no sense of where "the family" would strike next, though with a conviction that it had spread throughout the political thinking of the United States, if not the entire West, just as U.S.- and European-made military equipment has spread throughout the Third World, making itself ready for "war." Returning in January to ready the manuscript for publication, I felt painfully compelled to turn (however briefly, and with none of the certainty of hindsight) to the collaboration between "war" and "family" in the lurid staging of the "war in the Gulf." It is fair to say that familial discourse was used in the war against Panama to launch a personalized attack on Noriega that would single him out from the Panamanian people. Spanish-speaking America, and the family of man in general. By doing so, the U.S. government could claim to rescue the Panamanians from our mutual enemy and not from themselves. We are their kin, this logic implies, and Noriega is not. With Saddam Hussein, this strategy assumed exponentially grander proportions. Early on, in the purely verbal phase of the war in Iraq, the cards of the family were being dealt out to play a rather different game of hegemony. The defamilialization of President Hussein did not aim to single him out as a weak and aberrant individual so much as to make him into a monster capable of global pollution. It was on such discursive terrain that George Bush could equate going to war against the people of Iraq with preventing a madman rom raping Kuwaiti women and children. Within a few days of this speech we watched Israel donning gas masks in fear of missiles with disease-bearing warheads.

Nor can the Iraqi danger to "innocent civilians" be confined to the region of the world we call "the Middle East." The major networks routinely included reports by antiterrorist officials in Washington as well as local airport officials concerning the measures being taken to protect travelers against terrorist attacks. These reports told not only of restricting the appropriate sections of the airports to passengers but also of searching and interrogating Arab-looking individuals with Arab-sounding names who tried to board planes throughout the United States and Europe. This language made it both impossible to be "for" Hussein and possible to say virtually anything against him. To mention but one among countless examples, more than once in early January 1990 David Letterman's nightly "top ten" list included "Take a shower" and "Send out for McRibs" among the top ten things Saddam Hussein wanted to do before January 15. This particular attack on Islamic food codes combined with the racial slur against the personal hygiene of Arabs is hardly the most ingenious effort to link that culture's traditional notion of purity with our own notion of filth. There is only one conclusion to be drawn from this and countless other bits of information that saturated the media: The Iraqi military is inhuman. As such, it endangers humanity. Indeed, the implication is, we are not invading their country; they have invaded ours.

The effect of such intensive semiotic warfare is to portray the Iraqi military as the source of an infectious disease. Iraq cannot simply be singled out and exiled from humanity in the manner of lepers, however. It must be purified and reclaimed for "the family of nations" by measures reminiscent of those called forth in Foucault's example of "city under plague." That a solution can only be formulated in such terms is apparent, for example, in three articles appearing together on January 29, 1991, on a page of the Minneapolis *Star Tribune* under the label "War in the Gulf." Their titles read as follows: "Gulf May Be Nuclear Tinderbox Even Without Iraq," "Oil Slick Bears Down on Saudi Way of Life That's Centuries Old," and "Iraq's First Lady." To my mind, these articles can be used to understand the stakes in what will certainly prove an ongoing struggle. They identify Iraq as a cultural rather than a military threat. Together they imply that it is cultural difference alone which requires nothing short of an epic attempt at sanitation, supervision, and internal reorganization of the kind that only the Western family can provide. The first item contends that the danger of nuclear contamination in the Middle East remains unabated even though "Iraq's nuclear facilities now lie in ruins": "Over the last few weeks, Bush and administration officials and independent nuclear specialists have grown increasingly worried about new signs that Iran may be starting down the path of its Gulf rival, with secret efforts to buy nuclear technology and build nuclear weapons."[19] Where the first article keeps the threat of nuclear weapons and germ warfare alive despite the demolition of Iraq's military infrastructure, the second supplies proof that Iraq was hell-bent on global pollution. The article begins, "Any day now, the last fishermen of Safwa expect an ugly black island to wash up and blot out a way of life that has sustained them for centuries."[20] And finally, the *Star Tribune* suggests that these threats emanate from within the personal life of Hussein himself—his demonstrable hostility to the values of the family.

The reader's eye travels to the lower right-hand corner of the page to encounter a blurred photograph of the Iraqi President's first wife (Sajida Hussein is Iraq's "first" lady in a double sense) and an article that opens with this catalog of features from a grade-B X-rated movie: "She's a clothes horse. She's a bottle blonde. She's the headmistress of a girls' school. She's a jealous wife, and with good reason. She's the wife of a killer. She's her husband's first cousin."[21] Readers who wonder why the fact that her husband is both her cousin and a killer gives Sajida Hussein "good reason" to be a "jealous wife" must wade through half the article to discover that Hussein has replaced her, though she is his legal wife and mother of five children, with a second wife—or possibly, mistress—named Samira. (Never mind that the Saudi royal family practices polygamy.) "In either case," says the newspaper, "Hussein's relationship with Samira surely strained his family life." Yet, the same account suggests he never really had a family life, that even his first wife was a whore. Marriage with Hussein would therefore be unclean "in either case" because it is inherently hostile to the family.

How can the West deal with someone so filthy without risking infection to itself? Only by taking extraordinary health and sanitation measures. The coalition forces do not attack civilians but perform "surgical bombing" with "smart bombs" that can "take out" specified military objectives. We are being asked, in effect, to think of our military aggression as an act of purification: it cuts out the source of pollution as if it were a tumor, takes it out like trash. Caught in the intricate and subtle fabric of good-housekeeping discourse, even our least antiseptic maneuver can still sound like tidying up. After all, "carpet bombing" is what one does to rid a house of fleas. And when the Pentagon and Bush administration could no longer describe forces in Saudi Arabia as a "desert shield" (suggesting sanitary protection as well as chivalric armor), they switched to the apocalyptic language of "The Battle Hymn of the Republic" ("storm," "thunder," "lightning") with hardly any difficulty at all. The transformation posed no more of a contradiction than exists between such cleaning products as "Mr. Clean" and "Ajax," also known as "the white Tornado." For the fantasy that organized the Gulf War is the same one that organized the war on drugs and Foucault's city—a fantasy of ruthless sanitation in which everything is destroyed that cannot be contained within private households.

Since its lineaments cannot be distinguished from those of the family, I have tried to suggest, the discourse of war is entirely familiar, and yet it is also disturbingly new. There are many reasons for the family's uncanny power to reappear and polarize almost any political issue, not the least of which is its ability to exclude all information that would allow us to think our way out of the murderous abstractions it naturalizes. Indeed, I have encountered little information either at the university or in the media that would promote understanding of the historical forces that produced Iraq and constitute its present relationship to the nations around it. That no such supplement exists to counter the dehumanizing effects of the family is confirmed by a second effect. If familial discourse gives us no sense of the diverse ethnic and class composition of the "enemy," it is not much better at representing the character of a volunteer army that, on the one hand, seems to care little about the ethnic differences that shape official representations of the opposing army and, on the other, understandably feels resentment for the college kids and intellectuals opposing the war back home.

It is easy to see all the elements of the city under plague congealing once again—a demonic source of pollution, a susceptible population, a call for sanitary measures, and technologies that direct at once the flow of information and the disposition of bodies. It is far more difficult to describe adequately the operations of the family in contemporary political discourse. In calling attention to a few of its manifestations, I have tried to describe it as something like a disease in its own right, one whose fragmentation and dispersal has not brought recovery but something more like a cultural metastasis. I consider this essay only one small example of the kind of work that might be done at the intersection of critical theory, feminism, and cultural studies to show that the family does not provide a historical refuge from and antidote to "war" but rather its cultural anchor and moral justification.

NOTES

1. Christine Stansell, *City of Women: Sex and Class in New York 1789–1860* (Urbana: University of Illinois Press, 1987), p. 64.

2. In *Family Fortunes* (Chicago: University of Chicago Press, 1987), Leonore Davidoff and Catherine Hall have documented the separation of home from workplace. They argued that this new division of cultural space did not remove the family from the economy but simply changed its meaning. The demonstrable well-being of a man's household outside the city began testifying to the prosperity of his business downtown. Those men blessed by a substantial home in the new suburbs simultaneously solidified their hold over the English economy and established their own domestic life as the standard against which to measure other people. Different sexual practices denoted a lack of sexual regulation, especially in women. The same logic that said a man's family was healthy because his business was good thus implied that other cultures were poor because their women were bad. Groups whose women failed to display signs of domesticity consequently existed in the respectable imagination as places, in the words of Edward Said, "requiring Western attention, reconstruction, even redemption," *Orientalism* (New York: Vintage, 1979), p. 206.

3. Stansell, *City of Women*, p. 218.

4. For an analysis of black women's relation to the dominant gender codes, see Hazel Carby's *Reconstructing Womanhood: The Emergence of the Afro-American Woman Novelist* (New York: Oxford University Press, 1987). She described their appropriation of those codes to indict southern culture on grounds that a society's advancement could be measured by the way it treated women (including black women). She also explained that the same codes automatically set white middle-class feminism against women who could not politely detach themselves from the world of politics and work (see especially pp. 95–120).

5. Lydia Sargent's collection entitled *The Unhappy Marriage of Marxism and Feminism* (London: Pluto Press, 1986) dramatizes some of the exclusions that become apparent whenever feminism tries to extend its agenda beyond the upper middle class. Even when it restricts its definition of women to this class, feminism's tendency to collapse the household with the nuclear family and gender roles with those defined by the monogamous heterosexual can raise objections from lesbians and from members of ethnic groups accustomed to some other way of organizing the household. Despite more recent models of "women" based on "difference," "heterogeneity," or "subject positions," the problem exposed by Sargent's collection has not gone away. See, for example, Jane Gallop, "The Problem of Definition," *Genre* 20, no. 2 (1987): 111–132, and Linda Gordon, "On 'Difference,'" *Genders* 10 (1991).

6. *Women's Oppression Today: The Marxist/Feminist Encounter* (London: Verso, 1980), p. 211.

7. Notable exceptions to this rule are Michele Barrett and Mary McIntosh's *The Anti-Social Family* and Barrett's *Women's Oppression Today*, pp. 187–226. As Barrett cautions, "Unless we develop a more critical awareness of the family as a social, not a natural unit, we run the risk of mechanically assigning it to either 'cause' or 'effect' in the study of social change" (p. 188). Both designations are unsatisfactory because they reinforce "it," or the

idea of "the family," and with it the sexual division of labor, as a stable if not entirely natural entity: "Women's dependence on men is reproduced ideologically, but also in material relations, and there is a mutually strengthening relationship between them. It is not simply that an ideology of the family causes women to be used as 'reserve army' labourers and as cheap producers of labour power; nor is it simply that capitalism creates an ideology of gender difference to legitimate the exploitation of women. The ideological and material cannot be so neatly separated as either of these formulations would imply" (p. 211).

8. Michel Foucault, *The History of Sexuality: An Introduction,* Volume I, trans. Robert Hurley (New York: Random House, 1978). "The family, in its contemporary form, must not be understood as a social, economic, and political structure of alliance that excludes or at least restrains sexuality, that diminishes it as much as possible, preserving only its useful functions," Foucault explains. Rather, the family "ensures the production of a sexuality that is not homogeneous with the privileges of alliance, while making it possible for the systems of alliance to be embued with a new tactic of power which they would otherwise be impervious to" (p. 108).

9. Michel Foucault, *Discipline and Punish: The Birth of the Prison,* trans. Alan Sheridan (New York: Random House, 1979), p. 197.

10. Gina Kolata, "In Cities, Poor Families Are Dying of Crack," *New York Times,* August 11, 1989, p. 1.

11. Michael Decourcy Hinds, "Use of Crack Is Said to Stifle the Instincts of Parenthood," *New York Times,* March 17, 1990, p. 8.

12. "Change in the American Family: Now Only 1 in 4 is 'Traditional,'" *New York Times,* vol. 140, January 30, 1991, p. C20. The Census Bureau reports that "in 1970, 40 percent of the nation's households were made up of a married couple and one or more children under the age of 18. That proportion dropped to 31 percent in 1980 and to 26 percent last year. ... The number of single mothers (8.4 million of those 9.7 million single parents) was up 35 percent from 1980, as against an 82 percent increase in the 1970s."

13. See, for example, Lloyd Ohlin and Michael Tonry, *Family Violence,* vol. 2 (Chicago: University of Chicago Press, 1989).

14. Fox Butterfield, "Suspicions Came Too Late in Boston," *New York Times,* January 29, 1990, p. 25.

15. Ibid., p. 25.

16. Michael Massing, "The Two William Bennetts," *New York Review of Books,* vol. 32, no. 3, March 1, 1990, p. 29.

17. Ibid., p. 30.

18. Armstrong, *Desire and Domestic Fiction: A Political History of the Novel* (New York: Oxford, 1987), pp. 162–187.

19. Jim Mann, "Gulf May Be Nuclear Tinderbox Even Without Iraq," *Star Tribune,* January 29, 1991, p. 4A.

20. Associated Press, "Oil Slick Bears Down on Saudi Way of Life That's Centuries Old," *Star Tribune,* January 29, 1991, p. 4A.

21. (From the *Washington Post*) "Iraq's First Lady: Hussein's Wife of 32 Years Remains 'Mystery Woman,'" *Star Tribune,* January 29, 1991, p. 4A.

3

Not in Our Name:
Women, War, AIDS

ANN CVETKOVICH & AVERY GORDON

PART ONE
War Machines and Washing Machines[1]
Avery Gordon

I want to talk to you today from somewhere between the head and heart (and maybe the stomach, too) because they say that in times of war and peace, home is usually where women are, and they say that in times of war and peace home is where the heart is.* I'd like to suggest that what is at stake in the Gulf War is where and how we live at home. And, I want to ask you to think about three questions. These questions are: (1) What is the relationship between war machines and washing machines? (2) Where does war take place? and (3) How can we fight for a better home?

What's the relationship between war machines and washing machines? Some of you may be aware that during World War II, women entered the paid labor force, particularly in munitions work, in numbers historically unprecedented for white middle-class and working-class women. There they learned industrial and craft skills they had previously been denied and were thanked by government propa-

---

Editors' Note: The following two pieces are speeches that were given at rallies during the Gulf War in 1991. In addition to the war, they address issues such as disease and domesticity that have a bearing on the topics raised in this section of the book.

ganda films for their willingness to do their part for the war effort. Defending democracy and leaving the dishwashing to pile up, these Rosie the Riveters were sent home after the war to continue making their contribution to the building of the New American Century: to serve freeze-dried food on atomic dishware, to stockpile canned rations for the atomic age, and to become distinctly nuclear objects of desire—"dishes" and "bombshells."[2] Participating in the new war economy, what we now call the military-industrial complex, by tending to their washing machines, white middle-class women were asked to perform exactly the same function as the Pentagon: to be alert and on call for the preparation for war.

Today, America is at war to revenge what George Bush has called the "rape" of Kuwait and in order to prepare for the next New American Century. The next New American Century shares certain features with the last New American Century. Based on the equation of freedom and empire, today's language of the moral just cause masks the continuing patriarchal paternalism of an international military-industrial political economy. Proclaiming America the world's housekeeper, George Bush, the weak father, becomes strong by protecting his women from the bad father who raped his neighbor. Yet, in George Bush's housekeeping message (his 1991 State of the Union Address), the unpaid or underpaid women housekeepers—whether homemakers, secretaries, munitions workers, or prostitutes—who keep the house in order were invisible. The economic, bodily, psychic, and political violation of millions of American women is not, for Bush, a ground for waging a just war. Only the "rape" of a country, which is in our national geography halfway around "the" world, counts as a cause for national mobilization.

The imaging of the New American Century repeats a persistent gendered theme that confuses the family of nations with the nuclear family: patriotic marriages. Whether through public opinion polls that use women's supposed support for the war as evidence of widespread patriotism, even among those who are normally opposed to war, or through the deployment of figures such as Mrs. Norman Schwarzkopf, who function as unelected representatives for the "families of our men and women serving in the Gulf," women are being asked and are often volunteering to make patriotic marriages for the "hard work of freedom."

Generally speaking, feminists don't expect the state, newsmakers, or international policymakers to make explicit how "guns and money," the terms of war, rely on longstanding notions of masculinity and femininity. Feminists don't expect that men in power will explain how war requires "women as feminized workers, as respectable and loyal wives, as 'civilizing influences', as sex objects, as obedient daughters, as unpaid farmers, as coffee-serving campaigners, as consumers and tourists."[3] But I hadn't expected that some of the language and goals of feminism would be stolen and used as a justification for a war for an America that promotes freedom as patriotic marriage and patriarchal authoritarianism. The Pride is Back but this time because "our" women wear combat fatigues, drive jeeps, work sophisticated electronic surveillance equipment without veils, and maybe might actually kill people. Veiling the real news, *Newsweek* featured a short article on the first female POW. "For women in the military attaining equality may carry a heavy price," the story tells us. Transforming the desire for equality into a form of social control, this story reminds us that as women at home we support our sisters on the front while at the same time we resist their use as alibis for an unjust war. This war is *not* about America saving brown, black, and white women from rape, injustice and tyranny. In this context, it might not be a bad idea for us women at home to call ourselves Prisoners of War.

I have to tell you that I've been disturbed by the image of George Bush and the Pentagon as feminist. I'm disturbed about this because a name I claim is being cynically used for purposes I find unconscionable. And I'm disturbed because I thought that there was some connection between the historical convergence of the women's liberation movement, the student antiwar movement, and the civil rights and black power movements. I thought that they were fighting, sometimes together and sometimes not, to blow up both war machines and washing machines—to blow up the system of domination and privilege the war machine defends and the washing machine cleans. And I thought they were teaching us that there are wars at home and wars abroad and that they are not unrelated. Many of the participants in these movements felt they were already engaged in a kind of guerrilla warfare, motivated by the desire to invent something really different, and motivated equally by outrage, passion, and careful strategy. Sometimes making frontal attacks, sometimes laying in wait, sometimes camouflaged, sometimes out in the open, often fashioning weapons and alliances by taking what was found, we believed that a successful movement of bodies and ideas was a war worth fighting and maybe even winning.

And so my second question. Where does war take place? From the participants in the International Congress of Women in 1915, who took collective action across political boundaries during World War I to establish peace, to Virginia Woolf's important antiwar statement in 1938, to the women of Greenham Common, who left their homes in the early 1980s to live in protest at the missile bases, many women, asked to maintain the home front, refused to participate in a nationalistic and patriotic will to power. They also refused to play the role of a domestic peacemaker, and they refused to raise children as soldier machines, ready for that always future battle. And they also refused to accede to the so-called "gentle art of peace and nurturance," arts and crafts that keep women committed to both the "defense systems and the nurturant systems of [our] society."[4]

In 1938, after spending three years trying to answer a letter sent to her by an "educated" man who wanted to know how, in her opinion as a woman, war was to be prevented, Virginia Woolf answered with fighting words. Her answer, 150 pages long, was that women are already embattled, engaged in a struggle for dear life, a struggle against poverty, ignorance, homelessness, ill health, domestic violence, and violence in the streets. War is the procession of white men doing their business, she said, the business of violence, the business of imperialism, the business of exploitation and inequality between the rich and the poor, the business of oppressing groups and individuals.War is a very big business, she said, and so is "peace more than the absence of war." Peace requires recognizing the "complicity of war and social wrongs to entire populations."[5] Peace requires understanding that war takes place even during peacetime. But Virginia Woolf, tired and weary with no one listening to her, said this before she took her life at the banks of the river where she often walked:

> "Our" country ... throughout the greater part of its history has treated me as a slave; it has denied me education or any share in its possessions. ... "Our" country denies me the means of protecting myself, forces me to pay others a very large sum annually to protect me, and is so little able, even so, to protect me. ... Therefore if you insist on fighting to protect me, or "our" country, let it be understood soberly ... between us, that you are fighting to gratify a sex instinct which I cannot share; to procure benefits which I have not shared and probably will not share; but not to gratify my instincts, or to protect myself or my country. For, ... in fact, as a woman, I have no country. As a woman I want no country. As a woman my country is the whole world."[6]

These are the most famous lines in the book and they are powerful words of indifference, words of separatism designed to encourage women not to participate in the desire to "impose 'our' civilization or 'our' dominion upon other people."[7] These words were repeated in the activism of the women of Greenham Common. These were words that said: I refuse to agree to the logic of militarism. Such a logic could be translated simply as: Lie in peace, my women, I will fight the enemy to death for you. What Virginia Woolf was saying is that to be against war we need to oppose the tendency toward war, the war for the preparation of War. We need to oppose not just military men but military intelligence. We need to oppose the logic and the procedures following which a nation's potential is transferred to its armed forces in times of peace as in times of war. We need, in short, to oppose all those acts of war *not sanctioned* by capitalizing the letter W. war without War— war takes place everywhere and nowhere, she said. And in this way Woolf also suggested that, contrary to appearances, home is not always where the heart is.

There is much of importance in what Virginia Woolf wrote, but there is also the danger of believing that because war is mostly white men's business, because my country does things in my name I would rather disavow, because it's hard to be at more than one front at a time, or because we tend to respond most intently to what appears to be closest to home. ... Because of all these reasons, many women have believed that they could be women and not American women, that "as a woman, my country is the whole world." Because we cannot avoid being American women, let me encourage you to adopt instead the more difficult but still fighting words of Adrienne Rich who in 1984 rewrote what Virginia Woolf said.

> As a woman I have a country; as a woman I cannot divest myself of that country merely by condemning its government or by saying three times "As a woman my country is the whole world." Tribal loyalties aside, and even if nation-states are now just pretexts used by multinational conglomerates to serve their interests, I need to

understand how a place on the map is also a place in history within which as a woman, a Jew, a lesbian, a feminist I am created and try ... to create.[8]

What Adrienne Rich was saying was that as a white American woman, even as a feminist, she could not do otherwise than to be accountable for her Home, the United States, and what it does in her name both at home and abroad. And once you begin to study what America (and here I mean the United States because that is a long bloody history in itself that explains how the Americas became America, that is the United States) has done in my name and in your name as an American woman, it is enough to make you homesick in your own home.

One of the great conceits of our home, America, is the belief that everyone else wants to live here, or at least should have to live their lives for us—for our so-called security, for our "way of life," for our ability to consume disproportion-ately, for our dream of endless frontiers and silver screens. The "new world order" is unfortunately not so new. One has only to remember that the so-called dream of America was founded on the genocide of the Indian population, the capture and enslavement of Africans, and the silent labors and pains of many many women to wonder whether such a dream is not perhaps a frightening nightmare. Let's get closer to home. There is blood in the streets in the U.S. of A. There are unidentified dead women's bodies in the morgue and there are women missing in action. There are women who experience that they are living in a war zone, who are terrified to go out at night or terrified to stay at home. There is a war on drugs in which the U.S. government is the leading double agent and where mostly Afri-can-American women are being ordered by judges to take drugs as punishment for being what the state considers bad mothers. There are women dying because there are no rations for them. And you'd never know it because with the television blaring and all the self-righteous celebration of our seemingly great national ex-ports, freedom and democracy, it's easy to be wide awake with your eyes closed. Just what social order is this war supposed to defend?

This brings me to my final question. How can we fight for a different kind of home? If war is not just a limited problem but one fundamentally involving a logic of perception, the organization of resources, and most important, what we understand it to mean when we think we are living in peacetime, it can seem so overwhelming. And many many American women want to know: What does the struggle for a better home have to do with me? Yes, homelessness is a tragedy; yes, of course we don't really want to be killing other people or our own; I understand poverty is a terrible problem; I know it's horrible that women, blacks, gays, and chicanos, to name just the most visible targets, get killed just for being women, blacks, gays, and chicanos, as if that were all there were to being somebody. As a friend of mine reminded me, social justice is kind of an abstract idea when you're relatively privileged, when you're caught in a web of fears, including most signifi-cantly the fear of falling out of the promise of the American dream.[9] I know that right now you've got a lot of things on your minds—how to make it through school, how to be loved respectfully, how to make sure you do have a home and an income, how to acquire a little happiness. But, my question is: Do you want to reproduce the primary way in which the American government has dealt with the national anxiety about the decline of our empire? Do you want to attempt to se-cure against our own fears of falling by insisting with a force and a vengeance that our home will be everybody else's home whether they like it or not?

We are confronted not only by individual anxieties or problems. We face social problems requiring public and collective solutions. For George Bush, the individ-ual "volunteer" is the model citizen. In his housekeeping address he said that in the state of our union, it is sufficient to "get one addict off drugs. To convince one troubled teenager not to give up on life; to comfort one AIDS patient; to help one hungry child." Well, George Bush, America doesn't have just one AIDS patient, one hungry child, one troubled teenager, one woman raped, or abused, or screwed by corporate America who just needs to be "comforted." It has a society that at its core systematically beats us up in the name of loving discipline and our own desires and then pretends that it is our individual problem to bear and fix. And we all know who is primarily responsible for taking care of those messy household spills that men make!

Voluntarism is a way of managing dissent. It presumes the same kind of inevi-tability to social problems that the war has taken on. But neither War at home nor War abroad is inevitable and we must resist the equation that makes dissent trea-sonous and political resistance boring. If punks can wear combat boots, if the Pointer Sisters can do the neutron dance, if 300,000 French high school students could take to the streets in the fall (1990) because they saw the connection be-tween a rape of a young woman and the state's indifference to their education, if the women on this campus can work for a better home through organizing for peace, there's hope for a creative and playful, but deadly serious movement not only to get the troops out of someone else's house and bring them home, but to bring them into a better home, a just home where there's plenty of dancing. I'm here today to ask you to be accountable and responsible for what is being done in your name and to choose your alliances carefully. Because one thing is certain. Just as there is war, so there is resistance, whether underground or above ground. All of us will be asked to make choices: to decide with whom we will stand, from whom we will learn, and with whom we will participate in the project to create a better place to live. Thank you.

NOTES

1. What follows is a transcript of a speech I gave to students at the University of Califor-nia, Santa Barbara, on February 12, 1991, in Storke Plaza, an outdoor square in front of the student center that is used regularly by students as a public forum for teach-ins, open dis-cussions on various issues, informal music concerts, performances, graffiti art, billboarding messages, and so on. Rallies, teach-ins, sit-ins, radio programming, and infor-

national tabling and leafletting around the Gulf "Crisis" and War had been occurring regularly since the fall. Following a massive teach-in on November 14, 1990, several hundred students occupied Cheadle Hall, UCSB's administration building, during which I gave an earlier version of this speech. One hundred and ninety-six of the approximately 500 who occupied the building were arrested and tried. Some of these cases were in litigation for over eighteen months, although the FBI has ceased "visiting" the leaders of the student antiwar movement. The February 12, 1991, rally, organized by women, announced its war resistance with the title "Not in Our Name."

2. See Elaine Tyler May, *Homeward Bound: American Families in the Cold War Era* (New York: Basic Books, 1988), and Avital Ronell, "Starting from Scratch: Mastermix." *Socialist Review* 88 (April/June 1988): 73–85.

3. Cynthia Enloe, *Bananas, Beaches and Bases* (Berkeley and Los Angeles: University of California Press, 1990), p. 17.

4. Lela B. Costin, "Report on UNESCO's Report: The Role of Women in Peace Movements," in *Women and Men's Wars,* edited by Judith Stiehm (New York: Pergamon Press, 1983), pp. 313–314.

5. Ibid., p. 314.

6. Virginia Woolf, *Three Guineas* (New York: Harvest/HBJ Books, 1966), pp. 108–109.

7. Ibid., p. 109.

8. Adrienne Rich, "Notes Towards a Politics of Location (1984)," in *Blood, Bread and Poetry* (New York: W. W. Norton, 1986), p. 212.

9. See Barbara Ehrenreich, *Fear of Falling* (New York: Harper, 1989).

PART TWO

The War Against AIDS and War in the Middle East
Ann Cvetkovich

"Why don't people with AIDS get yellow ribbons?"   —*Skip Fulton,* ACT UP Austin

In memory of

John Hernandez   **Skip Fulton**

(December 2, 1962–January 19, 1991)   (September 19, 1955–November 15, 1991)

PREFACE: The following essay is a written version of material originally presented as part of the Progressive Faculty Group Teach-In Project at the University of Texas at Austin. In response to the Gulf War, members of the group organized a daily series of lunchtime teach-ins, which began on February 4, 1991, and ended on March 7, 1991. This talk was given on February 27, 1991, the same day that a ceasefire was officially declared. The date is important for two reasons. First, the problem of "linkages" explored in the talk seemed all the more important with the prospect of a so-called "end" to the war. As I suggest below, it is important to redefine the term "war" in order to understand the relation between the events in the Gulf from January through March and other political issues. It seemed particularly important to stress this point in order to explain why the ceasefire would only mean the cessation of "war" in the narrowest sense of the term. Second, the talk was one of the last in the series and is not so much a first impression of the conflict as the product of a series of experiences of "war" in the months of January and February that led me to ask about the nature of my connection to the war and my distance from it. I felt the urgency of contributing to the teach-in project as one tangible form of my commitment to antiwar activism, but I also wondered how I could claim to have any expertise as the leader of a teach-in, especially because the series was given the authority of scholarly knowledge. Eventually, though, my initial hesitation and confusion—my sense of anger, frustration, and powerlessness—came to seem symptomatic of the ways in which "experts" are defined and solicited for commentary during a state of "war." As AIDS activism has suggested, the so-called "experts" may be less than qualified to speak to the issues about which they are supposedly more informed than the general public. The distinction between the "experts" and the "people" must be challenged in order to allow everyone to speak, in order to prevent the silencing of groups by designating them as or presuming them to be ignorant and unqualified, and in order to give credibility to the opinions of those who dissent from the policies of the government.

It is difficult to know how to respond to the Gulf War without being forced to respond in terms set by the White House, the military-industrial complex, and the mainstream media. I say this because I am concerned, in the wake of many conversations with friends, students, and colleagues, about the way that antiwar activism places upon us the burden of having to *choose* between different issues and causes. As someone whose primary political involvements over the past few years have been teaching at the University of Texas and at Wesleyan University and being a member of ACT UP in Austin and in New York, I found myself in the difficult position last fall (and more so in January) of having to decide how to allot my time so as to be able to respond (both in words and in actions) to the Gulf War. As a member of ACT UP, that decision meant making a choice between going to ACT UP meetings and going to meetings of the Progressive Faculty Group (an already existing organization) and the Campaign for Peace in the Middle East (which began to organize in Austin in September 1990). My schedule was already overloaded and strained by the illness of a friend dying of AIDS. While most of the nation was glued to TV sets in order to watch what little the media had to report, I was attending my friend John's wake and planning the memorial ceremony to be held in his honor. These are not easy choices to make, and often one makes them only in practice and not in theory. How could I weigh the significance of Iraqi civilians being bombed by U.S. planes against the work of mourning John's death?

On the academic front, there were less stark but no less critical decisions to make. Should I spend my time conducting my professional business as usual, teaching classes and trying to finish my book manuscript? Or should I call these activities to a halt and spend classroom time on discussions of the war and the rest of my time attending antiwar meetings and rallies? And how could I put my academic training to work? I'm not an expert on foreign policy, on the Middle East, or on the military-industrial complex. What did I have to say about these issues that would constitute an informed opinion worth articulating publicly? It was only after some time had passed that I realized that, not only might I have something to say, but my sense of ignorance only played into the military-industrial complex's desire to control the discourse and the strategies of war. In fact, as both an AIDS activist and an "expert" in feminist theory and Marxist cultural theory, I had a position from which to speak, and I felt that it was crucial to remind people of the links between the war in the Middle East and other issues closer to home. I certainly did not want the links between my everyday life and the events in the Gulf to be filled in by Bush's or the media's calls to patriotism or to be signified by displaying a yellow ribbon.

So—how might it be possible to link AIDS, for me the most pressing personal and political issue at that moment, and war in the Middle East? To propose such "linkages" is already perhaps a transgressive political action, since George Bush is so loathe to accept the linkage between Saddam Hussein's venture into Kuwait and the Israeli presence in the Occupied Territories, which is enabled by U.S. support, or between Kuwait's rights as a nation and the Palestinian struggle for national self-determination. To create such links, it is necessary first to consider what we mean by the word "war." As a feminist, I have no trouble understanding the idea of a "war at home," a phrase that can be used to describe not just antiwar activism but other "domestic" problems. I am well aware that there is all too often a "war *in the* home" in the guise of the exploitation of women, whether it takes the overt form of sexual and domestic violence or the less visible forms of lack of access to abortion and health care, child care, and adequately paid work. And as a feminist interested in sexual politics, it is not hard to connect these women's issues to the issues raised by AIDS, the struggle against which has been hampered by the same moralizing and repressive attitudes toward sexuality, and especially homosexuality, that have so severely affected women.

To put it more crudely: Why are the already grotesquely numerous deaths of persons with AIDS (PWAs) considered less important than even the potential deaths of U.S. soldiers in the Middle East? Far more money has been poured into the protection of U.S. lives in the Middle East and into the killing of Iraqi citizens than has been spent on AIDS. And far more media coverage has been devoted to the "Showdown in the Gulf" than to the presumably less newsworthy deaths of PWAs (except when "innocent" children and white middle-class heterosexuals are dying). And far more people watch news reports about the war with sympathy and concern for their fellow citizens and family members than watch the news reports about AIDS (which often presume or encourage a fear of association with those who are dying). I find these discrepancies disturbing. Why do PWAs and their deaths remain invisible, while U.S. soldiers are not only highly visible but unavoidable, their absence from home marked by the proliferation of yellow ribbons?

There's a tie between the visibility of U.S. soldiers and the invisibility of PWAs insofar as George Bush would have us forget domestic problems in order to turn our attention to the supposed display of courage and power by the United States in the Middle East. If the money spent on war diverts funds from pressing needs at home, we are not to worry. In his January 1991 State of the Union Address, President Bush reassures us that our patriotism and rugged individualism will pull us through. Rather than the government being responsible for providing the funding and institutions that might remedy domestic problems, we are the "thousand points of light" that will provide local solutions to global problems:

> If anyone tells you America's best days are behind her, they're looking the wrong way. Tonight, I come before this house, and the American people, with an appeal for renewal. This is not merely a call for new government initiatives, it is a call for new initiative in government, in our communities, and from every American—to prepare for the next American century.
>
> America has always led by example. So who among us will set this example? Which of our citizens will lead us in this next American century? Everyone who steps forward today, to get one addict off drugs. To convince one troubled teen-ager not to give up on life; to comfort one AIDS patient; to help one hungry child.
>
> We have within our reach the promise of a renewed America. We can find meaning and reward by serving some purpose higher than ourselves—a shining purpose, the illumination of a thousand points of light. It is expressed by all who know the irresistible force of a child's hand, of a friend who stands by you and stays there—a volunteer's generous gesture, an idea that is simply right.
>
> The problems before us may be different, but the key to solving them remains the same: it is the individual—the individual who steps forward. And the state of our Union is the union of each one of us, one to the other: the sum of our friendships, marriages, families and communities.
>
> We all have something to give. So if you know how to read, find someone who can't. If you've got a hammer, find a nail. If you're not hungry, not lonely, not in trouble—seek out someone who is.
>
> Join the community of conscience. Do the hard work of freedom. That will define the state of our Union. (*New York Times,* January 30, 1991)

Bush's call to voluntarism conveniently sidesteps a number of problems. Indeed, many people with AIDS, and their friends and families, have survived through sheer force of will in the face of an often hostile or indifferent government and society. It is unlikely that the communities to whom President Bush referred include those networks of friends and lovers that support gay PWAs, who are often without the support of blood relatives and whose "marriages" go without benefit of legal sanctions. The "volunteer's generous gesture" is sometimes all that a PWA has to depend on, while the rugged individualism of America's military personnel receives the economic and social support of the government, the military, and a nation of patriotic citizens. The AIDS activist community does "the hard work of freedom" in the face of a government whose lack of action amounts to a declaration of war against its own citizens. The state of the Union and the "next American century" will include the loss of thousands of American lives to AIDS, a disaster that Bush apparently seeks to overlook or implicitly welcomes as the genocidal decimation of unwanted populations. The "war on drugs" and the "war in the Middle East" are also the names for a war against the American people and against the peoples of other nations. One of ACT UP's slogans is "Fight AIDS, not people with AIDS." Mr. Bush's wars lead to a state in which people with AIDS have to wage war not only against a disease but against government inaction and ignorance.

Out of respect for such battles, how might we stand to learn lessons from the war against AIDS that would apply to the war in the Gulf? Why do we continue to overlook AIDS deaths while continuing to watch obsessively the broadcasts that display the video screens of U.S. combat planes rather than pictures of dead and wounded U.S. soldiers and Iraqi civilians and soldiers? If we consider the links between homophobia and the public response to AIDS in this country, it is possible to see how ideologies of masculinity are constructed around the U.S. soldier and the U.S. war in the Gulf. The masculinity that is consolidated, legitimated, and celebrated when a soldier dies with honor or when the United States engages in military combat—a masculinity marked by virility, strength, freedom, and individualism—is precisely the definition of masculinity that a homophobic and sexist culture sees as threatened by homosexuality and AIDS. Rather than being depicted as a heroic fighter, the person with AIDS, and especially the homosexual person with AIDS, is depicted as a victim, a pervert, and a criminal. Rather than helping the person with AIDS, the government and the social structure continues to "blame the victim," holding homosexuals and IV drug users responsible for their illness because they have committed illegal or "immoral" acts. While mass culture represents the United States as the good father protecting the poor "raped" Kuwait from the bad father, Saddam Hussein, and happily disseminates the homoerotic spectacle of the United States "kicking ass" in the Gulf with its phallic bombs and planes, the image of sodomy at home is greeted with hatred, terror, and denial. Among the positive gains that might emerge from the AIDS crisis is the possibility that homophobia will be challenged and with it the ideology of masculinity that produces and is produced by homophobia. The same men so eager to kick Saddam's butt would probably also be more than glad to bash fags and dykes (and some will no doubt return home to rape, beat, or sexually harass the women in their lives).

There is much too that the antiwar movement might learn from AIDS activism. It is disturbing to see the media portray antiwar protests only by analogy with the anti-Vietnam protests of the 1960s. What is erased or ignored is the long history of feminist, antiracist, gay, lesbian, and AIDS activism that has marked the past thirty years. The AIDS activism of the past five years, for example, marks a significant shift in activist tactics. ACT UP was among those groups whose response to the war was swift. On January 17, an ACT UP affinity group named Action Tours managed to seize control of the CBS Evening News Report, appearing on screen holding signs saying "Fight AIDS not Arabs" before a startled Dan Rather had them whisked away. ACT UP has understood the importance of cultural politics, of intervening against mainstream media representations, whether literally, as in the case of the Dan Rather protest, or more indirectly, by getting media coverage of protests or producing alternative information in the form of videos, stickers and posters, and treatment and data reports.

ACT UP has also had to contend with the problem of linkage by analyzing how the problem of AIDS is connected to and exacerbated by sexism, racism, and homophobia. Originally composed primarily of white, middle-class gay men, ACT UP groups around the country have had to cope with accusations of sexism and racism from within the group and undertake the difficult task of doing outreach to other communities and social groups. There is much to be learned from their experience about how to form a direct action coalition and about the complexities of 1990s activism, which, having learned both positive and negative lessons from the 1960s, must respond to the demands of coalition politics. In arguing about whether to focus narrowly on AIDS or to expand to combat other issues, ACT UP groups have had to manage the difficulties of maintaining a unified struggle in the face of a diverse membership that includes many different perspectives and social positions.

Furthermore, because the AIDS issue is so centrally connected with issues of sexual politics, it opens up definitions of the "political." Just as feminists claimed that the "private is political," so AIDS activists have had to insist on the centrality of the bedroom, of issues of sexual preference, and of norms of sexual behavior in the construction of Western capitalist culture. Such a lesson should not be forgotten during a time when it is tempting to turn away from such apparently "trivial" or "decadent" concerns to the "hard-core" or "real" issues of international diplomacy and military combat. As a feminist whose work focuses on women's popular culture and sexual politics, I was at first ready to declare myself unable to comment on the men's world of war. It was only after some time that I realized that my AIDS activism and my feminism equipped me to offer a distinct position on the war and that I could understand the apparent irrelevance of my perspective as one more form of silencing and censorship.

One of the images most strongly associated with ACT UP is the slogan "Silence=Death" coupled with the inverted pink triangle. Just as AIDS activism suggests that "war" must be redefined, so too does it suggest that "death" needs to be redefined and that doing so can be a tremendously productive political gesture. Rather than attributing death from AIDS to biological and natural causes, ACT UP relocates the source of death in the silencing tactics of homophobia and in the social and political response or lack of response from government and medical institutions. If "Silence=Death," then, as ACT UP/LA proposes, "Action=Life." An AIDS diagnosis need not be a death sentence; as thousands of politically active PWAs have shown, it is possible to live with AIDS and to struggle against the effects of structural inequalities and epistemic violence.

The "War in the Middle East" began long before the events of January 1991 or the events of August 1990 and it will continue long after the ceasefire and long after U.S. troops leave the Gulf (if indeed they ever really do). If the linkage between the war against AIDS and the war in the Middle East is to have any impact, it will have to come from the continuation of forms of protest against the U.S. military-industrial complex and the mass media. There may be no more U.S. soldiers who die in the Middle East, but many more PWAs are going to die in the years to come, and all of us who survive both here and abroad will continue to live with the disastrous aftereffects of Bush's little war. It is important that the struggle continue through all the forms in which we wage political and cultural warfare. Act Up! Fight Back! Fight AIDS!

4

The Meaning of Property:
Real Estate, Class Position, and the
Ideology of Home Ownership

PIERRE BOURDIEU & MONIQUE DE SAINT MARTIN

Translated by Michael Hardt

THE RAPID INCREASES since 1950 in the rate of families that own or are gaining ownership of their residences (in the vast majority of cases, individual houses) both demonstrates and masks a very profound transformation in the strategies of accumulation and transmission of property among certain social categories. Upon analysis, this transformation reveals variations in the division between owning and renting houses and apartments according to social categories and generations.

Everything seems to indicate that there is a decline in the direct transmission of homes through inheritance. As Claude Taffin has shown, in 1984 recent owners who gained their property through inheritance or as a gift represented only 9 percent of the total of new owners.[1] Inversely, purchase on credit constitutes the most frequent mode of acquiring a principal residence (according to the 1984 study, 78.2 percent of the recent owners relied on loans). The amount of annual payments (which rose from 1,500 francs in 1978 to 35,700 francs in 1984) is continually increasing as a proportion of the household budget of those who become owners at a continually younger age and who do not expect to inherit the residence of their parents, which in the majority of cases is destined to be sold. Contrary to what we observe in older generations, where those who became owners did so almost always through inheritance or through the slow accumulation of savings,

___
The rules throughout this essay indicate that the authors wrote alternating sections of the essay.

45

the owners of the more recent generations treat the ability to gain ownership as a means to securing housing while amassing a family patrimony. At the same time, the rate of savings is continually diminishing—from 18 percent in 1970 to 12 percent in 1987—and this is not counterbalanced by a rise in homeowner credits, which in fact remained stable during the same period.[2]

But this overall picture of the growing percentage of people gaining ownership misses the essential point. It is undoubtedly true that the highest rate of ownership is still found in the sector of society characterized by the predominance of economic capital over social capital, and in particular among the owners of business and industry, both large and small, among the farmers and among professionals—all of these are categories that have participated only very slightly in this recent movement toward acquisition. The fact remains, however, that gains in residence ownership have been most marked in the portion of society defined by the primacy of cultural capital over economic capital, in other words, in all the upper-level categories of the public and semi-public sector (engineers, high-level managers); in the middle-level public-sector categories (technicians, middle-level managers, officer workers), with the exception of the artistic and intellectual professions; among the upper regions of the working class (foremen, highly skilled workers); and even among a nonnegligible segment of factory workers and manual workers (see Table 4.1).

Therefore, the overall process of growth in the rate of ownership is accompanied by a homogenization of two sectors that are opposed on the horizontal dimension of social space, that is, from the point of view of the structure of capital. One important segment of these categories, consisting of those who seldom managed to make purchase of a home a major form of investment in the past and would have offered a natural clientele for a policy favoring the creation of public rental housing (individual homes or apartments), has entered, thanks to credit and government assistances, into the logic of the accumulation of an economic patrimony and has become part, in the strategies of reproduction, of the direct transmission of material goods. At the same time, however, an important segment of the social categories situated at the opposite pole, consisting of those who had previously counted only on their economic inheritance to maintain their social position, has had to rely on the school system to negotiate the changes imposed by the rigors of competition. These two complementary and convergent movements undoubtedly have contributed more than anything else to the lessening of the distance and the antagonisms between the Right and the Left in society and, consequently, also in politics, replacing the different oppositions that divided the reality and the representation of the social world (liberalism and statism, owning and renting, private and public) with lessened oppositions between mixed forms such as co-ownership and multiple ownership.

In the first period of rapid growth in housing development, which stretched from 1950 to 1963–1964, high and middle-level managers turned toward ownership in great numbers while the proportion of owners rose almost as fast among

TABLE 4.1   The "First Owners" of Houses in 1984

	First Owner	Not First Owner	Total
Farmers	31.2	68.8	100
Specialized factory workers	49.8	50.2	100
Qualified factory workers	63.9	36.1	100
Foremen	67.6	32.4	100
Service workers	50.1	49.9	100
Retired workers	33.8	66.2	100
Craftsmen	59.2	40.8	100
Merchants	53.8	46.2	100
Retired craftsmen and merchants	39.7	60.3	100
Police and military	62.3	37.7	100
Private-sector office workers	48.0	52.0	100
Business administration	56.9	43.1	100
Public-sector office workers	59.1	40.9	100
Retired office workers	38.0	62.0	100
Mid-level private-sector employees	63.9	36.1	100
Mid-level public-sector employees	62.5	37.5	100
Technicians	68.3	31.7	100
Teachers	61.7	38.3	100
Retired mid-level employees	44.7	55.3	100
Executives	63.2	36.8	100
Private-sector management	56.9	43.1	100
Engineers	66.6	33.4	100
Public-sector management	66.6	33.4	100
Professors	46.0	54.0	100
Professionals	28.8	71.2	100
Artists	24.1	75.9	100
Retired management	47.1	52.9	100
Others	30.5	69.5	100
Average	50.5	49.5	100

NOTE: In the 1984 INSEE study, technicians, foremen, engineers, and public-sector managers were the most likely to be the first owners of the houses they lived in. This finding would suggest that these categories also had the most new house owners in the early 1980s.

SOURCE: INSEE study, 1984. Table prepared at the request of the authors.

workers and lower-level employees (who started, however, from a much lower rate) and decidedly less fast among professionals and business owners both large and small.[3] After the drop between 1964 and 1968, which affected all of the social categories but mostly the workers, the growth of ownership rebounded at a relatively rapid rate (though still lower than in the 1950s), principally among high and middle-level managers and among highly skilled workers and foremen; however, the office workers, factory workers, and manual workers remained at a very low level, and the business owners and professionals experienced a smaller growth than any of the other categories. After 1974, the growth of ownership of housing in general slowed down once again, even though ownership of individual homes maintained a steady level and even experienced a slight growth in the 1980s. This growth came about because at the end of the 1970s, new products introduced by the large industrial and semi-industrial construction firms arrived en masse in a market created by new forms of assistance and credit. These products were designed to attract new buyers and targeted principally the highly skilled workers, the office workers, and middle-level managers.[4]

The Determinant Factors of "Choice"

Having noted the broad evolution in the distribution of different modes of housing, we shall now describe the structure of the system of factors involved. One may call these factors structural because, through individual preference systems or tastes, they determine a person's inclination to resolve the issue of housing either by becoming an owner or a renter. We should not forget, however, that these systems of inclinations only become effective in relation to a certain state of the market and institutional conditions defining access to the market—in other words, in relation to the forms that continually reshape public assistance.

The explanatory model presented here aims to account, in a systematic way—and within the limits of presently existing data—for the "choices" that lead economic subjects to become owners or renters of an individual dwelling (a house) or a collective dwelling (an apartment) while integrating the principal determinant factors of the housing decision: economic capital, cultural capital, technical capital, the relative composition of these forms of capital, social mobility, age, marital status, family status, number of children, and so on. It seems appropriate to propose this model despite its insufficiencies and imprecisions because it can at least encourage research to balance the inherent limitations of studies that focus on *preconstructed populations* (low-income households, retired people, marginal populations, people who build their own houses, people who have recently gained ownership, etc.) but that overlook the group of objective relations that determine their relevant properties. The model presented here also avoids the simplifications characteristic of the partial explanations that usually satisfy statistical analyses.

For example, the investigation conducted by INSEE (the French national institute for economic statistics) at regular intervals (in 1955, 1961, 1963, 1967, 1970, 1973, 1978, 1984, and 1988) with large samples (29,233 households in 1984, 13,606 in 1978) grasps the housing situation, its evolution, the system of financing, the principal characteristics of the households, and so on, but it ignores equally important explanatory factors, such as the social mobility over several generations (or, at least, the profession of the primary wage earner). Furthermore, the statistical analysis proposed by the study does not give adequate weight to factors such as social or technical capital (although various researchers have focused on different factors or different populations—the new owners for one, the rental sector for another, etc.—comparing and synthesizing the data is still possible).[5]

An investigation conducted in 1986 by Catherine Bonvalet and her team under the auspices of the National Institute for Demographic Studies looked at the residential history of the generation born between 1926 and 1935 who live in the Paris region (n = 1,987 individuals). The study attempted primarily to determine the circumstances and the factors involved in their arrival in Paris, their position in the "housing circuit" and the constitution of property inheritance in the course of their life cycle, their retirement plans, and the frequency with which they had changed residence. Devoting a large part of the study to demographic and social factors, she accorded little attention to economic capital, social capital, or the politics and availability of housing. She focused on only one generation, one that could benefit from the transformations in home financing instituted in the 1950s, but by making use of a study conducted twenty-five years earlier by Guy Pourcher, she was able to pursue a comparative study of the transformation of explanatory factors and practices with regard to housing.[6]

A study of geographic and family origin, professional life, housing, and lifestyles was conducted by Nicole Tabard and her team at Credoc on 1,000 families who lived in the region of Essonne and had at least one child under twenty years old. The study focused primarily on the construction of a socio-professional typology of the towns and neighborhoods of the region and analyzed the relationships, on the one hand, between the morphology of the towns or residential neighborhoods and the behaviors and practices of the households with regard to housing and, on the other hand, between the social and geographic mobility of the subjects and their specific location within the region of Essonne.[7]

Since we find no better, we have had to construct the proposed model relying principally on the secondary analysis of a group of tables that were assembled at our request from the results of the 1984 INSEE study. These data allowed us to conduct a systematic comparison between owners and renters of houses and apartments according to the principal explanatory variables.[8] (See Table 4.2.) The interpretation of the statistics is supported by information and hypotheses gleaned from a group of extensive interviews (n = 45) that we conducted with owners of individual houses in the Paris region and in the south of France.

The opportunity to gain ownership of one's residence obviously depends on the *volume of one's capital.* But the propensity to buy one's residence, rather than rent it, seems to depend above all on the *structure of one's capital,* in other words, on the relative distribution of economic capital and cultural capital, and that structure or distribution is the principle of the constitution of the preference system.

TABLE 4.2 Owners and Renters of Houses and Apartments

TABLE 4.2A Breakdown by Socioeconomic Category of Head of Household

| | Owner | | | | | | Renter | | | | | | Average |
| | House | | | Apartment | | | House | | | Apartment | | | |
	Paris Region	Rest of France	France Total	Paris Region	Rest of France	France Total	Paris Region	Rest of France	France Total	Paris Region	Rest of France	France Total	
Farm workers	0.6	0.7	0.7	0.2	0	0.1	3.5	1.9	2.0	0.3	0.5	0.4	0.6
Small-scale farmers	0	1.1	1.0	0	0.4	0.2	0	0.2	0.2	0	0	0	0.5
Mid-scale farmers	0	1.2	1.1	0	0.1	0.1	0	0.4	0.4	0	0	0	0.5
Large-scale farmers	0.1	0.6	0.5	0	0.2	0.1	0	0.2	0.2	0.1	0	0	0.3
Retired farmers	0.3	3.9	3.5	0.2	1.4	0.9	0.4	2.5	2.3	0.1	0.8	0.6	2.0
Unskilled craftsmen	0.5	0.9	0.9	0.8	0.6	0.7		3.1	2.9	2.0	2.8	2.2	1.6
Unskilled industrial workers	1.5	3.9	3.7	1.4	1.5	1.5	5.6	9.3	9.1	3.8	7.8	6.6	4.9
Truck drivers	1.6	2.8	2.7	1.1	1.3	1.2	1.6	3.1	3.0	3.1	2.7	2.8	2.6
Skilled warehouse workers	1.2	1.5	1.5	0.6	0.6	0.6	3.0	2.5	2.6	1.6	2.1	1.9	1.6
Skilled craftsmen	3.8	4.8	4.7	2.9	4.3	3.8	6.5	8.4	8.2	5.5	7.9	7.2	5.8
Skilled industrial workers	4.8	8.7	8.3	3.4	5.2	4.5	6.5	9.7	9.5	6.6	9.5	8.6	8.0
Foremen	5.9	3.7	3.9	2.6	2.2	2.4	4.6	3.1	3.2	2.3	1.4	1.7	2.8
Sanitation workers	0.6	0.8	0.8	1.4	0.7	1.0	0.5	1.0	0.9	2.1	2.0	2.0	1.2
Retired workers	9.4	12.5	12.2	4.5	8.9	7.3	8.4	11.6	11.4	6.2	8.5	7.8	9.9
Craftsmen	3.0	4.0	3.9	2.0	3.5	3.0	4.6	2.3	2.4	2.1	1.8	1.9	2.9
Merchants	2.6	1.8	1.9	1.9	2.3	2.2	2.1	2.0	2.0	1.2	1.4	1.4	1.7
Retired craftsmen and merchants	2.6	3.9	3.8	3.4	6.4	5.3	0.4	1.3	1.2	1.1	2.0	1.7	3.0
Police	1.6	1.0	1.1	0.5	0.8	0.7	2.3	1.8	1.8	2.0	1.8	1.9	1.4
Private-sector office workers	0.4	0.6	0.6	0.5	0.7	0.6	2.5	0.7	0.8	1.7	2.1	2.0	1.1
Business administration	3.4	2.1	2.3	4.9	4.3	4.5	2.6	2.7	2.7	8.3	4.6	5.8	3.8
Public-sector office workers	1.8	2.6	2.6	2.1	3.0	2.7	2.4	2.3	2.3	6.3	5.3	5.6	3.6
Retired office workers	6.1	5.5	5.5	6.6	6.7	6.7	3.5	3.4	3.4	6.1	5.7	5.8	5.6
Mid-level business administration	5.8	3.0	3.3	7.2	3.8	5.1	6.0	2.9	3.1	5.6	3.2	3.9	3.7
Mid-level public employees	1.1	1.1	1.1	0.9	1.0	1.0	1.5	1.2	1.2	1.2	1.0	1.0	1.0
Mid-level health workers	0.9	1.2	1.2	1.5	1.5	1.5	1.1	1.0	1.0	1.8	1.9	1.9	1.4

	Owner						Renter						
	House			Apartment			House			Apartment			
	Paris Region	Rest of France	France Total	Paris Region	Rest of France	France Total	Paris Region	Rest of France	France Total	Paris Region	Rest of France	France Total	Average
Technicians	6.5	3.6	3.9	6.0	3.5	4.4	7.7	2.4	2.8	4.7	2.9	3.5	3.7
Teachers	1.2	1.7	1.7	1.6	2.3	2.1	1.8	1.1	1.1	1.4	1.6	1.5	1.6
Retired mid-level employees	7.2	5.3	5.5	6.1	7.4	6.9	0	2.3	2.1	2.9	2.6	2.7	4.4
Executives	0.4	0.6	0.5	0.8	1.2	1.0	0	0.1	0.1	0.2	0.2	0.2	0.5
Private-sector management	5.3	1.9	2.2	7.3	3.7	5.0	4.2	2.7	2.8	3.9	1.3	2.1	2.6
Engineers	7.1	1.9	2.5	8.2	1.4	3.9	8.2	2.6	3.0	3.0	1.3	1.8	2.5
Public-sector management	1.3	0.8	0.9	2.7	1.1	1.7	1.8	1.4	1.4	1.3	0.8	1.0	1.1
Professors	1.7	1.2	1.2	2.1	2.0	2.0	1.0	1.2	1.2	2.0	1.2	1.4	1.4
Professionals	1.6	0.9	1.0	1.9	2.0	2.0	1.4	0.8	0.8	0.9	0.6	0.7	1.0
Artists	0.5	0.2	0.2	1.4	0.3	0.7	1.3	0.5	0.5	1.2	0.3	0.6	0.5
Retired management	4.1	2.6	2.8	6.6	6.7	6.7	1.3	1.0	1.0	1.9	0.8	1.2	2.5
Others	3.6	4.9	4.8	4.5	6.9	5.9	1.6	5.4	5.1	5.0	9.6	8.1	6.2
Total	100	100	100	100	100	100	100	100	100	100	100	100	100

TABLE 4.2B Breakdown by Academic Degree

	Owner						Renter						
	House			Apartment			House			Apartment			
	Paris Region	Rest of France	France Total	Paris Region	Rest of France	France Total	Paris Region	Rest of France	France Total	Paris Region	Rest of France	France Total	Average
No degree	17.7	28.5	27.3	11.4	20.4	17.0	23.6	34.0	33.3	22.1	31.5	28.5	27.0
Primary education (CEP)	46.5	48.1	47.9	32.9	42.2	38.8	37.8	40.4	40.2	35.6	39.3	38.1	42.6
Vocational degree (BEPC)	14.3	9.5	10.0	15.6	14.5	14.9	11.4	10.9	10.9	14.7	12.2	13.0	11.7
High school degree (BAC)	7.2	5.8	5.9	12.4	9.2	10.4	10.8	5.8	6.2	10.9	7.9	8.9	7.6
Advanced vocational degree (DUT)	4.0	3.5	3.5	5.0	4.3	4.5	4.5	3.1	3.2	4.2	3.9	4.0	3.8
College degree (Licence)	8.0	3.1	3.7	16.9	6.4	10.3	7.8	4.7	4.9	8.8	3.6	5.3	5.2
Others	2.2	1.5	1.6	5.8	3.0	4.0	4.0	1.0	1.2	3.6	1.5	2.1	2.1
Total	100	100	100	100	100	100	100	100	100	100	100	100	100

TABLE 4.2C   Breakdown by Income

| | Owner | | | | | | Renter | | | | | | Average |
| | House | | | Apartment | | | House | | | Apartment | | | |
	Paris Region	Rest of France	France Total	Paris Region	Rest of France	France Total	Paris Region	Rest of France	France Total	Paris Region	Rest of France	France Total	
Less than 30,000 francs	3.5	5.6	5.4	3.5	5.1	4.5	4.2	7.3	7.1	4.3	9.1	7.6	6.2
30,000 to 49,999	7.3	10.8	10.4	4.9	10.3	8.3	7.3	14.4	13.9	7.7	16.5	13.7	11.7
50,000 to 64,999	5.3	9.8	9.3	6.2	9.3	8.2	9.3	12.9	12.7	10.9	15.9	14.3	11.3
65,000 to 79,999	4.6	9.6	9.1	6.9	10.6	9.2	5.9	12.2	11.8	12.0	13.5	13.0	10.8
80,000 to 99,999	8.2	12.7	12.2	10.5	12.8	11.9	12.3	16.3	16.0	13.8	14.9	14.5	13.4
100,000 to 119,999	7.8	12.6	12.1	8.4	9.4	9.1	10.4	11.9	11.8	11.0	11.0	11.0	11.3
120,000 to 149,999	15.2	16.1	16.0	14.8	14.8	14.8	17.6	10.6	11.1	16.1	10.8	12.5	14.1
150,000 to 199,999	22.0	13.6	14.5	18.0	16.6	17.1	17.0	8.2	8.8	13.3	5.7	8.1	12.0
Over 200,000	26.1	9.1	10.9	26.7	11.0	16.8	15.9	6.0	6.7	10.8	2.5	5.1	9.2
Total	100	100	100	100	100	100	100	100	100	100	100	100	100

NOTE: Paris Region refers to the Île-de- France.

SOURCE: INSEE study, 1984. Table prepared at the request of the authors.

The rate of ownership of housing in general tends to rise with the volume of economic capital, at least above a certain threshold (at around 60,000 francs a year in 1978 and 80,000 francs in 1984). Above this threshold, ownership seems to be independent of income. In 1978, 43.2 percent of the households with incomes lower than 15,000 francs were owners of their residence; 45.2 percent for the bracket between 35,000 and 45,000 francs; and 43.5 percent for incomes of 45,000 to 60,000 francs. Beyond this point ownership grew consistently, from 48.2 percent for the bracket between 60,000 and 80,000 francs, to 57.2 percent for incomes from 80,000 to 110,000, and to 65.2 percent for incomes over 110,000.[9] The rate of ownership for houses only grew a small amount with greater income. It rose from 35.2 percent for the lowest income bracket to 43.1 percent for the highest. The rate of ownership for apartments, however, varied very widely with income: It rose from 8.1 percent for the lowest income bracket to 22.1 percent for the highest.

It seems that a minimum volume of economic capital is necessary in order for someone to consider the project of becoming an owner, or rather that below a certain threshold people did not dare to imagine buying a house or apartment. When asked what prevented them from buying, 45 percent of office workers and 42 percent of all workers cited the lack of financial means as the primary obstacle, against only 24 percent of middle-level employees, high-level managers, and professionals. (See Sofres, *Les Français et l'immobilier,* March 1986.) The fear of being in debt when one does not know "what the future will bring" is also mentioned more by office workers (15 percent) than by members of other categories (8 percent). Craftsmen, merchants, and executives responded that real estate is no longer profitable enough much more frequently (18 percent) than high-level managers and middle-level employees (2 percent) or workers (1 percent).

Even though income does not seem very closely related statistically to the fact of owning a house, it is likely that it weighs very heavily on the decision to buy. When one focuses not on all owners and renters but only on those who have moved into a residence in the past three years, the correlation is clear. In 1978, in the lowest income bracket, 8.9 percent owned their house compared to 35.4 percent in the highest bracket. The proportion of owners of apartments rises equally dramatically with the increase of income.[10]

Everything leads us to conclude that the structure of capital plays a determinant role in the choice between buying and renting: In effect, if we leave aside the retired population, the proportion of ownership is highest among those categories of people who are decidedly richer in economic capital than cultural capital and who depend on economic capital for their reproduction (see Table 4.3). In 1984, 76.8 percent of executives were owners, as were 66.1 percent of craftsmen and 65 percent of farmers.[11] In contrast, the proportion of ownership is clearly lower in the categories with significant cultural capital. At the heart of the field of power, according to a logic already observed in several other domains, professors,

TABLE 4.3   Percentage of Owners and Renters According to Socioeconomic Category of Head of Household

	Owner			Renter				
	House	Apartment	Total	House	Apartment	Total	Others	Total
Farmers	61.3	3.7	65.0	8.9	7.6	16.5	18.5	100
Specialized factory workers	28.3	3.8	32.1	14.7	47.3	62.0	5.9	100
Qualified factory workers	39.1	6.4	45.5	10.4	38.8	49.2	5.3	100
Foremen	55.3	9.3	64.6	8.9	19.8	28.7	6.7	100
Service workers	21.7	7.6	29.3	5.3	47.6	52.9	17.9	100
Retired workers	47.4	7.9	55.3	8.7	25.2	33.9	10.8	100
Craftsmen	54.6	11.5	66.1	6.6	22.4	29.0	4.8	100
Merchants	44.4	14.1	58.5	9.0	25.9	34.9	6.6	100
Retired craftsmen and merchants	50.2	19.5	66.1	3.1	19.3	22.4	7.9	100
Police	25.8	4.5	30.3	8.7	37.5	46.2	23.4	100
Private-sector employees	21.5	6.1	27.6	5.6	57.2	62.8	9.6	100
Office employees	23.9	13.2	37.2	5.6	50.4	56.0	6.8	100
Public-sector employees	28.4	8.4	36.8	5.0	51.6	56.6	6.6	100
Retired office workers	39.1	13.1	52.2	4.8	34.0	38.8	9.0	100
Mid-level private-sector employees	36.3	15.4	51.7	6.6	35.7	42.3	6.0	100
Mid-level public employees	36.0	11.2	47.2	6.9	38.5	45.4	7.4	100
Technicians	43.4	13.7	57.1	6.0	32.2	38.2	4.6	100
Teachers	39.8	13.8	53.6	5.2	30.5	35.7	10.8	100
Retired mid-level employees	52.0	18.2	70.2	3.9	20.8	24.7	5.1	100
Executives	50.5	26.3	76.8	1.9	16.7	18.6	4.6	100
Private-sector management	36.1	22.4	58.5	8.8	27.7	36.5	5.0	100
Engineers	41.8	18.3	60.1	9.7	25.4	35.1	4.8	100
Public-sector management	32.5	17.4	49.9	10.1	29.6	39.7	10.5	100
Professors	33.9	15.8	49.7	6.5	32.7	39.2	11.1	100
Professionals	42.3	23.5	65.8	6.5	24.1	30.6	3.6	100
Artists	20.6	16.6	37.2	9.1	44.7	53.8	8.9	100
Retired management	46.6	31.1	77.7	3.3	16.3	19.6	2.8	100
Others	27.2	9.5	36.7	5.8	38.3	44.1	19.3	100
Average	39.7	11.1	50.8	7.8	32.9	40.7	8.6	100

SOURCE: INSEE study, 1984. Table prepared at the request of the authors.

artists, and public-sector managers, who are most often renters, are opposed to executives, who are most often owners. The intermediary position is held by private-sector managers, engineers (the closest to public-sector managers and professors), and professionals (the closest to the executives). Within the middle classes, we find an analogous structure, with one pole composed of craftsmen and merchants, most frequently owners, and the other of teachers and public-sector employees (administration and business employees are much less frequently owners than other categories).

The structure of capital, by means of the structuring action that it exercises on the constitutive inclinations of inhabitants, or rather, on the preference systems, is itself a *structuring factor of the action of other factors*. Therefore, although the rate of ownership is almost independent of income in the groups richer in economic capital than cultural capital, the two are strictly tied in the groups that are richer in cultural capital than economic capital, where there is greater recourse to credit for financing purchases.

Although 88 percent of executives having an annual income of less than 100,000 francs in 1984 were owners of a house, only 45 percent of those with incomes between 100,000 and 200,000 francs were owners. (This fact is undoubtedly linked to the fact that executives with lower incomes generally live in rural areas or small towns.)[12] Similarly, among the craftsmen, the rate of ownership was 56.5 percent for those with incomes below 50,000 francs, 54 percent for those with moderate incomes, and 54.5 percent for those with high incomes (over 100,000 francs). Small merchants and farmers with higher incomes are a little more likely to own houses than those with lower incomes. (Among professionals, who accumulate both economic capital and cultural capital, the likelihood of owning or renting a house or apartment is independent of income.)

Conversely, the variations are particularly strong among teachers and middle-level employees in the public sector. Less than 10 percent of the teachers with the lowest incomes (who are also the youngest) are owners of a house as opposed to more than 60 percent of those with incomes of over 150,000 francs; there is a comparable variation among middle-level employees in the public sector. Similarly, among engineers and managers (in the public and private sectors) the rate of ownership rises strongly with income.

Cultural capital exerts practically no visible effects on the rate of ownership within each social category, regardless of income. Nonetheless, in the lower categories, it seems that a minimum of academic capital (*capital scolaire*), such as the completion of primary education (CEP, Certificat d'études primaires) or vocational schooling (CAP, Certificat d'aptitude professionnelle), is the necessary condition for gaining ownership (undoubtedly in conjunction with ascetic inclinations that are also linked to a low reproduction rate). The probability of being an owner is lower among workers, office workers, technicians, and middle-level employees who are lacking basic education (CEP or CAP) than it is among those who have completed this early schooling. Those who hold only these basic educational degrees (CEP or CAP) are even more likely to own their residences than those in the same social category with a high school degree (BEPC or BAC).[13]

The category of those who have completed basic education (CAP or CEP) allows us to understand the effects of a particular form of cultural capital that are especially pronounced in the case of gaining ownership: *technical capital* ("handyman" capital), partially acquired at school and associated more or less with the possession of a CAP degree. Therefore, situated high on the hierarchy of manual workers, those in possession of a high degree of technical ability, such as foremen and supervisors,[14] can put the specific skills they acquired at school, certified by academic titles such as CAP or BP and reinforced by the course of their professional career, at the service of their ascetic inclinations. These inclinations, undoubtedly the source of their professional success, sometimes move them to accept the many sacrifices necessary to build their own houses, often with the help of friends or family members either partially or totally. (They are the "beavers" who construct their own habitat.)

The effect of the size of the community (taille de l'agglomération) is well known. But the fact is that it is specified according to the volume and the structure of the capital possessed. The gap between the social classes grows when one passes from rural areas to large urban areas, both with regard to owning one's own home and living in an individual house.[15]

Nicole Tabard showed that the gaps between managers or professionals and workers are more marked in the Essonne region than in France as a whole.[16] The apparent "democratization" of the access to ownership of individual houses in Essonne is essentially attributable to the fact that the higher segments of the working class usually reside in rural areas, or when they reside in a metropolitan area, they live in suburban zones. Our analysis of the 1984 study confirms that the percentage of those who own an individual house varies, within each category, in reverse proportion to the size of the community. Workers can gain ownership of housing almost exclusively in rural areas. Foremen, in contrast, are able to own houses even in the Paris metropolitan area (at a rate of 31.6 percent).

In general, the percentage of owners rises with *age* and is always low among those who are younger than thirty-five years old. Everything seems to indicate that (except for foremen, who show a 50 percent ownership rate between the ages of thirty and thirty-four), gaining ownership occurs later and later as one descends the social hierarchy. Thus, among unskilled workers, only those over fifty years old are more likely to be owners than renters, and gaining ownership often coincides with retirement.

   In fact, age itself takes on its full meaning only as a moment in the *cycle of domestic life:* The question of buying a house is posed with a particular force at certain stages of the cycle along with the concern for "settling down" or "starting a family," in other words, either at the time of marriage or in conjunction with the appearance of children in subsequent years.

Married couples, according to the INSEE study, are more likely than single people, regardless of age, to "choose" to own their principal residence and to take out loans to make the purchase. Nine out of ten people buying houses for the first time are married. In contrast, single people at age fifty are only half as likely to own their houses as married couples, and when they do become owners it is principally by inheritance or by outright purchase. The rate of ownership among divorcees is also low; divorce is often accompanied by a return to the rental market.[17]

The majority of Parisians born between 1926 and 1935 who have bought their places of residence had already constituted their family before buying. The purchases took place earlier in the life cycle for high-level managers than it did for workers or office workers. It seems that the former group was better able to manage the educational expenses of their children and the repayment of their mortgages.[18] It is probable that, for the subsequent generations, the purchase of a residence, which occurs at a younger and younger age, has constrained couples, including lower and middle-class couples, to deal simultaneously with educational expenses and the repayment of a mortgage.

The percentage of home owners among the salaried groups of the middle classes (office workers and middle-level managers), foremen, and the wealthy classes tends to grow with the number of children in the household. On the contrary, among manual workers, factory workers, highly skilled workers, and private-sector office workers, the relation is more complex, insofar as the propensity to buy a house is indissociable from an ambition to social advancement, which in turn is inseparable from a restriction on family size. Thus, in these categories, the households that have two children are more often owners of houses than those who have none or who have only one child and more often than those who have three or more children.[19]

In fact, as in the case for all fields of consumption, one can no longer completely account for the differences in the housing domain except by bringing into consideration not only the volume and structure of capital (which rules the dynamic of such factors as the size of the community of residence and the size of the family) but also the evolution of the stages of these two characteristics. One can grasp this evolution particularly well by looking at social and geographic origin, and it is often associated with changes of residence or changes from renting to owning. Although we have almost no statistics on the effects of social origin except for the information we have gathered from interviews (social origin is almost never taken into account in the studies), everything allows us to assume that gaining ownership (most often with the help of credit) has taken place mostly among those who have "arrived": in other words, those who have "newly arrived" in the urban society, those from the provinces who have "risen up to Paris" or, in the other large cities, those who have bought houses in the new suburban neighborhoods (since the old residents are more likely to live, often as renters, in the central urban neighborhoods).[20]

The likelihood of being an owner or a renter also depends on whether one is the son or daughter of parents who own or rent their principal residence. A comparative study of renters and of those gaining property in one group of thirty-nine-year-olds living in the Alpes-Maritimes region showed that two out of three daughters of owners became owners themselves (and that, after the age of thirty-nine), while the daughters of renters had a little less than one chance in two.[21] (The division between sons of owners and sons of renters is more or less the same.) Social origin (grasped here in an indirect and crude fashion) undoubtedly contributes to structuring the residential strategies of the households but only by means of an entire ensemble of mediations, such as the type of community, the stage in the life cycle, the profession and social origin of the spouse, and so on.

The salaried segments of the middle classes, great users of bank credit, and the upper segments of the working class have constituted an important part of those gaining ownership in recent years. According to the study conducted by INSEE in 1984, of all of those who owned houses, teachers, public-sector managers, technicians, middle-level public and private-sector employees, and highly skilled workers were the most likely to own a relatively new house (built in 1975 or later). Even if recourse to credit for the purchase of a house has become common to all groups, it is still most frequent among teachers, engineers, public- and private-sector managers, technicians, middle-level business employees, and foremen. (See Table 4.4.) The salaried segments of the middle classes are also among the most frequent to want to buy a house when they do not already own one. Among the apartment owners who envisage moving, those who most often express the desire to buy a house are the highly skilled workers, foremen, middle-level public-sector employees, technicians, and teachers. Finally, according to a study conducted by the Institut Français de Démoscopie in 1984, the percentage of those interviewed who stated that they "surely envisage" having an individual house built for their principal residence was highest among office workers and middle-level managers (19.1 percent of office workers and 13.7 percent of middle-level managers, as compared to 10.2 percent of all people interviewed).

An apparent democratization of the access to ownership is suggested by a rise in the overall rate of ownership: It grew fro 35 percent in 1954 to 45.5 percent in 1973, 46.7 percent in 1978, and up to 51.2 percent in 1984 despite, as Claude Taffin noted, unfavorable economic conditions. This apparent democratization, however, masks considerable differences marked by the location of the residences (the

TABLE 4.4 The Mode of Gaining Ownership of a House or Apartment

	House Owners					Apartment Owners				
	Inheritance or Gift	Outright Purchase	Credit	Other*	Total	Inheritance or Gift	Outright Purchase	Credit	Other*	Total
Farmers	37.5	22.9	38.8	0.8	100	54.1	18.3	27.6	0	100
Specialized factory workers	13.2	13.1	71.9	1.8	100	16.1	15.2	65.2	3.5	100
Qualified factory workers	7.6	4.7	84.1	3.6	100	8.2	10.3	75.7	5.8	100
Foremen	5.5	4.7	85.8	4.0	100	6.9	9.3	76.1	7.8	100
Service workers	19.4	19.0	61.7	0	100	22.2	22.3	53.1	2.4	100
Retired workers	21.1	35.1	39.3	4.4	100	17.2	42.2	35.9	4.7	100
Craftsmen	10.9	11.7	75.8	1.6	100	13.7	11.2	68.6	6.5	100
Merchants	9.5	16.1	72.7	1.8	100	25.2	16.0	53.4	5.3	100
Retired craftsmen and merchants	19.5	46.2	31.3	3.0	100	20.5	49.8	28.6	1.2	100
Police and military	5.3	10.1	81.4	3.2	100	8.0	12.4	75.2	4.4	100
Private-sector office workers	12.1	13.8	69.7	4.4	100	11.8	35.7	52.5	0	100
Mid-level administration	9.4	9.0	78.3	3.3	100	7.2	11.5	78.6	2.7	100
Public-sector office workers	7.4	9.8	80.8	2.0	100	14.2	8.3	74.9	2.6	100
Retired office workers	20.8	37.3	38.9	3.0	100	7.5	49.1	40.6	2.8	100
Mid-level private-sector employees	5.5	5.2	86.4	2.9	100	6.5	6.8	85.3	1.4	100
Mid-level public employees	5.7	7.1	85.1	2.1	100	7.4	10.3	78.5	3.8	100
Technicians	4.2	3.9	87.9	4.0	100	1.8	7.4	86.0	4.7	100
Teachers	2.9	7.5	89.0	0.6	100	11.6	11.5	76.9	0	100
Retired mid-level employees	15.8	33.1	48.9	2.2	100	7.5	40.5	48.7	3.3	100
Executives	3.1	11.3	83.1	2.5	100	14.2	29.5	56.3	0	100
Private-sector management	2.8	8.1	88.1	0.5	100	7.1	9.7	81.4	1.8	100
Engineers	4.4	4.7	88.9	2.0	100	1.5	12.8	83.3	2.3	100
Public-sector management	5.5	5.5	88.4	0.6	100	3.2	7.9	85.5	3.4	100
Professors	6.8	11.4	78.3	3.5	100	4.1	10.8	83.2	1.9	100
Professionals	7.7	15.8	76.0	0.5	100	4.0	9.8	84.2	2.0	100
Artists	2.3	10.2	87.5	0	100	7.6	17.9	74.5	0	100
Retired management	16.6	34.6	47.4	1.4	100	5.0	43.1	50.6	1.3	100
Others	28.6	37.0	31.2	3.2	100	21.9	34.1	42.6	1.4	100
Average	14.1	18.7	64.4	2.8	100	10.8	23.6	62.5	3.1	100

*Other: annuity plans, rental with the option to buy, etc.

SOURCE: INSEE study, 1984. Table prepared at the request of the authors.

opposition between suburban and city dweller having replaced the opposition between country and city dweller) and the characteristics of the residence itself (comfort, etc.). When combined, these factors determine enormous gaps in the ways of life associated with or imposed by various habitats.

The differences concern, first of all, the *real costs* of ownership, not only in terms of money and credit but also in terms of *time,* particularly labor time for managing the house, both in the case of foremen, who may dedicate their evenings and Sundays to "bricolage," to fixing and building things, and in the case of those in the nonmanual category who dedicate this time to study for night-school programs and crafts school. Time is also a factor in terms of waiting to become an owner or to be "really moved in," in terms of travel time to commute to work, and so on.

In the Paris region, gaining ownership of a residence is often accompanied by the move toward the suburbs. Therefore, in the generation of people born between 1926 and 1935 who live in the Paris region, 25 percent lived in Paris before buying a residence compared to only 14 percent after the acquisition. Among those who left Paris, almost two-thirds (63 percent) said that they missed the neighborhood where they used to live and would have preferred to stay.[22] What home owners increasingly lament, more than being far from their place of work, is being far from downtown. Between 1978 and 1984, the proportion of owners of individual houses who complained about being far from downtown more than doubled, rising from 10 percent to 20 percent for new owners and from 11 percent to 24 percent for other owners, while it remained relatively stable for the apartment owners (from 9 percent to 10 percent for new apartment owners and from 7 percent to 10 percent for others).[23]

If the transportation costs for commuting to and from work are particularly high for the owners among the salaried segments of the middle and upper classes, the costs in labor time in order to complete the house or the expenses to keep it up are particularly high for the workers. Nicole Tabard has shown how in the working class, and in particular in the lower segments of the class, "living in an individual house is a condition that favors domestic production."[24] The forms of energy consumed by the lower classes in individual houses is less costly than in an apartment because they "incorporate domestic labor." On the contrary, among the other social classes, the domestic expenditure of energy in an individual house is double what it is in an apartment, and among the wealthy classes it is even more.

The differences carry over into the *profits* associated with property and the eventual resale value: Obviously houses are very unequal in value because quality, beauty, and above all, location vary; there are significant differences in space and comfort; they are very differently furnished and differently situated *in relation to public or private facilities,* schools, cultural centers, shopping centers, places of work, and so on. Therefore, farm workers, unskilled industrial workers, and craftsmen are the owners of the smallest houses; executives and professionals own the most spacious houses. In 1984, 73 percent of professionals and 71.5 percent of executives who owned houses had more than 1,300 square feet of floor space, as opposed to 14 percent of the unskilled workers, 16 percent of the farm workers, and 17.5 percent of the foremen who owned houses. The differences that separate these classes are equally great when we consider the number of rooms in a house. In 1975, the proportion of uncomfortable residences among those that workers owned was 8.6 times higher than the proportion for the homes of professionals and high-level managers.[25]

This system of structural factors for determining preference systems influences the orientation of economic agents toward owning or renting and defines the limits within which these inclinations can act. But obviously, the execution of the concrete "choices" of these socially constituted dispositions depends at each moment on the economic means available to the agents, which, just like the state of housing availability, depends itself very strictly on the "politics of housing." In effect, through diverse forms of regulation and financial assistance directed toward favoring one group or another in such way as to create tastes with regard to housing, such as aid to individuals, loans, tax breaks, cheap credit, or aid to builders, governmental entities—and all those in a position to impose their orientations through the government—contribute very strongly to the *production of the state of the housing market*. In other words, they affect both the supply and the demand of land and housing both new and old, both individual and collective; in short they affect all the other forms that the market takes in the different regions and cities.

It follows that posing a systematic relationship between the evolution of the distribution of different modes of occupation in relation to residence ownership or rental and the evolution of the "politics of housing," as it is presented in practical terms in the experience of the agents, should allow us to understand how the properly political factors were able to affect the financial (and also emotional) investments of the different social categories in relation to housing. One would have to analyze this double process methodically: The two populations, owners and renters, are in effect united by a logic of communicating vessels, whereby any measure that reduces the availability of rental housing sends a segment of possible renters toward ownership, which is more or less attractive according to the amount of personal assistance and the cost of credit.

What is certain is that the politics decreed by the housing law of 1977 culminated an entire ensemble of actions aimed at influencing the "choices" of those in social categories previously the least likely to choose ownership in order to satisfy their housing needs and least likely to make the purchase of a residence a major investment. The legislation sought to influence them to choose ownership; in other words, in the spirit of certain of its founders, who associated collective and rental dwellings with collectivism and socialism, it was aimed at directing them toward a durable attachment to the established order, and therefore toward a form of conservativism. In one sense, the policy, which was aimed at offering a market to the producers of housing by producing owners attached to their property, was successful. But the petits bourgeois who thus find themselves constituted as small owners of small suburban houses have had access to these satisfactions only, for the most part, at such a high price that the liberal policies have certainly not delivered to its promoters the political benefits that they expected, even if these policies have contributed to the completion of a profound transformation of the social order.

The "New Owners"

Mr. and Mrs. P. have lived since 1977 in a Phénix house (an inexpensive brand of industrially prefabricated houses) in a housing development composed of 134 houses in Perray-en-Yvelines in the Paris region. They are among those who have recently gained ownership and who, possessing only a very small amount of economic capital but a relatively large amount of cultural or academic capital, purchased the land and the house with the aid of several loans. Mr. P., who was born in Tarbes of a father who was first a house painter then a delivery man for a store, moved to the Paris area because he could not find work in his region. Mrs. P. could not find work in her region either. She was born in Brittany, and her parents were building superintendents. Mr. and Mrs. P. rented an apartment for the first three years of their marriage but "always had the goal of buying a house, an individual house." Mr. P., who was thirty-five years old at the time of the interview (1985), has two vocational degrees (CAP), one as an electrician and another as a diesel engine mechanic. He has held several jobs in the automobile industry, first at Citroën, then at UNIT, next at IVECO, and finally at Renault's industrial vehicle division, where he is an automotive electrician. Mrs. P., who was thirty-two years old at the time of the interview and who completed her secondary studies without attaining her high school degree (BAC), worked as a secretary for a real estate agency for twelve years. She stopped working two years ago when their daughter was born; she plans to return to work when the child begins school.

At the time of the purchase, their resources allowed them only a limited choice; they "found themselves" at the Phénix office in Coignières. The other owners in the development were for the most part relatively close to them socially and would have had little chance of becoming owners during another economic juncture and during other market conditions. The owners were "rather wealthy" workers: office workers, postal workers, bank workers, insurance company workers, some middle-level managers and technicians, and a teacher. Two of Mr. P.'s colleagues lived in the same development. The houses were sold very quickly, in two weeks, in 1977; the sales agents "did not need to pressure" the clients.

Mr. and Mrs. P. spent a lot of time looking for their house. They "looked everywhere"; they visited model homes and went to the Paris house fair. They read all the real estate magazines and they sent in coupons for brochures on the different developments: "They were really only descriptive catalogues, not even giving the location of the houses." Having no land and very little savings (around 40,000 francs in 1976), they had to find both a plot of land and a house that were not too expensive. If they had bought the land first and then bought the house a few years later, it would have been "hard, because that would have made twice as much in loans." "We told ourselves, 'if we borrow money for buying the land we will have no money left for building the house.' And since you have to build in two or three years, we couldn't do it. So either we had to find something or do everything together, the land and the house."

They found a plot in Gallardon. "We didn't want it. It's really far away and cut off. There is a train in the morning and a train at night, even though now it's a little built up. So, we ended up at the Phénix office in Coignières. And there they told us, 'We have nothing available around here, but if you want in a year we are going to build a development of Phénix houses in Perray-en-Yvelines.' That was good for us. It was 15 kilometers further away [than Trappes, where they wanted to live], but oh well." Six or seven months later they received "a letter inviting [them] to the Phénix office in Coignières" to see a model home. They went back to the Phénix office, but they did not buy the first day. Mr. P. told the story:

> They offered us a four-room house next to the highway detour. We had come before and seen all the lots so we said, "We don't want one down by the highway." It wasn't done yet and there was only the embankment from the highway. ... That wasn't on the plans, or almost not at all. There was a little mark there on the plans and no one said that it was the detour for Route 10, which has a lot of traffic. The only plot that they proposed to us was that one near the highway. Aren't there any others? we asked. There were some others with oddly shaped plots, but we didn't want those either. ... So that day there wasn't anything. So we came back later and they offered us a five-room house. But we wanted a four-room house at first and found ourselves with a five-room we didn't want. ... Finally, the location was good, it was perfect, except there was one room too many. Well, it was a little more expensive at the beginning.

The house and the land together cost 270,000 francs in 1977. "The initial price wasn't expensive at all," Mrs. P. clarified. And her husband agreed: "It was relatively inexpensive with respect to the others." However, the actual price turned out to be much higher: "We're going to have to pay back twice as much," Mr. P. exclaimed.

Everything was done, however, to give them the impression that this was "a good buy." In 1976, they only had to pay a deposit of 2,500 francs. "We could have withdrawn our bid and we would have only forfeited 500 francs. So, really, it wasn't much of a risk," Mr. P. explained. Since they had about 40,000 francs in savings, they had to ask for a loan. Because they had been married less than five years, Crédit foncier (the state-financed real estate loan institution) gave them a loan "of about 126,000 francs, and they also had 50,000 francs in a home savings plan." "And then, since that wasn't enough," they applied for a loan of 50,000 francs from the company where Mr. P. worked. A former colleague of Mr. P.'s who had bought a Phénix house said he was happy with it. Mr. P., therefore, did not have any unfavorable bias. "Someone" had told them that the Phénix houses were "loud and resonant, they weren't very heavily built because they were made with concrete panels, they were prefabricated. So, all of that bothered me a little bit," Mrs. P. said. She added a little later, "But for us it wasn't very expensive at the beginning, and it was in a good location for us." Mr. P. explained, "We would have wanted something else, but we couldn't afford it." Making a virtue of necessity, they told themselves, "Well, it's not worse than other things." Both of them worked hard to put the house in order: landscaping, insulation, double-paned windows, vegetable garden—they even planted grass in the yard, which was bare in the beginning. Evidently, "the houses are a little too close together," and they complained that the dividing walls did not provide a sound barrier, the garages were too small, there was no basement and no space for a workshop, and the furnace made too much noise. The train station was far away. The sales agent had assured them that a new train station would be built in front of the development, but it was later rebuilt in the same location as the old station. The ground around the house was of very poor quality. When the developers were building the houses, "they took off all the topsoil and sold it. Then they brought in all the waste soil they could get" and added just ten centimeters of growing soil. It was much more difficult for Mr. and Mrs. P. to list what they liked about the house. They were satisfied with at least one thing: Their house did not exist in a catalog. It was not in the Phénix catalog because an architect had designed the houses specifically for this development.

They knew that they would probably always stay in this house, but they hoped to move in six or seven years, to have "something a little better." "Our goal," said Mrs. P., "is still to have a house for ourselves, alone." Her husband, who really wanted to have a basement, said, "1,100 square feet is enough, … for me, it's freedom." They did not want another Phénix house or any other prefabricated house. "The ideal would be to have it made by a craftsman and be able to tell him, 'I want it done like that.'" And if they have to call on a developer, they will be more "demanding" than they were the first time.

A Couple of Engineers in a Bâti Service House

Mr. and Mrs. B. bought a Bâti Service house (another brand of industrially made house) in 1980 in a development composed of forty houses in Les Essarts-le-Roi, not far from the forest and near Rambouillet. They too are part of the generation that has recently gained ownership, and even though they are also situated on the left of the social spectrum, they have more economic capital and, above all, much more cultural and scholastic capital than Mr. and Mrs. P. Mr. B., who was thirty years old at the time of the interview (1985), was born in Algeria where his father was in the military—"the equivalent of a high-level supervisor." He came to France in 1962 after having finished his high school and college education at the National School of Statistics and Economics Administration (ENSAE). He was hired as an engineer at an electric company (EDF) in Paris. His parents (his mother is a secretary) "had laid out a bundle for the education" of their children: His brother is a doctor and his sister a nurse. Mrs. B., who was born in Tunisia, is the same age as her husband. The daughter of the director of a small business, she received her master's degree in computer science at the university and attended the institute of business administration. At the time of the interview, she was an engineer for a large private firm. They had been married four years, and they had two daughters and hoped to have a third child "in the next two years."

They had rented an apartment in the suburbs at first, but as soon as they had "a little money put aside" (about 120,000 francs) they told themselves, "we're going to set ourselves up, we're going to buy something." They could not reconcile themselves to the tight spaces of Parisian apartments, so they did not want to buy into an apartment building. ("In an apartment building I don't feel at home. The fact of sharing things, of having things in common, like the elevator, I don't like that," explained Mr. B.) Since they had "decided to take the train," they began to look in Saint Quentin-en-Yvelines and its vicinity for "something around 400,000 or 450,000 francs." They almost bought a house in a project designed by Ricardo Bofil, a well-known architect, but at the last moment they said no, because several things bothered them: They did not like the layout of the rooms, there were no basements, and so on.

> One day in the apartment ads in our neighborhood, we saw Les Essarts-le-Roi. We knew Les Essarts and liked it very much. We told each other, "It is actually a drag—we would be a little further away from Paris than Mourepas." And then we went out to look at it. ... Well, there wasn't anything! It was still on the drawing board. There was a big sign that said Bâti Service and there was a little trailer with a little woman inside who was bored to death. She had a nice architect's model of the houses.

After having looked through a house like the one they eventually bought, they decided in a very short time. "From the point of view of the price it was a little more expensive (520,000 francs) than we thought, but finally we thought that we could tighten our belts a little." They easily got the necessary loans, signed the contract in 1980, and moved in 1981. They liked the neighborhood, and they made friends with the neighbors. Above all, "what we really liked was being alone ... and in addition you could put up a little wall. So we didn't have any illusions because we knew well that it was still a housing development and that there were co-ownership problems, but many fewer than there would be in an apartment building."

Their social trajectory, their successive changes of residence, and their professions had certainly influenced them toward a vision of housing that was to a certain extent disenchanted and functionalist. What they were looking for and what they liked in the Bâti Service house that they bought was "a functional thing, the rooms were easy to clean up and there was space to put things away. ... We wanted something well-lit, something simple. We went to the Bâti Service houses. Honestly, we didn't say, 'it's the greatest!' We said, 'it's o.k., it's sober it's standard.'" However, they would not have chosen a Phénix house: "Those reminded me of Merlin-Plage [a chain of cheaply made seaside vacation complexes], you know? It looks like a big version of a mechanic's garage and I think it doesn't age well."

Mr. and Mrs. B. followed the construction of their house very closely, and this allowed them to avoid several setbacks at the time of delivery. For example, they noticed that the kitchen window had been left out and installed in the garage. When they mentioned this to the site foreman he got angry, but two days later everything was put in place. They had many fewer problems due to poor workmanship than the other owners in their development. For example, a neighbor had a blocked drain pipe and had to break open his kitchen wall with a sledgehammer. Nonetheless, there were problems: electricity restrictions for everyone during the first two months, garages flooded during rainstorms, parking spaces so small and poorly designed that there were frequent conflicts, entire walls that came unfastened, and then the dogs—"between the dogs that barked and the dogs that pissed (laughter), there were dogs everywhere." The difficulties at the time of construction and the conflicts with the builder contributed to a kind of solidarity and mutual aid among the owners, but little by little relations got worse and tensions developed. Mr. and Mrs. B. were very careful to stay out of "neighborhood affairs" and out of the network of invitations, being "nice to everyone but superficial." The other owners were in general couples a little older than them, around thirty-five to forty years old, and had on average two children. It was a "group mostly composed of functionaries, with public-sector jobs. Many of them work for Renault, some for EDF [the electric company], some work for the post office, some are administrators for the tax bureau or the police, there is middle-level management. ... In many couples, both work."

Mr. and Mrs. B. knew well that they would not stay in the development all their lives. In about four years they would think about moving, and they did not want to return to another housing development. "I want a house all alone with walls around it. Period. I would prefer something really individual," declared Mr. B., while his wife hoped that the next house would not be too isolated or too far from the schools and the city center. They wanted to stay in the same area; from an aesthetic point of view, they preferred "an old house with nice stonework," but considered modern houses "more functional. You are sure that things work because there are no surprises. And, ideally, if we could design the house ourselves that would be a rather interesting experience. But, I don't know. I'm a little hesitant."

Technical Capital and Ascetic Inclinations

Mr. and Mrs. R. and their three children live in a house that Mr. R. designed and built himself on land that his father and grandfather bought in the hills around a mining village in the Aix-en-Provence region. Mr. R. is from a family of miners and was raised by his grandparents, who both had worked in the mine (his grandmother worked at sorting and cleaning the coal). Mr. R., who was thirty-five years old at the time of the interview, is chief of equipment at the mine. He said, "I am at the bottom, at the working face. I make coal, sure with today's modern methods, but finally the mine will always be the mine." His father, too, worked for five years in the mine before settling down in a large city nearby, where he first worked in a tax inspector's office before opening his own hardware store.

Mr. R. accumulated a diverse technical capital over a period of several years. Between the ages of sixteen and thirty, he had obtained as many as five vocational degrees (CAP), studying in the accelerated learning centers at the mine. He said, "If you start at the beginning, first I did body work (in an auto garage). Next, I passed a CAP in painting, then a CAP in industrial design, next a CAP in mining, a CAP in welding, and finally I passed a CAP in electro-mechanics. That allowed me to do electrical work, plumbing, heating systems ... and on top of that I taught myself how to lay roofing tiles." Mrs. R. exclaimed, "It's crazy, I really ask myself with all those CAPs that he has, we should be millionaires [laughter], but me I don't have anything. I don't even have one CAP." Mrs. R., the daughter of a rather modest family repatriated from Algeria, has never worked outside of the home but is raising their children, who were five, six, and fourteen years old when the interview was conducted.

After having lived for the first six years of their marriage in a public housing project (HLM) in a large neighboring city, and then in a company house near the mine where they did not have to pay rent, Mr. R. began to build their house. Thanks to a strong technical capital, set into action by the ascetic inclinations that he shares with his wife ("Both of us, we're work ants," Mrs. R. said), he was able to complete his project with a very small initial amount of economic capital: about 40,000 francs, and no loans:

> With 40,000 francs you can do a lot, you know. Back then, the bondstone for the walls cost 1.75 francs each and so you could buy 5 or 6,000 of them and make two houses. So, we bought only what was necessary at the beginning. ... With the first 4,000 francs, I completed the entire septic tank, the ground floor pavement, I put the walls on the first story and I began on the second. With that first amount of money, I managed to do all the walls, all the rough work, without counting the woodwork and all that.

For five or six years they economized as much as possible so that they could buy the necessary construction materials. "Little by little as he worked, the money came in. We were thrifty and we bought more material," Mrs. R. explained. Having decided to "do everything for the house," they did not buy anything that was not absolutely necessary. "We didn't buy a dinner plate, really nothing. It was food for dinner, two pairs of jeans and two sweaters each year. During five years we put everything into the house, but into the interior because my husband is still working on the exterior now. We limit ourselves much less than we used to." Mr. R. did practically everything himself in the house, except for the plaster on the ceiling, the construction of the stairs, and the installation of the central furnace for "the good reason" that it would have taken four or five months to do it and that would have held up their moving into the house.

The construction of the house, which in total cost 220,000 francs, required strict economy, but also and perhaps more important, a considerable investment of time. "When I was working on my house, I worked eighteen or nineteen hours a day. Sometimes I got up at 3:30 in the morning and went to bed at 9:30 at night, working nonstop with only a sandwich between 12 and 2. It was like that for three years. And I never knocked off, Saturday and Sunday too, Christmas and New Years' too." For this, Mr. R. was not "an exception, no, because those who work in the mine, in any case, in principle, they're hard workers, no question. Without that, you wouldn't go to the mine." It took a lot of time to do the work, but it also took time to choose the craftsmen that would do the work that Mr. R. did not do himself and to find good-quality materials at the lowest possible prices. "Before contracting someone to come here, we spent two months, you see. We found out everything about him, to see if he was a responsible worker, to see if he had to re-do a job three times, because in that case it's not worth it. It's not even a question of money, it's the loss of time," explained Mr. R. He added later, "We always nego-tiated the price with all the suppliers, her because she's a pied-noir [a person of European descent and French citizenship who was repatriated from Algeria], and me because it's always been like that. We always try to get by." But, in the case of the floor tile, "we couldn't save very much, maybe 10 percent at the most, and that was figuring on the least expensive tile. We went to look everywhere, at all the stores. That requires a lot of time and, in the end, we often didn't save very much. But we always tried to have the best material, not very expensive, or rather as cheap as possible."

Clearly, the house gave them a great deal of pleasure. "It's true that our house has a history, each part of our house has a history, while some people buy a house just like that, with the keys in hand, as they say …" Mrs. R. did not finish her sen-tence, which left a lot implied and unstated. A little later, however, she added that taking a loan for twenty years to buy a house was too long and that, moreover, it was "not honest" because "you pay almost three times the cost of your house." "Or rather, what also happens is that the father and mother both work to pay off the debts and the children unfortunately … you see, my oldest there, he just got out of school, it's 3:20. He knows that his mother is there and he comes home." "We are proud of the house," she said. "We would talk to you about it for hours."

The history of their house was inseparable from the history of their family. Its construction was planned long ago; they had "always talked about it," and Mr. R. said he had known since he was "very young" that he would build his own house in that area. They wanted "their children [to be] all {born]" before Mrs. R. was thirty years old. That way, the costs of the house and the educational expenses of the children, particularly high during adolescence, would not come at the same time. The hardest period of privation is over. Sometimes they go out to a restaurant: "Rarely, but it happens, always with our children because we are so used to having our children with us that when we go somewhere we always bring them with us. If something were to happen to us, well, morally we're a family and we would face up to it. That is very important to us. Our children are part of us, and we are part of them, and the house and everything fits together," explained Mrs. R. When, after six years dedicated to the construction of the house, they went on vacation in Corsica, they went as a family to a "vacation village." They went out at 9:00 A.M. to go fishing, and the others in the village never saw them. "Really, it's stupid, but that's the way it is. We didn't participate at all in the group activities— except my oldest who went dancing one or two nights—because we had enough just with each other."

The internal organization of the house was planned with an eye toward the future, toward old age. The bedroom and bathroom would be on the ground floor when they could no longer climb the stairs. Mr. R. planned to take his retirement when he is fifty-three and hoped to take advantage of it in order to travel and "to live as a couple" for the first time. When they met, Mrs. R. already had a son from a previous marriage. They said they never stop thinking "far ahead"; they were already thinking about dividing their land in three parts so that they could build a house for each of their children or so the children could build houses themselves. Certainly, "today work requires that you move around" and perhaps their children would not be able to live there, "but what is certain is that we would like our kids to have a house in any case, so as to have a roof over their heads."

NOTES

1. C. Taffin, "L'accession à tout prix," *Economie et statistique* 202 (September 1987), pp. 5–16. The direct transmission of property, however, is much more significant than the figures indicate: Family assistance functions in several different forms (interest-free loans, gifts of land, partial down payments, etc.).

2. See L. Crétin and P. L'Hardy, "Les ménages épargnent moins qu'il y a quinze ans," *Economie et statistique* 219 (March 1989), pp. 21–26.

3. C. Topalov, *Le logement en France* (Paris: Presses de la FNSP, 1987), particularly pp. 305–314. The rate of farmers and industry and business owners who are the owners of their residences, already very high at the beginning of the period, rose much more slowly.

4. The logic of exploiting more and more intensively a "well" that was drying up undoubtedly led the banking institutions to push back the limits of reasonable risks. Because of this, the crisis has struck hard on the lower classes. For example, of the fifty-one houses

put up for sale between 1981 and 1983 by the high courts of Rennes and Saint-Malo as a result of disputes between a new house owner and a lender, twenty-one of the owners were workers, of which nine worked in construction and public works, five were office workers, and three were farmers. (The socio-professional category of the party involved was ignored in twenty cases.) See "Agence d'urbanisme et de développement intercommunal de l'agglomération rennaise," *Les accédants à la propriété en difficultés financières* (Rennes: February 1986).

5. The most systematic attempt was conducted by Pierre Durif and Sylvie Berniard on the basis of the 1967 housing study, which they compared in particular with the 1963 study. See P. Durif and S. Berniard, "Les Français et la maison individuelle," *Economie et statistique* 7 (December 1969), pp. 3–16. See also P. Durif, "Propriétaires et locataires en 1967," *Economie et statistique* 3 (July-August 1969), pp. 41–56.

6. C. Bonvalet, A. Bringé, and B. Riandey, *Cycle de vie et changements urbains en région parisienne. Histoire résidentielle d'une génération* (Paris: Ined, June 1988).

7. N. Tabard, *Relations entre la structure socio-économique de l'espace, la production de l'environnement et les conditions de logement. Analyse de l'enquête Essonne* (Paris: Credoc, 1987).

8. Even though here we are principally interested in the system of explanatory factors of the purchase or rental of a house or apartment as a principal residence, we are aware that one should also take into consideration the ownership of other residential properties. The study directed by Catherine Bonvalet focusing on Parisians born between 1926 and 1935 shows that 42 percent of this generation own some other residence in addition to their principal residence and 30 percent use the additional residence as a secondary home. Upper level managers, executives and professionals have the highest rate of ownership of a second residence (more than 60 percent) and office workers the lowest (especially those in the public sector: 27 percent). The inheritance of property often deals with a secondary residence or some other residential property, especially in the case of people living in residences that fall under the rent control law (the law of 1948) or in residences paid for by the employer. It may be in the interest of some people to continue to rent in order to live in the inner city even while they own a secondary residence or some other residential property: The highest percentage of people owning a second residence was among the interviewees who had a residence that fell under the rent control law (51 percent) and among those whose rent was paid by another party (58 percent). Even among those who rented in public-housing projects (HLM), there was a significant percentage (27 percent) of interviewees who had a second residence. See Bonvalet, Bringé, and Riandey, *Cycle de vie et changements urbains en région parisienne*, pp. 113–115 and 137–142.

9. Pierre Durif and Sylvie Berniard have already highlighted this phenomenon: The relative proportion of purchases of individual houses in cities of over 100,000 inhabitants and in the Paris metropolitan area were highest in the middle-income groups. This was the case both in 1967 and in 1963, when the phenomenon was particularly pronounced because there was a particularly large number of individual houses on the market for sale prices.

10. M. Villac, G. Balland, and L. Touchard, "Les conditions de logement des ménages en 1978," *Les collections de l'INSEE,* M. 85.

11. We know, in a general way, that the business and industry owners invest more than all the other categories and that they invest, in every sense of the term, in the *possession of material goods:* houses, luxury cars, etc. They are great readers of specialty magazines, such as car magazines, that are permeated by an ideology of private property and ownership.

Everything allows us to assume that, because these categories with a very strong professional heritage depend very heavily on *economic heritage* for their reproduction, they are predisposed to think of the residence as a transmissible patrimony and to make it a secure family investment (*le placement de père de famille par excellence*).

12. In this category the rate of ownership is also independent of age.

13. The rate of ownership of apartments seems more tied to academic degrees than does the rate of ownership of houses, at least in certain categories. But certainly one should look at the effect of *urbanization*. The owners of apartments are most common in the large cities where there is also a higher percentage of academic degrees.

14. The foremen with the lowest incomes (less than 65,000 francs a year) are much more often owners of their residence (39.5 percent) than office workers (16.5 percent) or the middle-level managers (8.2 percent) who have the same resources.

15. Villac, Balland, and Touchard, "Les conditions de logement des ménages en 1978," no. 38, pp. 161–166. In addition to the size of the city, one must also take into consideration the region. Pierre Durif has shown that in 1968 there were significant regional disparities, notably between western and eastern France: The proportion of individual houses was over half in western France and was particularly high in the north; in contrast, collective dwellings were dominant in the center, the east and particularly in the southeast. See Durif and Berniard, "Les Français et la maison individuelle," particularly pp. 5–7.

16. Tabard et al., *Relations entre la structure socio-économique de l'espace, la production de l'environnement et les conditions de logement.*

17. Bonvalet, Bringé, and Riandey, *Cycle de vie et changements urbains en région parisienne,* p. 121.

18. Ibid., pp. 125–126.

19. On the relation between birth rate and social ambition, see P. Bourdieu and A. Darbel, "La fin d'un malthusianisme?" in Darras, *Le partage de bénéfices* (Paris: Les Editions de Minuit, 1966), pp. 117–129. Also see P. Bourdieu, *La distinction* (Paris: Les Editions de Minuit, 1984).

20. This hypothesis is confirmed by the initial results published in the study directed by Nicole Tabard in the Essonne region and should allow us to refine our knowledge of the effects of social trajectory. She showed particularly clearly the connections between social origin (notably for managers and professionals) and living in a more or less "well-off" city.

21. See P. Culturello, *De la location à l'accession,* research report of the CNAF (Nice and Marseille: GERM-CERCOM, 1989).

22. See Bonvalet, *Cycle de vie et changements urbains en région parisienne,* p. 131.

23. See M. Eenschooten, "Le logement de 1978 à 1984. Toujours plus grand et toujours mieux," *Economie et statistique* 206 (January 1988), pp. 33–43.

24. N. Tabard, *Consommation et inscription spatiale. Synthèse et perspectives* (Paris: Credoc, 1984).

25. See Topalov, *Le logement en France,* p. 315. The analysis of the 1984 study, which should be continued, will allow us to see to what extent these gaps have been reduced.

5

Homelessness and Poststructuralist Theory

DENNIS CROW

I HAVE BEEN FASCINATED by the theoretical and practical relationship between culture and public administration for a long time. Since 1981, I have been involved with neighborhood groups, housing coalitions, professional organizations, and municipal government while teaching public administration and urban planning at the university level. Over the past five years, my practical interests have focused on problems of homeless persons and my scholarly interests have been continually focused on the application of critical cultural theory to problems of public administration and urban planning. Between 1985 and 1987, after teaching in Austin and San Antonio, Texas, I taught urban planning at Mankato State University in Minnesota and volunteered in many capacities with the organization that operates the Welcome Inn Transitional Living Center. Since 1988, I have been employed by the U.S. Department of Housing and Urban Development (HUD) in Washington, D.C. I would like to describe some of the details of my practical and theoretical activities these days.

Since August 1989, I have worked for the Office of Special Needs Assistance Programs (SNAPs) at HUD. This office manages the bulk of HUD's assistance to the homeless, including the Emergency Shelter Grants Program (ESGP), the Supportive Housing Demonstration Program (SHDP), and the Supplemental Assistance to Facilities to Assist the Homeless (SAFAH) program. These programs financially assist state and local governments and nonprofit organizations to provide shelter and social services to the homeless. Having come to HUD after helping to manage a shelter, I was surprised to find that the handful of people directly involved in writing the original legislation and regulations had accepted information from homeless advocacy groups and arrived at reasonable program designs.

Specifically, I am responsible for managing the existing grants for transitional and permanent housing for the handicapped homeless, reviewing applications

72

for new funding, and helping to write regulations and other materials involved with managing these grants. Before the payment system was automated, I made sure that organizations were paid by the Office of Finance and Accounting and that they, in turn, complied with the laws and regulations governing the programs. In 1990, my work focused on about fifty projects in the area between the Caribbean territories and the State of Mississippi, and now it focuses on about thirty projects from Arkansas to Nevada. I am now also responsible, in part, for running ESGP nationwide and for doing basic research to design the allocation process and some program guidelines of a new set-aside of ESGP funds for Native Americans.

Most SNAPs and HUD field staff members push paper that results in the Department of Treasury depositing substantial sums of money in shelter providers' bank accounts. In addition, the SNAPs staff amends grants and writes, changes, and waives regulations to try to encourage quality shelter programs and to try to decrease the practical burden of regulations on shelter providers. Our work constantly involves interpretation of the statutes that establish the programs, the regulations that govern them, and shelter providers' efforts to finance and run their programs as they think best. The SNAPs staff largely tries to both enforce the regulations and accommodate shelter providers' needs within the limits of the laws and of the priorities set by the political leadership. The most frustrating part of the job, ironically, is coping with mistakes and reprinting documents to add other offices' grammatical changes, which delays completion of the paperwork. I have had opportunities, from my first day in this office, to offer policy advice drawn from my experience and to try to make our policies responsive to planning and architectural issues. If I had not been the principal fund-raiser during a financial crisis period at a shelter, I would think that these efforts were far removed from actually benefiting homeless people. Despite the scandals at HUD, SNAPs is an exciting place to work.

In addition to my full-time job at HUD, I am involved with other organizations that assist the homeless and promote academic and scholarly work in the humanities and social sciences. Through the Washington Ethical Society, I have driven the House of Ruth van to deliver sandwiches, tea, fruit, and clothing to people on the streets of D.C. and have joined a Habitat for Humanity construction crew that is building a duplex for low-income families. I also am founding member of the Institute for Advanced Cultural Studies and Maisonneuve Press, an international publishing venture specializing in left cultural studies and urban studies.

I do not consider my theoretical training in cultural theory or my graduate training in public administration planning any match for or help in my everyday work. I have only learned how the government works through being part of it—as a planning intern, as a nonprofit service provider "outside" the bureaucracy, and as a civil servant "inside" its webs. Nevertheless, left critical scholarship in cultural studies, political science, or architecture, whether empirical or theoretical, still seem accurate to me but largely uninformed by the practical exigencies of running a shelter, a community clinic, a neighborhood revitalization effort, a neighborhood literacy or job training center, or an NEA-censored art exhibition. These activities require enormous efforts by people throughout the world but do not have the visibility and media coverage of the demonstrations and social movements that have occupied the left's image of political practice for most of its history. Furthermore, theory should be informed by practice (and probably the reverse less so), particularly through attention to the empirical and theoretical effects of international divisions of labor and practices of neocolonialism anywhere. In my own scholarly work, in *Philosophical Streets* (1990), I have attempted to do this. In the following paragraphs, I want to explain how these experiences have shaped my thinking on the theoretical relationship between criticism and community development.

Michael Ryan (1982) provided a sense of a politics emerging from the lessons of deconstruction. He argued: "If such a politics has a starting point at all ... , it would be those historical, social, institutional networks that produce consciousness and truth-as-meaning-intention as determinate effects, networks characterized by their resistance to axiomatic foundationalism." Though I disagree with some of Ryan's conclusions, this one is important still. My experience has led me to emphasize networks that produce financial and physical results more than the "effect of the real" in consciousness. There are more lessons to be learned in practice about the construction of social "problems," their official putative solutions, the strength of the real labor of politics in grass-roots community development, and the very asymmetry of theory and practice (e.g., Wallis 1991).

R. Radhakrishnan (1989) provides an account of a theoretical poststructuralist politics that considers these effects of practice. His practical point is quite simple: The "identity" of the "agent" of political action is negotiated through the action of shifting coalitions or networks. He argues that the practice of the Rainbow Coalition historically and theoretically precedes any attempt to theoretically interpret it in terms of the politics of "differance" or heterogeneity. Radhakrishnan cleverly suggests that practice precedes theory and that theorists' attempts to comprehend it cannot keep up. Even though the inability of poststructuralism to produce a prescription for political action is usually interpreted as a fatal error or worse, instead it advises us, as Radhakrishnan implies, that the progressive coalition building practiced in the past is still with us and cannot be undone so quickly by theory alone. Advocacy by urban and rural coalitions to change political and administrative practice is still viable. His attention to the Rainbow Coalition as a practical electoral force suggests that a poststructuralist politics cannot anticipate political innovation in the face of changing opportunities for coalition building around employment, housing, health care, and education. Furthermore, Radhakrishnan recognizes that theory alone can neither undo previous approaches to political change nor create new ones ad hoc without acknowledging existing and developing political, administrative and cultural approaches to social justice.

The limitations and opportunities for thought and action are much greater than Radhakrishnan states. First, though theorists' attention to the "Rainbow Coalition," which probably has a different identity in Chicago, Los Angeles, New York, Philadelphia, and Washington, D.C., is short-sighted, it points to the expansion of old coalitions from ones based solely on political parties and labor organizations. Second, though the focus of critical theorists still seems confined to empirical demonstrations of coalitions' viability in urban electoral politics, their theoretical contribution requires the deconstruction of the oppositions of politics versus administration or politics versus planning as well as analyses of coalitions formed to address housing, income, health, and environmental issues in nonelectoral advocacy and service delivery actions. Such coalitions challenge the boundaries of existing institutions and preconceptions about the centrality of electoral politics. Third, careful criticism of the academic disciplinary boundaries might provide an intrinsic rationale for the collaboration between university personnel and such professional, political or service coalitions. Fourth, poststructuralist analysis, combined in particular with political economy and traditional planning analysis, can inspire analysis of local versus global or rural versus urban oppositions that limit interpretation of economic practices. We can learn from practical experience a vigilant attention to the practical details that necessarily elude theory, however sophisticated, and to the specific differences among theories that enable or disable coalitions among theorists and practitioners.

REFERENCES

Crow, Dennis. *Philosophical Streets: New Approaches to Urbanism* (Washington, D.C.: Maisonneuve Press, 1990).

Radhakrishnan, R. "Poststructuralist Politics," in *Postmodernism, Jameson, Critique*, ed. Douglas Kellner (Washington, D.C.: Maisonneuve Press, 1989), pp. 301–332.

Ryan, Michael. *Marxism and Deconstruction* (Baltimore and London: Johns Hopkins University Press, 1982), p. 115.

Wallis, Brian, ed. *If You Lived Here: The City in Art, Theory, and Social Activism* (Seattle: Bay Press, 1991).

6

Orphans' Dreams:
Panic Wars
and the Postmodern

JACKIE ORR & STEPHEN PFOHL

PREFACE

This is a story about PANIC, popular cultural DOUBLES and the fateful destiny of becoming PARTIAL HIStorical orphans. This is a story of war and of the violent white effects of being contradictory subjects who are also subject to the imperial NETWORKINGS of a technologically advanced form of capitalist and patriarchal TELECOMMUNICATIONS. Imaginarily and in the body. We are (w)riting in relation out from within the story of not wholey or as One. This (w)riting is (dis)eased and marked by gaps and incompletions. Within this (w)riting we both encounter and pose questions concerning a critical theatrical (ab)use of psychoanalysis and the ritual demands for ones (who are (k)not One) to pass through the HORRORS of being orphaned. How best to enact this panicked scene, this drama of transference without transcendence and without escape? Without heroics or the call to PATRIotic war? Being orphaned by the dance of social psychoanalytic practice. Being orphaned by tears (or tears) and laughing matters. Like a serpentine skin passing out of time shedding one's ego. Not killing or being killed but being orphaned beyond (or beneath) belief and beyond (or beneath) interpretation and proper grammar gone SYNTACTIC.

THE FIRST DREAM
Theaters of Panic

This text begins repeatedly in the wake of a dream recurring.

The desert was on fire. I was standing in the red grey
storm with my troops and around us Pan god of panic pip-
ing blue notes across the windy shifting theaters of war. I
dreamed that the desert was on fire and positive feedback
Pan god of panic piped blue luminous sound flakes falling
softly on Los Angeles, Baghdad, Rome, Tel Aviv, Baghdad,
Bashra. Shifting theaters of war. Panic loosed through
streets of images. Satellites of sound.

> *I was trying to write this text when I was taken by the
> dream that follows. I am bathed electric in this dream's pale
> blue light and wet. I am about to take my seat in a lush, red
> and velvety theater. This theater seems Chinese. Maybe it's
> not far from Tiananmen Square. It strikes me that vam-
> pires may be circulating within this theater.*

(By   inadventure,   they   unfortunately
left a gap in the analysis
of the dream.)

Somebody had of course yelled "Fire!" The horror in the
theater auditorium was beyond all description. ... [I]t was
inside the house that the greatest loss of life occurred, especially on the stairways leading down from the second bal-
cony. Here most of the dead were trampled or smothered,
though many jumped or fell over the balustrade to the
floor of the foyer. In places on the stairways, particularly
where a turn caused a jam, bodies were piled 7 or 8 feet
deep. ... Many bodies had the clothes torn from them, and
some had the flesh trodden from their bones.[1]

> *Before entering the theater, I encounter a grey-faced white
> man who presents me with a program and the words*

> *BETWEEN THE PLANS AND THE HANDS THAT*
> *BUILD, THERE MUST BE A MEDIATOR. "This was all so*
> *strange and uncanny that a dreadful fear came upon me."²*
> *The cushioned red seats in this theater are arranged in a*
> *semi-circle and I find myself looking down upon the stage*
> *from this my given vantage point in history. This is a the-*
> *ater of doubles and time is running out. There is panic.*

Over 600 people died trying to escape the fire in the Iroquois Theatre one winter afternoon, December 30, 1903. It
was the largest loss of life to date in a disaster of its kind.
What unsettled some observers of the scene was that the
deaths were seemingly caused by the panicked flight of the
audience, and not by the real danger of fire. For some theorists of panic, the disaster presented a compelling problem:
how to explain humans' fatal attempt to escape not death,
but the apparent face of death, conjured by the cry of a single word. What occurred in the Iroquois Theatre after
somebody stopped the play yelling "Fire!" was, apparently,
an other, strangely staged piece of theater—with no thing
cast for certain in the role of death but every body playing
the part, and panicked, of death's victim. The scene that
ensured seemed not far from suicide, with this unnerving
difference: nobody, apparently, desired to die.

> *In the theater there is panic and a precession of seven dou-*
> *bles: one HIStorical mode of producing and consuming im-*
> *ages after another. Before me lies the image of a woman*
> *waving at the image of the man on a screen waving back*
> *into the NETWORKS. Then FLASH BACK into the future.*
> *there's another double, another man. He's racing across a*
> *sea of LIQUID CAPITAL without a LICENCE TO KILL but*
> *real bodies (still) fall behind the screen as he speeds by. Nic-*
> *aragua. El Salvador. Guatemala. Panama. Iraq. He's in a*
> *cigarette boat but it's not James Bond. It's the U.S. presi-*
> *dent. It's George Bush.*

In the United States of America, in the two decades following World War II, panic theory burgeons into a full-
blown body of sociological literature, as well as a sustained
topic of investigation by the U.S. government and Department of Defense, and a dramatic concern of popular public
discourse. While theater fires become a relatively rare event

(deterred by rigorously regulated and enforced fire codes
and more effective technologies of prevention) the terror of
sudden, catastrophic death assumes a new form. If the theaters of war in World War II witness the panicky disappearance of the difference between military and nonmilitary
targets of death, the theaters of post–World War II and
postatomic bombings observe the disappearance of the
boundaries of the "theater of war" itself.

> *December 1989. Thirteen months before the screening of
> Operation Desert Storm. I've been trying to complete this
> text by the deadline but am distracted, detoured, led astray.
> Maybe it's just bad timing for theory. I have been working
> with othersThese last to counter the terrible U.S.-sponsored
> violence against the people of El Salvador. We publicly raise
> questions about the virtual media WHITE OUT concerning
> such matters as the murderous bombing of San Salvador's
> poorest neighborhoods, the suppression of a wide range of
> popular religious and humanitarian organizations and the
> insidious use of weapons such as U.S.-made white phospho-
> rous bombs (a powdery explosive with effects much like
> NAPALM).*

In the new social time and space of a forever Cold War,
the terror of a sudden molten blast of death becomes incorporated into the everyday "peacetime" of millions of Americans. As screams of "Fire" cease to interrupt the staged
reveries of an American public at play, the U.S. government
introduces the repetitive wail of air-raid sirens to regularly
interrupt the daily programming of American citizens at
school, in the streets, at home. The imagined possibility of
a sudden nuclear attack extends the theater of war into the
imaginary peacetime of everyday American life.

> *On stage in the theater the fifth double has just completed a
> good performance. This was the theater of representation, a
> drama of words and things in passing. A sixth double be-
> ginning to screen its play. The audience is thrilled. The war
> continues. This is a perfect copy of what's gone on before;
> an exact mechanical reproduction. The audience is thrilled.
> Suddenly I notice a grey mattered shape moving fast and
> leftward across the row before me. This ghostly figure glides
> nearly transparent to the periphery of my vision and then*

dis-appears. I am greatly alarmed by the almost weightless movement of this shape and re-cognize it as that of a seventh double. The remarkably invisible performance of this double seems already always in process; unannounced, unheralded, unnamed. It slips beyond the confines of modern language into the smooth and digitally coded abstractions of what's sheerly signed. The audience, still entranced by the reproductive theatrics of the sixth double as it repeats HIStory, seems oblivious. It is as if this seventh double lies beyond the body of theater as "we" know it. It is nevertheless playing its part, enacting its (w)rite, disseminating a particular functionality. I sense its drama oozing deadly if unseen into the space in which I find myself transferred and terrorized. I brace my body for the struggle that lies ahead.

The U.S. government enthusiastically sponsors this reconfiguring of the borders of the theatre of war. The newly formed Federal Civil Defense Administration (FCDA) and its local agencies begin to circulate vivid, but calculatedly manageable, images of nuclear holocaust. Horrific images of nuclear attack are widely distributed through the FCDA-produced film "Survival under Atomic Attack," which sells more copies than any other film to date. The U.S. Air Force collaborates with radio networks to broadcast dramatic simulations of Russian attack. Through a series of "Operation Alert" exercises begun in 1954, participatory simulations of Russian nuclear attack take place in dozens of American cities: as imagined bombers approach the town, real sirens wail and people clear the streets seeking safe shelter. Photographs of the town's empty streets are circulated in the local press the next day. In 1953, the government invites hundreds of media people to witness an atomic explosion in the Nevada desert. Three-quarters of the nation's population reportedly hear of the test or witness it on television. National magazines and TV carry photos of the mangled bodies of mannequins, their destruction staged, then filmed in the living rooms and kitchens of houses built near the test site by the U.S. government.[3]

This is a theater if simulation. It strikes me that vampires may be circulating within this theater. Vertigo spins contagious within this space that's really no-where while episodic

*bursts of panic activistly drive a mass of sex and racially
coded spectators beyond the boundaries of what's modern.
It seems dangerously impossible to reflexively glimpse and
collectively re-present what or who's being sacrificed so viciously to program such special effects. Outward into hyper-
space. Inward into frenzy. This theater seems ominously capable of blurring material and imaginary distinctions between what's real and what's other. This is the theater of
the SEVENTH DOUBLE and within its ritual framings
there's no telling fact from fiction. As my I's/eyes move left-
ward in dramatic pursuit of this final doubling the borders
of the invisible stage that constitutes this theater begin to
dissolve into odorless, test bans of tasteless silent color:
RED, WHITE, BLUE. This dream is ending. This dream is
beginning again.*

DREAMING THEORY:[4] The Actress emerges from the
bathroom. White linen dress. Red lips. Lovely. She emerges
from the bathroom and stands before him—a bombshell.
She performs for the Doctor from her latest script, swirling
white skirts. She reads him the last lines of her final scene,
laughing, "The panic theorist's problems are, dare I say,
real."

In a white linen dress. Red lips. Lovely. She winks.

The Doctor blinks. It's time for his scene. His imaginary
8:15 A.M. scene. He imagines his work now embodied in
bombshells. Bad timing for a theory produced in connection in Mozart, to reflection, to reading, to writing sheets
and sheets of white paper? Bad timing for theory not in
connection to (sur)real other bodies.

[In the elevator, the Indian goes alone up and down.]

*As citizens of the New World Order, the collective represen-
tations by which we narcissistically advertise ourselves to
ourselves have little to do with the material exigencies of
our actual HIStories. Little is ritually remembered about
who ate whom for dinner on Thanksgiving, the first and
perhaps most cynical of all New World holidays, or of the
economic foundations of American democracy in genocide,
slavery and the subordination of women. Unto death do us
part. One boatload of refugees, escapees, prisoners, outlaws,*

and fortune seekers after another. Claiming the land, seiz-
ing the time, one cemetery, lynching tree, and ghetto blast-
ing moment of HIStory after another. Without the pre-
Capitalist constraints of residual medieval institutions, ar-
chitecture and folkways. American the Beautiful. Sacrificial
America. Without the constraints of having white men's
bodily aggressions HIStorically modulated by a lack of
seemingly limitless spatial frontiers. The westward expan-
sion of the USA was, for well over a century of moderniza-
tion, unencumbered by the formal or legal fictions of colo-
nial discourse. And within this magnetic expanse, U.S.
white men begin to cut their ties with European modernity,
as each day "our" ancestors enacted rites such as regularly
carrying a gun, purchasing women for male-ordered plea-
sures and sticking metal knife blades into the scalps of other
living human animals. And cutting. All for the pleasures of
power, conquest and terror. The joys of the wild west—
manifest destiny and the like.

Bombshells embodied become for him real. An explosion of glass panes—a billion splinters of glass in his eye,
buried in her lips, round her neck, across her (lovely)
breasts.

She becomes for an instant a sheer pain of glass—the
spin of her white linen skirts now red staining—flesh
sharded to slivers—(his eye splits wild open)—and forced
to the bone in one final shatter, a shudder of flesh all one
wound for an instant before the next blast that burns now
her flesh gone to nowhere, she is blasted to nothing no
bone of a memory left for some wild beloved who searches
this circle of white light destruction. Who walks through
this ruin with eyes split wild open, unweeping, searching
the ruin for some familiar bone.

(This is the image in which she was born and is dying,
   sharding him down to the bone of his eye.)

The Doctor blinks. The scene passes. She stands before
him again—a bombshell he (barely) knew.

With a wave (or a particle?) of her hand
        she, laughing
                disappears lightly.

*I grew up as a little boy playing cowboy, rolling in imagi-
nary struggles for freedom on the floor of a room in a house
that my father had purchased and enacting intense and
transferential rites of feeling the manly virtues of sticking it
to a televisionary enemy of we who are whites and memory-
less. What white lies behind this deadly color coding? Afterwards, in bed, I would close my eyes and imagine that a car-
load of suburban white girls, maybe cheerleaders, would
sneak up to my window and climb into my mind. They
would tie my hands behind my back and strip me of every
bit of clothing. I would bask in submission and arousal. I
would watch myself watching. The girls would then pirate
me out of my father's house into their father's AUTOmobile
and drive me around. With abandon. What transferences
with what senseless futures are young American boys today
feeling standing quarter to quarter in relation to a video-
game named CONTRA, OPERATION JUST CAUSE,
OPERATION DESERT STORM, FREEDOM FIGHTERS,
KICK ASS. A white Rambo look-alike totem dashes across
the screen blinking digital. He is powerfully armed and fires
laser beams into brown-skinned iconic men in mustaches.*

Now I walk along home, along Satellite Beach
   there are waves and waves high tide and the ocean swells
somewhat over the edges where I lie, I listen, I lie. And as I listen
   at the edges I hear another high swelling and over our heads
where we lie sunning on Satellite Beaches they fly
   one two three four five black bird-planes
and smaller than the pelicans.

They circle over Satellite Beach in a high
   swelling tide.
How they roared, mama, how loud they roared
   one two three four five over my head
     over your head
Are you listening mama?
Did you count them coming flying low, shrill,
   insistent black and swelling the edges, mama,
     of Satellite Beaches?

(AND OUT OF THE CORNER OF MY EYE I SAW THEM
MAMA, TO THE LEFT AND MOVING ACROSS THE FRAME

FILLED BY YOUR SWELL FACE MAMA. SHADED BY A
WICKER HAT WITH YELLOW RIBBON ROUND THE BRIM
AND FIVE BIG BLACK-ROAR BIRD-PLANES FLY ACROSS
THE FRAME, ACROSS THE GREY SKY BEHIND THE WIDE
WICKER BRIM OF YOUR SUN HAT MAMA

DO YOU THINK IT WILL KEEP YOU FROM BURNING?)

*During the first 48 hours of the FMLN offensive armed Sal-
vadorans attacked more than 50 military positions spread
over half of El Salvador's 14 provinces. Under the cover of a
virtual media WHITE OUT the government responded to
these military actions by dropping U.S.-supplied bombs
from U.S.-supplied aircraft upon the poorest slums or bar-
rios of its CAPITAL city. During the last one hundred hours
of Operation Desert Storm the bombing is laser guided and
more intense. Perhaps as many as 150,000 fleeing Iraqi
troops are not allowed to flee. I am watching TV. A show
called "Inside Edition" honors what it designates as the
true heroes of the Gulf War as it broadcasts images of a
stealthy band of American Natives transubstantiating into
Apache Helicopters. Within these black metallic bird-planes
pilots sit eyes wed to the camera and fingers to the fire. Un-
counted corpses lie scorched under HIStory's sun while back
in the U.S.A. yellow ribbons abound.*

How they roared, mama, how loud they roared
        one two three four five black roar bird-planes
                over my head.
Are you listening mama?
Did you count them coming flying low, shrill,
    insistent black and swelling the edges, mama
        of Satellite Beaches?

THE SECOND DREAM

Network Wars and the Deconstructive Kinship of Orphans

1. TV (for) Dinner?

What does it mean to (w)rite that a critical practice of social psychoanalytic theorizing might assist ones (who are (k)not One) to become orphans? It's not that we hadn't been trying before. It's that socially deconstructive strategies of (k)not knowing have encouraged our descent out from within a set of HIStorically specific disciplines into the material imaginings of some others. With the help of our friends. After all, you can befriend an orphan but never become her kin; or his. What we mean is this—deconstructive methods may assist us in partially loosening the hegemonic stranglehold of those kinship patterns that are currently being supported by the activities of metropolitan based men of corporate power. Worldwide. Not simply the nuclearized family as kin, but also the close-circuiting of sacrificial ritual relations that seduce people into feeling a kinship with automobiles, shopping malls, sports arenas, office towers, football teams, and Patriot Missile totems. For it is within these dense and frenetic sites of social structuring that people are today increasingly being trans-nationalized into pre-packaged identities, pledged allegiances, public health syndromes, and anxious desires for more and for less.

This is a new and post-familial meaning of networks. Today, kinship is increasingly defined not so much by blood as by material networks of signed reproduction and totemically charged moral impulses. Hence, "one" can and does speak in the name of the global family of CBS, NBC, ABC, CNN, Time Incorporated, and Disney. Thus it appears that increasing numbers of people may receive more ritual sustenance from involving themselves in the imaginary family feuds, intrigues, worries, and desires of TV and media personalities than they do from flesh and blood relations. Given this state of affairs, it is vital that those of us concerned about the future of human social relatedness begin to re-theorize the meaning of kinship. Transferential identifications with electronically screened characters—this is hardly the same as being subject to "the name of the Father." Or if it is, it's transference in the name of such a disembodied or abstract father that many of us are literally made orphans in the sociological sense of the word.

The pains of being orphaned—this may indeed be a terrifying aspect of the postmodern scene. More horrific, however, is the possibility that masses of people are today being teleconverted into mutant subjectivities whose primary connections to feelings of kinship are digitally sampled then relayed through the media itself. Those who keep statistics on these matters inform us that there are fewer "father-mother-children" families dining at the Parasite Cafe each evening. And fewer parent-headed families of any type. Within the confines of the *USA Today,* children are regularly confronted with having to give up routine contacts with one in a series of "parents." On the other hand, virtually nobody is asked to divorce oneself from ritual contact with the mass electric and trans-sexual parentage that the media has become.

For the American middle classes this mutational situation is rapidly becoming a "real time" situation, at least since the advent of mass-marketed "TV dinners." And by the 1990s the truly "post-familial" realities of everyday life are becoming more pronounced and more costly.

2. Panic Through the Networks

Live on screen, a young girl in braids and braces sits on the couch next to her mother. She doesn't know what neural networking activity is, really, but in front of the camera she calmly tells the talk show host and today's home TV viewing audience about her first attack of panic. The sudden terror, a pounding heart, sweaty palms, shortness of breath—the same dramatic symptoms her mother experienced in her twelve-year battle with panic disorder. The camera swings to a grey-suited man seated in a swivel chair. Dr. Gerry Rosenbaum, psychopharmacology unit chief of Massachusetts General Hospital in Boston, describes panic disorder as a biochemically based disease, explaining how genetic vulnerability to the problem can be passed through the family. Before the commercial break, the talk show host assures home viewers who believe they might suffer from this disabling disorder that they are *not* alone—for more information, viewers may phone the number (highlighted at the bottom of the screen) of the ANXIETY RESEARCH UNIT at Massachusetts General Hospital. Studio audience applause; a quick shot of a young girl in braids and braces, smiling; the phone number flashes again. Break to commercial.

WITH MCI´S SPECIAL TOTAL TELEPHONIC PACKAGE YOU GET

SOMETHING OTHER COMPANIES ONLY DREAM OF GIVING.

COMMAND

    CONTROL

        COMMUNICATIONS.

IT´S YOUR CHOICE. CALL NOW AND GET ONE MONTH FREE.

Over 300 people phone the Anxiety Research Unit within two weeks of the airing of the local Boston TV talk show. From among the pool of panicked callers, screened by a twelve-item questionnaire administered over the phone, a handful of subjects with appropriate profiles are chosen to participate in Massachusetts

General Hospital's clinical research program on panic disorder. MGH runs the largest U.S. clinical study on the cause and treatment of panic, a recently discovered "disorder" that reportedly affects about 5 percent of the American population at any one time, the vast majority of them women.[5] The medical research at MGH is sponsored by Upjohn, a transnational pharmaceutical company that manufactures Xanax, a new and widely prescribed drug for panic and anxiety.[6] Upjohn also designed and sponsored the Worldwide Panic Project, an international clinical study of panic disorder in fifteen countries involving over 2,000 research subjects—and the most extensive global clinical research ever conducted by a transnational drug company.

She doesn't know what neural networking activity is, really. But she knows what it's like to experience sudden attacks of terror when she's crossing the street, turning over to sleep, eating in a restaurant, shopping in the mall, watching TV. She knows what it's like to receive a panicky relay of screened information, to phone the Anxiety Research Unit and respond to a voice across the electric wires. … On a scale of one to ten: how severe was your most recent attack? Yes or no: any thoughts of suicide? Never, sometimes, frequently, a lot of the time: fear that something is wrong with your mind?

She knows what it's like to become a voluntary participant in a clinical research program and hear the young doctor tell her that a panic attack is like "a brain misfiring." His words offer a short-circuited re-call of the overtly militaristic models of neural activity used a hundred years ago by Sigmund Freud to chart the "defence systems," the "contact-barriers" of the not-yet-central nervous system. An explosive geography now displaced, within the conceptual-technological fall-out of two world wars, by the contemporary and supposedly "nonviolent" language of the "communications" model. This new model of neural activity evokes a seemingly neutral and nonaggressive landscape of NEURO-TRANSMISSION to ground the elusive materiality of just *how* the human nervous system functions. The central activity of the system becomes the relay and reception of biochemical INFORMATION. In this model dis-orders of the central nervous system are represented as the transmission and reception of irregular or deviant information. In the 1984 Upjohn Co. corporate annual report, a caption for an illustration depicting an intricate network of human nerve cells reads:

> Information passed along a nerve cell's axon is assimilated by the dendrites or cell body of the receiving cell through synaptic connections. Neurotransmitters (chemicals) are released from the axon into a very tiny space (the synapse). They then diffuse across this space and bind to receptors on the receiving cell, and the message has been delivered. Contemporary neuropharmacology seeks to modify aberrant messages that occur in certain disease states.

She feels her brain misFIRE. Perhaps it's the sketch of the Brooklyn Bridge, a memory framed and hanging on the young doctor's office wall. Dry throated thoughts race anxious through her brain reminded. Misfiring. She doesn't know exactly what neural nets are but she knows she's deeply entangled. Splattering neurotransmissions, untidying the office. She is posing patient within the orderly office in the Anxiety Research Unit when suddenly a message is delivered. Traveling red white and blue-blooded, faster than a speeding bullet, it reads: beware the Bridge and the panic of trying to cross over.

A memory misfiring: it is July 4th, 1986, New York City. It is the day of the bicentennial celebration and Lady Liberty's about to be unveiled. Thank you President Reagan. Hats off to Vice President Bush. It is July 4th, 1986, in New York City and she joins the flow of surging bodies across the Brooklyn Bridge. The free fireworks begin at sunset. Millions stalk the horizon seeking clear sight for the spectacle; thousands move en masse across the Brooklyn Bridge, pursuing the perfect view. She joins the flow of surging bodies when, halfway across the Bridge, the bodies in front stop moving, the bodies behind keep coming. In the crush of the holiday crowd turning wild, halfway between language and neurotransmissions gone awry, she feels her brain begin misfiring. There appears no escape and panic takes its pleasure, signaling wave upon wave of terror as the crush of bodies surge before the sunset and the fireworks explode above within without. The message has been delivered: LADY LIBERTY is alive but dis-eased, channeled senseless through the networks. She feels her senses pulsing almost weightless. The bodies surge. Her brain misfires. Wired live, electric in a crackling sea of unveiled fear without horizon. There appears no escape, and the panic takes its pleasure. It is the 4th of July, 1986. The major networks aired the action and the fireworks were free.

3. Taxation Without Re-presentation

George Bush addresses a multinational and multinetwork television audience with the following words: READ MY LIPS. This is corporate CAPTIAList semiology, sign-work for profit. In issuing this command Bush announces his position in a long and violent precession of metropolitan men of power covering their traces. To follow Bush's command sign or signal is to become (a) subject to an escalating taxation by a nearly instantaneous substitution of one dominant and domineering mode of communicative economy by others. This is the material force of Bush's base attraction: a masterful MORAL REPULSION of other economies of logic, feeling, and action. By itself this dramatic erection of authoritarian moral boundaries is no-thing new. It has been a feature of patriarchal state societies since their violent ascension to power. What is new, at least since the western HIStorical production of what's modern, is the increasingly instantaneous nature of telecommunicative fixation. In this Bush may genuinely be a pioneer. Racing across an oceanic surface of photo opportunities in his spy-thriller-secret agent-cigarette boat, Bush may, in actuality, herald the end of the theatrical representation and the advent of a pure and cynical screen play of power. Operation Desert Storm: the first "real time" TV war. Reagan, who, after all, was really only always an actor, may have promised the theatrical terror of the simulacra. But with Bush it's time for an efficient corporate execution of models that function transferentially without rehearsals and with only the shortest of digital delays. An eclipse of re-presentation into the model. Instantaneous communicative categorizations: READ MY LIPS.

4. Military Intelligence?

The emergence of communication technologies as increasingly dominant transmitters within a post–World War II network of bioengineering-electronic-chemical-computer research and theory signals a profound shift in the United States central(ized) nervous systems. Remembering that the symbol for post–World War II military operations theory is C^3I: command-control-communications-intelligence, it becomes HIStorically urgent to consider a new postmodern trinity of fields: military intelligence; corporate communications technologies; and medical models of the NETWORKings of a human nervous system. At the social and symbolic intersection of these three fields may rest some possibilities for understanding how "individual" human perceptions are increasingly modeled after and constituted by communications networks effecting a sustained militarization of New World Ordered bodies. If, indeed, "Our dominations don't work by medicalization and normalization anymore; they work by networking, communications redesign, stress management,"[7] then fighting such domination requires a radical re-configuring of how OUR BODIES, OUR SELVES are represented and reproduced. There are, possibly, all the grounds in the world for contesting these medical representations as cultural weapons in a war to militarize all (possible) perceptions of our selves in relation to others.

"There is no war without representation ... weapons are tools not just of destruction but also of perception—that is to say, stimulants that make themselves felt through chemical, neurological processes in the sense organs and the central nervous system."[8] When first developed, pharmaceutical pills were called "magic bullets" for their ability to target their effects on certain body processes. The seductive effectivity of these chemical weapons can easily silence any questioning of those dominant representations of our bodies that enable corporate/medical research and drug development to progress, and certain forms of CURE to control our perceptions of what possibly can transform our dis-ease. What *is* being communicated in a communications model of the central nervous system? What military intelligence is involved when a body knows to panic, even if it doesn't understand neural networking activity? What effective ignorance might we call upon to resist the sophisticated corporate/medical/military modelings of our dis-orders? "The priveleged pathology affecting all kinds of components in this [bio-technological] universe is communications breakdown."[9] But if the panicked body experiences a breakdown in NORMAL neurological communication—then where are the deviant signals coming from? And how should anybody respond?

5. Double the Pleasure. Double the Fun. Docu-drama.

As man is (w)riting. Television waves pass through this man's body. This is HIS-tory. On screen there is a double of a woman whose trembling wet body is being dragged naked from the shower by a man before the camera. This image is relayed PRIME-TIME before another man's eyes/I's. This show is *Rescue 911*. This show is a docu-drama, an "educative" theatricalization of "real life." This is entertainment, a seductive male fantasy that parasitically assumes the shape of information. This show operates in prime-time to doubly connect a panicked television audience to the police. To doubly connect the man before the screen to the man before the camera committing a crime?

For the man engulfed in a commercial radiation of heterosexist imagery, it is difficult to take his eyes off the screen, off the terrorized naked form of the double of the white woman on the verge of being raped. Aesthetically raped on prime-time in the shape of inFORMation. This show is obscene. He watches the man drag the double of the woman to her bedroom and pin her to the sheets thrashing. The double appears nearly naked. As a viewer, he is invited to follow the camera as it studies the woman's exposed thighs spread and bared shoulders, inching toward her breasts. Each camera shot promises more exposure, more information. Each camera shot is cut by a frame of the doubled woman's baby in the next room unaware. Is he actually going to see the woman's breasts, the rape? This show operates for profit. Whose profit?

The *reel* violence of this obscene spectacle shifts in focus. The doubled woman-victim of this (a)morality play now outsmarts her would-be monster-rapist. She tells him that if only he'd allow her to phone in late for work he'd have plenty of time to rape her without anybody noticing. The monster-rapist says "ok." The the doubled woman outsmarts him by quietly phoning her normal-male friend Scott, and Eva, a woman police dispatcher at 911. Since the monster-rapist is listening, the doubled woman has to use coded language like on television. Within seconds the woman's name, address and vehicle registration appear on Eva's screen at 911—Police Headquarters—and help is on the way. Soon the screen is flooded with good, authorized and normal white men who catch the monster and save the doubled woman from being raped. Except aesthetically. She was saved by the 911 police from the monster but not from the eyes/I's of the man before the screen (w)riting his watching eyes/I's.

Time for a commercial break. On screen there is a double of a white woman whose trembling wet body is being filmed naked in the shower before the camera. This woman seems ecstatic, enthralled by the possibility of becoming cleaner than ever for only a few pennies more per shower. This is entertainment, a seductive male fantasy that parasitically assumes the shape of information. This show operates in prime-time to doubly connect a panicked television audience to the police. To doubly connect a man before the screen watching to a man before the camera committing a crime?

6. Lilly WHITE Drug Wars

In the spring of 1980, during his first campaign for the U.S. presidency, George Bush resigned from his position as corporate director of Eli Lilly and Company, America's fifth largest transnational drug company.

It is spring 1990. Information transfers cold, white and blue across the airwaves. There is a television and the drug wars and an image of U.S. drug czar William Bennett. The story publicly signals some new ideas Bennett has to build a nationwide network of orphanages. These orphanages are to safeguard the children of parents who've fallen through the CRACKs. This man is no bleeding heart. This man's boss is George Bush.

Please don't panic little orphans.

Please don't panic.

7. Media Mutants, Byte by Byte

And at exactly the same time in HIStory, we are also presented with a nostalgic (if erroneous) image of the drug-free nuclear family as the only true source of "real time" telecommunicated kinship. This is the image of the family evoked by a moral army of reactionary forces opposed both to "the liberation" of women and children from heterosexist family roles and to the so-called breakdown of the family on the part of the racially stigmatized and economically vanquished. Both occurrences are said to be related to crime, drug abuse, and a host of other deviant behaviors.

Calls for bolstering the endangered family are also increasing elements of an alleged "progressive" political agenda. Without minimalizing the very real pains of peoples victimized by the political and economic abandonment of traditional family networks, it is, nonetheless, far from clear that efforts to save the modern western family will prove either just or strategic. Consider the global operations of transnational corporate power as it is telecommunicatively decentered into the ritual materiality of everyday life. The most immediate site of this transfer involves the hyper-electric tactics of mass-mediated socialization. In this, there is little evidence that family units, as sociologists have traditionally defined them, have been at all effective in resisting this ultra-modern transformation of kinship structures.

Family members who weep with Oprah and share the intimacies of terror with Geraldo may have little to emotionally exchange with each other in the flesh; little that is but the panic of not being able to live up to the simulated ideals of media icons that have virtually no reference to anything outside the screen and its information. Better, perhaps, to be sociologically orphaned than mutant members of the new and fleshless family of the corporate mediascape. At least orphans might know the pains of the HIStorical disappearance of their fleshly parents, just as they may dream of the aboriginal possibility of reconstituting some new and less hierarchical structures of kin. For telecommunicative mutants the future is in the past. What mutants screen play as the basic nuclearized family is no-thing but the re-runs of an old and exhaustive patriarchal drama. Only that this time there's a new talking head at the mutant's dinner table and it's consuming the flesh of everybody else. Byte by byte. This is the Parasite Cafe. Maybe it's better to be an orphan.

THE THIRD DREAM
V for Vendetta: The Orphans' Revenge

It is the Fourth of July in the world's most a-mazing shopping mall fantastic. It is the day of the orphans' revenge. The orphans catch President Bush in a televisionary crossfire, or so the story goes.

TAKE TWO: 1-0, 1-0, 1-0. "Digitality is with us. It is that which haunts all these messages, all the signs of our societies. The most concrete form you see it in is that of the test, of the question/answer, of the stimulus response."[10]

QUESTION: Why a second beginning to this HIStory?
ANSWER: **V for Vendetta: the Orphans' Revenge**

It is the Fourth of July in AMERICA. It is the day of the orphans' revenge. Bush travels to the world's most a-mazing shopping mall fantastic. He appears to witness a video project of the U.S. Flag onto a vast screen composed of the digitally reconfigured body images of exactly 50,000 Indiana school children. Each child is dressed in painted white canvas and is posed individually. Each with her or his own life-size white mask stands obliged before a perfectly white backdrop. To the eye of the camera it is virtually impossible to tell the difference between each white costumed child and the pure white backdrop. Photographs of each child are snapped out of time. In these images each child appears only to disappear. No figures remain visible within these photographs; nor grounds.

Slides are made of each photograph then projected in sets of fifty. These projections are then rephotographed as slides that are again projected in ever larger configurations until a purely white composite of the images of all 50,000 children, now strictly miniaturized, is at last achieved. This image is then projected onto the backside of the huge screen that drapes the luxurious central boulevard of the fantastic shopping mall itself.

It is in-dependence day in America and onto the frontside of the giant video screen is projected a seamless high-density image of white stars shimmering against an electric blue background and the unfurled red and white stripes that in combination signify the constitutionally insured integrity of this totem, this flag, "old glory." Bush is there to celebrate the flows of what New World Order of freedoms this emblem sets in motion. Globally. Free Trade. Free Enterprise. Free Kuwait. The freedom to die homeless alone and in panic. He waves his arms and smiles into the converging networks. He offers words of heartfelt thanks to that great mass of shoppers from the home state of Vice President Dan Quayle who worked so tirelessly in securing the purchase of that HIStoric landmark in representational politics—the end-of-this-century passage of a U.S. constitutional amendment guaranteeing the death penalty to FLAG ABUSERS. The crowd goes wild. Yellow ribbons abound.

Ecstatic tears smear the makeup of prominent TV news personnel while sales skyrocket higher than ever. The crowd goes wild. But then in an intense, sudden, and televisionary instant shadows mar the screen and Bush's kind and well-tailored body is shred from head to toe by a rain of exploding industrial projectiles. It is the orphans and they are signaling REVENGE.

It is the Fourth of July in America. It is the day of Bush's Assassination. It is the end of all coded empiricities, of all modeled flesh remade. It is the day this dream begins again and again and again and ...

NOTES

1. There is a description of the Iroquois Theatre fire in E. Foy and A. F. Harlow, *Clowning Through Life* (New York: Dutton, 1928), p. 113.

2. Bram Stoker, *Dracula* (New York: Dell Publishing Co., 1978), p. 19.

3. Spencer Weart, *Nuclear Fear: A History of Images* (Cambridge, Mass.: Harvard University Press, 1988), pp. 129–133.

4. The scenes depicted in this passage offer one (transferential) reading of Nicolas Roeg's film "Insignificance." Roeg cinematically staged a chance encounter in 1950s America between Albert Einstein (The Doctor) and Marilyn Monroe (The Actress). The film operates here as a screen on which to explore my own project(ions): a panicky exploration of the imaginary and material relations between heterosexuality and (post)modern nuclear warfare.

5. David Sheehan, M.D., *The Anxiety Disease* (New York: Bantam Books, 1984), p. 11.

6. Massachusetts General Hospital's clinical research programs on panic disorder and panic disorder with depression are funded by private grants from Upjohn Co. (conversation with J. Sidari, Anxiety Research Unit, MGH, August 1987).

7. Donna Haraway, "A Manifesto for Cyborgs: Science, Technology, and Socialist Feminism in the 1980s," *Socialist Review*, no. 80, 1985, p. 69.

8. Paul Virilio, *War and Cinema: The Logistics of Perception* (London: Verso, 1989), p. 6.

9. Haraway, "A Manifesto," p. 82.

10. Jean Baudrillard, *Simulations*, trans. Paul Foss, Paul Patton, and Phillip Beitchman (New York: Semiotext(e), 1982), p. 115.

PART TWO

DRUGS
HYSTERIA
PAIN

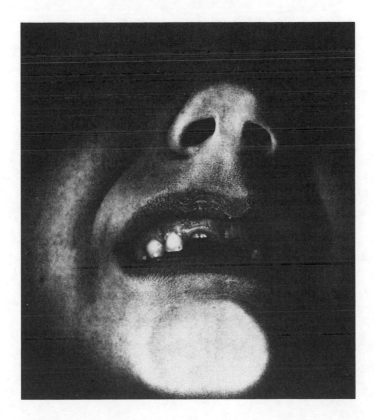

7

A Short HIStory of the Parasite Cafe

STEPHEN PFOHL

THE DECOR RESEMBLES an abandoned theme park. But don't be nostalgic. At the threshold to the cafe floats a ghostly white sheet draped over a black plastic dreamscape. Above the sheet hangs the white head of a pumpkin face smiling. At least I think this pumpkin's face is smiling. Things here seem a bit uncanny and it's difficult to be positive about what's being signified. To get to the tables, which look like wasted school desks, you have to pass beneath the floating sheet. It's only then that you realize that one side of this sheet is doubling as a screen for an image being projected. The image appears to be a composite of two additional images, one dissolving into the other. Along the outside is a facsimile of a white woman's face fractured with the words NOT YOURSELF. Perhaps this is an image once worked on by Barbara Kruger. Imploding within the center of this first image appears the second—a shameful snapshot of naked black male bodies held at gunpoint. In my search for meaning I find a caption that reads, BK PARASITE VISITS ATTICA.

I'd heard this cafe was postmodern, but this seemed a bit much for an introduction. Nevertheless, having agreed to (w)rite up a short review of the place, and feeling really hungry, I said to myself—*Ok, why not some thought for food*—and began to chew things over. I decided to begin with the menu. Right away you realize this place is all about eating cheaply. But at whose expense?

Appetizers Anybody?

For a first course, *Parasite Cafe* offers two tempting morsels—*Possession of the Reaganheads* (October 27, 1984) and *Terror of the Simulacra* (November 1, 1986). The menu indicates that these items, like all *Parasite Cafe* concoctions, even the solo performances, represent a process of collective production. More intriguing is the admission that some of the cafe's performances have been more (politically) reflexive about this matter than others. This menu, it seems, is not without its contradictions.

Since some friends and I sampled both of these appetizers, let me tell you a bit about each. Both involved Halloween and things that are frightening. *Possession of the Reaganheads* took place in a house overlooking Griggs Park in Brookline, Massachusetts, and was attended by over 200 masked people. Live music drifted between jazz, punk, and noise and a three-part "video-text" was staged with accompanying theatrics. The video itself depicted the mechanical reproduction of *the ghost of Marty Martin,* a kind of populist figure clothed in the supposed innocence of a 1950s childhood gone yuppie, and the telecommunicative conversion of that figure into the much publicized image of Ronald Reagan. Set to a weave of found sounds, industrial music, and rap, the video was the product of a long week's labor by a group that included Boston area artists and sociology graduate students from Boston College, Brandeis, and Harvard. Thanks to time parasited from the Boston Film and Video Foundation, editing was completed just prior to the evening's revelry. During the screening of the third segment of the video, with its sped-up sampling of a debate between Reagan and Mondale, overdubbed with the voices of John Wayne and Dick Van Dyke, about 100 people wearing Marty Martin masks challenged what appeared to be an equal number of Reaganheads. Everybody danced all night, but the following Tuesday George Bush was again elected vice president.

Terror of the Simulacra enacted related themes. Only this time, two years had passed and the image of Reagan had recessed further into the media, eating away at what by-passes the body as memory, byte after byte. Set within the spacious confines of an old three-story warehouse on the border between Jamaica Plain and Roxbury, this *Parasite Cafe* event hosted over 450 people. On the first level of the warehouse, people could ebb and flow to the experimental rock sounds of the *Bent Men* and *the Jesus Christler Corporation* (whose "hit song" *Terror of the Simulacra* made Jean Baudrillard a parodic household name for a (k)night, and be exposed to or confronted by a variety of local performance artists. Cries of festival rang out and the police made a dutiful appearance near daybreak. The second floor was reserved for dancing, while on the third, films from the Weimar Republic betrayed hints of discomforting parallels with earlier periods of facism. Literature was available for the taking, and more than a few words were offered about why, after six Halloweens of Reaganomics, some people continued to ask whether postmodernity really existed. So much for the appetizers. On with the meal.

Entrees, Served with Fresh Word-Salad

Here, things may become a little harder to swallow. This much may be said of main courses prepared by the *Parasite Cafe*—each appears performatively seasoned at the crossroads of *sociology, literature, social-psychoanalysis, and HIStory.*

Each also attempts to conjure a reflexive (dis)taste for the ritual reproduction of the economic, sexual, and racial hierarchies its members find themselves caught up within in relation to others. And a distaste, as well, for the modern Western HIStorical distinction between art and science. Materially and in the imaginary realm. There's a lot to choose from here, so I can only give you a sampling of the cafe's more engaged offerings. These begin with the video-text *Criminological Displacements*. Written by two members of the *Parasite Cafe* and produced in collaboration with a third, this 35-minute VHS tape re-presents a deconstructive reading of Michel Foucault's several investigations of the genealogy of the human sciences. Offering a sociological HIStory of criminology in terms of the whitemale narrative pleasures of sadism, surveillance, and the reduction of otherness to a variable unit of the selfsame, *Criminological Displacements* was first shown at the meetings of the American Society of Criminology in the fall of 1985. Thereafter, it has been presented at a variety of universities and professional conferences, including the Cork Film and Video Festival in Ireland and meetings of the Popular Culture Association, the Marxist Literary Group, and the Society for the Study of Social Problems. Composed as a critical collage of words, "found" sights and sounds, this video-text attempts to displace both the formal structure and the visceral experience of much contemporary theoretical discourse. This is a characteristic of most *Parasite Cafe* productions—an effort to give notice to the aesthetic form by which social science makes its appearance known.

Shortly after producing *Criminological Displacements*, several members of the cafe presented a version of *Death of an Author* at an evening of feminist-oriented performances hosted by Fem Core Space in Boston's South End. A drama structured by the interplay of "live" voices and *memorex*, this meal begins with a recitation of disquieting parallels between sociological positivism, pornography, and photo-realism. It ends with the noisy disclosure that: "In theory, the *Parasite Cafe* is situated just to the left of the dominant Judaic-Christian narratives within which its members had been reared and guarded: ritual sites of desire and snapshots, the institutional apparatuses from which Oedipus masters the riddle of the Sphinx blindly and without blood."

But what became of the Sphinx once the young sovereign's sex became latent and Greece became some city-states? Did she cry out or coyly pose? The final scene of *Death of an Author* re-searches this question by juxtaposing images of Oedipus's socio-logical conquest with the sacrifice of Marilyn Monroe and the U.S. bombing of Libya. This is what seemingly makes the *Parasite Cafe's* (w)ritings so different. Each attempts a partial refusal to disconnect the (telecommunicative) calling of its own socio-logical practices from the materiality of rituals that position all claims to knowledge as simultaneously claims of power. John Wayne makes an appearance at the close of this performance, while a trinity of jerking bodies suckle fluids transformed by solid-state electronics into images of each performer's own deadly cinematic destiny. This, I believe is a good example of why so many items on the *Parasite Cafe* menu are labeled "postmodern." Each not only refers to questions about the HIStorical emergence of post-modern culture but also makes critical assumptions about the sociology of linguistic representation that challenge modern social science thinking.

Treat social facts as things and represent them as objective entities that might be measured and compared accordingly! Most contemporary U.S. sociology still follows this edict, treating the problem of language as little more than the task of adequately operationalizing variable aspects of objects being represented. If only the imprecisions of discursive language could be translated into less ambiguous terms! Each item on the *Parasite Cafe* menu takes issue with the objectified character of such sociological representation. Each also departs from subjectivist approaches that are typically posed as "humanist" alternatives to positivism.

For a truly parasitic entree, consider *Desire for Allegory,* a 1986 text slicing scenes from Nazi Germany with recollections of contemporary U.S. HIStory. This dinner comes topped with an "early warning system's sauce." Mixing words from Walter Benjamin with those of Anne Rice, this text is about corporate vampirism in its televisionary phase. Or, for those with a feminist taste for parasitism, I recommend *Panic Diaries* (1987), a disturbing narrative of a woman writer's struggle with "anxiety disorders." Tossed upon a bed of dreams, with a subtext of corporate pharmaceutical control, this text is served with images of its author's own biography sauteed with patriarchal violence. Or maybe it's televisionary space travel that makes you salivate. If so, try tasting *Explosions/Implosions: It's All the Same to Me,* a 1988 performance pairing the death of Christa McAuliffe with the incantations of Jean Baudrillard. But if it's ghosts you're longing for, and for making critical connections between gendered forms of social science (w)riting and the ways in which women's texts are marked by race, class and imperial power, you'll certainly want to try a piece of *Ghostly Memories: Feminist Rituals of Writing the Social Text* (1990). This offering comes in multiple courses, but if you're hungry for a good introduction, and it's something subtle that peaks your interest, this text may prove a meal in itself. And, for a story of U.S. "drug wars" south of the border, seasoned with a critique of "nasal passages" in James Bond, William Bennett, and Immanuel Kant, there is nothing like the aroma of *A Nosography and Nosegrammatics of Male Hysteria* (1990). And finally, for those who find it difficult to pass the evening without radio, there is *Skull Bubble* (1990). A video-textual meditation on the cultural HIStory of twentieth-century airwaves, this piece is served with a dash of connotative technology and an earshot of channels changing what it means to be a "man."

By playing with, cutting up, and/or mirroring back upon the social scenes out of which they themselves are served, each of these *Parasite Cafe* productions search imperfectly for a language that reflexes upon the "fact" that "we" are simultaneous authors of and authored by the languages in which we find ourselves trying to communicate. This task is, of course, impossible. Thus, it may be at precisely those places where the culinary "know-how" of this strange cafe appears most likely to fail or slip or falter that hungry readers may be called upon, not merely to complete their meals, but to enter into a dialogue with troubling questions that no one (w)riter can answer on her (or his) own. In this way, each *Parasite Cafe* performance suggests, if somewhat differently, that the production of objects of knowledge, although involving the interpretive labor of reflexive human (animal) agents, neither begins nor ends with the subjective experience of fully conscious actors.

This critical "anti-humanism" is not antiexperiential. Nor does it suggest that social actors are "cultural dupes" of some prearranged structure. Nor is it "antihumanitarian." Quite the opposite. According to the socio-logic guiding the cafe's multiple meal plans, it is the binary division between being either objective or subjective that is itself antihumanitarian. This division may also be whitemale western and modern. It privileges the cultural prerogatives of allegedly autonomous human agents over the remainders of nature, viewed either as passive objects or subjective constructions of "man himself." Meals at the *Parasite Cafe* are prepared to partially subvert this binary distinction. They do so by decentering interpretive experience back into the ritual folds of social science language itself. Not language as expressive of some pre-given relation between a (potentially) all-knowing subject and a fully knowable object; but language as a ritual practice that materially gives (and takes away) particular objects to and from (HIStorically specific) subjects; language that constructs and reconstructs experience within and between the bodies of those it depends on or feeds off. This is a paradoxical power of language. It forcefully (w)rites us, just as we actively speak it.

To view language in this parasitic fashion is to understand that all representations are partial in a double sense of the word. They are partial because they, like we, are forever incomplete, interdependent or "overdetermined" by the material and imaginary conditions of their use. And they are also partial because they are political, and they are political because every instance of language forecloses the HIStorical possibility of being elsewhere for the moment. To glimpse this aspect of language is to reflexively resist modernist divisions—not only between what's objective and what's subjective, but between fact and fiction as well. This is not to suggest that there is no difference between fact and fiction, but that what differences there are LIE within, not outside, the material effects of specific linguistic practices. This performative theorization of facts as nothing but powerful forms of fiction is, for members of the *Parasite Cafe*, a key strategy in a social movement toward postmodern social science. By reflexively doubling back upon the fictive construction of their own factuality in (w)riting, *Parasite Cafe* offerings try to give notice to the partiality of their own positionings within the very situations (of action) they labor to represent. It is for this reason that *Parasite Cafe* texts frequently employ collage strategies of (w)riting. By juxtaposing scenes of autobiography, historical narrative, and sociological observation with found texts, visual imagery, and theoretical analysis, *Parasite Cafe* productions commonly invite those who dine upon them to actively collaborate in the construction and reconstruction of a text's own meaning.

Thus, while enacting claims to factuality, *Parasite Cafe* productions routinely appear open to other possibilities, other fashionings of social science method. Each somewhat differently embodies a style, form, or aesthetic of critical social science (fiction) (w)riting that plays seriously with an awareness of its own partial positioning within the material dynamics of language itself. For this reason, the *Parasite Cafe's* "deconstructive sociological" menu may initially seem difficult, demanding, or simply weird. More than a few times I have (over)heard the question, "I can see it as some form of *avant-garde* art of literature, but what use is it to sociology?" At other times the response of critical readers from a variety of different backgrounds has been far more encouraging.

Content aside, there is today a growing appetite among those of us whose parasitic tastes fall theoretically between or across traditional disciplinary divisions. Such readers recognize, in the aesthetic form of "realist" sociological writing, an unreflexive complicity with the profitable language of professional academic discourse. This is a discourse without passion; a normative discourse that appears to believe its own words are anything but symptomatic of unspeakable relations of material social contradiction. But what of the tastes of readers eating at the margins of a given set of disciplines, or those who have been marginalized by disciplinary norms, as such? It is to the appetites of these readers (and others "we" have yet to even dream of dining with) that the menu at the *Parasite Cafe* is directed. With this in mind, wait until you see what they're offering for dessert.

For a Meal to Re-Member

Composed, at various times, by five to seven core participants and a host of contributing others, the *Parasite Cafe* has been described (somewhat erroneously) as a site of theoretical and practical intervention within and against the telecommunicative confines of whitemale and transnationalized CAPITAL. Situated at the borders of the university and postmodern culture, its activities involve various modes of (w)riting, including performance art, social theory, manuscript construction, music, radio theater, video production, college teaching, filmmaking, collective drifting, painting, xerox, dance, graffiti, and other forms of political activism. In Boston, the *Parasite Cafe* has also sponsored several film series and the appearance of various writers and performers, including Kathy Acker, Luisa Valenzuela, David Crockett Smith, Arthur Kroker, Pele Lowe, Kim Sawchuk, and Gail Faurschou. Although originally situated in Boston, *Parasite Cafe* events today also occur in Santa Barbara, Oakland, and Santa Cruz, California, as well as New York City and Stony Brook, Long Island.

Occasional manifestations of the *Parasite Cafe* occur under the sign of related associations. For instance, since July 4, 1990, the day after the U.S. Supreme Court's decision on *Webster, Parasite Cafe* members have joined with other Boston area artists and activists in forming *Sit-Com International*. Sit-Com activities have included performative, poster, and graffiti actions against the heterosexist, racist, and imperialist materializations of CAPITAL in the USA Today. Examples include the unauthorized pasting a sixty-six-part text onto the walls of Boston's Institute for Contemporary Art during the opening of its 1989 show in the Situationist International. In solidarity with other Central American activists, Sit Com also organized a series of "Shopping for Democracy" actions, involving the "sign work" of more than seventy George Bush–masked participants in several of Boston's major department stores during both the height of the 1989 Christmas shopping season and the FMLN offensive against the terroristic and U.S.-funded government of El Salvador.

Upcoming *Parasite Cafe* projects include the publication *Orphans' Dreams: Panic Wars and the Postmodern, Death at the Parasite Cafe: Social Science (Fictions) and the Ultramodern* and *Sociology Is Stupid* (a long-awaited issue of the *Parasite Cafe Review*). Texts by several *Parasite Cafe* members are also featured in the November 1990 issue of *Social Problems*. For correspondence and a "take-out menu" of "cheap eats" write: *Parasite Cafe,* c/o Department of Sociology, Boston College, Chestnut Hill, MA 02167.

8

James Bond and Immanuel Kant's War on Drugs: A Nosography and Nosegrammatics of Male Hysteria

MARK DRISCOLL

Federal drug czar William Bennett said in a speech that he would find it perfectly accept-able to have drug dealers beheaded. "There is no moral problem there," he said, "I used to teach Kantian ethics—trust me."

> —*San Francisco Guardian*
> December 27, 1989

To which organic sense to we owe the least and which seems to be the most dispensable? The sense of smell. It does not pay us to cultivate it or refine it in order to gain enjoy-ment; this sense can pick up more objects of aversion than of pleasure (especially in crowded places) and, besides, the pleasure coming from the sense of smell cannot be other than fleeting and transitory

> —Immanuel Kant, *Anthropology*

THE VIGILANTES and border police of transgressions of the nose leading to the noose—or worse in Bennett's redemption of the *supplice* from the third section of Foucault's *Discipline and Punish*—occupy an honored epistemology whose Kant-ian traces or, uh, lines, are most carefully laid out and cut on the Georgetown cof-fee tables of figures like drug czar Bennett and various other moral law Kantians in Bush's State Department and CIA.[1] What appears to be another Bush dissimu-lation, considering the intensity of the spin of the media toward the Fukuyama Hegelians with their conservative reading of Kojeve[2] and subsequent interdepart-mental memos trumpeting the end of History, reading "West is the Best, the

Commies lost," is quite logical when exposed as to its genealogy of male hysteria, which I will nosographize here. It is my contention that inscribed in the discourse of neoliberal disciplinarians practicing what Doug Henwood calls a sadomonetarism[3] is a repression of the sense of smell and phobia of nasal penetration—a sign I call a nosegramme; the practice, nosegrammatics. A nosegrammatics is present in the Kantian ethical foundation and its scent gets picked up by Freud, who describes the suppression of olfactory sensation—anosmia—as the ground for hysteria, with the discovery of the unconscious resulting from repression to follow.[4] Freud further locates the repression of smell and oral sensation as the cause whereby Homo erectus rose up to biped from its quadruped animality. Finally, my tracks will show me mapping this narrative onto the Bush/Bennett war on drugs and the ways in which spectacle fictions—the James Bond film *Licence to Kill* in particular—have been searched and deployed into ideological trouble spots to aid in the anosmiatic drug war. Contemporary representations of male hysteria resulting from olfactory repression and fears of nasal penetration will prove themselves to be the proud (nose)heirs of a long male hysterical tradition.

Surely, a critical strategy that mobilizes the James Bond film *Licence to Kill* to read Kant's *Critique of Judgement* and *Anthropology* could be guilty of something like a hysterical symptomatology itself, you are thinking to yourself as you start to turn your own nose upward. Possibly. But how will my tics and conversions articulated as questions to James Bond allow a clearer understanding of both Kant and the present manifestation of a Kantian decapitationary ethics? What will the practice of nosegrammatics reveal in Immanuel Kant and James Bond?

As a Central America solidarity worker deeply troubled by the 92 percent approval rate of the invasion of Panama in December 1989, I felt that it was necessary to refigure the ways in which hegemony had been fixed to allow the naturalization of this most recent rattling of the U.S. imperial saber. What machinic structures of imperial desire had been turned loose in the summer so as to quilt themselves together paralogically just in time for the Christmas "jingo bells"? What desiring machines only became signifiable when their lines of affect slid under the bar of Signifier's common sense and became the spectacle of Panama in the mode of a future anteriority? Lines of desire congealed so that the U.S. invasion—combined with a reintroduction of Drug Enforcement Administration (DEA) personnel, death squads, and panoptic technologies in Peru and the blockade of Colombia by nuclear-powered cruisers—will have been, or produced a present that made sense of events then past.[5] Powerful constellations came together to produce a deadly imperial logic. The breakdown/fracture of the U.S. metanarratives of political liberalism—the ever-expanding cultural accumulation, the growing sense of entitlement, capital and labor accords, etc.—seems to be represented as symptom in *Licence to Kill* at a conjunctural moment when their staging speaks to an intensification simultaneous with the metanarratives' partiality becoming generally accepted. Despite their partiality, these metanarra-

tives cannot be completely abandoned without risking a severe loss of legitima-
tion/regulation, and their representation seems weirdly put on in some Charcot's
theater of postimperial hysteria.

The symptomatology of the broken/cracked imperial metanarratives in the
summer and fall of 1989 situated a hyperactive Bond on a male hysterical continuum with Pee Wee Herman, Sam Kinison, Axl Rose (is a rose is a ...), and, just
possibly, George Bush himself. The hysterical male body can be defined as a desexualized topos of oscillation between masculine and feminine identifications, in
the case of "dead ringers" Pee Wee and Sam Kinison, and an embodied site both
omnipotent and unfindable—Freud's definition of the hysterical body—in the violently covert cases of Bush and Bond. Although the covert body, desexualized,
omnipotent, and impossible to locate (Remember "where was George?"), is the
body that best represents the case of Bond, the body elided between male and female identifications needs to be exposed also. This second body is evidence of a
terroristic staging of homophobic and misogynist "tics." Axl's racism and
homophobia—every day is a grisly October Surprise, as in Halloween—is superseded by Kinison's gay bashing: his often repeated theory of the origin of the HIV
virus claims that "faggots got tired of fucking each other's assholes so they went
out to fuck monkeys." Even with Pee Wee Herman we need to ask why women and
working-class people are usually the victims of his hysterical laugh. Who gets on
the guest list for entry into the Playhouse of the Signifier and who is excluded
from access to signifying play?

Psychoanalytic protocols stipulate that the hysteric's line of desire is barred/ex-
cluded from signification and exiled from the potential ideational partners of
those lines within Symbolic structures. The apparatus, fully or partially triggered,
can't cathect or discharge affect where its machine structure wants. That which
gets played out on the landscape of the body takes the place of a discourse that
can't be spoken, of desires for which Symbolic structures can't provide transla-
tions. Male hysteria is evidence of the disarticulation of prior narrative/Symbolic
logic and its displacement by the oscillating ability to occupy a plurality of subject
positions—an everywhere and nowhere, overt and covert at once—in a
heteroglossing of postimperial logics. Hence the Christmas triple intervention of
Panama by 26,000 troops, the blockade of Colombia's coastline by two nuclear-
powered cruisers, and the forced reintroduction of U.S. military radar sites in Peru
and Bolivia. (Not to mention the stiff neck Bush came down with for the first three
days of the invasion, a hysterical symptom that staged itself most famously during
his press conference—intoned with his nefarious nasality, at times almost apho-
nia—where he performed a David Byrne–like stiff-necked dance on national television as the split screen coverage showed the first U.S. casualties being brought
home in body bags.) The same Christmas week, the summer's James Bond success
Licence to Kill was released to the imperial audience at home in video format. This
fourth intervention/tic is by no means less important than the others.

Licence to Kill is haunted by a Theweleitian[6] phantasmagoria of rifle women, *vagina dentata*, liquid quicksands, and fully differentiated badguys. These demons are to be obliterated by a hermetically sealed, un-Bonded Baudrillardian bubbleboy.[7] James Bond is the CIA eugenicist responsible for plugging up the nasal passages and purifying Latin America of drugs, sexuality, and the ideological virus of independence from the demands of transnational capital imposed by the International Monetary Fund (IMF).

Like Dora, Bond associates sexuality with filth and disease. His sexual/viral politics is grounded on what Monique David-Menard has called the knowledge framework of hysterics: an "epistemology of disgust."[8] This disgust gets played out in gruesome fashion. Bond lowers a badguy into a shark pit, mobilizing a *Jaws* intertext, explodes a drug dealer's head in a pressure chamber, guns down a North Korean, and uses explosives to level the Panamanian druglord's refinery/hideout to the ground (U.S. Southcom would have called it a "witches' den.") Despite his immersion in cocaine powder and paste, Bond doesn't get high. In the crucial scenes where Bond puts his life on the, uh, line to destroy the white stuff, he makes sure his olfactus is protected; he wears a scuba diving mask in one scene and a makeshift veil in the drug refinery, and he uses handkerchiefs to protect his face during other times where there's danger of nasal penetration. A total of forty-three narcoterrorists are reduced. The bittersweet satisfaction of having vengeanced and saved the honor of both the U.S. DEA and CIA doesn't seem to still the sadomasochistic violence of Bond. Freud, in his case study of the hysteric Elizabeth von R.,[9] observed that the hysteric indulges in an orgy of pain. Bond's monological pursuit of the drug menace leads him to risk his life on two occasions while in the act of personally destroying cocaine, demonstrating his willingness to sacrifice himself to the neocolonial narrative logic.

Kant Sings "America, the Beautiful" at Halftime

In *The Critique of Judgement*,[10] Immanuel Kant attempts to resolve the problem of reason, which he had set up in the first and second critiques. Here in the third critique, it seems that it is through art that Kant works out the problem of how reason can know and how reason can act good. Kant asks, "What will aesthetically guide one to know what is really real and let one know that one isn't on the wrong track, the selfish track, etc.? How does one really know the difference between what is really beautiful and tasteful and what is simulational of the truly beautiful? How can we have a transcendentally ironclad rule that will position us so that we can be guided to the correct image of the beautiful that will then guide us to knowing whether it is real and right?"

The faculties of knowledge through understanding and of reason through desire need to be supplemented and sutured by sensation. Judging, through sensation, turns out to be the dealer/middleman/pusher whose role as intermediate faculty is to fix something between intellection and desire, between theoretical understanding and practical reasoning. This capacity as Kantian dealer is called, in the soul, the faculty of pleasure and pain, and in knowledge is called the faculty of judgement.

The Critique of Judgement begins to locate and fix a hierarchy of senses—which articulate judging in different relations to the outside—that sets up an anosmiatic repression and depriviliging of the olfactus. The beautiful, of course, enjoys an essential relationship with vision. Next comes hearing. But taste and smell interrupt the faculties of apprehension. Smell seems to destabilize and make hysterical even Kant's *sensus communis,* the epistemological ground for the moral law post–third critique. Kant points out that people find themselves compelled to postulate this sensus communis to account for the agreement they share in their appreciation of beautiful objects. But watch Kant put in his noseplugs: "To say that 'this flower is beautiful' is the same as to assert its proper claim to satisfy everyone. By the pleasantness of its smell it has no such claim. A smell which one man enjoys gives another a headache."[11] Later, he defines smell/smells as characterized by a "certain want of urbanity ... that extends its influence further than is desired."[12] "The man who pulls his perfumed handkerchief out of his pocket attracts the attention of all around him, even against their will, and he forces them, if they are to breathe at all, to enjoy the scent."[13] Even the suppression of the original odor from the nasal discharge threatens common sensing, and by extension, the moral law. The nose piercings get worse in the *Anthropology.*

Can't You Smell That Smell?

To further telescope and set his sense hierarchization, Kant defined objective senses as those that give us a mediated or disinterested relation to the outside; sight and hearing are only exposed and polluted by light and air, respectively. Against sight and hearing, taste and smell penetrate the organ and get mixed in with saliva and nastier things and thus cannot preserve their objective subsistence. Repeating a thematic form from the third critique, he notes nasally that, "Smell is taste at a distance and other people are forced to share in it whether they want to or not. Hence by interfering with individual freedom, smell is less sociable than taste. Filth seems to awaken nausea less through what is repulsive to eye and tongue than through the stench associated with it. Internal penetration through smell is even more intimate than through the absorptive vessels of mouth and gullet."[14] This inscribed nosegramme, articulated as a phobia of nasal penetration, defines sniffing and smelling—the odoramatics of the judging faculty—as threatening the social itself. Is this hysterical symptom similar tropologically to desires driving contemporary fears of nasal and oral drug penetration—in particular cocaine and glue—and contamination? Maybe only the nose Knows.

Your Parallel Tracks Are Showing

One could argue that genre shifts in spectacle fictions—Bond, Batman, and disaster films—operate on a parallel track with shifts in which the ideological articulations through which hegemony had been previously "fixed"—the junkie metaphor is deliberate; think of the Lacanian *point de capiton* as that which secures both dealer and what is dealt/condensed—are no longer operating to produce consent. During crisis periods, when the cry goes up "that throne and altar are in danger," the International sung by male hysterics everywhere (Sigmund Freud, "Fetishism"; this cry as castration anxiety also displaces attention upward to the olfactus, where the nose knows its famous shine). Spectacles are often more effective as rapid deployment mechanisms for effecting necessary ideological adjustments in "trouble spots" than more organically rooted institutional structures. Organic modes of ideological production are not as conjuncturally pliable as the special operational force of spectacles; spectacles can be put into operation rapidly in search and deploy/destroy missions. These missions can function to condense new elements, displace older ideological forms that have lost their pulling power/signifying currency, and introduce opportunistic infections into the invaded body politic. As market mechanisms, spectacle fictions can be judged quickly as to their "street value" by the mood indicator of box-office sales.[15]

007, Having Aced Drug Czar Bennett's Ethics Course ...

The parallel tracking of spectacle genre shift and ideological crisis dovetails nicely with the figure of James Bond in *Licence to Kill*. The ideological crisis that grounds the new Bond turns on the tensions of capital accumulation with the growing demands for entitlement from dispossessed groups, demands that must not simply be contained by economic elites but must be "rollbacked," or regulated, in the language of the French regulation school,[16] and in a new way. Not unsympathetic with regulation school theory, Stuart Hall suggests that democratic institutions become markedly/marketly less democratic when the needs of accumulation dictate. Hall claims that "public opinion is tutored in social authoritarian postures by the method of sponsored 'moral panics.'"[17] The Reagan monarchy was famous for its staging of panics and *grand peurs*: Libyan assassins were reported operating inside our imperial boundaries; we were reminded that Harlingen, Texas, was only a two-day drive from an expansionist, Marxist Nicaragua, etc. Protecting the country from these more than normal contaminating agents required more than normal modes of social control in addition to greater states of vigilant readiness. Hall adds that "the repertoires of 'hegemony through consent' having been exhausted, the drift towards the more repressive features of the state comes more and more prominently into play."[18]

The second aspect of the parallel track, that of the shifting genre of spectacle fictions, which floated/airlifted and then parachuted[19] onto an ideological test site, is one ideally suited to the figure of James Bond. Since the first Bond film, *Dr. No,* released in 1962, Bond has functioned as an icon that puts into fictitious crisis a certain Western geopolitical imaginary and then works toward the resolution of said crisis in a new way. Bond operates historically as an ideological blender where conflicts get shaken, not stirred, and poured out into the martini glass of hegemony, usually with a bartender's steady hand. The 1960s Bond was, after an early Cold War scripting, given as a representative for detente. He was given a law-and-order inflection in some of the early to mid-1970s films (*Diamonds Are Forever*) in answer to the crisis of Western capitalist interpellation caused by OPEC and the withdrawal from Vietnam, then rearticulated into an increasingly comic mode necessary for a pre-Thatcher Britain and the Billy Carter media saturation (*Moonraker*). His remobilization for the resurgent Cold War of the Reagan 1980s brings us to the film under discussion, where Bond is a black-tie Oliver North in the service of the Bush/Bennett "war on drugs" and the counterinsurgent U.S. militarization of Latin America.

Policing My Desire

Why the fascination with Bond? What is driving my intense cinematic transference? When I saw *Licence to Kill,* I cathected intensely and weirdly to Timothy Dalton, the new James Bond. I couldn't figure it out, but the seduction by the brooding, slightly Byronic Dalton was thorough. It wasn't until much later, actually right before the invasion of Panama, that I was able to locate and excavate some kind of history of this transference.

It seems that Dalton had disappeared from big budget films after playing Heathcliff in the last Hollywood production of *Wuthering Heights* in 1971 to become a Shakespearean actor. When he landed the Bond role in 1986, he hadn't appeared on screen in fifteen years. It just so happens, and my mother confirms this, that the same teen production of *Wuthering Heights,* with Dalton as Heathcliff, was the first "adult" film experience for me when I saw it with my seventh grade English class in 1972 in a four-screen mall theater. I vaguely remember the battle going on over my erotic investment between the broodingly beautiful Dalton/Heathcliff and my seventh-grade girlfriend Sharon. Poor Sharon probably never stood a chance. Is it total left paranoia to suggest that the James Bond producer of thirty years, Alfred "Cubby" Broccoli, refunctioned the last mass media Heathcliff into James Bond? (But not to go so far as to follow this conspiratorial line all the way to Bush's disavowal when he declared on the nation's front pages that "I hate broccoli, and I've always hated it.") It is interesting to note that many reviewers of the Bond film unconsciously articulated this same imaginary identification dredged from U.S. popular memory; there were two or three mentions of Dalton's "Bronte-like" mien, and *Village Voice* reviewer Amy Taubin defined Dalton's hairstyle as "Olivieresque," Laurence Olivier being the popularly identified pre-Dalton Heathcliff.

To playfully suggest that Heathcliff is sacrificed from one capitalist regime only to return as a leaner and meaner James Bond when the dictates of bloody Taylorism and flexible accumulation demand is to loosely follow a Marxist trace left by George Bataille in his *Literature and Evil*. Bataille's reading of the Bronte text is that it speaks to a desire excessed beyond the margins of a bourgeois sexo-semiotics. The passion play of Heathcliff and Catherine Earnshaw occupies a borderlands splitting desires of expenditure and demands of accumulation. The transgressive subjectivity of Heathcliff—so dangerous because he has mastered the narrative of nascent industrial capitalism only to refuse and resist it—is binarized against the stockpiled ego of Edgar. My take on Bataille's reading of the story is that Heathcliff must be sacrificed to a new mode of regulation allowing for a shiny new regime of accumulation.

The Other Side of the Parallel Tracks

In addition to the Bond iconography's spectacular occupation of the ideological test site, he plays an important role as educator/facilitator for the behavioral codes of Western capitalism. The Bond films, from the beginning, were designed to educate spectators into the signs of the demand structures of consumption. The 007 of the 1960s is a sumptuary consumer of the first order. Within a representational habitus that features what Roland Barthes calls a "relaxed imaginary," Bond drinks rather heavily, displays the grooviest new military-industrial hardware/software, and advertises a desublimated sexuality qua classless Club Med international playboy. The mid-1970s Bond was still very much desublimated, and the license to kill was still primarily a license to consume, but there were signs that the big output and massive consumption of the 1960s, the height of the Fordist post–World War II wave and boom, were coming to a close. And the relaxed imaginary of the Bondian cinematic address was beginning to get more stressful.

(A) Pink Freud(ian) Smells a Rat

Freud's work on conversion and the symptomatology of hysteria in *Studies on Hysteria* led to the important discoveries of psychoanalysis, the unconscious, repression, and transference. But it didn't happen without glitches. Freud was struggling to break with Charcot's theory of hysteria, the associative theory, which was grounded on a causal relation between psychic pain and its associative articulation somatically registered to be "read," directly off the body synchronically.

Freud's breakthrough, and the subsequent discovery of the unconscious, allowed him to give voice to the *history* of the hysterical symptom. Monique David-Menard suggests that, in the case of smell, sensoriality is somatic but informed by the ways in which the history of the symptom is organized by desire.[20] Symptoms can no longer be read off of the body in the doctor's office. The desire to fit and match associatively somatic pain and its relational hysterogenic place on the body is rejected by Freud. And this important breakthrough comes as a result of Miss Lucy's case of hysterical anosmia, which might be diag-nosed as the Kantian suppression of smell. Miss Lucy had "entirely lost her sense of smell and was almost continuously pursued by one or two subjective olfactory sensations."[21] By concentrating on nasal blockage and illicit contaminations of the nasal passages, Freud found that olfactory problems didn't fit as well as motor problems into the causal and associative schema. Hysteria became a problem of nasal and olfactory repression, then was extended into all repression—that is, until 1926, when Freud mapped hysteria onto the Oedipal model, making it for women only.[22]

Covert Bodies, Stealth Bombers

The raiding of the icon of Bond from a British nationalist imaginary and flown Stealth-like onto the U.S. geopolitical airstrip can't be factored completely without the notion of empire. The 1960s Bond was employed to massage the declinist British psyche of post-empire while educating Brit and Western consumers into logics of mass consumption. Bond decoded and recoded the English narrative of chauvinistic nationalism by successfully playing out roles of competitive individualism and civilized violence; the Brits could really show the West how the consuming and counterinsurgency games were supposed to be played. Bond's role as damage-control expert for declining empires has been put securely into the service of the U.S. intelligence community and the DEA.

Within a narrative of a declining position—the postnasal drip of empire—in international trade and finance, some predict a raking, weeding, and mowing of our backyard under the sign of the war on drugs and the remilitarization of Latin America. The DEA's counterinsurgency operations in Peru and Colombia, coupled with the invasion-devastation of Panama, confirms suspicions of the future anterior mode that ideological productions often hegemonize. The will-have-been of the Bond film works as a mode of predicting/producing military logic and initiating spectators' suture into imperial common sense. Bond is a covert secret team player and counterinsurgency operator responsible for revenging the honor of the humiliated U.S. intelligence corps by apprehending a Panamanian druglord/caudillo who is the man in charge of the country of Panama. Bond, of course, accomplishes his mission through proper CIA derring-do and also by blowing up a small city.

The fast and dirty designation of Bond as male hysteric needs to be mapped onto other hysterical phenomena. What Freud called anesthesias, negative hallucinations, seems at first to be a motivation by the hysteric to produce his or her own pain. Freud suggests that all cultural production is the material effect of projected hallucinations and as such a hysterical deficiency in the subject's symbolization of her/his own body. The painful representation of hysteria in the Bond film results from a staging of a *jouissance en abyme;* the hysterical challenge to language through violent and rapid movement and the excess of hysterical demand speaks to desire split off from demand. The hysteric demands something of us, but we know that the *en abyme* structure/splitting of demand from desire prevents us from responding to the demand correctly. This floating response mechanism is possibly the key designator separating male hysteria from female hysteria. Female hysterical demand is always questioned as to the letter of the demand—What does woman want? The response to male hysterical demand never attempts to cleave the demand from desire. Most don't ask: What does Bush/Bennett/Bond really want? For left critique, are we destined forever to just respond on cue to contemporary male hysterical demand that is never what it seems?

The letter of the hysterical war on drugs demands a cleansed social body practicing a clearing up of stuffy nasal/market passages, a Dristan McCarthyism. Symptoms relating to this demand can be easily located in *Licence to Kill*. Freud's rewriting of the Dora case locates two aspects of the hysterical symptom: anosmia, which is the repression of olfactory sense, and a positive hallucinatory replacement for this repression. Any recreational cocaine user trusts his nose not just for snorting cocaine—Freud of course knew this—but for its smell. James Bond and all DEA agents reintroducing low-intensity war in Latin America must suffer from anosmia as an occupational hazard. Is the smell of blood the hallucinatory replacement for the olfactory taboo against cocaine? Does Kant's own valorization of war in the category of the sublime in the third critique suggest precisely this displacement? Keep your eyes on the shrinking stocks of cold and nasal remedies in your local pharmacy for answers.

NOTES

While I am on the topic/tropic of the historicization of the symptom, I should thank Parasite Cafe for their big fat lines of intellectual and emotional affect. They should know that the countertransference is still operating. Alex Michaels helped me write this in many more ways than he is aware.

1. I'm thinking of the major contender for the governorship of Massachusetts, Boston University President John Silber. Silber took a sabbatical year in 1988 to write his second book on Kant. Doug Kellner informs me that Silber directed drug czar William Bennett's Ph.D. dissertation on Kant. Both were faculty in the Philosophy Department at the University of Texas at Austin.

2. It is astonishing how much of contemporary political theory is grounded in a debate, heretofore unknown to me, over Alexander Kojeve's reading of Hegel. The conservative genealogy goes back from Fukuyama through the very powerful legacy of Leo Strauss. Before Professor Peter Euben informed me of this current in Anglo-American political philosophy, I thought that we only read Kojeve as a result of his importance for Bataille, Lacan, and later, Michel Foucault.

3. *Left Business Observer* (November 1989), p. 2. Henwood writes on economic affairs for the *Nation*.

4. Sigmund Freud and Josef Breuer, *Studies on Hysteria: Standard Edition of the Complete Psychological Works of Sigmund Freud*, edited by James Strachey, Volume 2 (London: Hogarth Press, 1953–1974).

5. See Slavoj Zizek's wonderful *The Sublime Object of Ideology* (London: Verso, 1990).

6. Klaus Theweleit, *Male Fantasies* (Minneapolis: University of Minnesota Press, 1987).

7. See Jean Baudrillard's discussion in *The Ecstasy of Communication* (New York: Semiotext, 1988).

8. Monique David-Menard, *Hysteria from Freud to Lacan* (Ithaca: Cornell University Press, 1989), p. viii.

9. See Freud, *Studies on Hysteria*.

10. Immanuel Kant, *The Critique of Judgement* (New York: Hafner Co., 1966).

11. Ibid., p. 123.

12. Ibid., p. 174.

13. Ibid.

14. Immanuel Kant, *Anthropology from a Pragmatic Point of View* (Carbondale: Southern Illinois University Press, 1978), p. 44.

15. I am deeply in debt to the excellent Birmingham Center Study by Tony Bennett and Janet Wollecott, *The Popular Life of a Popular Hero* (London: Routledge, 1985).

16. See, for example, Alan Lipietz, *Mirages and Miracles*, translated by David Macey (London: Verso, 1987).

17. Stuart Hall, *The Hard Road to Renewal* (London: Verso, 1989), p. 24.

18. Ibid, p. 33.

19. George Bush was a paratrooper in World War II. His parachutes were made of hemp, a product that the U.S. government was *pushing* "patriotic" farmers to grow more of to do their part in the war effort. A U.S. government twenty-minute propaganda film called; *Hemp for Victory* describes how farmers are needed to grow hemp for their country to destroy the fascist beast. Marijuana comes from the hemp plant. It would not be stretching my point to suggest that pot plants saved George Bush's life on many occasions while he was on parachute duty.

20. David-Menard, *Hysteria from Freud to Lacan*.

21. Freud, *Studies on Hysteria*, p. 106.

22. Hayden White put me on the scent to Jacques Derrida's reading of Kant in his "Economimesis," in *Diacritics* 11 (1981). Derrida reads the notion of disgust, degout, as upsetting the ground of taste, or gout, in the Kantian system.

9

AlphaBet City:
The Politics of Pharmacology

I COME FROM A COUNTRY in which the largest party, in power since 1948, has started its campaign for the upcoming elections—marked by a political instability that defies Italy's already elastic standards—by blaming the specter of "a freedom to take drugs" on the opposition parties. I live in a country in which "a war on drugs" has been going on for some time, a country that refuses to sell hypodermic syringes over the counter while feigning concern about AIDS. And I grew up at a time when many regarded (some) drugs as purveyors of alternative physio-psychological behavior. From this triple perspective, I will use "drugs" as a point of departure for political information and cultural reflections. The vastness of the topic, however, the polymorphous perversity of drugs' effects on both users and nonusers, makes it impossible to develop a linear argument. The alphabetically structured, collage-format of this piece is at once a response to my wish for a totalizing order and an attempt to respect the multilateral nature of the subject.

AlphaBet City

Academia. The question of drugs does not seem to be on the political agenda of the humanities. Perhaps it is for the best. At least there's no risk of "political correctness."

Enthralled by "the sexual fix" (see Stephen Heath's book by that title), we (academics in the humanities) have long chosen sexuality as the central metaphor for our discourse(s) on the body. When we talk about the politics of the body, pleasure and desire, we immediately think of sexuality—even the pleasure of the text is patterned after it. Sexuality is to us what the steam engine was to Marx and Freud, a mold giving shape to our theories. In fact, desiring mechanisms and libidinal investments could be explained by a recourse to other models, such as addiction. This is what Avital Ronell implicitly suggests in *Crack Wars: Literature, Addiction, Mania* (University of Nebraska Press, 1992). Showing that Nietzsche and Heidegger gave the subject of addiction serious thought and using Flaubert's Bovary as an example of an addicted body, Ronell argues, by means of an exuberant, postmodern textuality, that literature and addiction have more in common than it seems. But, she points out, "it is actually becoming impolite to enter areas of conflict."

Of course, the silence on the topic of drugs is partially due to the illegal status of drug (ab)use, which keeps people from being personal and prevents the formation of a symbolic sphere on the topic. Social subjects whose existential, intellectual, and physical state is overdetermined by the past or present assumption of illegal substances do not share the value of their experience(s). At best, you confess to your addictions and experiences during moments of friendship and intimacy. At worst, your substance abuse becomes the subject of gossips in the halls of your school or in the corridors of hotels hosting professional meetings.

Social scientists and M.D.s, notoriously addicted to quantifying people and behaviors, are usually the only academics treating the topic. In their works, however, addicts become numbers, abstract figures. In 1986, during an international conference on subcultures held in Milan, some adolescents parading the insignia of punk subculture approached a group of sociologists and cut themselves with razor blades: "This is our blood. Now you can study it!"

Bibliography/Burroughs/Body. William Burroughs is a bibliographical must for no other reason than the pleasure of stumbling upon genial symbolizations of the body's dark side:

> "Junk yields a basic formula of 'evil' virus, *The Algebra of Need*. The face of 'evil' is always the face of total need. A dope fiend is a man in total need of dope. Beyond a certain frequency need knows absolutely no limit or control. In the words of total need: '*Wouldn't you?*' Yes you would." (*Naked Lunch*)

> No conscious tabulation of the disadvantages and horrors of junk gives you the emotional drive to kick. The decision to quit junk is a cellular decision, and once you have decided to quit you cannot go back to junk permanently any more than you could stay away from it before. (*Junky*)

The "algebra of need" is *la scienza nuova,* an investigation of the psycho-physical equations leading to "cellular decisions." What do we need? What are the positive numbers in this algebra? Why are they positive?

And why is a dope fiend usually a man? Is it for sociohistorical reasons (women having been more sheltered) or is it that they (women) have better ways of incorporating total need?

Cyberpunk. The bloated world of cyberspace is gravid with information and the characters in it have long lost any sense of what is normal psycho-physiology. Their bodily and mental systems function with implanted chips and transplanted organs. Drugs in cyberpunk fiction are high-tech substances produced by pharmaceutical companies to enhance our performances—something in the line of steroids. "They don't make you happy, they don't give you pleasure, they are not addictive but they change the human body's potential. They transform the body into something else, like nothing else does" (Bruce Sterling). And "then the street finds its use for them" (William Gibson).

The "cyberhippies" of *Mondo 2000*, a "far-out" journal published in California, blend the New Age slightly hypocritical and self-righteous search for balance with the futuristic epistemology underlying the idea of Cyberspace. Theirs is the idea of "smart drugs," a search for and with substances that are legal and that improve your mental performance (see *Mondo 2000*, no. 2).

In the cyber-perspective, the world is the result of all the representations of those who live in it, their projections, their images. We can stop giving mental energy to ideological representations we dislike and seek new avenues, new energetic constellations. "What is to be changed is no longer the *world*, but our *in*sight, the rules according to which we construct and enter the territory around us" (Bifo). Hence the myth of mutation and secession. The desiring machine called human body—a body that includes the mind as one of its functions—can use substances, which exist on the borderline of legality and silence, to engender new forms of humanity, new tribes in metropolitan interstices. "Renaissance presupposes secession, and secession involves a process of cutting loose, already prefigured in the camps and caravans of the vast contemporary desert. Nomadic mobility permits an exit from the most devastating consequences of the crisis, finding residual conditions for residual life" (Bifo). Now that the big wave of drugs has subsided, addicts to the various drugs will constitute mutant tribes, subjects of research for a monadology *and* nomadology. They are monads and nomads, members of a subculture with its own oppositional ethos, value systems, and life-styles. The subcultural approach seems the most fruitful theoretical approach to the understanding of drugs.

Derrida. The French philosopher was asked to contribute, not too long ago, to the debate on drugs for the excellent monographic issue of *Autrement,* "*L'Esprit des drogues*" (April 1989). After stating the opacity of the very concept of drugs and the impossibility of it being purely theoretical or theorizable, Derrida argues that the topic lent itself to two equally possible and plausible views:

> a) Since "drugs" and "dependency" are normative concepts, institutional evaluations and prescriptions, we ought to minimize this artificial situation. Let us return to the true natural freedom. Natural right requires that we let people free to manage their own desire, their soul and body, as well as the thing called "drugs." Let us rid our-

selves of the law so deeply ingrained in the concept of "drugs" by the history of ethical norms and conventions. Let us rid ourselves of this repression and return to nature.

b) We recognize that the concept of "drugs" is an institutional norm. Obscure in its origins and history, this norm does not rest on a scientific concept of natural toxicity. And it never will, however hard we may try. Still, in fully accepting the logic of this prescriptive and repressive convention, we believe that *our* society, *our* culture, *our* conventions require this prohibition. Let us enforce it with consistence. The health, the productivity and the functioning of these very institutions are at stake. These institutions protect the very possibility of the law in general by means of that supplementary and basic law which, by prohibiting drugs, ensures the integrity and responsibility of the subjects of the law, the citizens, etc. There is no law without conscious, vigilant subjects, masters of their actions and their desires. This law then, this prohibition, is not an artifice among others, but the condition of the possibility of a general respect for the law in our society. It is not true that a prohibition must be bad; it is not necessary for it to take brutal forms; its ways can be symbolically overdetermined, but one cannot deny that the survival of our culture includes this prohibition.

Derrida's view of the two best possible positions interests me because, in spite of its elegant subtlety, it is fairly typical: a liberal intellectual giving a fair chance to both antiprohibitionist and prohibitionist arguments, a balance that can oftentimes result in either an abstentionist or a repressive position (Derrida himself confesses to opting for the latter). In fact, his views entail a gross idealization, that is intellectualization, of both of the positions involved.

As to the first position, Derrida visualizes an enthusiastic, libertarian anarchism as the motor of antiprohibitionism. Although not entirely wrong—nobody ought to interfere with my private desires, even if I wish to self-destroy; the right to die is the last (in time) political battle to be fought—he seems to ignore the existence of another philosophy behind antiprohibitionism, a sort of hard and bitter realism that is more respectful of the actual rights of the disenfranchised— as most drug addicts are. As a rule, European antiprohibitionists are not so much in favor of drugs as they are against criminalizing drug users. Antiprohibitionists merely seek to cope with the fact that *there are* drug addicts and that they should be treated democratically. Society can try to limit the phenomenon but also must learn how to live with them. This is the line of conduct adopted by Holland and by several European cities (Zurich and Hamburg, for example) in the conviction that it is the illegality of drugs that breeds the huge, dirty profits *and* the criminal underworld associated with drugs.

As to the second position envisaged by Derrida, an enlightened prohibitionism, it is very far from the actual reality of societies in which repressive stands are the law. Prohibition entails the creation of positions of power; a bureaucratic network with funds being channeled into offices run by state officials and their "experts"; a restriction of personal freedom (random urine tests, more power to the police); a war not against drugs but against drug users. One of the merits of David Cronenberg's *Naked Lunch* is its choice of the metaphor of bugs. For a puritan ideology, drug addicts ought to be exterminated—with AIDS acting like the scourge of God. The war on drugs as war on bugs.

The link between prohibitionism and its ideological motor is provided by a Roman wall in the rightwing neighborhood of Prati: "*Drogato crepa!*" (Drug addict drop dead!), it says. Blue paint on a beige wall, this graffiti epitomizes the attitude of those who wish the sale of syringes restricted. A large swastika next to these words reveals who the most vociferous supporters of the war on drugs are. If you are a prohibitionist, at least know who your allies are.

Europe. What will happen with the creation of the European Community? I feel sorry for the Dutch and the other antiprohibitionist strongholds, for it is likely that they will have to uniform themselves to the harsher laws of other members of the EC such as Italy (see below).

Film. When Italian television broadcast *Midnight Express* (1978), Alan Parker's film about a young American man's tribulations in a Turkish jail after he gets caught smuggling hashish, somebody thought it wise to censor the scene in which the protagonist's father, visiting his son in jail, remarks: "I know that for your generation smoking a joint is the same as for me is a glass of scotch."

It would be interesting to compile an exhaustive list of films touching upon the subject of drugs, from Louis Gasnier's *Reefer Madness* (1938, a mythical docuidiocy on the "dangers" of smoking pot) through Otto Preminger's *The Man with the Golden Arm* (1957, the first major movie on heroin addiction) and Roger Corman's *The Trip* (1967, on LSD as the dangerously mighty "problem child"[1]) all the way to Ken Russell's *Altered States* (1980, about one man's *need* to go beyond "the doors of perception"[2]) and Cronenberg's *Naked Lunch* (1991, a film in which addiction and literary creativity intertwine their sticky fingers).

One of the most seductive portrayals of the pulsating indeterminacy that pervaded the generation that "discovered" marijuana is to be found in *Blow-up* (Antonioni, 1966). In one of the final scenes, after a narrative about displacement and distraction, that is, about the sudden eruption of something Other into the mainstream, Thomas goes to a party in which many joints are being passed from hand to hand. There he sees Verushka, who just a few hours earlier had told him that she was leaving for Paris. "I thought you were in Paris," says Thomas, visibly piqued, to which Verushka replies: "I *am* in Paris."

In the past few years, the film industry has become increasingly reluctant to deal honestly with the image and the sound of getting high. It is the "clean and sober" ideology that monopolizes the screen now. Notable exceptions are a handful of films that explored the misery and the weird beauty of drug addiction: Alex Cox's *Sid and Nancy* (1986) where Eros and Thanatos meet under the sign of H; Lech Kowalsky's *Gringo* (1985), on Alphabet City's junkies, perhaps the most neorealistic film ever made; Gus Van Sant's *Drugstore Cowboy* (1989), with the great old man William Burroughs making comments about narcotics and hysteria; and Joseph Ruben's *True Believer* (1989), a thriller in which the hero-lawyer (James Woods) smokes pot all the time. When his young assistant, blatantly irritated by this habit, tells him: "Oh come on! Do you really have to do that!" the lawyer laconically answers: "Have to?"

In your eyes it is "I want to." In their eyes it is "you have to." At which point are you right? At which point are they right?

Generation(s). It is common to romanticize a generation (the mythical 1960s) that provided some of us (not even the majority, only the most vocal—across national boundaries however, the first symptoms of a *global youth*) with the feeling of being *one*. For many men and women, back then drugs were the cement. The newer generation, free from the romanticizing of drugs that afflicted my generation, ought to be in a better position to judge pragmatically. In fact, Western culture is at last ridding itself of the romantic myth of drugs as an intrinsically mind-opening experience. It took a generation of lives blown in and by the wind, waiting for the man, seeking to be heroes, just for one day: a day in the life. And among the failures of my generation, perhaps one ought to add this one too. As with political extremism, one can play the *pentito* (repentant) role, that is, feel guilty about having made a mistake and accepting the reasons of the opponents. Or one can see things historically, reiterate that the reasons behind the drug culture were valid *then* and that they need simply to be readjusted to a new historical context. Shall we forget having once known that some drugs are not dangerous and become so only insofar as they are illegal? Or having once known that cannabis induces introspection rather than violence, fear rather than arrogance? (I see people fighting at rock concerts when they drink too much. I hardly ever see a fight at reggae concerts, where people are usually high on cannabis.) Or having once known ...

Health/Hysteria. In the age of compulsive fitness and cardiovascular awareness, the concept of health becomes the obscure object of hysteric desire. Work a lot and then work out. Know your proteins and vitamins.

This is good for you, this is bad. Inevitably, when a myriad of experts pontificate about health from the pulpits of mass culture, the heavy-handed offer of bodily and mental role models is the result. It is as a challenge to this health hysteria that drugs become interesting.

"Narcotics have been systematically scapegoated and demonized. The idea that anyone can use drugs and escape a horrible fate is anathema to these idiots. I predict in the near future rightwingers will use drug hysteria as a pretext to set up an international police apparatus." (William Burroughs as Father Murphy in *Drugstore Cowboy*)

Italy. Italy has a forty-five-year-old tradition of being one of the most servile followers among the U.S. colonies. With very few exceptions (e.g., the stand on the

Palestinian issue in the early 1980s), Italian leaders have managed to ape their "benefactors" in a way that a few hundred years from now historians will regard as an example of neofeudalism. Italy's zeal has of course been rewarded: The transition from a poor country to one of the world's leading economies has been possible also thanks to its position on the Western chess board. Italian legislation regarding drug use changed as soon as the Reagan and Bush administration launched the war on drugs. Explicit references to the United States were made by Craxi, the socialist leader who, with congresswoman Jervolino, devised the new law. Under the old law (1979–1989), possession of small quantities for personal use was not punished. Also, distinctions were made between soft and hard drugs. The new law shifts the focus to the users: They become criminals to be arrested no matter what drug they possess or how much. The result, so far, is far from brilliant: crowded jails, interminable waiting periods before trials, and above all, imprisonment for people who, in some cases, would have been better off outside. An eighteen-year-old man, found with 20 grams of hashish, hung himself in jail. He was not a hard-drug user.

Meanwhile the deaths from overdose have not decreased and the police have more power.[3]

Just Say ...

... Know.

Liquid Sky. Although in the film by this title a junkie refers to heroin as *liquid sky*, this ought to be the name for alcohol. In some sense alcohol is *l'éminence grise* of the whole politico-legal discourse, because it is so clearly a drug and yet gets special treatment in legislation. Alcohol is the true liquid sky because its legality stretches all over the world. It is the liquid paradise in which we are allowed, when not invited, to swim and drown.

The prohibition of alcoholic beverages in the United States (18th Amendment, passed in 1917 and in vigor from 1920 to 1933) provoked a popular reaction that reclaimed its availability and pleasure. It is one of the greatest and most successful popular rebellions of our century. We cannot celebrate it, however, because its heroes were gangsters.

Mother. On Tuesday, November 26, 1991, fifty-five-year-old Jolanda Ozzone from Savona, Italy, killed her thirty-year-old son by smashing his skull with a hammer while he was asleep. A junky since 1978, her son would often ask her for money and had violent fits if she refused to give it to him. After the killing, she called the police: "Please come. I killed my son. I could not take it any longer." Between fury and compassion, this Italian mother's gesture weighs heavily on the scales of the drug reality.

Narcotic Acts.

The Harrison Act of 1914 was the legal watershed from which all subsequent drug laws have descended. It banned over-the-counter sales of narcotics and instigated a pattern of underground and criminal drug trade which continues to this day. As time went on, subsequent laws such as the Marihuana Act of 1937 prohibited some drugs specifically not covered by the Harrison Act. New drugs were developed and eventually banned, like LSD, which was outlawed in 1967. But some drugs with powerful political and economic clout—tobacco for instance—remained completely legal until very recently. … The Comprehensive Drug Abuse Prevention and Control Act, which Nixon signed in 1970, replaced all previous drug laws and included the infamous Controlled Substances Act, which ranked drugs according to their potential addictiveness. Completely lacking in medical substantiation, it was a conservative reaction against the hippies and college students, who were demanding an end to the Vietnam War, and ethnic urban minorities, who were threatening open rebellion. Marihuana and psychedelics were classified with heroin as belonging to the most dangerous, or "Schedule 1," substances, while cocaine and opium (not fads at the time) were considered to be less dangerous "Schedule 2" drugs. (John Strausbaugh, in *The Drug User*)

Opium. Sir Patrick Hehir, a London M.D., wrote this ballad—"Opium Eater's Soliloquy"—in 1894:

I'd been cheered up, at my chandoo-shop, for years at least two-score,
To perform my daily labour, and was never sick or sore,
     But they said this must not be;
     So they've passed a stern decree,
And they've made my chandoo-seller shut his hospitable door.

If I'd only cultivated, now, a taste for beer and gin,
Or had learnt at pool or baccarat my neighbour's coin to win,
     I could roam abroad o'nights,
     And indulge in these delights,
And my soul would not be stygmatized, as being steeped in sin.

But as mine's a heathen weakness for a creature-comfort far
Less pernicious than their alcohol, more clean than their cigar,
     They have sent their howlings forth
     From their platform in the North,
And 'twixt me and my poor pleasure have opposed a righteous bar.

Politics/Personal. It is a well-known fact that in both Italy and the United States, the massive introduction of heroin in the drug market was accomplished with the more or less active participation, if not support, of the government. The desire for transgression that animated much of the counterculture in the late 1960s and early 1970s situated many young people in a mental and urban space very near to drugs. All one needed to do was to make heroin available. In Italy, the 'heroinization' of political antagonism took place at a time when the politicization of an entire generation had reached disquieting proportions (late 1970s). The Italian antiterrorist police were able to trace the Red Brigades' hideout, where NATO General Dozier was being held captive, thanks to the information supplied by an addict.

Then there are the most obvious problems of AIDS, urban violence, huge profits, the Mafia, Noriega, dirty-money-laundering in Swiss banks, the dream of fast money in an economic recession. ...

The use of certain drugs may be condemned on rational and pragmatic grounds. But what makes *some* addictions to *some* drugs dangerous is only the apparatus that surrounds them (high costs, black market). The main battle ought to be fought against the money-making machine, which is why the war on drugs will not be won. In fact, the war on drugs has been somewhat successful with cannabis only, and for two reasons. The people who consume cannabis are more easily scared by illegality, and the profits to be made with cannabis are minimal compared to those from hard drugs. As long as there are billions to be made on cocaine and heroin, the war on drugs will only result in an extension of the class struggle: The losers will end up in jail and entire neighborhoods will be occupied by the police while people who can afford to use drugs in a clean and safe way will indulge their "private vices."

On a personal note, I know people here as well as in Europe, in academia as well as in the "real world," who are productive and make a habitual use of cannabis and have occasional experiences with other substances (ecstacy, LSD, methedrine, mushrooms, etc.). If they were caught, they would be forced to participate in rehabilitation programs. One of these people, an Italian manager of a multinational corporation that submits its employees to random urine tests, once told me: "I would like to go to the police, turn myself in, and ask them what kind of rehabilitation program they have in mind for me: I have a degree, a well-paid job, I read one book a week, I have family and ..."

But then again I know people who went down the drain.

Did they want to go down the drain? (For an enlightening survey on wanting to go down the drain as a political act, see the controversial French book *Suicide: Mode d'Emploi,* which, however, does not mention drugs.)

Romanticism/Rock/.

Here are the young men, a weight on their shoulders
Here are the young men, well, where have they been?
We knocked on the doors of hell's darker chambers
Pushed to the limits, we dragged ourselves in

Watched from the wings as the scenes were replaying
We saw ourselves now as we never had seen
Portrayal of the traumas and degeneration
The sorrows we suffered and never were freed
                    ("Decades," by Joy Division, 1979)

Rock music has sealed the romantic image of drugs that was initiated by literature (Coleridge, Baudelaire, Poe, De Quincey, Cocteau, Artaud, Michaux, etc.)
and furthered by jazz. The experience of musical limits in certain types of rock
music (not in your average MTV or college radio fare, though) is often coexten-
sive with the use of some drug. Today the music industry is trying to manufacture
a drug-free image for rock music. After he celebrated putting "a spike into his
vein, let me tell you, things are not the same" in 1967, Lou Reed is now appearing
on MTV dissuading kids from trying drugs. "You can be just as bad," Bonnie
Raitt says, "even if you do not use drugs." What is disturbing is not so much the
inconsistency of older people denying youth their rights to "walk on the wild
side" as the implicit prescription of what being "bad" means, the official rock culture pontificating on the safe way of being negative.

Semantics. *American Heritage Dictionary:* "Drugs 1. A substance used as a medicine in the treatment of disease. 2. A narcotic, especially one that is addictive."
People who use n. 2 seek cure from the disease caused by a social and legal discourse that produces and enforces the distinction between 1 and 2.

Unlike Italian, which uses the word "*medicina*" for n. 1 and "*droga*" for n. 2, English retains a semantic ambiguity that threatens from its very start any discourse
on drugs. What is at stake, in a true Derridean fashion, is a question of good
pharmakon and bad *pharmakon*, the latter always already threatening the former
with the specter of parasitism.

Tenure. Would I have written this piece if I did not have tenure?

Urban Geography. The drug generation in Italy was an essentially urban phenomenon. Italian hippies (*fricchettoni*, bastardization of the English "freak") may
have dreamt an escape from the city, but their critique of the order breathed the
air of the metropolis. The psychedelic drug culture (drugs as a means to avoid
playing the game) was then replaced by heroin. As heroin became the number one
product for fast profit, it spread to small towns and villages alike. Many small
towns in the south never knew the hippie stage and were hit by heroin all at once.
Like all southern towns, Matera has its junkies. They mostly hang out in the
hauntingly beautiful old section called *I sassi* (where Pasolini shot *The Gospel According to Matthew*). But they cannot buy dope in town, for the big families have
decided that the town has to be drug-free. Profits, however, are too alluring to be
given up. Heroin is thus sold in the neighboring villages, agglomerates with a
population of about 10,000 and a florid heroin business.

Valium. "The medicinal substance most sold in the world cures spiritual rather than bodily diseases. It is *Valium,* a tranquilizer that has earned a fortune to the Swiss pharmaceutical company *Hoffman-La Roche.* Every year, American doctors fill something like 60,000,000 Valium prescriptions" (*THC,* a Genoese fanzine).

Workaholics Anonymous. The part of the world in which I live is addicted to a powerful narcotic called work. It eats your brain, consumes the pleasure cells, and is irretrievably bound with the maintenance of the dominant libidinal economy. It makes the experience of love more difficult. It segregates people by restricting their socializing: You live with colleagues. I once told an academic friend that I was in love and he asked: "Great! Is she in literature?"

X, Y, and Z.

According to a survey conducted recently by the *Washington Post* and ABC News, 62 percent of Americans would be willing to give up "a few freedoms we have in this country" to significantly reduce illegal drug use; 55 percent said they favored mandatory drug tests for *all* Americans; 67 percent said all high school students should be regularly tested for drugs; 52 percent said they would agree to let police search homes of suspected drug dealers without a court order, even if houses "of people like you were sometimes searched by mistake"; 67 percent favored allowing police to stop cars at random and search for drugs "even if it meant that cars of people like you are sometimes stopped and searched"; and fully 83 percent favored encouraging people to report drug users to police, "even if it means telling police about a *family member* who uses drugs."

President Bush said in his television address not long ago: "Our outrage against drugs unites us as a nation." (William Burroughs, in *Drug User*)

NOTES

1. *LSD: My Problem Child* is the title of a booklet by Dr. Albert Hoffman, the researcher who accidentally experienced the first LSD trip on April 19, 1943, in his laboratory at Sandoz Pharmaceuticals in Basel.

2. *The Doors of Perception* is the title of a book by Aldous Huxley.

3. Since the composition of this essay, the drug law discussed above was repealed by referendum.

10

The Broken Self: Fetal Alcohol Syndrome and Native American Selfhood

MARGIT STANGE

"PATIENTS WITH FAS/FAE [Fetal Alcohol Syndrome/Fetal Alcohol Effect] are often raised in alcoholic families who are unable to protect their children from neglect, physical abuse, sexual abuse, sexual promiscuity, violence, maternal death, and abandonment," writes Ann Streissguth in her manual on Fetal Alcohol Syndrome among Native Americans. Streissguth and her research colleagues at the University of Washington–Seattle are largely responsible for provoking and supporting, with their statistical and etiological pronouncements, the current concern about Fetal Alcohol Syndrome and its milder relation, Fetal Alcohol Effect. In this discourse of FAS, as Katha Pollitt has pointed out, not only is responsibility placed on the "family" (usually a single woman) rather than on oppressive social, economic, and medical conditions, but it is possible to see the deaths of Native American women from alcoholic and other disease—that "maternal death" Streissguth mentions—as first and last the woman's failure to live up to the responsibility of providing adequate maternal nurture.[1]

For Streissguth and for Michael Dorris, author of the bestseller *The Broken Cord,* maternal failure—like maternal nurture—is crucial to the Native American community as a whole. When Dorris thinks of his Native American ancestry, what comes to his mind is the succession of husbandless women, "strong, capable mothers, aunts, and grandmothers," who bore the children and made the homes, who nurtured and acculturated the younger generations.[2] The fact that it is women who were, and are, largely responsible for carrying on the physical and cultural legacies of Native American life does not make the Native American community unique. However, the growing alarm over FAS—an alarm whose context includes the devastating alcoholic impairment of Native Americans—has meant that Native American women are often singled out for scrutiny and condemnation. The FAS discourse, as used by chemical dependency professionals, imagines alcoholic impairment as a negative endowment that "society will need to address" if it wishes to forestall "a legacy of medical, legal and social problems."[3] For Dorris and other writers on Native American struggles, this notion of alcoholic disease as a legacy passed on by the female bearers of children has enabled an etiology of Native American distress in which woman is both the medium of infection and, through her sexuality and fertility, an infectious agent in her own right.

The fight against alcoholism and its effects is being waged with special urgency in Native American communities, and success is both possible and necessary: An example is the recovery of 95 percent of the Alkali Lake Indian Band, which was initiated and inspired by band member Phyllis Chelsea's commitment to sobriety.[4] In this chapter, I take issue not with the movement to fight alcoholism in Native American or other communities but with aspects of the underlying logic of today's antialcoholism discourse that allow for its misogynist deployment. I place Dorris's representations of Native American adversity and struggle in the context of this antialcoholism discourse—not just the Fetal Alcohol Syndrome discourse but also the meta-antialcoholism discourse developed by Alcoholics Anonymous (AA), the American Medical Association (AMA), and popular self-help writers. I trace the strain of antidisease logic, which enables a healing discourse to become an antiwoman discourse, which at the very least focuses blame and which might well increase the sufferings of alcoholically impaired women and men. My criticisms, far from being meant to disable the antialcoholism movement, are friendly to its tradition of productive, dialectical self-criticism as practiced by professionals and others who are dedicated to fighting alcoholism with whatever paradigms are available. These paradigms—for example, "codependency" and the disease model of alcoholism as well as the important refutations of these models—have themselves arisen out of critical opposition to existing treatment models and practices. Through this dialectical process, the scrutiny of the female pathology created by the misogynist impetus of the FAS discourse and calls for resistance, such as I offer here, may be part of a process that finally brings empowering attention to the neglected needs of women alcoholics.

Women are the objects of suspicion and speculation in the discourse of Fetal Alcohol Syndrome. In a February 4, 1990, *New York Times Magazine* article entitled "When a Pregnant Woman Drinks," writer and physician Elisabeth Rosenthal described watching a laboratory test of an eight-year-old girl with FAS. The test is a "game" whose rules require that the girl, before rewarding herself with a cookie, unwrap two boxes and remove a cookie from each box. "Clearly not up to this most elementary task," Rosenthal writes, the girl is finally rescued by her mother, who opens one of the boxes. With the second box still sealed, the "grinning child pops a cookie in her mouth."

"'Ugh. This is too painful to watch,' exclaims Dr. Claire D. Coles, the center's director. 'Look at that nice little girl. Her face is dysmorphic. ... What's worse, look at the mother. She's also mildly dysmorphic'" (p. 30).

Looking at the mother—and at the future mother, the mother's daughter—is the central gesture of FAS discourse. FAS is defined as a constellation of birth defects thought to be caused by intrauterine alcohol exposure. Its main symptoms are mental retardation and retarded physical and motor development. (Researchers speculate about the existence of a related, relatively widespread syndrome, Fetal Alcohol Effect/FAE, which is indicated by poor judgment and a history of maternal drinking.) FAS was identified by Seattle researchers in the mid-1970s, when FAS studies and reports began to appear in professional journals. According to Michael Dorris, by 1979, 200 studies had been published in the professional press and by the mid-1980s the field had grown greatly: In 1985, 2,000 articles on the subject were published in professional journals (Dorris, p. 143).

Since 1989, FAS has gained a popular audience through mass media exposure, mobilized in part by the appearance of Dorris's *The Broken Cord,* which came out in summer 1989, made the *New York Times* bestseller list, received the National Book Critics Circle Award, the Christopher Award, and honors from the American Library Association and *Library Journal;* the book was issued in paperback in 1990 and was dramatized in a two-hour ABC television movie in February 1992. Dorris, who is half American Indian, is the husband of writer Louise Erdrich and a professor of Native American studies at Dartmouth. *The Broken Cord* tells how, as a single man, Dorris adopted a three-year-old South Dakota Sioux boy who turned out to be retarded. Finally told that his son, Adam, had FAS, Dorris went on to discover that FAS was widespread in the Native American community, especially among the plains tribes. His book was motivated by this discovery and aims to spread the message that FAS is a threat both to the society at large and, particularly, to Native Americans.[5]

According to a 1990 article in the *Minneapolis Star and Tribune,* U.S. government researchers now believe that, in the nation at large, one in 1,000 children is afflicted with FAS. (Many researchers and clinicians, including almost all the Europeans in the field, think this number is vastly inflated; the European consensus is that FAS is relatively rare.) The government researchers also estimate that among plains Native Americans the incidence of FAS is ten to thirty times higher than in the nation at large. The *Star and Tribune* article reports that South Dakota Senator Thomas Daschle (D) has called for a congressional investigation of FAS and its effects among plains tribes, saying "it's clearly at the epidemic level. I call it genocide."[6]

In fact, the existence of an epidemic—that is, a rising incidence—is not clearly established. It is indisputable that alcoholism is, and has been for some time, endemic and devastating to Native Americans and that fetal damage caused by substances, along with inadequate prenatal and lifelong medical care, malnutrition, environmental adversities, and other hardships, is not uncommon. No significant changes in this situation have been clearly documented. What has changed is the focus and the rhetoric regarding alcoholism. In the rhetoric used to discuss FAS, the discourse of alcoholism has shifted so that it intersects in new ways with the discourses of race and gender. Now, looking at alcoholism as a social problem means scrutinizing the bodily reproduction of a defined and delimited population of alcoholically impaired persons. From the viewpoint of FAS discourse, these persons—like the alcohol problems they embody—are reproduced by mothers.

FAS is an effect of reproduction. Thus, in order to be, as Senator Daschle calls it, an "epidemic," FAS must be a disease of propagation; there must be a rise in the proportion of FAS births, or a rise in the overall birth rate, thus causing a coincident rise in the number of people born with FAS. Yet, to Daschle, FAS is above all "genocide"—that is, the decimation of the racial populace, the decline of Native American births relative to deaths. Daschle, then, uses "genocide" to mean not a decrease in the number of persons belonging to the race but a decrease in the absolute amount of the abstract racial essence: There may be more Native American persons around, but there is less Native Americanness left in the world.

This split between the Native American person and the Native Americanness of that person depends upon a certain notion of disease. In its use of this notion of disease, FAS discourse reveals its origins in the American discourse of alcoholism and addiction. Since Americans "discovered" addiction in the late eighteenth century, the discourse of addiction has been concerned with the status of the self.[7] Originally focused on questions about the agency of the self—Are will and desire the same thing? Is compulsive behavior truly compelled?—this concern is now being reformulated as a problematic of the identity of the self as framed by the delineation of "disease": as the AA self-help formula puts it, "I have a disease, I am not my disease."

James Milam, M.D., explicates the grounds and consequences of the identification of alcoholism as a disease. For Milam, to say that alcoholism is a "true physiological disease" is to say it is not a symptom of something else and that there is no limit to the power of the disease of alcoholism—it is a disease "which transforms its victims, leaving them with little or no control over their behavior."[8] The behavior of the alcoholic is not symptomatic of the underlying causes of the disease, but instead expresses only the effects of the disease itself: The physical compulsion to drink, combined with the deleterious effects of drinking on organs and systems, produces a characteristic pattern of behavior. In effect, the person becomes symptomatic of the disease.

Milam's viewpoint has been attacked on the grounds that it effaces the agency of the alcoholic. However, in mapping the unlimited power of alcoholism on the self, Milam recuperates the self: His main point is that the alcoholic is "not responsible" for the disease and that, at the level of identity, the person who becomes alcoholic retains his integrity and is untouched by and unsignified by the disease. Not only behaviorally but also at the level of consciousness, it is the disease and not the person that is being manifested. Thus, in an active or withdrawal stage alcoholic, feelings of remorse and guilt or "insights" brought on in interpretative therapy are the effects of random neuron firings caused by chemical imbalances and are appropriately ignored or treated with Librium (Milam and Ketcham, p. 151–152). For Milam, the scientific truth of alcoholism allows the alcoholic to recuperate an untouched selfhood.

Milam writes as a credentialed research scientist. He shares his commitment to defining alcoholism as a disease with the AMA and the U.S. government. In self-defined contrast (but not, as we will see, in total contrast) to this position are the popular self-help writers who are influenced by AA and committed to a grass-roots, experiential healing process. They see self-help as the deployment of what Foucault calls "local knowledge": For example, old AA members who have found their way to sobriety "come back" to lead new members to health. Anne Wilson Schaef, a writer of self-help books on addiction and codependency, represents the cutting edge of the popular discourse on self-help for addictive disorders.[9] In a September 1989 speech to the California Council on Alcohol Problems, Schaef recounts a confrontation with the elitist, medicalizing, unifying discourse of alcoholism "specialists": She has an argument with a psychiatrist who wants to, but cannot, deny the effectiveness of AA and who finally dismisses it as "good for people who can't afford better treatment." Schaef dismisses this psychiatrist and his viewpoints with the withering indictment, "he treats alcoholics with *chemicals!*"[10]

Treating alcoholics with chemicals is a tragic joke to Schaef because, in her view, alcoholism is already an imposed, foreign presence that can only be excised by the triumphant emergence of the true, endogenous self. Paradoxically, although Schaef positions herself in opposition to the medicalizing discourse, the disease model is central to her approach. In her speech to the California Council she repeats the dictum, "I have a disease, I am not my disease." But Schaef politicizes addiction disorders: The disease model becomes an infection model—our foreign diplomacy, our government, our schools, our families are characterized by a pathological will to truth and a drive for "control" that the individual internalizes. Control is exercised through "objectivity," through unifying discourses of interpretation, and through the scientific, instrumental approach to truth, such as that of the psychiatrist with his chemicals. Healing means extricating the true "I" from this matrix of power whose internalization is reflected in alcoholism and in parallel forms of compulsive behaviors to which Schaef has given the name "addictions" (including "workaholism, rushaholism, sex and relationship addiction").

For Schaef, then, alcoholism is a loss of self-sovereignty that amounts to the colonization of the self. Women's oppression is a major example of this colonization. Schaef, who is one of the theorists of codependency (a disease-like byproduct of alcoholism), argues that the socialization of women constitutes them a codependents. Codependency is usually manifested by repetitive, self-destructive relationships with addicts that involve the codependent in managing the unending problems of the addict; as a metaphorical disease in its own right, codependency, like alcoholism, means the failure (to use Sartrian terms) to live as and for oneself. In order for the alcoholic or codependent to heal herself—in order, that is for her to recuperate her own, nonsubjugated selfhood—she must activate what Schaef calls "her own healing process." She must be free from authoritative intervention; interpretation (which Schaef calls "rapey") and other imposed "treatments" are further invasions and counters to self-realization. The successful confrontation with addiction and/or codependency, as Schaef sees it, leads to the restoration of a sovereign self unjustly subjugated.

For Schaef, it is the notion of "disease" that makes it possible to differentiate between the alcoholic or codependent behavior and the true self of the person. Indeed, disease is what enables the person to posit and claim a self at all: If disease is the subjection of the self, "I have a disease" means "(therefore) I have a self." For Schaef as well as for Milam, the disease model leads to an "undiseased" sovereign self constituted as an object o knowledge by the identification of disease. While Milam prescribes medical intervention to aid recovery from alcohol's presence and effects, Schaef advocates the identification and liberation of the true self of the afflicted; her speech to the professional convention aims to inspire and guide her audience of alcoholism specialists in their dedication to this mission. At one point during this speech, however, she pauses and seems to ad lib: "And I wonder," she asks almost parenthetically, "how many of us are FAS? And I wonder what this means for our culture. And what this means evolutionarily."

FAS does not logically fall into the category of power-induced "addictive" behaviors of which we must heal ourselves by allowing our "own healing process" to take over. It is (defined as) an irreversible disorder in the constitution of the body and brain. Yet Schaef's politicizing metaphorization of disease allows her to imagine FAS as a disease of culture and of race, an infection of the social self, a deforming disorder of the communal sphere—as well as a disorder of the individual self for the person wondering if he or she "is FAS." Indeed, for Michael Dorris, his son Adam's FAS is all of the above. Dorris repeatedly characterizes the FAS/FAE person as "stuck," unable to advance on the road to selfhood. His son, he writes, "had been deprived of the miracle of transcendent imagination, a complex grace that was the quintessence of being human" (Dorris, p. 167). This lack of imagination means that "he doesn't ask who he is, or why" (Dorris, p. 264). To see several FAS victims together in a room, Dorris writes, is to see the "transformation of disparate individuals into the same general category." FAS displaces identity. While Adam Dorris may not ask who he is, Michael Dorris does ask—asks not only who Adam "really" is, but who Native Americans really are. His narrative tells the story of what he uncovers—the "ballooning emergence of FAS among Indian people" (Dorris, p. 137).

In fact, Dorris's parenting has always been part of an inquiry into his Native American identity. Dorris's decision to adopt the Sioux boy is a gesture toward recuperating this racial identity (as another part of this project, he has himself renamed at a Lakota ceremony that he attends with his son). Like many Native American children, Adam has had a traumatic infancy. Dorris, a self-described "nurture man," writes, "I had no doubt that I could give Adam back the life of independent choice, of unbounded possibility, that he was entitled to live." But *The Broken Cord,* as a title, figures the failures of connection and reconnection: Dorris finds only paternal frustration as he runs up against the "legacy" of Adam's "genetic history"—a past whose main feature is an alcoholic mother who immutably deformed Adam within her womb (Dorris, p. 79). Dorris provides his nurture, but no reinstated "Adam" emerges: Adam has seizures, cannot remember or connect events and information, has no sense of time or causality, responds repetitively and mechanistically to his environment, and fails to develop in any identifiably "human" direction. Dorris, like another FAS parent who says "we can't reach them, they don't think like we do," finds himself unable to be a nurturing parent, for the FAS child "will never be human" (Dorris, pp. 208, 168).

Dorris's discovery of the blight upon his son became his discovery of the blight upon the Native American. He traced this back to the infecting colonization by Europeans bearing alcohol that begins with the introduction of alcohol and drinking protocol to the native people. Through alcohol, the invasion of Europeans into Native American life was coterminous with an invasion into the sanctum of the self: Dorris explained that one reason for the ready adoption of heavy drinking by the Lakota people was its apparent usefulness in the traditional Lakota "vision quest," a visionary ritual that yielded "an identity" as the quester's irreducible self dramatically emerged (Dorris, p. 82).

While Dorris concludes that "alcohol, over the past 150 years, has become so absorbed into the social systems of many Native American groups that it could not easily be excised" he finds that in the alcohol use of Native American women, the invasion is making new—and possibly excisable—inroads (Dorris, p. 94). One day while he was looking out on the openness of the Sioux territory around Pine Ridge, South Dakota, Dorris is drawn to the sight of two approaching figures "walking on the bank of the highway. ... They staggered, were propped against each other for support. They were women. ... I watched while [one of them] stepped without notice through a large puddle. ... [T]hey argued loudly in a language I didn't understand." Dorris watches the drunken women scream and bat at each other as they slosh through the mud of the embankment; he records that one of them apparently "said something so funny that both women laughed and had to grip each other for balance." He finally decides that "their features were similar" and concludes that "they had the look of a mother and daughter" (Dorris, p. 169). Dorris closes the chapter in which these women appear by lamenting that on every road of the Pine Ridge Reservation, "I trailed those two women ... my oldest son, all of us, in their erratic wake" (Dorris, p. 170).

Dorris sees a rising rate of drinking and alcoholism among Native American women in the past ten years; he attributes it to rising resistance to traditional gender distinctions and a rising rate of alcoholism in the overall population. He finds in this new site of invasion the possibility of excising the disease by cutting off the reproductive transmission of alcoholic impairment. The discourse of fetal rights here comes together with the politicizing metaphorization of disease. If the alcoholism of the sick women is not to be excised from them, they themselves can be cut out, stopped from making racial and social inroads, from passing on a legacy of infection to the racial body. Dorris quotes Jeaneen Grey Eagle, director of an alcohol treatment program on the Pine Ridge Reservation: "We need to get some of those women in jail" (Dorris p. 165).

Jailing is only one possible solution: Sterilization of repeat offenders is another. Though jailing these mothers seems to be an act that deprives Native Americans of their rights, and though sterilizing Native American women would seem a genocidal move, to Dorris these measures would strengthen Native American rights and preserve the racial essence. To Dorris, the confinement of pregnant mothers, even the resort to sterilization, is justified by the sovereign right of Native American children like Adam to be themselves. This right coincides with the sovereign right of the tribe: Dorris explains that tribal law is sovereign on the reservation. Thus, tribes have been able to take measures against drinking mothers that the U.S. Constitution would not allow (Dorris, p. 176).

Dorris's belief that more Native American persons does not mean more Native Americanness depends upon—but reverses the logic of—an important aspect of the identification of alcoholism as a disease: the discovery of the inheritability of alcoholism. In James Milam's exposition of the disease of alcoholism, the inheritability of alcoholism means that alcoholism and population rates decline together. Comparing the relative percentages of alcoholism in different ethnic populations, Milam hypothesizes that genetically alcoholic subgroups reproduce more slowly than nonalcoholic subgroups due to early death, infant mortality, and so on, making alcoholism subject to "the principle of natural selection whereby those people with a high genetic susceptibility are eliminated over many generations, resulting in a lower susceptibility rate for the entire group" (Milam, p. 45). Because the genetic traits that result in alcoholism are slowly removed from the gene pool, populations that have been exposed to alcohol over many generations have much lower incidences of alcoholism than those which, like Native Americans, have been introduced to habitual drinking fairly recently.

But Dorris states—without substantiation—that there is population growth both of Native Americans as a whole and of alcoholically impaired Native Americans, and he presents this propagation as both the deployment and the effect of the devastating infection of white colonization.[11] Accepting the medical data that indicate the inheritability of alcoholism, Dorris inserts into this hypothesis his notion of FAS and FAE as alcohol-induced impairments brought about and manifested by reproduction. By collapsing FAS/FAE with alcoholism (Dorris sees in the maternal drinking that causes FAS/FAE the legacy of genetic alcoholism), Dorris imagines alcoholism as a form of behavior that reproduces itself sexually. Alcoholic and FAS/FAE women and men, having poor judgment and no sense of consequences, reproduce faster than the non–alcohol-impaired population. "If a predisposition toward ethanol dependency was inherited … and … [if] men and women were less likely to use contraception … when drunk, … then a substantial swell in a group's drinking behavior often resulted in a population explosion. … Such conditions propagated themselves, in every sense of the word" (Dorris p. 91). For Dorris, alcoholism and FAS, collapsed together as effects of reproduction, cause a rise in the number of Native American persons coincident with a rise in the incidence of "disease"—which in this context means a diminishment of the true, pure racial essence of Native Americanness.

FAS enters the discourse of the metaphorization of addictive disease to effect a more radical split between the self (racial and/or individual) and the disease. If for Schaef the disease of alcoholism produces the identification of a true self that is "not the disease," this true self could be reseated as the body's sovereign when the healing process succeeds. But for Dorris, the deformation of FAS produces a body that can never be the expression of the self and a self that is always denied or forestalled. The FAS person is always a diseased person; the self that is not the disease is a wholly ideological self existing outside the body, beyond the reach of both disease and power.

For Dorris, then, the racial healing process meant reconstituting and passing on an undiseased racial self separated from biological bodies and sexual reproduction—and thus purified of female input. Dorris made the decision to become a father—which was also the decision to affirm his identity as a Native American—in a moment he negatively invokes as a self-constituting vision in the tradition of the Lakota vision quest. To be more precise, this is a moment of *re*vision, for he writes that it was "not … a vision of any sort, but rather [a moment in which] my mind was temporarily cleansed, made ready for new writing." Dorris's vision is the absence of mothers: The new "message" he receives tells him he wants to adopt a male baby without fathering it biologically or imagining a female coparent. In his fatherhood, Dorris imagines, he is continuing the "tradition" of single parenting practiced by many generations of his widowed female ancestors—women whose husbands all died young, leaving them to raise their families alone, "strong, capable mothers, aunts, and grandmothers" (Dorris, p. 3). To emerge as a product of this line of female parents, it turns out, is to imagine the recuperation of a legacy of identity realized by forestalling female parenting and replacing it with nonbiological male parenting. His task, as his book recounts, is a further revision in which he discovers the infecting legacy of FAS and excises it, cutting the umbilical cord between mother and child to reinstate the sovereign Native American self.

In Dorris's fantasy of the restoration of the true racial self by the excision of women from the racial body, we can trace one trajectory of the disease model of alcoholism. To my mind, it's the wrong trajectory but not necessarily the wrong model, for the disease model can be a tool of resistance to the marginalization of the alcoholic: It was developed in resistance to moralizing attributions such as the innate characterological or cultural inferiority of the alcoholic, and it posits recuperation from impairment through a rational individual and collective struggle for empowerment. But through metaphorization—especially the extension of "disease" to non-substance-based behaviors—disease has itself become a totalizing attribution that allows for the discounting and punishment of pathologized behaviors, relationships, and populations. The FAS discourse sounds an alarm about women alcoholics because women alcoholics have babies, but we can use the disease model and its logic of the self (as, indeed, it has been used) to insist that women are worth attending to in themselves, and not just in their relational roles—whether or not their performance of these roles has been affected by disease. Treatment programs could find—and are finding—ways to respond to women's self-defined needs and to further equality between the sexes, in contrast to the FAS discourse, which, hiding behind its urgency, pushes aside any programs for sexual equality, especially for equitable sharing of childrearing. Nonetheless, by focusing attention on women alcoholics, FAS discourse may, finally, help bring about these improvements. The cultural weight Dorris attributes to women as the custodians of racial and cultural continuity could also help produce greater concern for the needs and entitlements of women. Dorris's vision of significant and lasting legacies passed on from mother to daughter acknowledges women's power and may even be a model for women's collective struggle against disease: Phyllis Chelsea, the Shuswap woman who initiated the remarkable recovery of the Alkali Lake Band, claims that she gave up drinking at the insistence of her young daughter and has remained sober to keep her daughter at home.

NOTES

1. Ann Streissguth, Robin La Due, and Sandra Randels, "A Manual on Adolescents and Adults with Fetal Alcohol Syndrome with Special Reference to American Indians," publication of the Department of Psychiatry and Behavioral Sciences, Child Development–Mental Retardation Center, and the Alcoholism and Drug Abuse Institute, University of Washington, Seattle, July 1986 (Supported by Indian Health Service Contract), p. v. Katha Pollitt, "'Fetal Rights': A New Assault on Feminism," *The Nation* 250, no. 12 (March 26, 1990), pp. 409–418.

2. Michael Dorris, *The Broken Cord* (New York: Harper & Row, 1989), p. 3. Subsequent references will appear in the text.

3. Metro Council for Chemical Abusing Women and their Children, "Treatment Focus Subcommittee Report," Minneapolis, MN, June 1989, p. 11. For providing me with expert insight and information—including this document—I am indebted to Eugene Hoffman, senior chemical health counselor, Hennepin County (Minnesota) Chemical Health Division.

4. Veronica Taylor, "Special Populations: The Triumph of the Alkali Lake Indian Band," *Alcohol Health & Research World* 12, no. 1 (Fall 1987), pp. 57–84. The story of the band's recovery is documented in the film *The Honour of All*, available from Alkali Lake Indian Band, P.O. Box 4479, William Lake, B.C., Canada V2g2V5.

5. Michael Dorris's adopted son, whose real name was Abel, died on September 22, 1992, from injuries received when he was struck by a car while walking at night on a freeway ramp. Abel was twenty-three. His brain was sent for examination and analysis to FAS researcher Sterling Clarren of Children's Hospital, University of Seattle, Washington. Clarren hopes to find and identify the brain abnormalities that underlie FAS. As of May 1993, Clarren's office reported that this work had not yet been done.

6. Pat Doyle, "When He Was Born, He Was Drunk," *Minneapolis Star and Tribune*, August 26, 1990, p. 12A.

7. Harry Gene Levine, "The Discovery of Addiction: Changing Conceptions of Habitual Drunkenness in America," *J. Studies on Alcohol* 39, no. 1 (1978), pp. 143–174.

8. James R. Milam and Katherine Ketcham, *Under the Influence: A Guide to the Myths and Realities of Alcoholism* (New York: Bantam Books, 1981), p. 6. Subsequent references will appear in the text.

9. Anne Wilson Schaef's books include the following Harper & Row paperbacks published during the 1980s: *The Addictive Organization, When Society Becomes an Addict, Women's Reality,* and *Co-Dependence: Mistreated, Misunderstood.*

10. Anne Wilson Schaef, address to the 14th Annual Conference of the California Council on Alcohol Problems, September 1989. Audio recording published by Conference Recording Service, 1308 Gilman St., Berkeley, California 94702. All subsequent Schaef quotations are from this recorded speech.

11. Dorris thus reverses the trope of native decimation that he had invoked a few pages earlier in writing that "the truth of the matter [is] that alcohol threaten[s] the million and a half contemporary Indian people as virulently as, five hundred years ago, a plethora of Old World diseases had decimated Western Hemisphere populations, eliminating by infection, in some cases, nineteen out of twenty people" (Dorris, p. 87).

PART THREE

POLITICAL
BODIES

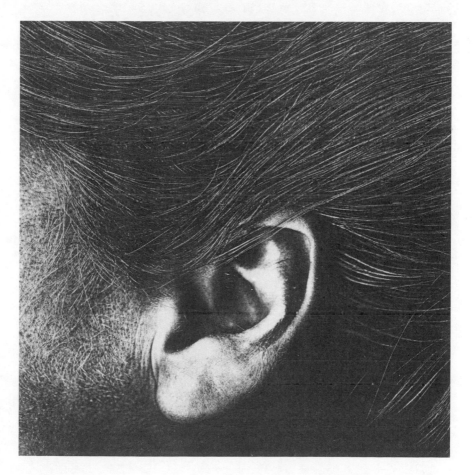

11

George Bush, or Homosocial Politics

THOMAS DUMM

In May of 1988, while seeking the Republican nomination for the American presidency, George Bush spoke at Twin Falls, Idaho. Referring to his relationship with Ronald Reagan, Bush said,

> "For seven and a half years, I have worked alongside him, and I am proud to be his partner. We have had triumphs, we have made mistakes, we have had sex ..."
>
> There was a stunned silence in the audience, and Mr. Bush hastened to add, "We have had setbacks." After a roar of laughter, the Vice President observed: "I feel like the javelin thrower who won the coin toss and elected to receive."[1]

The report from the *New York Times* suggested that Bush misspoke. But something quite the opposite may have occurred. If Freud is correct, if verbal slips, like dreams, expose secret wishes, perhaps Bush's slip exposed his wish to have sex with Ronald Reagan. The follow-up joke that Bush made is interesting evidence of such a wish, once some of the codes of desire that are involved in his slip are deciphered. But to do so requires that one also understand the seeming paradox at the heart of the Bush campaign, how a "decent" man could behave so "viciously," how the raising of "differences" between Bush and the Democratic Party nominee Michael Dukakis, especially on the "issue" of prison furloughs, could reflect a fear that informs the American polity as its members seek to understand how power is exchanged and represented in their society. What was Bush wishing for in wishing to have sex with Ronald Reagan? To even begin to think about the issues that are involved in that question requires examining an arena of politics not directly addressed by most of the journalists who "cover" politics or those political scientists who seek to understand problems of "leadership."

To study the problem of American politics by inquiring into hidden motives of its practitioners leads one onto the slippery terrain of consciousness and unconsciousness and of secrecy and its exposure. If one presumes to engage in such an activity of unmasking, one will necessarily be asking questions that are, for very troubling political reasons, still taboo among American men. How do men love each other in the United States? How do codes of desire inform their interactions? How do their games relate to the violence of representation? These questions become important when the way in which desire is constituted as a political field intensifies the violence that is usually involved, more or less, in the hunger for pleasure that ordinarily is called sexual. It may be that an entire dimension of politics is not addressed by most of those who profess to study it because they have failed to follow one of the most important lines of inquiry that informs the motivations of those who seek and practice leadership. This dimension might be outlined by taking seriously what is one of the most common metaphors used by men of power to describe how they relate to each other, usually that of "fucking each other over."

In post-Freudian America it is a commonplace to note that sex and power are closely related to each other, but the orientation of most studies concerning the relationship of sex to power in the United States still employ a fairly standard Freudian scheme of causality in which a return of the repressed *explains* the character of the persons involved.[2] I wish to pursue a different line of argument. But because the difference might be (deliberately or accidentally) misunderstood, and because the misunderstanding could be damaging precisely to people whom I wish to aid and abet at the outset I must attempt to clarify what eventually becomes blurred, namely the boundary drawn in American culture between homosexuality and homosociality.

Eve Kosofsky Sedgwick sustains a distinction between the homosexual and the homosocial in her important study of nineteenth-century English literature. In that study she issues a caution: "To assume that sex signifies power in a flat, unvarying relation of metaphor or synecdoche will always entail a blindness, not to the rhetorical and pyrotechnic, but to such historical categories as class and race."[3] She suggests that the connections that might exist between the homosocial (which she describes as the typically exclusive male realm of social relations where male bonding occurs) and the homosexual (in which men have sexual intercourse with other men) are bound to vary from one historical situation to the next. Citing a variety of writers on the subject, she points out how historical specificity has informed the extent to which the relationship between the realms of the homosocial and homosexual have been constructed as a continuum.

Sedgwick suggests that in contemporary American society the continuum between the homosocial and the homosexual is discontinuous. "In fact," she argues, "for the Greeks, the continuum between 'men loving men' and 'men promoting the interest of other men' appears to have been quite seamless. It is as if, in our terms, there were no perceived discontinuity between the male bonds at the Continental Baths and the male bonds at the Bohemian Grove or the board room or the Senate cloakroom."[4] Indeed, in American society, homosociality is homophobic, that is, antihomosexual.

She also notes that homophobia directed against men is just about invariably misogynist.[5] Following Gayle Rubin's argument concerning the traffic of women, Sedgwick suggests that the construction of homosocial bonds is a realization of the defeat of the feminine. This pattern seems to be an especially appropriate model for the pattern of relationships in the United States: the construction of a homosocial realm that must be profoundly homophobic and misogynist in order to sustain itself, and consequently the existence of an intense discontinuity between the homosocial and the homosexual.

Sedgwick's argument is compelling, but one might ask if the construction of the gap between the homosocial and the homosexual in the contemporary United States is arranged as neatly as she seems to suggest. One might, in fact, construct some very strong continuities or linkages between homosocial and homosexual desire in the United States. These connections, neither essential to homosexual identity nor exhaustive as an explanation of the performances of political actors, serve nonetheless to raise questions concerning the motives of participants in American national politics. One need not look too closely at such minor but exemplary political actors as Terry Dolan, or Fritz Chanell, or Roy Cohn, or Father Bruce Ritter in order to think about broader questions concerning the frustration of desire, the rituals of humiliation, and the secrecy of male bonding—and the impact that such psycho-social arrangements have on the judgments of powerful men.

Death by AIDS already has had the tragic effect of exposing some of those most likely to suffer added, gratuitous pain from exposure, namely, New Right political activists, Catholic priests, and macho matinee idols. I am not interested in engaging in what traditionally might be called an *exposé*. But even a careful exposition of exposure risks misinterpretation at the outset because it may be perceived as being homophobic. In this context, the various associations that have commonly been made in the United States between homosexuality and homosociality are retrograde.

While hopefully not extending such clichéd discussions, I wish to suggest that there are ways in which the order of politics in the United States in the last half of the twentieth century has depended upon the maintenance of *secrecy* concerning desire among men in power, a secrecy that has complicated and made tendentious public discourse about politics and has enabled an associated secrecy involving the political culture of the national security state. More broadly, I wish to suggest that the politics of the late twentieth century in the United States is a politics most concerned with cover-ups and that the politics of secrecy that have to do with cover-ups is the politics associated most clearly with the intense violence of making the body the site of hidden importance. This secrecy is not the stuff of conspiracy, but neither is it easily recapitulated by such psychoanalytic categories as repression, or the Marxist version of repression, false consciousness.

Of course the relationship between President Bush and his most recent antagonist, Saddam Hussein, was one forged in secrecy. Bush and Saddam Hussein first encountered each other "from a distance" when they respectively headed the American CIA and the Iraqi secret police in 1976.[6] At the time, Saddam Hussein was, with the tacit approval of the American State Department, repressing the Kurds of Iraq. One might also recall that the now incarcerated General Manuel Noriega, the last one to be so demonized by Bush, also enjoyed a secret relationship with the CIA. Secrecy here is an indication of the brotherhood that men enjoyed. Having undergone ferocious rituals of manhood (all having engaged in combat, all having participated in purifying their countries against "others"), the relationships they enjoyed were "in the closet."[7] The personal sense of betrayal that is entailed when codes are violated (as Saddam Hussein did when he overreached in Kuwait) gave the energy of personal indignation to Bush in his prosecution of war, which is why he insisted on a "personal" statement of concession from Hussein before ordering a cease-fire at the end of the war.

But such a scenario by itself begs the question—What *do* men want? Feminists are now turning to that question.[8] But the most appropriate path to follow if one wishes to understand the resentments of American men is not the one that leads to the Freud of libidinal drama but the one that leads to the Freud of the disenfranchised, of the ridiculous, the Freud of jokes. That Freud is the one who inspires the reading that follows.[9]

Jokes

What is one to make of the following joke? The joke is related by Norman Mailer in *The Executioner's Song* and is told by Gary Gilmore to his girlfriend Nichole. The joke is important for several reasons, but most importantly because of the role that Nichole's laughter plays in the joke's resolution. I wish to propose that Nichole's laughter is culturally continuous with the political dynamic that compelled George Bush to reveal his desire to have sex with Ronald Reagan.

One needs to understand that this joke is told in the narrative of *The Executioner's Song* at a point when Gilmore had already started to shoplift with regularity, and it was making those who knew him and worried about him nervous. They worried that he would be caught by the authorities, among other things. They also worried that he was losing control, but they were more worried for him than about him. One day when Gilmore returned from a shoplifting spree, Nichole became upset.

> As if he sensed it, he then told her the worst story she ever heard. It was supergross. Years ago, while still a kid, he pulled off a robbery with a guy who was a true sadist. The manager of the supermarket was there alone after closing and wouldn't give the combination to the safe. So his friend took the guy upstairs, heated a curling iron, and rammed it.
>
> She couldn't help herself. She laughed. The story got way in. She had a picture of that fat supermarket manager trying to hold on to the money and the poker going up

his ass. Her laughter reached to the place where she hated people who had a lot of things and acted hot shit about it.[10]

Freud might have called this a tendentious joke. Nichole is enlisted in Gary's resentment. Nichole has her own resentments at those people who have a lot of things. Both of them are very poor. Both understand themselves to have only each other, but Gary especially sees himself as dependent upon Nichole emotionally. His appeal to her is to a third party to whom he can state his resentment against the bosses who run things.

But is this an obscene joke? Here one might note that the audience for the joke is a woman. Her participation is sought, and her approval seems to operate as a compensation for Gilmore's inability to meet the "true" object of his hatred, the men who run the world. But I use the term "truth" quite loosely here. It is precisely the truth of the matter that is elusive in this text and that might be explored if one is able to go further into the context provided by Mailer in this book and into the supplemental texts that so fundamentally inform this true life story. To take but one example, Gary may himself have wanted to have sex with that supermarket manager.

One might ask if Gilmore's story, whether "true" or "false," is an example of the pornographic imagination at work. But to place Gilmore's story into the genre of pornography does nothing to resolve the problematic status of this joke. It instead complicates the picture enormously, despite what one might think of former Attorney General Meese's attempt to enlist pornography as a clarifying *political* explanation concerning the status of the dangerous individual.[11] Indeed, precisely Meese's pornography problem underlies the problematic status of the culturally determined "truth" of this matter.

William Connolly's observations concerning the Marquis de Sade help one to understand how the pornographic is entangled in efforts to make politically "normal" situations true. In an analysis of *Philosophy in the Bedroom*, Connolly suggests that "[T]he pornographic dimension ... advances as the text proceeds through the induction of Eugenie into the connections between pleasure and cruelty to the closing scene in which Eugenie takes revenge against her mother for being her mother. Desire is now assimilated with revenge in a mixture which becomes ... definitive of the pornographic."[12] For Connolly the Sadeian texts are attempts to give expression to that which is created by the codes of reason at the core of the modern political project. He writes, "The tightening and intensification of the affirmative standards of reason, order virtue and responsibility creates a subordinate space within which pornography attacks this entire network of ordering concepts."[13] The problem of pornography is that the text of vengeance it acts out is always an incitement to further ordering on the part of the agents of order. Under the old regime the Marquis was confined in prison, and under the revolutionary regime he was declared insane. In this intensely frustrating manner, the tactics of the pornographer are understood only to mirror those of the order that the pornographer putatively opposes.[14]

One might note that the 1989 death row confessions of mass murderer Ted Bundy, who claimed that reading pornography was the pivotal moment in his life's path, is consistent with the notion of pornography as a writing of the word. Bundy declared that eventually he needed to satisfy his imagined desires by enacting them upon bodies. But if one takes Bundy seriously, one must then ask how the pornographic imagination varies from that of the normal. To ask that question is to answer that the two are the same, which is precisely the problem that conservative ideologues such as Edwin Meese are unable to cope with.[15] The dissolution of the genre distinction between pornography and other writings, say for instance, this essay, undermines both the attempts to censor pornography and, ironically, also and always whatever liberating possibilities pornography might contain. The issue of pornographic right, when reduced to that of freedom of expression, provides a disciplinary limit to discussion by shifting focus from the content of the writing to the degree of flexibility of the state in "allowing" certain liberties, whether they be based in community standards or in a broader, more abstract, but in the final analysis, limited polity.

In her essay on the Meese Commission, Susan Stewart has noted an important parallel between classic pornographic writing and the writing of pornography's detractors. For her, both pornographers and their critics come up against a limit that is articulated as a form of imprisonment. But this imprisonment has reference to the terror of the choice impelled by the binary of boundedness versus boundlessness, specifically within the context of a range of contaminations that are very much on the minds of those who both fear and participate in pornography. After noting a particularly lurid passage in the Meese Commission *Report* describing booths in porn shops (a description remarkably reminiscent of prison cells), she then observes:

> The suffocating stench and the scandalous hole—here as always in the *Report,* is the terrifying return to, and absorption in, the sexual orifices. In these passages, the possibility of action must be limited to the efflorescence of fantasy itself. Hence this architecture of pornography always emphasizes boundedness and contamination as a way to eroticize the boundary: eroticization of bodily orifices and cavities; the eroticization of class and occupation; the eroticization of gender and race. ... Hence we find in pornography an eroticization of those positioned on the boundary, acting out the impossibility of fantasy realized. And we discover the importance of the *pose* here; being poised, the pornographic actor waits on the cusp of the moment between representation and realization.[16]

This indefinite moment is one that any politician in the United States must know. Between representation and realization stretches the boundary of what is possible and what is not. Because politics is necessarily about the creation of meaning, the meanings that are both repressed and reinscribed in public discourse as marginalia take on critical force and importance as their "naturalness" becomes threatened by those who are not content to remain within the bounds of conventional politics.

Tough Baby

Like Bundy, Gary Gilmore can be understood merely as being a misunderstood man. But that is only the start. One must also understand better how it was that he saw himself as a criminal.

But curiosity about that self-imagined criminality is not innocent, either. There are many barriers to the successful negotiation of the codes, of law, of desire, of laws of desire, that contributed to making Gilmore the criminal/subject that he became. And of course many people are weary of rehearsing how "society makes criminals." To be sure, the degree of reflexivity inherent in the habits that constitute the modern person makes even the most simple of observations concerning someone such as Gilmore tendentious. Nonetheless, how else is one to try to know who Gilmore is?

To take a relevant example, in attempting to comprehend more fully the politics of fascism, Klaus Theweleit has proposed that the rank and file of the German Nazi party were motivated by a deep hatred of women. He also has cautioned against understanding this misogyny by applying the popular term "latent homosexuality." In an excursus on the idea of homosexuality, he notes that prejudices shared by such left "kulturcritiks" as Theodor Adorno and Bertolt Brecht in regard to homosexuality, citing in particular a passage from Adorno's *Minima Moralia*, in which Adorno equates totalitarianism and homosexuality.[17] Theweleit writes,

> Within the context of Adorno's own system of values, this assertion can be seen to amount to an annihilation of those who were the victims of this totalitarian disease. To direct an accusation of this kind against Adorno appears particularly justifiable in relation to a proviso of his own insertion, in which his masculine allegiances come to light. For him, the "tough guys," despite their alleged hatred of effeminacy, are "in the end ... the true effeminates." Are we then dealing with competition among men to determine who is the "real man"? Is effeminacy the worst imaginable shame?[18]

Theweleit's rhetorical question—Is it a contest about who is the real man?—provides a different entrance into the issue of gender identification. The truth of masculinity becomes but a subcategory of the question, what is the truth of sex? This question is what animated Foucault in his study of sexuality as well.[19] The construction of the body is at stake in the development of fascism. But how?

Paradoxically, Theweleit does not pursue Adorno far enough. If Adorno naturalizes this question at one level, at another he describes with great clarity the acts of violence that are required for the formation of masculine identity. Adorno suggested in that aphorism (in the English translation, "Tough Baby") that there is a particular kind of violence at work in the creation of the tough guy. His model was cinematic, quite possibly Humphrey Bogart, or even more likely, given the bourgeois patina he places on it, Cary Grant. The objects with which such men surround themselves are those of "smoke, leather, shaving cream." "The pleasures of such men," Adorno wrote, "... have about them a latent violence. This violence

> seems a threat directed against others, of whom such a one, sprawling in his easy chair, has long since ceased to have a need. In fact it is past violence against himself. If all pleasure has, preserved within it, earlier pain, then here pain, as pride in bearing it, is raised directly, untransformed, as a stereotype, to pleasure: unlike wine, each glass of whiskey, each inhalation of smoke, still recalls the repugnance that it cost the organism to become attuned to such strong stimuli, and this alone is registered as pleasure.[20]

There is no denying that by applying dialectical logic to the habitual experience of pleasure and pain, by elevating the hedonistic calculus to the psychodynamics of a "named" neurosis, sadomasochism, Adorno succeeded in naturalizing the phenomenon he described, suggesting that the "he-man" is the "true" effeminate.[21] But one need not follow Adorno to his conclusion. Instead, one can think, as Theweleit does in regard to other pieces of evidence, about the description itself.

That description places a body at risk in the continual reinscription of a code of desire through small acts of violence. The strong stimulation of whiskey (an "acquired taste," one might note) is but one example of the various damages that are done to the body in order to construct a particular range of pleasures in resistance to the organism. So while Adorno suggests that "He-men are thus, in their own constitution, what film plots usually present them to be, masochists,"[22] that masochism can only be read as such if one ignores the ambiguity of the term "constitution." That the constitution of masochism is culturally specific is implicitly suggested in Adorno's text by the fact that he constructed his aphorism as a joke.

The title of Adorno's aphorism on the he-man is "Tough Baby." Perhaps because the American man is the quintessential tough baby, the ironic inversion that Adorno exercises here is summed up in two words that are specifically American slang, juxtaposed. A tough baby is literally a contradiction in terms. But tough takes on many meanings in American English—for instance as a synonym to unfortunate—and so does baby, referring to women in a diminutive sense, to fellow men in black English (Hey, baby), so that there can be a register of meaning ranging from the most masculine man to the most feminine woman depending upon the way in which the reader negotiates the juxtaposition of the two words.

Adorno's assertion of the "truth" of the constitution of masochism and homosexuality's relationship to totalitarianism belies a specifically *political* problem underlying his joke title. Adorno must have recourse to some truth that will enable him both to understand the problem of a totalitarianism he despises (and yet which he replicates in his worse moments) and a homosexuality that he explicitly loathes (but which he secretly might aspire to). The dialectic ironically enables him to be less responsible for his politics than he otherwise would need to be. Rather than inhabit the observation concerning the bifurcation of the world of men into intellectuals and tough guys, he encompasses both sides in order to throw them both away, tough baby with bathwater. By shifting poles at just that moment when one expects that he would embrace a conclusion (totalitarianism as an aggressive principle gives way, in the final analysis, to a "feminine" passivity and the intellectual becomes the "real" man, not unlike Clark Kent/Superman), he escapes his own judgment of homosexuality. Homosexual desire is subsumed under the more tragic problem of fascism; it becomes fascism's shadow. Adorno thus followed the path of least resistance, failing to stand against the sexual reaction that informs the cold-war politics of fear.

A Bunch of Punks

Rather than abandon the political space of the tough baby, Norman Mailer has chosen instead to inhabit it. In *The Executioner's Song*, Mailer pursues the sexuality of Gary Gilmore unto death. He suggests how Gilmore came to be invested in some sort of evil having to do with sexual deviance. First, in his relationship with Nichole, Gilmore wanted her to shave her pubis, and when she complied he was more easily aroused.[23] He seemed to prefer anal intercourse with her.[24] Also, he called her "pardner," after making love.[25]

Second, there is a larger context, that of the seasoned convict, a life-world where power is equated with rape. Mailer quotes one of Gilmore's letters to Nichole:

August 20

What a bunch of punks. I'll bet I could take any one of them posse punks and fuck him in the ass and then make him lick my dick clean.
I was interviewed by a couple of psychiatrists today. They wanted lurid details.[26]

The juxtaposition of the imagery of violent domination with an observation concerning the vicarious interest of health professionals in his case indicates Gilmore's understanding that the inmate code is shared by those of the upper classes. And of course it is. That the universal language of violent domination in American culture is that of sexual domination is barely reportable. "Fuck you." "He really fucked him over." "We got screwed." "Asshole." Such ordinary colloquialisms might be understood as the smutty compensation in language for the frustration of a desire, as Freud would claim. But Freud didn't note such a bonding of obscenity with hostility in his analysis of the objective of jokes. To understand Gilmore's joke, a joke that is not so rare as one might like to think, only requires that one credit Gilmore with a will to transgress boundaries, a will not evenly distributed through American democracy.

Gilmore recognized that the psychiatrists "wanted the lurid details." Foucault has noted that generally in Western societies the need to know who a criminal is has replaced the question of what acts a criminal may have committed as the determining factor in penalty. The specific entry of psychiatry into the question of criminality was occasioned precisely by a desire on the part of authorities to understand and control violence. As Foucault put it, "the psychiatrization of criminal danger" was invested in a series of concerns about the development of laboring and dangerous classes of people.[27] The role that psychiatry played was less one of establishing an imperialism over determinations of guilt and innocence than it was that of securing a modality of power, a power that, as long as it remained mysterious to the social order, operated as a threat to that order. By demonstrating the existence of something called a "homicidal mania," psychiatrists intervened in the juridical process in such a way as to prevent juridical administration at one level, because penalty is suspended in the case of insanity. But at another level, they operated to validate justice, because in the purest form, homicidal mania presents the citizenry with "proof" that there does indeed exist something that might be called purely criminal behavior, or as Foucault put it, "that in some of its pure, extreme, intense manifestations, insanity is entirely crime, nothing but crime."[28]

The pure criminality of Gilmore motivated the desire of the psychiatrists for lurid details. But Gilmore's letter is very ambiguous. What did the psychiatrists seek details of? Gilmore's murderous acts or his sexual desires? His tendentiousness or his obscenity? Nothing could be more purely criminal within the context of the culture that Foucault delineates in his essay than homicidal mania. But Mailer suggests that Gilmore operated on the edge of criminality worse than that of the homicidal maniac. The problem, it seems, is that of man/boy love.

In these times, despite the fact that only rarely is a death involved, the pedophile is considered to be perhaps the worst case of homicidal mania because for those who so imagine the crime, the pedophile commits a harm that is imaginably worse than death. As a criminal type, the pedophile is the invisible criminal, the criminal who most thoroughly characterizes the infinite deviousness of the criminal act, and hence the ubiquitous horror of a potentially infinite harm that can underlie a criminal act. The construction of this monster is the result of the enablement of a particular term, one that appears in French law under the rubric "*attentat sans violence*," and which perhaps in English is best characterized by the term "statutory rape," in that the crime is not defined by the use of force but by a supplemental factor, in this case age. (The tired excuse of the statutory rapist is an innocence concerning age: "But judge, she may have been twelve but she acted thirty.") Foucault noted a peculiar characteristic of sexual legislation of the nineteenth century, that "it was characterized by the odd fact that it was never capable of saying exactly what it was punishing. *Attentats* (attacks) were punished; and *attentat* was never defined. *Outrages* (outrageous acts) were punished; nobody ever said what an outrage was."[29] This peculiar event occurred because the specific truth of the offense was not what was at stake. Instead, the establishment of laws of sexual morality concerns the construction of what might be called "vulnerable populations." The establishment of children as such is the first step in a process by which this political strategy is enacted. An intervention will be enabled to a far greater extent than in any other criminal commission because the vagueness of the offense is matched by the felt vulnerability. The entity called "society" thus is threatened; juridical power intervenes.

In one of his letters to Nichole, Gilmore mentioned his attraction to a thirteen-year-old boy.

> He was real pretty, like a girl, but I never gave him much thought until it became apparent that he really liked me. ... One time he ... asked if he could read this Playboy I had. I said sure, for a kiss. ... He was one of the most beautiful people I had ever seen, and I don't think I've ever seen a prettier butt. Anyhow, I used to kiss him now and then, and we got to be pretty good friends. I was just struck by his youth, beauty and naivete.[30]

In an extraordinary moment of sympathy for Gilmore, Mailer recreates the thought of a writer, Barry Farrell, as Farrell dwelled upon the meaning of this letter, of an interview with Gilmore in which he requested some child pornography (an art book called *Show Me,* of which Gilmore claimed, "It's not a piece of smut"[31]), and finally, of the events leading up to Gilmore's savage murders. Farrell's character is made to think,

> Could it be that Gilmore's love for Nichole oft depended on how childlike she could seem? That elf with knee-length socks, so conveniently shorn—by Gilmore—of her pubic locks. ... You could about say it added up. There was nobody in or out of prison whom hardcore convicts despised more than child molesters. The very bottom of the pecking order. What if Gilmore, so soon as he was deprived of Nichole, so soon as he had to live a week without her, began to feel impulses that were wholly unacceptable? What if his unendurable tension (of which he had given testimony to any psychiatrist who would listen) had something to do with little urges? Nothing might have been more intolerable to Gilmore's idea of himself. Why the man would have done anything, even murder, before he'd commit that other kind of transgression.[32]

One is left here with a fuller understanding of Gilmore's joke, but the joke is on Gilmore. The play of vengeance in which he was involved implicated him in the role of the pederast. Gilmore's denial of the pornographic dimension of the photos of boys ("It's not a piece of smut") came too late to recuperate his image. He goes down in Mailer's book, on the basis of the presentation of evidence, as a pornographer. And his pornographic imagination is what led him to his death. He is just another punk.

"Take My Vice President, Please!"

The irony of the security state must be that it leads its protectors into temptation. The temptation to confess as well as to seek vengeance are parts of this structure, parts of this struggle. One might think that George Bush's Freudian slip is indicative of the resentment of the vice president, the second banana, the potential leader, so to speak. The vice presidency, as once described by one of the holders of the office, "isn't worth a warm bucket of shit." As the excremental office, the office of the anus, the vice presidency is the perfect office from which to gain a perspective on the operations of justice in an age of decline.

Bush, as the potential leader, performed a rite of self-abnegation in pursuit of ideal office. He did not resist the terms of his apprenticeship; he declared undying fealty to a man he once had contempt for (recall his statement about "voodoo economics"). Bush becomes the man punishing the boy for wanting approval from a father who is never there when he needs him and is always judging him when he doesn't need judgment. Bush's father is someone whom Bush can never satisfy—first because his father the senator was someone who Bush only superseded in stature with his own rise to the presidency itself—and second because his father the movie star/president is a man whose own defense against the primary source of pain in his life (his own drunken father) was to withdraw from all potentially painful relationships.[33]

The estate of the desperate debtor, Thomas Hobbes suggested long ago, is a dangerous state of being. It results in resentments that are very deep and that reflect the tensions of those who know that beneath a patina of civilization, tenuously held in check by the sword of an authority, every man must lock his door at night and his strongbox all the time. Hobbes's description of this estate makes no distinction between public and private: It is a distinction perpetuated in the wake of the establishment of authority, and must always be guarded against. Americans know that Bush could not express his hostility to Ronald Reagan, but the drama of American politics lies precisely in the artifice of civility that always threatens to slip away. When Bush makes a joke, such as "read my *hips*" (told in a moment when he was slipping in public esteem), he risks exposure. Jokes precisely make resentments and desires accessible in a form that walks a fine line of acceptability. Bush insulated himself from criticism by directing the force of the joke at himself. As the winner of the javelin toss who elected to receive, he has truly fucked himself, if only in the interest of power.

Bush chose a pretty young man, a DKE brother, to be *his* vice president. And he kept him as his running mate in 1992, even though polls indicate that switching to someone like Colin Powell would help lead to a Republican realignment. Loyalty is the first virtue of a fraternity brother. And yet to be a brother is to defer, in important ways, the passage to adulthood. One continues to move in a world inhabited by adolescents. So shortly after the 1988 presidential election, Bush returned to his ancestral home in Kennebunkport, Maine, and announced that his father (the senator) would have been proud of "his little boy."[34] He further exposed his desire to remain a child by refusing to eat his broccoli, insisting that, because he is president of the United States, he doesn't have to eat what he doesn't want to eat. His favorite dietary items include pork rinds dipped in hot sauce and Heath Bars (candy bars) crumbled over breakfast cereal.

In a curious way, the parallel between criminal and president is complete with this insistence. Gary Gilmore and George Bush are brothers. Both have, in a sense, been raised by the state. Both have sought out father figures throughout their lives to guide them. Both have suffered the abuse of childhood. Both became killers, in time. Both have run all their lives from their most secret impulses by way of a pornography that allows them to enjoy vicariously a pleasure that is otherwise unallowable. The primary difference between them seems to be that as president, Bush doesn't have to eat his vegetables, and Gilmore, while alive, had no control over his diet, being in prison. But even in this difference one might note a similarity—for his last meal, Gilmore sent out for pizza.[35]

In one of only two breathtaking moments of the 1988 presidential debates, Michael Dukakis disparaged as meaningless Bush's employment of the phrase "a thousand points of light," thus threatening, if only briefly, to rip aside the tattered veil that enabled Bush to weave his spell. But that disparaging comment was not enough. Another code evoked at the beginning of the second presidential debate destroyed whatever chance Dukakis had of being elected president. When Bernard Shaw of CNN asked Dukakis if he would reconsider his opposition to the use of the death penalty if his wife were brutally raped and murdered, Dukakis lost the election.

It might be worthwhile to examine that moment, because it represented a peculiar watershed of American national politics. Bernard Shaw is the first black anchorman for a network, in this case the Cable News Network (unlike his predecessor, Max Robinson of ABC, who at his peak was a coanchor), and was the only black man to participate in the presidential debates. His question was all the more damning for Dukakis because of that fact, in two senses. First, that a black man asked this question underlined the concern with crime that is shared by black Americans, who suffer most severely from the consequences of both violent street crime and the more systematic crimes perpetuated by corporate violators of law. But second, and more important, Shaw symbolically stood in for Willie Horton. His question was a figurative mugging. The question was very "personal," it questioned Dukakis's "manhood," and it demonstrated his impotence against the threatening Other, as represented by black men. That Dukakis's answer was perceived by most Americans as inadequate is a reflection of the weakness of his answer, of course, but it is difficult to claim what answer to that question would have been capable of overcoming the impression of domination that Shaw's question established.[36] Had Dukakis attacked Shaw, he would perhaps have repaired the breach, but that action would have undermined his image in reference to his sympathy to the black community. His retreat to legalism gave Bush victory in the debate. Bush had demonstrated throughout the campaign that the category of the "legal" must be disregarded in the name of strength. To refer to legality is to refer to weakness, in foreign policy, where strictures such as the Boland Amendment had "tied the hands of the president" in fighting communism. But legality also tied the hands of the president in "the fight against crime." The demands of security require tough guys to carry it out, wild enough to violate law and smart enough not to get caught. Dukakis's appeals to legality attempted to do what Adorno did, to substitute one "real" man for another. But that strategy does not seem to work in a culture as frightened of uncertainty as is the United States at this time.

In 1951, Adorno thought he was witness to the ultimate degradation of a form of civilization in the wake of Auschwitz. He subtitled his collection of aphorisms, "Reflections from Damaged Life." He concluded that study with an observation on the task of thought: "Perspectives must be fashioned that displace and estrange the world, reveal it to be, with its rifts and crevices, as indigent and distorted as it will appear one day in the messianic light. To gain such perspectives without velleity or violence, entirely from the felt contact with its objects—this alone is the task of thought."[37] The violence that Adorno sought to escape through the thought of redemption, despite his denial that the reality or unreality of redemption is at stake in this impossible exercise, lies implicit in the very force of the thought itself. The felt contact with objects requires a move that is inevitably violent. Fraternity brothers, however, are not interested in such mediations. They seek the violence itself as a validation for being, as a means of knowing who they are, as loyalists of the home team.

The democratic process might still inspire a movement away from the codes of desire that insistently impose themselves upon the bodies of men and women as monological alternatives to each other. In other words, it might be possible to think less messianically than Adorno, to think through the more banal tensions that afflict the possible futures of a particular society. A large part of that future is not constituted by the homosocial politics of desire as it is defined by/confined to white men positioned in hierarchies of subordination in business and government. Indeed, one future concerning the problematic of homosociality might be found in the ongoing response of women in the United States to the paradoxical fact that their rape has nothing to do with them at the same time that it has everything to do with them.

But in the meantime, the banality of American national politics continues to disguise the violence of its organization. The discourse of American national politics depends upon the forms of subordination in which it engages in order to achieve its coherence and order. As such it speaks a language of love in the commission of death. While such a language may once have contributed to and have been commensurate with a rich and complex political world, even if that world depended upon the exclusion and denigration of a majority of the human race, the events of the first half of the twentieth century make its continued appearance in the second half a new kind of obscenity, if only because the wish of such a politics is now too easily fulfilled, thus putting at risk the future for all of humankind.

NOTES

1. Report on George Bush, speaking in Twin Falls, Idaho, reported in the *New York Times*, May 12, 1988, p. A32. "George Bush, or Homosocial Politics" is a fragment of larger work in progress, *The Body Politic in America*.

2. A recent example of the valuable use of psychoanalysis is Michael Rogin's *Ronald Reagan, The Movie, and Other Studies in American Political Demonology* (Berkeley: University of California Press, 1987).

3. Eve Kosofsky Sedgwick, *Between Men: English Literature and Male Homosocial Desire* (New York: Columbia University Press, 1985), pp. 10–11. Also see her essay "Across Gender, Across Sexuality: Willa Cather and Others," *South Atlantic Quarterly* 88:1 (Winter 1989). In that essay, Sedgwick attempted to build further distinctions between sexuality and gender. Finally, see her *Epistemology of the Closet* (Berkeley: University of California Press, 1990), which further extends her argument.

4. Ibid., *Between Men,* p. 4.

5. Ibid., p. 20.

6. For a trenchant analysis of the realpolitick background of the war in Iraq, see Christopher Hitchins, "Why We Are Stuck in the Sand," *Harper's,* January 1991.

7. On the rituals of hazing in American fraternities and their association with women hating see Peggy Sanday, *Fraternity Gang Rape* (New York: NYU Press, 1990).

8. See, for instance, Kathy Ferguson, *The Man Question* (Berkeley: University of California Press, forthcoming).

9. See *Jokes and Their Relation to the Unconscious,* translated and edited by James Strachey (New York: W. W. Norton, 1963).

10. Norman Mailer, *The Executioner's Song* (New York: Warner, 1979), p. 149.

11. See the Meese Commission Report. On the dangerous individual and the psychiatrization of violent crime, see Michel Foucault, "The Dangerous Individual," in *Politics, Philosophy, Culture,* edited by Lawrence Kritzman (London: Routledge, 1988).

12. William Connolly, *Political Theory and Modernity* (New York: Basil Blackwell, 1988), p. 79.

13. Ibid., p. 83.

14. In this sense, one can think about the old joke employed so well in the various movie and stage versions of "Little Shop of Horrors" concerning the sadistic dentist who is frustrated when he has a masochist as his patient. The paradox is not so dissimilar to that of the pornographer. It is perhaps similar to the famous example upon which much of modern formal theorizing is based, the "prisoner's dilemma."

15. For a brilliant analysis of the Meese Commission's report, see Susan Stewart, "The Marquis de Meese," *Critical Inquiry* 15 (Autumn 1988).

16. Stewart, "Marquis de Meese," p. 170.

17. Klaus Theweleit, *Male Fantasies: Volume 1. Women, Floods, Bodies, History,* translated by Steven Conway in collaboration with Erica Carter and Chris Turner (Minneapolis: University of Minnesota Press, 1987), pp. 55–56.

18. Ibid., p. 55. The passage under discussion is from Theodor Adorno, *Minima Moralia,* translated by E.J.N. Jephcott (London: Verso, 1974), pp. 45–46.

19. See, for instance, Foucault's preface to *Herculine Barbin* (New York: Pantheon, 1980).

20. Adorno, *Minima Moralia,* p. 46.

21. For a contrasting view of the function of the *practice* of sadomasochism, see Foucault, *Politics, Philosophy, Culture,* edited by Lawrence D. Kritzman (New York: Routledge, 1989), "Sexual Choice, Sexual Act," p. 299.

22. Ibid., p. 46.

23. Mailer, *The Executioner's song,* p. 142.

24. Ibid., pp. 363–364.

25. Ibid., p. 155.

26. Ibid., p. 335.

27. Foucault, *Politics, Philosophy, Culture,* "The Dangerous Individual," p. 128.

28. Ibid., pp. 134–135.

29. Foucault, *Politics, Philosophy, Culture,* "Sexual Morality and the Law," p. 275. The comment on *attentat sans violence* is borrowed from Guy Hocquenghem in the same interview, p. 278.

30. Ibid., pp. 853–854.

31. Ibid., p. 485.

32. Ibid., p. 855.

33. On Bush and his relationship with his father, see Sidney Blumenthal, *Pledging Allegiance, The Last Campaign of the Cold War* (New York: Harper Collins, 1990), pp. 56–57. The details of Reagan's life are best described by Reagan himself. See Ronald Reagan, with Richard Hubler, *Where's the Rest of Me?* (New York: Karz-Segil, 1965). It is worth noting that Reagan spends a total of two paragraphs discussing his marriage and divorce from Jane Wyman, including the children they had together. Michael, an adopted son, he notes, suffered the most pain. But he doesn't ask why, and doesn't seek to explain himself. In that regard, he states, "I have never discussed what happened, and I have no intention of doing so now" (p. 202). Reagan throughout demonstrates his unquestioning attachment to and loyalty for older men who in his mythical rendering unerringly gave him advice on how to advance through life. Never in the entire book does he question authority, except in the context of demonstrating the error of his ways and the goodness of their ways.

34. Michael Shapiro brought this incident to my attention.

35. Mailer, *The Executioner's Song,* p. 882. One might note that since he had not specifically put the pizza on his list for his last meal, Gilmore was not allowed to eat it, even though his visitors were.

36. Some have suggested that if Dukakis had responded by saying that he would have wanted to kill the rapist, but that he is thankful that here in the United States rule by law prevails so that justice prevents private vengeance, that such a statement might have done the trick. (Two very thoughtful correspondents, George Kateb and Jean Elshtain, have made precisely that argument to me in response to a draft of this essay.) But such a response, it seems to me, reflects a nostalgia for a situation when people better understood or even popularly knew of a gap that exists between private and public discourse. I think that such a gap has been appropriated so cynically at this point, most significantly by corporations but by other private interests as well, that few members of the voting public are prepared to accept the legitimacy of such a claim as the one Dukakis might have made.

37. Adorno, *Minima Moralia,* p. 247.

12

Postmortem on the Presidential Body, or Where the Rest of Him Went

BRIAN MASSUMI & KENNETH DEAN

THE REAGAN presidency reintroduced the body of the leader as an effective mechanism in U.S. politics. Reagan worked. And to a surprising extent, he worked through the vehicle of is body. It will be maintained that he is still at work even after his practical withdrawal from the political scene, and he will continue to be at work even after his belated death. U.S. policy under Bush mimed the political course set by Reagan blow by blow, Panama for Grenada, Saddam Hussein for Kohmeini. Bush staged an even more crowd-pleasing Middle East hostage drama than his mentor had, escalating from threats to open war as he merrily set about trying to bomb his way to the mother of all reelections, in bloody one-up-manship over the behind-the-scenes negotiations with Iran that had crowned Reagan's first-term inauguration (Gary Sick, "The Election Story of the Decade," *New York Times*, April 15, 1991, A15). Reagan's ghost is in the patriotic machine. The goal of this chapter is to identify the remains.

Reagan made unification his political mission—a *reunification*, to be precise—of a "spiritual" rather than territorial nature. The 1960s had torn America apart at the seams. Ronald Wilson Reagan would heal the "wounds" of Vietnam.

Close-up to Infinity

"The story begins with a close-up of a bottom." That is the opening line of Reagan's first autobiography, written in 1965 for use in his campaign for the governorship of California. At the dawn of his political career, Reagan signposts the body that would serve him so well. "My face was blue from screaming, my bottom was red from whacking, and my father claimed afterward that he was white."[1]

Reagan points to his body, and it is familial. His body is one with his family, and both are one with the country by virtue of their color scheme—red, white, and blue. Reagan habitually draped himself in the flag. It was a constant of his career. One need only think of the decor at Republican conventions. Individual body, family, and country are presented as having a common substance: the fabric of the flag. Their combined strength is embodied in it. It is their sum. Their sum, plus some. For there is a remainder to the equation. Body, family, country add up to a whole greater than the sum of its parts, just as a pattern of stars and stripes adds up to more than a cloth. The flag is not only a materialization of unity; it is the fabric of greatness. In it, three are one. Not just any one: Number One—"the greatest nation on earth." The flag is the repository of an excess attributed to terms in an equation. Outside of the equation, the same terms would be noticeably lacking. They would have only an incomplete, more or less brutish existence. The flag elevates and animates them. It is the material embodiment of their "spirit"—the "American spirit" incarnate. Those it enthralls attribute it with almost magical powers to bring forth and replenish. It is the objectified presence of the subjective essence shared by three interrelated terms in the patriotic equation. As such, it is more precious than the merely mortal terms it brings together. "I don't give a damn," said the veteran, "whether it's the protester's civil right or not. I fought to protect the American flag, not to protect him" (*Newsweek,* July 3, 1989, p. 18).

Body, family, country share a common substance that unites them but at the same time seems to exist on a higher plane than they. The substance that unifies paradoxically inhabits a world apart. One, two, three, plus unity makes four: body, family, country, Flag. Multiplicity is a stubborn thing. No problem. Four, and many more, will be as one in a second kind of unifying substance. "I have heard," Reagan's autobiography continues, "more than one psychiatrist say that we imbibe our ideals from our mother's milk. Then, I must say, my breast feeding was the home of the brave baby and the free bosom." The motherland. Now body/family/country not only have a common substance but a shared energetic principle or generative fluid: mother's milk (five). The flag brings forth and replenishes because mother's milk soaks its fabric like blood flowing in the veins of the newborn baby. The nation's procreative fluid is not seminal. It is maternal, and the maternal is presented as sexless. Nations reproduce by nonsexual means.

More than four: The flag is not the only common substance pumped with procreative fluid. The motherland got a "facelift" for American Independence Day in 1986: Schoolchildren across the country were asked to contribute their lunch money to scrub and refurbish another spirit of America, chaste "Miss Liberty." The unveiling of the new and improved Statue of Liberty coincided with one of the peaks in Reagan's popularity. Reagan himself was the prime-time master of ceremonies for one of the most expensive and self-indulgent displays of patriotic fervor in living memory. "WOW!," ran a cover of *Newsweek* announcing a "Portrait of Miss Liberty on Her Birthday Bash" (July 14, 1986). In this and countless other exultant press stories, every alleged American virtue and victory was described as Miss Liberty's personal accomplishment. Reagan, a kind of spiritual bridegroom bathed in a fountain of youth of floodlights and fireworks, stood faithfully by her side—when he wasn't standing on her pedestal. A *New York Times* illustration of a statuesque Reagan wearing Miss Liberty's crown was a typical image of the period.[2]

What at first seemed to be a simple, stable structure of three homologous terms turns out to be much more complicated. The would-be substance of unity takes its place in a proliferating series. It is as though the structure were undermined by an imbalance it could not permanently correct. A lack in the brute materiality of the three base terms is compensated for by a supplementary term operating in a higher dimension. The supplementary term succeeds in filling the lack, but it overfills it, turning it into an excess. The imbalance is still there but has changed signs, from a negative to a positive.[3] There is always a remainder of spirit that cannot be contained in a given substance of unity and must therefore be absorbed by another: from flag to statue. The excess haunts the reunification series, turning up again at each successive term. Its omnipresence is acknowledged in an image of a life-giving fluid suffusing all solid states of unity, acting as the energetic principle of their serial progression. The minus sign of brute human existence has become a series of pluses embodying the flow of the American spirit in fateful progress toward the pinnacle of history. Progress as a serialized redundancy of Number Ones. Plus, double plus.

Triple plus. Reagan's own body functioned as a substance of unity. He was not content to take his place as one in the multiplying series. He would be the preeminent term, simply by virtue of his greater mobility. A man can stand on a statue's pedestal, but a statue can never fill a man's shoes. If Reagan stood on every pedestal presented, and draped himself in every flag in sight, the entire series of national icons would converge toward him. He would be catapulted out of their already elevated plane to an even higher one: He would be the substance of the substance of unity, the essence of the essence of subjectivity. He would be what made mother's milk wet. All he had to do was remain in perpetual motion, circulating from one hallowed site to another, not just arrogating to himself their life-giving powers but raising them to a higher power. Now it is no longer one substance of unity being added to another; they begin to multiply exponentially.

The foundation provided by embodiment of the national spirit is in continual slippage. It begins to recede from the three material terms it purports to ground into loftier and loftier dimensions. The substance of unity becomes a substance of the substance of unity in a potentially infinite regress that can be controlled only by transforming the process of exponential multiplication back into one of simple addition: in other words by finding a way of managing the ever-excessive virtue of the American spirit by continuing to move laterally between terms on the same level instead of moving up into ever higher powers or dimensions. Above Reagan, the only personifiable unifying substance left to appeal to is God, and He rarely gives photo opportunities. Once Reagan's body had circulated long enough for the magic of all earthly national icons to rub off on him one after the other, after he had become their subjective sum, he had only two choices: ascend to the heavens or begin circulating among himself. The asexual reproduction of the country culminates in the mechanical reproduction of the image of its leader.

The most striking instance of this process was Reagan's legendary acceptance of the presidential nomination at the 1984 Republican Convention. His image was piped in larger-than-life on a huge video screen suspended above the podium. The imposing screen presence created a feeling of imperial aloofness that only highlighted Reagan's bodily absence. A heroic Nancy tried to compensate by hailing his talking head as if he could see her—as if they occupied the same space and level of reality. The image on the screen was repeated countless times around the red-white-and-blue bedecked convention hall in portraits held aloft by the adoring crowd. The giant screen, Nancy, and the proliferating close-up of the leader were united on the surface of the home viewer's TV screen. So there is a unifying substance higher than Reagan but not quite God: TV. But the TV-promised land is nowhere. It is everywhere. The screen unifies incommensurable dimensions—portraits, Nancys and delegates, other screens with giant talking heads, political discourse, advertising. But it does it by the millions. In his moment of triumph, at the height of his unifying powers, Reagan is diffused to infinity. He disappears into an infinitely fragmenting video relay.

Stumped

Reagan's body is struck with an inescapable contradiction. It is trapped in a dialectic of immanence and transcendence that can have no synthesis. The closer the nation comes to embodying its own unifying subjective substance, the farther that substance recedes into another dimension until it approaches the vanishing point. The more exalted the unifying substance, the more ethereal it is; the more ethereal it is, the more painfully inadequate it proves in unifying the heterogeneous material terms for which it strives to provide a common substance. The unification drive leads only to disappearance and fragmentation: The physicality of the unifying body disappears, leaving only its image, which is then relayed to infinity, composed, decomposed, re-membered, and dismembered.

Each move to a higher unifying substance requires the new Number One to subsume all preceding terms. That substance must therefore subsume in one way or another its own conditions of emergence. Every image of unity contains within it a trace of the dialectic of immanence and transcendence that produced it. Since the dialectic takes the form of an alternation between a lack and an excess inscribed in the unifying substance, images of that substance will also alternate between those two poles.

Reagan's body was lacking in a big way. Reagan was a walking amputation. A preamputation. He was always already lame. A preoccupation with feet occupies a prominent place in Reagan's first autobiography. The title was taken from the movie *King's Row*. In Reagan's words, he played the part of a "gay blade" named Drake "who cut a swathe among the ladies." Drake it seems, took to dating the daughter of a prominent doctor, who was not at all pleased with the arrangement. One day Drake was injured in a railroad accident. When he regained consciousness, his legs were gone. The father of the woman he was dating was the doctor assigned to treat him. "*Where's the rest of me?*" Drake cries.

Reagan presents this scene as his most challenging role and the acme of his acting career. "A whole actor would find such a scene difficult; giving it the necessary dramatic impact as half an actor was murderous. I felt I had neither the experience nor the talent to fake it. I simply had to find out how it really felt, short of actual amputation." So he consulted physicians and commiserated with cripples. But, he says, "I was stumped." In the end, he manages. "I had put myself, as best I could, in the body of another fellow"; in becoming a good actor "I had become a semi-automaton." He is now a real-life amputee. And at that point he realizes that half of him has always been missing, he was always just limping along through life repeating his lines. He finds the rest of him in the mother's milk of patriotism and conservative ideals. What he does not say is that for the analogy to be complete, this second, real-life healing would logically take the same form as the first: He would become whole by taking over "the body of another fellow." Now the other body a *president* would have to take over to make himself whole is—every body. The body politic. Reagan verges on saying outright that the political magic he would work is akin to national possession: countless bodies unified by the same American spirit, one glorious body politic repeating in unison an old actor's favorite lines. Instead, he reminisces about his father, a shoe salesman who "spent hours analyzing the bones of the foot." It comes as little surprise later on when we learn that after being delivered with divorce papers by his first wife, Reagan went out and promptly broke a leg. And that what attracted him to his second wife, Nancy, was hearing that her father was a prominent surgeon. Years later, the most positive thing biographer Kitty Kelley would find to say about Nancy was that she had the "ability to embrace physical deformity."[4] *Where Is the Rest of Me?* ends with a quote from Clark Gable: "The most important thing a man can know is that, as he approaches his own door, someone on the other side is listening for the sound of his footsteps."[5] His better half. Nancy will keep Reagan whole ("Mrs. Reagan Defends Her Role as the President's Protector," *San Francisco Chronicle,* June 10, 1988). But the series of minuses proliferates at a pace with the pluses. Any antiamputation device is no more than a stopgap measure. The Reagan era was a theater of bumbling and ill health punctuated by his prostate gland and polyp-beseiged rectum. Being shot got him one of the highest ratings in the polls he ever achieved.[6] The most visible press coverage given him in the months after he left office was for having hand surgery (January 1989), falling off a horse (July 1989), and having water drained from his brain (September 1989). Even in the best of times, any inadequately planned close-up revealed that his supposedly ageless face looked like it was rotting on its bones.

Reagan manifested his amputational nature by disappearing into his ceremonial residence. His mode of being in the White House mimicked the transcendental nature of the substance of unity he continued to be despite his tendency to lose bits and pieces of himself. His comment about building a Great Wall around the White House was directed at the press corps, which he was likening to invading Asian hordes. But it could just as well have referred to the ground-to-air missiles and elite combat units ringing the White House to ward off attacks by terrorists. Or to his increasing deafness ("Reagan's New Hearing Aid Has a Remote Control," *San Francisco Chronicle,* February 11, 1988) and the hearing aid he would shut off to avoid reporters' questions ("Reagan Feigns Laryngitis to Avoid Query," *New York Times,* March 3, 1985). Or to his overall lack of accessibility to the press—despite his reputation for being a media president, he had fewer press conferences than any president since the advent of radio ("The Disappearing Presidential News Conference," *New York Times,* October 17, 1988, A20). Or to his ever-increasing aloofness and lack of engagement in the everyday running of the country ("President 'Strangely Passive,'" *The Australian,* May 10, 1988; "Memo Suggested 'Inattentive' Reagan Be Removed: Book," *Montreal Gazette,* September 16, 1988, A10). Or his tragicomic propensity to nap during meetings and international crises and his growing inability to distinguish politics from film scripts.[7] When the body of unification is not being cut up, it is cut off, separating itself from that which it unifies.

Reagan repeatedly drew attention to the structural homology between his body and the body politic ("Reagan's Nose Could Change the Whole Face of the World," *International Herald Tribune,* August 10, 1987). Any difficulty he encountered was apt to be expressed in somatic terms. His triumphant first address after his assassination centered on a metaphor linking his recovery to that of the economy ("Reagan Appeals to Congress for His Economic Plan, Saying He Is Recovered but US Isn't," *New York Times,* April 29, 1981). Criticism struck him physically, with hysterical regularity if not anatomical accuracy ("Reagan Lashes Out: 'There Is Bitter Bile in My Throat,'" *Time,* December 8, 1986, cover).

A consequence of the structural homology between the body of the unifier and the body politic it unifies is that the country sets up a defensive self-other boundary analogous to the skin. Any uncooperative element appears in one of two ways: as a rival body attacking boldly from without, threatening to pierce the body's protective shield, or as a disease that slips in through the pores to enter the country's bloodstream and sap its strength from within. The military-industrial complex under Reagan strove to produce a technological skin. Star Wars was to be a skin prosthesis made of lasers.

National unity oscillates between paranoia and hypochondria. It is in any case a sickness. The hypochondria is written into the paradox of the substance of unity. A seamless whole has to have parts, otherwise it would have nothing to totalize;

but it cannot have them, otherwise it would not be a seamless whole. The whole is continually undermined by its parts. The body politic is always under attack by its own organs in one form or another. That is why it has such a pronounced tendency to want to cut them off.

Patchwork President

It was a common assertion that Reagan owed his influence to his appearance of youth and vitality. But Reagan was in fact so closely associated with illness and injury that one of the favorite ways his detractors found to parody him was to depict him as he was supposed to appear: young and strong.[8]

A vulgar Freudian corollary to the "youth and vitality" theory had it that Reagan was a charismatic leader who presented the nation with an image of self-assurance, wholeness, and health: the perfect ego ideal. It is difficult to see, on close inspection, what there was to identify with.

Sometimes Reagan seemed to beg for psychoanalysis. "I was the hungriest person in the house," he writes in *Where Is the Rest of Me?*, "but I only got chubby when I exercised in the crib; any time I wasn't gnawing on the bars, I was worrying my thumb in my mouth—habits which have symbolically persisted throughout my life." Identify with that, and you get a nation of thumb-suckers. Hardly a worthy adversary for the "Evil Empire."

But the there was always the anal option. On the foreign policy front, Reagan's libidinal economy was on a permanent war footing that could be described as anal-aggressive. His body sucked attention and energies inward toward the government and its architectural seat, then redirected them outward at the enemy. When Reagan disappeared into an increasingly retentive White House, he was disappearing into the black hole of his own anus. Never was he closer to that ultimate immaterial state of godlike transcendence than in his role as Prime Sphincter.

His phallus was fuzzy. Reagan *could* play the role of a father figure. But when he did, he was more like everybody's uncle than a mighty patriarch. And as we saw at his home birth, he had a propensity to embody the motherland. As a matter of fact, he did not customarily have a penis. During his prostate saga, the *New York Times* published an anatomical chart of the presidential body (December 18, 1986). Despite the proximity of that gland to his alleged genital apparatus, the executive organ fails to appear. Reagan does get *both* an anus and a rectum, suggesting a tendency of the phallic to disappear into the anal. Reagan agenitality, however, just as often veered toward the vestal virgin roles of the Statue of Liberty genre. In antigenital mode, he did not even tolerate the sexual activity of others ("Ardent Dogs Killed as Risk to Reagan," *San Francisco Examiner*, October 19, 1987).

If the citizenry indulged in phallic phantasies in relation to Reagan's body, they were not likely to imagine him having what they wanted. Rather, they became what he lacked. Whenever his anthem played, they would pop up proudly erect and pledge allegiance to his magic fabric. If dangerous marauders (like Grenada) loomed on the horizon, they would shoot off their missiles in eager defense of Miss Liberty. Reagan's followers, like Hitler's, *stood in* for his phallus, which was detached from his body and multiplied, as scattered as his TV image.

Reagan's vital body parts were distributed across the social field in different, always changing, constellations. His body was infinitely decomposable and recomposable. It could not only bridge the gap between the individual and the collective; it could travel across age and gender boundaries with postmodern ease. A postcard marketed at the beginning of the first term shows Ronnie and Nancy wearing each other's heads, and looking eerily comfortable in them.[9]

Reagan *could* be the virile father of the nation, as when he bombed Libya; but he could just as easily be its favorite daughter (despite having killed Khadafy's). His political effectiveness did not depend on sustaining any particular symbolic configuration. Any one would do—as long as attention remained focused on his body. That was the bottom line. It didn't matter what symbolic connections were made to his body—only that *some* connection to it be made. CBS News correspondent Lesley Stahl recalled receiving a phone call from the White House press secretary thanking her for doing a highly *negative* story about Reagan. It didn't matter what the content was, he said; broadcasting images of Reagan, any images, could only help him. ("Speaking of Everything," with Howard Cosell, May 10, 1988). The White House press corps itself seemed to argue against any theory of Reagan's political success being based on citizen identification with positive qualities associated with his visual image.

If we give in to Reagan's invitation to psychoanalyze we miss the novelty of how his body effectively functioned on the political level. As substance of unity, his collectivized body guaranteed a structural homology between the three fundamental terms of individual body, family, country. In a system of homologies where each term mirrors every other, no term is central and no event can be deemed originating. A system of equivalences is set up vertically between the part and the whole and horizontally between parts or wholes on the same level. This authorizes an infinite circuit of symbolic relays that can be traveled any number of times in any direction: Thus the famous structuralist principle of reversibility. What it means is that every possible symbolic permutation is an a priori of the system. A symbolic interpretation can at most activate a term that is already present. It cannot critique. It can only fill predesignated gaps. Speculation on whether Ronnie and Nancy still "did it" and jokes about Reagan's virility and its sublimation in displays of military prowess were commonplace during his presidency. A psychoanalytic interpretation might triumphantly unearth a series of risqué associations, ignoring the fact that they were already on everybody's lips. In the age of Reagan, Oedipus came out. What was once repressed was now on the surface.

It is precisely as a *surface* that Reagan's body functioned. There was no depth to it for an unconscious to hide in. The "Teflon president": all shimmering surface.

As we have seen, a substance of unity functions by combining in a homogeneous medium heterogeneous terms drawn from a multiplicity of levels. It does that by extracting or abstracting certain qualities and not others and projecting them onto a single surface. In Reagan's case, the qualities were predominantly visual, and the ultimate surface was the TV screen. That particular surface is almost omnipotent in its combinatory powers. Logical and symbolic associations pertaining to what psychoanalysis calls the secondary processes get equal billing with what normally would be considered primary processes. The primary processes become visible. Reagan's public pronouncements consistently displayed distortions characteristic of the dreamwork. Nicaragua, for example, was displaced to a threatening position just south of the Texas border. Film and TV residue from past viewings were condensed into present perceptions, such as when Reagan called his dog "Lassie," or when he told a story about a heroic fighter pilot drawn from a movie he had seen as though it were a true story. In Reagan's America, the psychoanalytic distinction between the unconscious and the conscious, and the ideological distinction between the fake and the real, ceased to be pertinent. Everybody knew that Reagan couldn't or wouldn't tell the difference between them. But it didn't matter. He simply did not operate on that level. Fantasy, logical contradiction, and fraud were authorized. That did not make Reagan psychotic or even cynical. He operated on a level at which those terms have no meaning. On that level, he was perfectly functional. His presidency worked. Reagan almost single-handedly turned the ideological direction of the country around. He was able to produce ideological or Oedipal *effects* by nonideological and non-Oedipal means.

The plasticity and manifestness of Reagan's body unbalances not only a traditional Freudian approach but more recent paradigms as well. It is difficult to see him in this postideological dimension, following the suggestion of a Baudrillardian critic, as a hyperreal male who "could always satisfy our iconic interests." He can only be perceived as a "satisfying" simulation of masculinity (a "hologram" of the American male) if vast stretches of his image production are ignored.[10] A Lacanian analysis might find him the embodiment of the phallus, constituting subjectivities by distributing plenitude and lack, all the while remaining tragically absent to itself. This interpretation would privilege his amputational aptitudes, placing them under the sign of castration. But the cut of the scalpel can be seen as a positive power of plasticity as easily as it can be seen as the playing out of a primordial lack. Given Reagan's organs' ability to regenerate and mutate, amputation could actually be considered an enablement: a precondition for migration and reconnection on a surface of variation.

It is perhaps less useful to say that Reagan was neither a father figure, a phallus, nor a simulation than to recognize that he was all of these things. He was not *fundamentally* an actor in a family romance projected on a nation, nor the constitutive agent of an intersubjective structure of lack-in-being, nor a hyperreal optical effect. He was a surface on which all of these processes had equal play, like different channels to which a viewer's brain could turn as at a press of the remote control. His screen-body was the interface in a many-dimensioned interactive medium.

The Kinetic Geography of the Quasi-Corporeal

For all the fluidity, there was one constant. "Unity." Unity in neutral, in itself nonpsychoanalytic, nonideological, nonsimulatory. More abstract than any of these modes. Simply topological.

But if, as was asserted earlier, a unity always exists *in addition to* and *alongside* the multiplicity it unifies, then it stands to reason that there is something more inclusive than unity and more abstract than the simply topological: an interconnecting mechanism that defines the relation between the unifying substance and what it unifies. Subtending and surrounding the body and body image of the national unifier and the bodies and images they bring together, there is another kind of body that has no image—that can never have one because it is only ever *in-between.* There is a body without an image that inhabits the gaps. It occupies the spaces under, above, and between bodies and images, residing in the *interrelation* of all that is. It does not extract (dismember) or abstract (unify). It is effectively all-inclusive. *The* interactive medium: the "body politic" in its fullest extension, at once infra-concrete and super-abstract. A void where no anus can go. But where the proper name "Reagan" can, and does.

> It has taken me many years to get used to seeing myself as others see me, and also seeing myself instead of my mental picture of the character I'm playing. First, very few of us ever see ourselves except as how we look directly at ourselves in a mirror. Thus we don't know how we look from behind, from the side, walking, standing, moving normally through a room. It's quite a jolt. (*Where's the Rest of Me?*, p. 79)

To see yourself as others see you. But not as in a mirror. Not an inversion or reversal. A surrounding—of the body in motion. From all angles simultaneously, and in all qualities of movement, front, back, walking, standing. To leave "my" self-perspective, but not for "yours." Not for the Other's I; for *others'* eyes. To see oneself as "*one*" would see one: an impersonal perspective conceivable only as the sum total of subjective perspectives. To be the division, not only between the "I" and the "you," but between all Is and all yous at once. To be "one"—in all its multiplicity. Unity as a super-topological overlay of all possible inter-geographies of bodies in motion. Subsumed by a name.

A nagging question is how "Reagan" could produce a wholeness or wellness effect in spite of his evident mental and physical deficiencies, what his so-called 'charisma' consisted of. At first what seemed the most plausible hypothesis was that it was his hairdo. But it became increasingly clear that the 'magic' "Reagan" worked did not have to do with his body itself, or any of its organs, or any power of interpersonal magnetism they had. It seemed to have to do with two quite mundane things.

First, his gestures. On a good day, Reagan was a master of the smooth move. His movements drew pleasing figures in space. It was as if his entire body were a cartographer's pen drawing an invisible map of some atmospheric utopian realm. He surveyed an invisible space of well-being that was attached not to its body, but its movement, its transitoriness, its fluidity. The body would some day rot, perhaps was rotting already, but 'Camelot' would remain in the traces of his passing. Wholeness and wellness was not *on* his body; it was not *in* his body. It was *around* it, in his wake. It was like a *negative trace* of his body: his body grasped not as an object or an image of an object but as a set of ordered motions *between* unlocalizable points suspended in the air. 'Wholeness' and happiness could be had by inhabiting the same virtual space as "Reagan." We could make our personal space coincide with his by going through the same motions. Of course, any repetition of the 'same' passages between points that are by nature unlocalizable will be different, a translation, an impersonation (a personification of the unpersonifiable subsumed by the Reagan name). Repeating "Reagan's" gesture with a difference, we actualize a quadrant of his virtual geography in our neighborhood, overlaying his super-abstract kinetic map on our terrain, like an invisible image of all we could be (were we as inhuman as he).

Second, the "Reagan" 'magic' seemed to inhere in his voice, his reassuring, mellifluous voice. His voice also drew patterns. Or rather, it set down rhythms, wrote musical notes in tune with the national anthem.

The insufficiencies of Reagan's brain, body, and body-image were compensated for in *abstract figures:* gestures and trajectories; and rhythms. These were *without content, nonvisual,* and *suprapersonal.* The word "figure" is therefore misleading. Call them *processual lines.* "Reagan"'s political effectiveness was to be found on that presymbolic, prelogical, *quasi-corporeal* level: in his ability to construct a *body without an image,* to "meld image and body in a space where they cannot be separated."[11]

I should have said his political effectiveness "is" to be found. "Reagan"'s body is still at work. Think of George Bush. He had the distinction of being the first candidate to win an election with a slogan he never spoke. "Read my lips" ("NO NEW TAXES"). Bush, lacking his predecessor's 'charisma,' resorted to reading his lines. It was Reagan who first rejected a tax increase by quoting Clint Eastwood (in 1985). A quote of a quote whose speaker remains unidentified: free indirect discourse. The campaign-period Bush, with his annoyingly squeaky voice and staccato, windmill-like gestures at the podium, was not a rousing orator. He had no choice but to be Reagan's "other fellow," to let himself be possessed of the spirit of Reagan-America, giving free indirect voice to it like a ventriloquist's puppet. The lack of symbolic or ideological cohesion evident between Reagan press sessions, or even from one phrase of Reagan's discourse to another, was telescoped into a single sentence of "Bushspeak," as though Bush were trying to master his master by condensing his permutational power into the smallest possible space. The second great political issue Bush campaigned on was the pledge of allegiance to the flag. He draped himself in the flag, as if the residual magic of its last occupant would transfer itself to him. He repeated Reagan's motions.

That is where the rest of "Reagan" went. Into Bush's body. Bush strove to make his personal space coincide with Reagan's virtual geography. Had Bush stood on his ground, he would never have had a chance. He was not 'presidential material.' So rather than trying to stand on his own two feet, he became "Reagan"'s better half, patiently waiting by the White House door for the footfalls of his master's missing limbs. but Reagan's ghost deserted him. Bush made one permutation too many in the fall of 1990 when he voiced that lipsynched phrase, almighty in its negativity but now flipped into the affirmative: "new taxes." He had already learned to talk in complete sentences and control his spastic oratorial style. He had become a man. A mere mortal, with an image problem. In other words, with an image. He lost what connection he had to the body without an image. He fell into direct speech in the first-person singular. As a consequence, his popularity plummeted to historical lows from which only Saddam Hussein could rescue him, and then only temporarily. No one likes Bush as a person.

The body without an image is the agency of political possession in us all. Reagan's body image is the measure of his archaism. Reagan's contemporary functioning, like that of every leader, resides in the body *without* an image.

A quick summary and some random conclusions:

The body is substended by a superabstract, quasi-corporeal space that has no content or qualities proper to it. It is nevertheless a full space. It has two dimensions: gesture/trajectory and rhythm. Better, potential gesture/trajectory and potential rhythm: lines on an invisible map and notes on a silent score. Actual gestures/trajectories and rhythms arise from it, or come to it—in any case embody it.

A particular body's qualities are defined by which and how many potential gestures/trajectories it incarnates. Its body image is their visual residue. A body image is less a static outline of the body in a typifying posture than a cumulative afterimage of its successive displacements. It is essentially kinetic (the body-as-motion, rather than the body-as-object).

A body's discourse is its vocal residue. That discourse is under no obligation to obey rules of logical cohesion. It is composed more as a musical composition whose phrasal variation responds to contextual cues than as a rational discourse ordered by a logos.

Symbolic associations and ideological contents arise at the mobile intersection of a body's visual and vocal residues. Just as there is nothing in principle requiring cohesion on either side, there is no a priori logic to their coupling. This does not mean that there can be no regularity in a given body's symbolizations and ideations. It means that where there is regularity, it is extrinsically determined. A body has the possibility of producing an infinitely varied play of meaning. But in practice, it is always circumscribed.

What limits it is the body of the leader. The body of the leader occupies a preeminent, quasi-corporeal space. It has social prestige, not for its inherent qualities or the superiority of its symbolizations and ideations but simply because its kinetic geography is more far-reaching. Its opportunities for leaving afterimages are more numerous and varied: It has almost unlimited media access. Its surfaces stretch forever and loop back on themselves. Its heights are higher, its multiplications more numerous. It can see itself as "one" would see it, occupying every pronoun position simultaneously. It can stand on every pedestal and don every flag. It is exemplary. It inhabits most fully the collective gap. Its name sums up the in-between of all bodies.

Just as the prestige of the statue or flag can rub off on the exemplary body, some of its accumulated prestige can rub off on a common body that makes its kinetic geography coincide with a quadrant of the leader's virtual space. The body of the leader raises its permutational potential to the highest power only in order to limit that of others. It uses its prestige-value to garner an apparent monopoly on infinity. A common body pales in comparison with the glitter of the riveting political polestar. What can a poor body do but share the glory of the leader by actualizing in its own neighborhood a restricted set of the leader's gloriously expansive permutations? The common body is reduced to imaging a selected set of gestures-trajectories and sounding a selected set of rhythms authorized by the body of the leader and in coupling them forms a 'private' world of symbolizations and ideations in unity with the national destiny. This is not identification per se. Identification is when the symbolizations and ideations are given regular enough patterns that the body can consistently and relatively unambiguously locate its "I" in them. The base selection of symbolizations and ideations of which identification is the regularization is more a line of continual variations than a subject position. It is a function of a technology of attention, not a structure of subjectivity. It is made by remote control: Because the image and words associated with the body of the leader have been made to be everywhere, and to be on average alluring ("prestigious"), some will inevitably be picked up then patterned, by institutions such as school and army, into socially affirmed self-positionings. Positioned subjectivity is the result of a presubjective technological seduction that is also an induction into a curtailed region of potential. If subjectivity has a structure, it is that of a collectively contracted bad habit.

"Reagan"'s body is in the last analysis not a body at all. It is a quasi-corporeal space emanating from bodies and with which bodies can be made to coincide. It is in the first and last instance impersonal. It adheres in essence to no body in particular, not even "Reagan"'s. It lures bodies. It possesses them.

The system of symbolic permutations actualized by the body of the leader may contradict itself. As may the system of ideational or ideological permutations. And the system of symbolic permutations may contradict the system of ideological permutations. It doesn't matter. Once again, their cohesion is assured on another, supplementary level that is presymbolic and prediscursive. Visual images and linguistic contents translate or recapitulate, at least indirectly, that quasi-corporeal level *and* its supplementarity. The exemplary body is simultaneously present and absent: present in its audiovisual permutations, absent in the super-abstract dimension of quasi-corporeality from which those permutations arise. In special circumstances, this simultaneous presence and absence can be given a direct image: For example, in an infinite video relay at a Republican Convention that simultaneously multiplies and disappears it. Most images of the leader's body are less ambitious. They focus either on its presence or its absence and contain the elided term implicitly or as an aftereffect. All images of the leader's body are unstable. They do not necessarily add up to a structure, even a decentered one. A common body *may* select a structural approach to the body of the leader or be structured by its lack. However, its subjectifying powers of absence, no less than its vaunted unity, will always remain in the I of the beholder.

But ...

The infinite permutability of the body of the leader and its followers is not as free-flowing as I have made it out to be. Two facts have been bracketed:

1. The image of the body of the leader, in spite of its fluidity, has a base gender: masculine. By "base gender" is meant: the gender the body most often returns to, just as batters in the sport figuring most prominently in American political discourse—baseball—always get another chance to come to the plate again, if not in this inning, then the next, if not in the next inning, then at least in the next game. Masculinity is the body of the leader's home base. This, in concert with institutional mechanisms at work on other levels, skews the ability of common bodies to share equally in the glory of the body of the leader. Bodies gendered feminine rarely come to bat. They tend to be placed on the "absence" side of the body, equated with the body without an image as "matrix" of existence, symbolically translated into the mother-womb. This means that they tend to be written out of series of actual permutations composing the substance of unity (or written into the substance of unity as a version of originary lack). As a consequence, they are relegated on average to lower prestige value and a smaller share of the social product whose distribution is indexed to it.

2. There is an apparent dissymmetry in the two dimensions of quasi-corporeality. The rhythm of the voice often takes precedence over gesture-trajectory. The symbolizations and ideations associated with the body of the leader can be controlled to a certain degree by the repetition of phrases. Privileged symbolizations and ideations form by dint of verbal redundancy. These are coupled with stereotyped gestures-trajectories, which exert a powerful impact on the selections made by common bodies. An amazing level of conformity is observed, in spite of the formal possibility of open-ended permutation. Common bodies tend to regularize their audiovisual actualizations into clichéd subjectivities and life's paths.

"Reagan"'s contemporaneity is also his despotism: his ability to monopolize the body without an image, obliging other bodies to limit themselves to a scant repertory of bodies with an image. A predictable image. A controlled image.

"Reagan"'s functionality is as a converter of the sightless, silent in-between to images and meanings embodying control.

It may seem odd that an essay that has insisted throughout on bodily potential for invention and has argued consistently against structural and poststructural paradigms that ground "one"'s potential in a constricting a priori (whatever its nature: whether a normalizing family drama, an irresolvable metaphysics of absence/presence, or the cynicism of simulational free-play) should end with an evocation of social control. Control, as it is conceived of here, is not a structural hegemony. It is philosophically contingent—even if it can be asserted that it is empirically ubiquitous. The theoretical gambit has been to conceive of determination as extrinsic. Not in order to deny the reality of such limitative mechanisms as forced gendering and social inequality. In order to be able to imagine a future without them.

In spite of the conservative, even fascistic, turn "Reagan" effected in American politics, the country overall remained strongly pluralistic throughout the 1980s. If anything, the ethnic, religious, and sexual multiplicity it encompassed increased. The heterogeneous terms that a substance of unity homogenizes on its chosen surface always retain their heterogeneity on another level, though muted. Despite all the rightwing rhetoric, Reagan-Bush America has fortunately not been willing to make the political decisions that would be necessary to force the social field into a strictly disciplined homology between body, family, and country. In the 1990s, relatively large sectors still remain, in spite of it all, unsubordinated to the symbolism of the unifying body, its regularizing ideology, and the self-satisfied aestheticism of contenting oneself with noting the hyperreality of both. If these bodies are to have a future as ample as their present, they will need a logic that can grasp the processes of seduction/induction threatening to curtail them as simultaneously determining and extrinsic to their potential.

Cultural circling of the kind that turned large swathes of the 1980s into a rerun of the 1950s, and threatens to turn the 1990s into a rerun of the 1980s, is a powerful political force in late capitalist society. It occurs anytime an attempt is made to subsume multiplicity in a shared substance or project it onto a common surface. Wherever there is a drive for unity, there will be a driving tension between past and present, presence and absence, immanence and transcendence, played out in a serial recycling of off-balance images whose only solidity is provided by a structural homology between levels and desires designed to erase their particularity. Such is the patriotic equation. Red, white, and blue. The body is the nation. The nation is a family. The family is a motherland. The spirit of the nation is in mother's milk. It is in the air we breathe. The mother is the father. The father is sexless. He is virile. He has a phallus, or doesn't, or we are it. The baby is a flag. The leg is a phallus. The president is an anus. All true. But it doesn't really matter if it's true or false. Because the symbolic circling is not the only thing going. Ideations are also circling. And the symbolic images and ideological contents meld into a mega-feedback loop that reaches an even higher power of infinity than either one alone, blurring the very distinction between conscious and unconscious, real and fake, true and false.

Yet in the giddy swirl of that vicious circle, there is always a region of clarity, at least locally, at least for a moment, when a particular image or idea is actualized. And one always is, however transitorily. Where one is, there is always at least a hint of body. Because the anus is *also* an anus, and a leg *in addition to* being a phallus is still a leg. No, we are not preamputated. Our cuts enable reconnection. We are not regressed. Our holes are new and for the future.

Only when we can learn to say that with conviction will the circling stop. Only when we make permutation a compounding of differences rather than a reductive equation between like terms will the body of the leader die. Only then will the master's masculine body-image and voice lose its seductive-inductive powers of conformity and curtailment.

There is always body. *Il y a toujours du corps.* There is always an excess no image or idea can contain. It is not above, in a higher realm we might attain. It is not below, as the ground we stand on. It is inter-. Liminal. It is not material, but it is: in its wake. Suspended in the air we will not breathe. It is our only homeland. We cannot come to it because we are already there. In kinetic geographies so particular they defy abstraction. In superabstract gesture/trajectories and rhythms that coincide irrevocably with the movement of a life. Neither leg nor anus has general existence. A leg, anything of body, is never reducible to an image or idea, even if it is never completely detachable from them. Bodiness is *this*. It is the here-and-now of images and ideas, compounded and disjoined.

A modest proposal: Consider a logic of the quasi-corporeal, understood as the synthetic thisness of body-in-motion, as a possible way out of the broken record of the symbolic, the ideological, the cynicism of their mega-feedback loop, and the social control in symbiosis with it all. Revive the body—without an image, and in excess of any unifying substance. Uncouple it from seductive and inductive powers of the body of the leader by deducting from it masculinity and voice. Come to "one"'s impersonal potential. Dispossess.

NOTES

This essay is an abridged and modified version of Chapter 3 of *First and Last Emperors* (New York: Autonomedia, 1992).

1. Ronald Reagan, with Richard B. Hubler, *Where's the Rest of Me?* (New York: Karz Publishers, 1981), p. 3.

2. Photograph by Tina Paul of a sculpture by Adam Kurtzman, *New York Times,* October 7, 1986, editorial page.

3. Reagan was the "thumbs up" president (in the same way that Winston Churchill was a "V for Victory" man). The thumbs up sign expressed Reagan's supposed restoration of America's confidence in itself, which is still regularly cited as his greatest achievement. An illustration printed on the editorial page of the *New York Times* (January 5, 1987, p. A17) replaced the fingers of a fist making the thumbs up sign with Reagan's facial features, graphi-

cally representing him as a multiplicity of appendages adding up to a First Digit rising proudly above the others. It may be noted that this preeminent thumb replaces Reagan's most admired body part: his hairdo. Hair dye is another embodiment of the all-powerful life-giving fluid (the fountain of youth has not only been found, it has been bottled).

4. Kitty Kelley, *Nancy Reagan: The Unauthorized Biography* (New York: Simon & Schuster, 1990), p. 358.

5. The preceding statements from Reagan and Hubler, *Where Is the Rest of Me?* are to found on pp. 3–8, 301. Many are quoted in Michael Rogin, "Ronald Reagan, the Movie," *Ronald Reagan, the Movie, and Other Episodes in Political Demonology* (Berkeley: University of California Press, 1987), pp. 17–27, 32–33. This essay owes much to Rogin's suggestive essay, which provided a number of leads on Reagan body parts (but is written from a very different theoretical viewpoint).

6. According to a *New York Times* (January 18, 1989, p. A14) chart of Reagan's approval ratings, his popularity peaked twice in the upper 60's percentile range, once after the attempted assassination, and again after the bombing of Libya, which occurred during an extended period of consistently high ratings following his second inauguration.

7. Rogin, "Ronald Reagan, the Movie," provides a number of examples.

8. Examples are a *Gone with the Wind* poster, widely distributed during his first term, showing Ronald "Rhett" Reagan carrying Margaret "Scarlett" Thatcher in his arms; a postcard featuring a "Portrait of Ronald Reagan as Centaur" (photo of an oil painting by Komar and Melamid, 1981–1982, Editions Vormgeving, Rotterdam); and a "Mister America" postcard entitled "Our Ronnie" depicting Reagan as a body builder (City Sights, Boundhead, Ontario).

9. "Unofficial White House Photo," copyright 1981 by Alfred Gescheidt. Distributed by the American Postcard Co.

10. Diane Rubenstein, "This is Not a President: Baudrillard, Bush, and Enchanted Simulation," *The Hysterical Male: New Feminist Theory*, ed. Arthur and Marilouise Kroker (Montreal: New World Perspectives, 1990), pp. 253–255.

11. Giorgio Agamben, *La communauté qui vient. Théorie de la singularité* (Paris: Seuil, 1990), pp. 54–55 (forthcoming in English translation from University of Minnesota Press).

PART FOUR

TORTURE, KNOWLEDGE, & THE STATE

13

Subjected Bodies, Science, and the State: Francis Bacon, Torturer

PAGE DUBOIS

IN HIS ESSAY "Of Adversity," Francis Bacon enacted a characteristic move evocative of his allegories of ancient myth, of his psychology, of his scientific method, and of his practices as a servant of the Elizabethan and Jacobean state: "Certainly virtue is like precious odours, most fragrant when they are incensed, or crushed."[1] Phenomenologically, this observation seems to be a particularly telling one; for Bacon, exemplar of enlightenment, the quintessences of persons and things emerge under aggressive, even violent treatment.

Theodor Adorno and Max Horkheimer's *Dialectic of Enlightenment* begins with an invocation of Francis Bacon. The authors, citing Voltaire, call him "father of experimental philosophy" and allow him to set forth the program of enlightenment. Bacon named the obstacles that stand in the way of a scientific understanding of the world—idols of the theater, of the marketplace, of the tribe, and of the cave. His program was meant to enable human beings to overcome these obstacles and thus achieve a position of dominance over intractable matter. "The human mind, which overcomes superstition, is to hold sway over a disenchanted nature."[2] For Horkheimer and Adorno, those great thinkers of the contradictions and impossibilities of life in the twentieth century, Bacon stands for the irresistible and terrible process they delineate, the progress of knowledge and domination leading always and inevitably to an ever-greater alienation of human beings from nature. Bacon is the initiator of the early modern phase of the process, taking up the task from those earlier thinkers who replaced myth with philosophy, animism with monotheism, who carved out of the most archaic life a dominating, objectifying, alienating human existence that proceeded to enslave all human beings because of their need to maintain their distance, their separation from nature.

Bacon serves Horkheimer and Adorno as a historical figure, as an eloquent spokesman for the dialectic of enlightenment. Bacon exemplifies the individual in search of control over nature and stands as one compelling moment in Horkheimer and Adorno's elegant argument concerning the price all human beings pay for civilization. The rhetorical figure they employ, the *exemplum,* in Greek *paradeigma,* is treated in Aristotle's *Rhetoric* as a device of persuasion; Aristotle contrasts the example with the enthymeme, as a form of induction.[3] He further divides argument by example into two kinds—"the use of a parallel from the facts of history," and "the use of an invented parallel."[4] He uses, as an example of the invented parallel example, a fable that curiously recapitulates the theme of domination over nature that runs through my own essay. He recalls Stesichorus' telling of this fable, to convince the people of the city of Himera not to give the tyrant Phalaris a bodyguard: "There was a horse that had a meadow all to himself, until a stag came and began to spoil his pasturage. Thirsting for revenge, the horse went to the man, and asked: 'Could you help me to punish the stag?' 'Yes,' said the man, 'if you will let me bridle you, and mount upon your back with javelins in my hand.' The horse agreed, and was mounted; but, instead of getting his revenge, he became the slave of the man." So enlightenment seems a project of liberation; it enslaves as it seems to liberate. Stesichorus' fable, like many another example, works to engage an audience in sympathy through a sort of identification; we imagine ourselves bridled and domesticated like Stesichorus' horse.

Example is a particularly powerful and double-edged instrument of argument. Its dangers lie in the fact that a single counterexample can refute an argument based on a series of examples, and also in that a listener, a reader, can herself interpret an example, can turn it, make it prove more than the argument in question or something quite otherwise. I want to touch here on this rhetorical figure, considering not only the ways in which the rhetoric of example functions in Bacon's work itself but also how Bacon's work can serve as an example for us of a totalizing early-modern program of domination. In particular, I want to consider Bacon's rhetoric concerning inquisition—how it draws on and justifies his legal service to the Elizabethan and Jacobean state and how legal inquisition itself derives justification by a sort of rhetorical adjustment of legal discourse during the time of Bacon's service. At the center of my analysis will be torture, corporeal and metaphorical.

Natural Philosopher, Man of Science

I will focus initially not on torture of the body per se but rather on the use of rhetorical references to torture, to Bacon's many figures of speech and exempla that rely on torture to support his view of the proper role of the natural philosopher or scientist-to-be. Again and again Bacon returns to a description of the man of enlightenment, the practitioner of his new methods, as an inquisitor engaging in the torture of nature. Let me consider first Bacon's text called *De Sapientia Veterum,* published in 1609.[5] This little book consists of a series of thirty-one parables, short narratives recounting the myths told of various characters from the domain of Greek mythology. After telling their stories, Bacon interprets the narratives in terms of his own concerns, parting the "vaile of fiction" that had interposed itself between the mysteries and secrets of earliest antiquity and the current day. He means to interpret these "fables," "parables," "allegories," "tropes," and "similes" so as to tear aside the veil from ancient fictions. They are "sacred reliques or abstracted ayres of better times"; their interpretation is an "inlightning and laying open of obscurities."[6]

In a revealing passage glossing the myth of Typhon, in a section called "*Typhon, or a Rebell*," Bacon describes the battle between the master of heaven and the rebellious Typhon: "This Fable seemes to point at the variable fortune of Princes, and the rebellious insurrection of Traytors in a State."[7] When the prince's power is challenged by the people, "there followes a sort of murmuring or discontent in the State, shadowed by the infancie of *Typhone* which being nurst by the naturall pravitie and clownish malignitie of the vulgar sort (unto Princes as infectious as Serpents) ... at last breakes out into open Rebellion, which ... is represented by the monstrous deformity of *Typhon*."[8] Bacon, being a man of law and order, rejoices in the allegorical suppression of such rebellion, as Jupiter crushes Typhon under Mount Etna.

This text's sixth book contains another elaborate allegory concerning Pan as the representation of Nature itself, Pan who is said to have bound Typhon. Bacon glosses this mythological episode in the following manner:

> To the same may be interpreted his catching of Typhon in a net: for howsoever there may sometimes happen vast and unwonted Tumors (as the name of Typhon imports) either in the sea or in the ayre, or in the earth, or else where, yet Nature doth intangle in an intricate toile, and curbe & restraine, as it were, with a chain of Adamant (*Reti inextricabili implicat, & coercet, & veluti catena adamantina devincat*) the excesses and insolences of these kinds of bodies.[9]

Pan's binding of Typhon—Nature's chaining up such rebellions and "tumors" as the monster represents—naturalizes both the process of bondage and the suppression of rebellion against princes.

In the thirteenth section of this text, on Proteus, the polymorphous god of the sea is said to stand for Matter. Here too, we find the motifs of binding, control, and domination in language that recalls the practices of torture. Bacon recalls that anyone who desired to consult with Proteus, "he who desired his advice in any thing, could by no other meanes obteine it, but by catching him in Manacles, and holding him fast therewith (*nisi eum manicis comprehensum vinclis constringeret*)."[10] Bacon uses this exemplum to describe the efforts of the "Minister of Nature," that man who seeks to know the secrets of matter. He points out that the pursuer vexes and urges matter, but she flees and changes herself into strange forms. Matter is consistently here represented by the feminine pronoun; the male god Proteus is metamorphosed in Bacon's explication and becomes a female subject to misogynous male pursuit.[11] He concludes, apropos of the techniques of this pursuit, "The reason of which constraint or binding will bee more facile and expedite, if Matter be laide hold on by Manacles, that is, by extremities."[12] The exemplum of the *Odyssey*, Menelaus' interview with Proteus, is made retroactively to testify to the necessity of constraint of matter.

Prometheus, in *De Sapientia Veterum*, is called "the state of man, *Status hominis*." This figure is one of the most elaborately commented upon of all those creatures from classical mythology adduced in the text to support Bacon's view of nature and man's relationship to it; like many others, Prometheus undergoes domination at the hands of his master. Bacon explains that what brought about the torment of Prometheus, chained to Caucasus, was his attempt to deflower the virgin goddess of wisdom, Minerva. He interprets this moment in the myth as an argument for grasping the difference between humanity and divinity and for respecting the divine, not attempting to subject it to "sense and reason." Prometheus, like Typhon and Proteus, exemplifies necessary subjection, resistance subjected to proper authority:

> At last *Iupiter* laying many and grieuous crimes to *Prometheus* his charge … cast him into chaines, and doomd him to perpetuall torment (*& ad perpetuous cruciatus damnavit*): and by *Iupiters* command, was brought to the mountaine *Caucasus*, and there bound fast to a pillar that he could not stirre; there came an Eagle also, that euery day sat tyring upon his liuar, and wasted it, but as much as was eaten in the day, grew againe in the night, that matter for torment to work upon might neuer decay.[13]

Bacon glosses this parable not as an example of the workings of the divine intelligence upon nature or matter, nor as an example of the noble rebel, the ally of humankind, against tyranny. Rather, following his naming of Prometheus as the state of man, he construes the narrative in terms of the contrast between the man of prudence, Prometheus, and his improvident brother, Epimetheus. The torments of the Eagle are the cares and troubles and "intestine feares" with which men of prudence torment themselves: "For beeing chained to the pillar of necessitie, they are afflicted with innumerable cogitations (which because they are very swift, may bee fitly compared to an Eagle) and those griping, and, as it were, gnawing and devouring the liuer, unlesse sometimes, as it were by night, it may bee they get a little recreation and ease of mind, but so, as that they are againe suddenly assaulted with fresh anxieties and feares."[14] The man of science, the natural philosopher himself, must be rescued from torment (*supplicium*) by Hercules, who exemplifies fortitude and constancy of mind. The labor of the mind is itself occasion for torture in Bacon's view; he sees torment everywhere—in the relationship of the philosopher to matter and nature, in the relationship of the thinker to his own consciousness. The intellectual occupies more than one position, tormenting and tormented both. Intellectual man must enslave himself, engage in self-domination; the tortured experimental philosopher inflicts pain on himself even as he chastises nature. And the pain inflicted by the philosopher on himself can further serve as justification of the pain of others who serve the philosopher, whose labor provides the material support for his philosophy.

Glossing the myth of the Sphinx in *The Wisedome of the Ancients*, Bacon intermittently refers to the monster as male, although the classical Sphinx was a dreadful and murderous female creature. Science, says Bacon, is a monster like the Sphinx, having sharp and hooked talons (or "talents"), because science fastens upon the mind and holds it, because wise men's words are "like goads" and "like nailes driven farre in."[15] The effects of science, when it proceeds from pure knowledge to practice, similarly torment the studious man:

> for so long as there is no other ende of studie and meditation, then to know; the understanding is not rackt (*nec in Arcto ponitur*) and imprisoned, but enjoyes freedome and libertie, ... but when once these *Aenigmaes* are delivered by the Muses to *Sphinx*, that is, to practise, so that it bee sollicited and urged by action, and election, and determination; then they beginne to be troublesome and raging; and unlesse they be resolved and expedited, they doe wonderfully torment and vexe the minds of men, distracting, and in a manner rending them into sundry parts. (*animos hominum miris modis torquent & vexant, & in omnes partes distrahunt, & plane lacerant.*)[16]

Bacon returns to these scenes of torments, or racks, imprisonment, rending, and dismemberment; on the side of matter, nature, and the natural philosopher, the knower and the known are described again and again in terms of violence, punishment, and coercion. Although it could be said that ancient mythology itself abounds in such themes, it is remarkable that many early modern readers and rewriters of Ovidian myth focused on themes of erotic desire, pursuit, rape, and metamorphosis rather than on these scenes of torment and punishment that seem to fascinate Bacon.

In a famous allegorical reading, Adorno and Horkheimer interpret the myth of Odysseus and the Sirens in their *Dialectic of Enlightenment*. "Odysseus recognizes the archaic superior power of the song even when, as a technically enlightened man, he has himself bound."[17] Pleasure tempts the seeker after enlightenment, who must constrain himself, that nature in him, his body. For Adorno and Horkheimer, Odysseus' ambivalent posture, his listening to the Sirens even has he has himself bound to the mast, is a perfect emblem of enlightened man, who faces temptation, acknowledges it, is pained and tormented by it and nonetheless responds by dominating his own impulses toward pleasure, by binding himself and resisting temptation.

Bacon too considers these ancient singers. His treatise on the ancients, his mining of the significance of ancient myths, his explication of the emblems of antiquity, ends with "The Sirenes, or Pleasures." His theme is, as we might expect, resistance to pleasure. While the "meaner and baser sorte of people" will need to stop their ears when confronted with "the wicked enticements of pleasures," the heroic Ulysses bound himself to the mast and survived the Sirens' song; this same Ulysses who "so peremptorily interdicted all pestilent counsels and flatteries of his companions, as the most dangerous and pernicious poisons to captivate the mind."[18] Like Ulysses, Orpheus succeeded in resisting the Sirens, he by out-singing them, hymning the praises of the gods; Bacon finds this to be the most admirable approach to seductive pleasures. The Sirens must be opposed in the name of a higher good; divine meditations will subdue "all sensuall pleasures." Bacon's world is full of dangers, racks, torments, coercions; the natural philosopher must enchain the natural world lest he be enchained or enchanted by it.

The scientist's position in relation to nature, as teased out of ancient mythology, reflects a disposition on Bacon's part to see his inquiry as inquisition, to conceive of the relationship between nature and himself as one of temptation and punishment. In contrast to the Catholic's reliance on penance and confession, Bacon exhibits a Protestant faith in self-mastery, self-abnegation, and abstinence. Men must master their own fallen nature. And in the struggle between human beings and nature, adversity reveals essence. In his discussion of the "Prerogatives of Man" in *De Augmentis,* Bacon praises various historical figures for their demonstration of the highest "points" in human nature. The great Caesar, under the press of Roman state affairs, could dictate to five secretaries at once. The example Bacon uses of intellectual virtues is Anaxarchus, whose mind controlled his body to such a degree that "when questioned under torture, (he) bit out his own tongue ... and spat it into the face of the tyrant."[19] He continues in this vein by discussing the torture of the Burgundian who murdered the Prince of Orange: "being beaten with rods of iron and torn with red-hot pincers, he uttered not a single groan; nay, when something aloft broke and fell on the head of a bystander, the half-burnt wretch laughed in the midst of his torments."[20] The victims of torture, like the dictating Caesar, show their mettle under stress; like nature pressed hard by the intellectual inquisitor, they demonstrate unalloyed their refined qualities.

The fascination with scenes of torment, the belief that torment *produces quintessence, is* extended to Bacon's programmatic statements concerning his scientific method, and to his descriptions of particular experimental techniques. In discussing the similarities between animate and inanimate bodies, for example, Bacons uses these words: "as animals are liable to many kinds and various descriptions of pains (such as those of burning, of intense cold, of pricking, squeezing, stretching, and the like), so is it most certain, that the same circumstances ... happen to inanimate bodies, such as wood or stone, when burnt, frozen, pricked, cut, bent, bruised, and the like."[21] Although in the argument here Bacon seems almost to imagine sensation in the inanimate, and therefore to empathize with tormented matter, nonetheless the desire of the scientist to work upon matter with techniques of violence recurs throughout the corpus. Bacon returns to the figure of Proteus to justify his methods, to insist that the "straitening" of nature should be the task of the natural philosopher. He argues: "For like as man's disposition is never well known or proved till he be crossed, nor Proteus ever changed shapes till he was straitened and held fast; so nature exhibits herself more clearly under the trials and vexations of art than when left to herself."[22] The Burgundian revealed himself under torture, just as the ancient mythological figure held fast by Menelaus finally resumed his natural shape under punishment, just as nature reveals herself to the scientist. Bacon establishes an atmosphere for inquiry radically different from that of the Aristotelian scientific works, in which the reader finds the natural philosopher engaged in patient observation of nature, and also from the alchemical texts in which the operative methodological analogy is often one of seduction, the wooing of recalcitrant matter to perform the tasks required by the alchemist.

Earlier in *De Augmentis,* Bacon speaks of nature, again in the feminine, and describes a particularly intrusive version of his method, meant to force nature, to straiten her, to drive her to reveal her essence: "For you have but to follow and as it were hound nature in her wanderings, and you will be able, when you like, to lead and drive her afterwards to the same place again. ... Neither ought a man to make scruple of entering and penetrating into these holes and corners (of sorceries, witchcraft, etc.), when the inquisition of truth is his sole object."[23] If the alchemist seduces nature, the actions of the natural philosopher verge on rape. Here nature, the woman, practicioner of sorcery, contains secrets that must be hounded and penetrated by the man of science. The division and hierarchy between mind and nature is, as often, inscribed as a gender hierarchy, and the violence and coercion enacted toward women resonate in the allegory of domination.

Bacon the rhetorician is quite conscious of the ways in which his metaphors and figures of thought in general play on the analogy between judicial interrogation and his inquisition of nature. The classical exempla afford him the opportunity to gloss in detail the relationships between master and subject, between tormentor and tormented; he sees represented in the myths of antiquity, in the ancient representations and allegories of nature, a vulnerable terrain, available like nature itself to be mined, confined, chained, and tormented by the natural philosopher, who is in turn endangered by similar forces, the torments of his own ideas, the seductions of pleasures.

Lord Chancellor, Man of State

In the "Preparative Towards a Natural and Experimental History," Bacon wittily alludes to the analogy he often draws between the interrogation of matter and the forensic practices of the Tudor and Stuart state. Summing up his project, he says: "I mean (according to the practice in civil causes) in this great Plea or Suit granted by the divine favour and providence (whereby the human race seeks to recover its right over nature), to examine nature herself and the arts upon interrogatories (*super articulos*)."[24] This is the language of the court. In legal discourse, an interrogatory is "a question formally put, or drawn up in writing to be put, to an accused person or a witness." (*OED*) Bacon sees himself as putting questions to nature, interrogating her as an accused, as a witness. His scientific method depends on the analogy between these two differing realms of the search for knowledge, that of the search for the truth of matter, and that of the pursuit of truth in judicial inquiry.

Beginning in the fifteenth century, part of the process of interrogating witnesses and accused persons in England, in some kinds of legal proceedings, was torture.[25] Although torture had long been employed in continental ecclesiastical and civil prosecutions, based on Roman law, it seems to have been less frequently employed in England in part because of the common law's ban on self-incrimination. Nonetheless, by the time at which Bacon writes of putting nature to the question, of putting her on the "rack," he refers to a current instrument of torture. In *Measure for Measure,* the Duke (in disguise) is threatened with racking:

> ESCALUS: To the rack with him—We'll touze you joint by joint But we will
> know this purpose—What! Unjust?
> DUKE: Be not so hot; the duke dare no more stretch this finger of mine
> than he dare rack his own. (V, 1)

("Touze" means to handle roughly, "to pull out of joint, to rack.")[26] The rack was, according to James Heath, "a rectangular wooden frame, with transverse rollers, one near each end, with bearings on its sides, ... deep enough for the rollers to be turned when it was standing on the ground."[27] The accused, or the witness, was placed on the rack and stretched, sometimes left in this position after those supervising the torture had left the torture chamber. William Allen recounts various incidents of torture on the rack in a text published first in Rheims in 1582. He describes in some detail the experiences of Alexander Briant as reported to him. Although allowances must be made for the rhetorical occasion of Allen's text, the ostensible motive of exciting sympathy for Catholic martyrs in England, the scene is rather vivid: "He was even to the dismembring of his body rent and torne upon the rack. ... Yet the next day following, notwithstanding the great distemperature and soreness of his body, his senses being dead, and his bloud congealed (for this is the effect of racking), he was brought to the torture againe, and there stretched with greater severitie than before."[28] Heath also notes that, according to the contemporary Diary of Edward Rishton, Briant was interrogated on March 27, 1581, "sharp needles being thrust under his fingernails."[29]

We know that Bacon supervised torture and defended torture as a legal instrument. On February 2, 1597, a warrant was issued to "Mr. Frauncis Bacon" and others concerning William Tomson, "a very lewde and dangerous person, ... charged to have a purpose to burne her Majestie's shipps, or to doe some notable villanye." According to the Acts of the Privy Council, the letter said: "if by faire meanes or perswasions he shall not be moved to reveale unto you the whole truth in these matters, then you shall by vertue heerof cause him to be put to the manacles, or the torture of the racke, as in like cases has been used, thereby to force him to declare the truthe."[30] Similar letters and warrants noted by the Council's records and addressed to Bacon commanding him to torture "one Gerratt, a Jesuite" and Valentin Thomas.

In fact, although there was considerable doubt and debate concerning the use of torture in English law because common law did not allow the accused's own testimony to convict him, Bacon takes for granted the use of torture as a means of "discovery." In a text called "Certain Considerations Touching the Better Pacification and Edification of the Church of England," written to King James in 1603, Bacon, discussing the governing of bishops, reviews the legal authority of the bishops. He brings up a point that he considers needs reform, that is, the oath *ex officio,* which had been used to require accused persons to accuse themselves and plead guilty to unnamed charges, or "blanks," rather than to specified charges and accusations. In the course of arguing against this practice, Bacon explains his position on torture in relation to such cases: "By the laws of England no man is bound to accuse himself. In the highest cases of treasons, torture is used for discovery, and not for evidence."[31] That is, a confession exacted under torture goes against the law against self-incrimination, but information gathered by torturing the accused can be pursued and used to incriminate others. Bacon has no objection to torture per se, but only to its improper use when it is employed in violation of the traditions of English common law.

And indeed, in a subsequent case, prosecuted during the rule of James, we find Bacon again receiving a letter and warrant authorizing torture and asking him to witness it this time in person. A clergyman named Edmund Peacham had made charges against his own bishop; his house was searched and there was found a sermon warning of imminent judgment, the king's death, slaughter of his officers, and rebellion among the people. The Privy Council considered these papers treasonous and sent Peacham to the Tower. He was examined by the Privy Council and, although he admitted that the papers were in his own handwriting, he was found to give insufficient information concerning the possibilities of a general conspiracy. On January 18, 1614, the members of the council sent a warrant addressed to Bacon, among others:

> These shall be therefore in his Majesty's name to will and require you and every of you to repair with what convenient diligence you may unto the Tower, and there to call before you the said Peacham, and to examine him strictly upon such interrogatories concerning the said book as you shall think fit and necessary for the manifestation of the truth, and if you find him obstinate and perverse and not otherwise willing or ready to tell the truth, then to put him to the manacles, as in your discretion you shall see occasion.[32]

The nineteenth-century editor of the *Letters and Life* of Bacon, contained in the *Works,* points out that such a warrant, although not often issued during the reign of James, would not have excited resistance, since such warrants were relatively common, at least thirty-eight having been recorded during the reign of Elizabeth:

"the Crown then assumed the right to put any commoner to torture for what it judged to be obstinacy in refusing to answer interrogatories."[33]

The manacles and their use are described by James Heath: "Two wrist-irons were put onto the examinate, each iron having, at right angles to its own aperture, a fixing-ring. When the examinate's arms were above his head, a rod ... was slipped through one of the fixing rings, through a staple projecting from an upright—or, no doubt, from a wall—and through the other ring and then secured by dropping a pin into a hole."[34] The accused was then often suspended clear of the ground, hanging by his hands, and in one recorded case, left with his heels strapped to his thighs. This particular method of torture is reminiscent of crucifixion, the practice of which is recalled in Bacon's remarks in Latin in *De Sapientia Veterum* on Jupiter's binding of Prometheus: "*& ad perpetuos cruciatus damnavit.*" There Bacon also speaks of Proteus as bound in *manicis ... vinclis.*[35]

Although some historians have disputed the claim that such torture actually occurred, saying that the accounts of torture depend on the evidence of the accused alone, and especially on lurid narratives of Catholic martyrs, in the case of Edmund Peacham a document testifies not only to the warrant's having been carried out but also the presence of Bacon at the torture and interrogation. This document consists of a list of the "interrogatories" upon which Peacham was to be examined, both general and particular. It concludes: "Upon these interrogatories, Peacham this day was examined before torture, in torture, between tortures, and after torture. Notwithstanding, nothing could be drawn from him, he still persisting in his obstinate and insensible denials, and former answers."[36] The document is signed by "Fr. Bacon," among others, and dated January 19, 1614.

There is some evidence that the king was worried about the outcome of this case, perhaps fearing that the judges might acquit Peacham. The victim's susceptibility to torture might have been assumed to be great; in a subsequent letter the king describes him as "an old, unable and unweildy (*sic*) man."[37] Bacon, two days after the torture session, wrote to the king in a slightly cryptic letter, suggesting not only that the king's people must stick together in this time of crisis but also underlining his own loyalty in the cause:

> It grieveth me exceedingly that your Majesty should be so much troubled with this matter of Peacham, whose raging devil seemeth to be turned into a dumb devil. But although we are driven to make our way through questions (which I wish were otherwise,) yet I hope well the end will be good. But then every man must put to his helping hand. For else I must say to your Majesty in this and the like cases, as St. Paul said to the centurion when some of the mariners had an eye to the cock-boat, *Except these stay in the ship ye cannot be safe.*[38]

The rhetoric of this letter is especially interesting. Bacon makes a little joke about Peacham's dumbness. Although he had admired the exemplary Anaxarchus for his self-mutilation in the face of torture, Bacon does not extend his admiration of the intellectual virtues to the silent Peacham. He expresses regret about the necessity for torture, a common topos among torturers, a topos that blames the victim for obstinacy and for requiring the unwilling agent of the law to resort to unpleasant methods.[39] (The nautico-Biblical language of the last lines reminds me of nothing so much as the last days of the administration of Richard M. Nixon, when there was much talk of who was "on board," of leaving opponents to "twist slowly in the wind," of "rats deserting a sinking ship.") A few days later still, Bacon again addressed the king in the matter of Peacham: "First, for the regularity which your Majesty ... doth prudently prescribe in examining and taking examinations, I subscribe to it; only I will say for myself, that I was not at this time the principal examiner."[40] Is this a rat deserting the sinking torture ship? Further on in the text Bacon says disparagingly of Justice Haughton, one of the judges of the King's Bench who was to deal with Peacham's cause, when he wanted to confer with the other judges against Bacon's wishes, that he was "a soft man." (Reminiscent of Margaret Thatcher's epithet, "wet," to apply to the more "liberal" members of her party?)

Although the case of Peacham clearly aroused some controversy, the use of torture continued in the reign of James. We find, for example, the case of Samuel Peacock, accused of affecting the king's judgment by means of sorcery. Bacon, by then Lord Chancellor, in a letter to the king dated February 10, 1619, advocates torture: "we proceed in Peacock's examinations; for although there have been very good diligence used, yet certainly we are not at the bottom. ... But I make no judgment yet, but will go on with all diligence; and if it may not be done other wise, it is fit Peacock be put to torture. He deserveth it as well as Peacham did."[41] The fact that Peacham is mentioned here, after a five-year interval, suggests that the use of torture for these cases of treason was relatively infrequent, and that Bacon may have felt uneasy about advocating it and desirous of locating a precedent for Peacock's torture. It is probable, however, that this suggested torture was carried out in fact, according to a letter written by John Chamberlain, who reports: "One Peacock, sometime a schoolmaster and minister (but a very busy brained fellow) was the last week committed to the Tower. ... He hath been strictly examined by the Lord Chancellor, the Lord Coke, ... and others; and on Tuesday was hanged up by the wrists; and though he were very impatient of the torture and swooned once or twice, yet I cannot learn that they have wrung any great matter out of him."[42]

The effect of these scenes of torture, in particular a century and a half of legal torture committed especially in the names of Mary, Elizabeth, and James, is to subject the bodies of the monarch's subjects, to establish their subjection. Those gradually subordinated to the domination of the absolutizing monarchy come gradually to understand that their bodies are vulnerable not only to confinement or death, but also to torment.[43] Torture is not punishment; it allows the torturer access to the secrets of the tortured and violates the subject's body and mind in ways that newly inscribe the subject in a regime of control. Bacon himself, as an agent of the state and of new forms of monarchy, serves as a torture instrument;

he subjects his victims' bodies for king and state, just as he imagines domination over nature, nature subjected, nature in the service of man. And Bacon, as agent of the state, as a subjected servant of the king, is a cog in the gradual process of state formation. He disciplines and curbs himself in the king's service, subjects himself to tormenting thoughts and intellectual difficulties, torments himself in the great project of liberation from the domination of nature, a project aptly termed the dialectic of enlightenment.

Bacon's philosophical writings, his disquisitions on antiquity, on nature, on his own scientific program, use metaphors and exempla that serve to naturalize torture. If the natural world and the self can only be approached, understood, and mastered by techniques that curiously resemble torture, then torture is an appropriate technique in other realms of human inquiry. Bacon is making the world safe for torture by presenting a scientific program that assumes violence and coercion to be essential for the domination of nature.

Although Bacon relies at times on antiquity for justification of his natural philosophical program, he does not cite the practices of the ancient slave-owning societies, which routinely engaged in torturing slaves and foreigners in legal investigations. Yet he mines, in ancient myth and heroic narratives, scenes of bondage and torment that he allegorizes to explain the necessary alienation between experimenter and matter. The exempla from antiquity that he glosses bolster and authorize his position in relation to recalcitrant nature; he is Jupiter binding Prometheus, Menelaus interrogating Proteus, Oedipus victorious over the Sphinx. His reasoning concerning these ancient exempla extends both to his scientific practices and to the juridical inquisitions over which he presided.

Bacon's exempla work toward the naturalizing of techniques of torture. Can the rhetorical figures of metaphor and catachresis usefully be applied here as well? Catachresis is the rhetorical figure called by the Renaissance rhetorician George Puttenham *abusio*, or "the figure of abuse":

> But if for lacke of naturall and proper terme or worde we take another, neither naturall nor proper and do untruly applie it to the thing which we would seeme to expresse, and without any iust inconuenience it is not then spoken by this figure *Metaphore* or of *inuersion* as before, but by plaine abuse, ... as one should in reproch say to a poore man, thou raskall knave, where *raskall* is properly the hunters terme giuen to young deere, leane and out of season, and not to people.[44]

As Patricia Parker points out, the distinction between metaphor and catachresis slips and blurs in rhetorical writings.[45] Catachresis is defined as the use of an improper word, the enlisting of a proximate term to supply the deficiency in a language. This rhetorical figure is relevant to my enterprise here, in that one could see the English employment of torture, when it seems to be more characteristic of continental legal practices, to be an improvised, *ad hoc* practice. In her fascinating essay on torture in Renaissance England, in which she distinguishes between the truth discourses of Protestant torturers and the Catholic tortured, Elizabeth Hanson offers a description of the employment of torture that seems analogous to rhetorical catachresis:

> [T]orture seems to have had no proper discursive ground. Its legal foundation was the lack of an express prohibition against it and the immunity of the sovereign from prosecution. Its language was borrowed from Continental jurisprudence, but not its rationale. Its justification as a political tool was borrowed from its de facto status as a tool in some criminal investigations. An aberrant, quasijuridical, quasipolitical phenomenon, it occupied a discursive space opportunistically fabricated from absences and borrowings.[46]

In Hanson's view of torture, we see a social institution developed as a sort of catachresis, a cobbling together of existing forms to produce a new one. In the case of torture, the *abusio*, the abuse, is abuse not only of language, not only of the legal traditions of England, but also of the body. Bacon's use of metaphor, of exempla, is another kind of abuse, a rhetoric that naturalizes, that renders quotidian and ordinary, techniques of violence and coercion enacted against human bodies, material, natural bodies made analogous to the matter against which the scientist struggles.

One could deconstruct Bacon's text by discovering in it a return of the repressed, a questioning of the project of domination in Bacon's natural philosophical program, self-doubt about the use of torture, a reliance on the resources of classical rhetoric even as he expresses profound ambivalence about poetry. Engels, although he appreciated Bacon's program for the mastery of nature, found Bacon's rhetoric too aphoristic, his reasoning too allegorical. There are fissures in Bacon's discourse of mastery, moments in which the reader can detect a self-reflexive, contradictory impulse in the text.[47] But to celebrate this double discourse, to offer a reading that locates the material, the sensual, the pleasurable in Bacon's writing, would be to write another essay. I am not here interested in an exercise in formalism, nor in an exploration of the complexities of Baconian thought. I have tried to read Bacon's work in a way that responds to a tradition of idealizing readings, readings that see Bacon's as a purely liberatory project.

In discussing what she calls a discourse of "discovery" in sixteenth- and seventeenth-century England, Hanson compares the contemporary striving for truth in torture and in voyages of exploration, seeing in both "a separation between the knowing mind and the object of its knowledge." There is an initial resistance to discovery, but "in the crossing of seas or the parting of flesh, the mask is stripped away, making knowledge and sight seem equivalent."[48] What is most striking to me, however, is not the epistemological homology between the enterprises of geographical or scientific discovery and legal torture. Bacon, advocate of the new science, of the inquisition of nature, of the new epistemology in which "the encounter with truth depends on a separation between the knowing mind and the object of its knowledge,"[49] was himself deeply implicated in the legal procedures of torture. Yet somehow, scholarly discipline has often allowed for a separation of the historical study of the law from a historical study of natural philosophy. In a valuable discussion of Baconian method and rhetoric, John C. Briggs, without mentioning legal torture, concludes from a passage in *De Augmentis* that: "Bacon's inquirer becomes a kind of inquisitor. He uses his endurance and his separation from others to take on their corruptions and discover the innermost weaknesses and resistances of their nature."[50] Kenneth Cardwell, in an essay entitled "Francis Bacon, Inquisitor," shows how Bacon's legal experiences with "inquisition" affected his conceptualization of work on matter: "[I]n administrative inquisition Bacon found a structure appropriate to his scientific enterprise."[51] Yet except for a brief mention of Ernst Cassirer's discussion of Bacon in a footnote,[52] in which Cassirer says that Bacon said that "nature must be 'put to the rack,'"[53] Cardwell does not even mention the fact that in England at the time when Bacon worked as an examiner for the Privy Council and as lord chancellor, "inquisition" often meant torture.

Those who write about Bacon in the twentieth century seem to focus either on his life, his work for James I, his tenure as lord chancellor and his correspondence concerning his duties to the king, correspondence that included such matters as his views on torture, or on his natural philosophical works, his meditations on antiquity, on Plato and Aristotle, on rhetoric and its place, on the program for experimentation laid out in his scientific treatises. It has been difficult to think about both Bacon's practical life, his engagement in torture, and his theoretical life—his use, for example, of the metaphor of torture to explain the enlightened man's relationship to nature. Literary critics write about Bacon's art, historians of science about his scientific writings, legal historians about the moral questions raised by the practice of torture in Elizabethan and Jacobean England. Rarely does any scholar consider the man's work as a historical entity, fearing perhaps disciplinary ignorance, fearing a naive fall into the biographical fallacy of generations past to bring to bear what Bacon did on what he wrote.

Is this difficulty a product of modernity, of that separation of science, morality, and art described by Max Weber and recalled by Jurgen Habermas?[54] One of the most compelling motives for historical study is its capacity to register difference, to demonstrate to us the ways in which we assume without question the categories through which we organize experience. If Bacon thought about both science and the law, saw the same techniques operant in both domains of practice—indeed, as his rhetorical practices indicate, saw no reason to separate these realms from one another—reading his texts reveals to us how difficult it is to reassemble a world in which these questions are not yet differentiated.

Bacon uses, as examples to delineate the proper relationship between intellectual and nature, figures from classical mythology who illustrate the necessity for a world of torment, of adversity, of bondage and pursuit. Bacon himself serves as an example, a historical figure who for Adorno and Horkheimer demonstrates the irreversible process of enlightenment, the loss of connection to the pleasures of the body, the self-mutilation, sacrifice, and alienation entailed in mastering nature. I want to read the example of Bacon also in another way, to see him as a man whose right hand knew what his left hand was doing, who had not yet been modernized, classified, and compartmentalized, an example of the torturer tortured, one who begins to think about science as he begins to think about the law, as regimes that require the torture of nature, the torture of natural bodies.

We citizens and subjects of North America in the twentieth century have difficulty thinking all at once about the fight against pornography, the "war on drugs," the medical establishment's conceptualization of the immune system's fight against the AIDS virus, Israeli torture of Palestinians supported in effect by American aid. All these antagonisms seem to exist in autonomous spheres of culture, medicine, domestic and international state policy. Bacon, Renaissance man, engaged in all these spheres simultaneously, laying the ground for Enlightenment culture's thinking in terms of aggression and conquest. We need to think more about how our own twentieth-century rhetoric, our figures of war, domination, and subjection, although seemingly operating in discrete realms of cultural, political practice, support estrangement from one another, from the natural world, from our own bodies and the bodies of the subjected.

NOTES

1. *The Works of Francis Bacon, Lord Chancellor of England,* ed. Basil Montague, vol. 1 (London, 1825), 16–17.

2. Max Horkheimer and Theodor W. Adorno, *Dialectic of Englightenment,* trans. John Cumming (New York: Herder and Herder, 1972), 4.

3. Aristotle, *Rhetoric,* 1356b.

4. See John D. Lyons, *Exemplum, The Rhetoric of Example in Early Modern France and Italy* (Princeton: Princeton University Press, 1989), and Annabel Patterson, *Fables of Power: Aesopian Writing and Political History* (Durham, N.C., and London: Duke University Press, 1991).

5. Francis Bacon, *De Sapientia Veterum* (London, 1609), translated as *The Wisedome of the Ancients* by Arthur Gorges (London, 1619); New York and London: Garland, 1976.

6. Ibid., "Preface," unnumbered pages.

7. Ibid., 5–6.

8. Ibid., 6.

9. Ibid., 34.

10. Ibid., 67.

11. On the gendering of nature, see Carolyn Merchant, *The Death of Nature: Women, Ecology, and the Scientific Revolution* (San Francisco: Harper and Row, 1980), esp. "Dominion over Nature," 164–190.

12. *Wisedome,* 69–70.

13. Ibid., 122–123.

14. Ibid., 138.

15. Ibid., 150.

16. Ibid., 151–152.

17. Horkheimer and Adorno, *Dialect of Enlightenment,* 59.

18. *Works,* ed. Montague, vol. 4, 175.

19. *The Works of Francis Bacon,* ed. James Spedding, R. L. Ellis, and D. D. Heath, vol. 4 (London, 1860), 374.

20. Ibid., 375.

21. *Works,* ed. Montague, "Novum Organum," vol. 14, 134–135.

22. Ibid., "De Augmentis," vol. 4, 298.

23. Ibid., 296.

24. Ibid., 263.

25. See James Heath, *Torture and English Law: An Administrative and Legal History from the Plantagenets to the Stuarts* (Westport, Conn., and London: Greenwood, 1982).

26. *Oxford English Dictionary* (Oxford: Clarendon-Oxford University Press, 1971).

27. Heath, *Torture and English Law,* 181.

28. William Cardinal Allen, *A Briefe Historie of the Glorious Martyrdom of the xii Reverend Priests,* ed. J. H. Pollen (London: Burns and Oates, 1908), 48.

29. Cited in Heath, *Torture and English Law,* 122.

30. Ibid., 225.

31. *Works,* ed. Spedding *et al.,* vol. 10, 114.

32. Ibid., vol. 12, 92.

33. Ibid., n. 2. Eight such cases were recorded during the reign of Mary, two during that of Edward VI.

34. Heath, *Torture and English Law,* 183–184.

35. Bacon, *Wisedome.*

36. Cited in *Works,* ed. Spedding *et al.,* vol. 12, 93–94. The copy is from Balfour MSS., Advocates' Library, A.1.35/33.1.7, vol. ii.

37. Ibid., 106; this text is said to be copied from a letter in the king's handwriting.

38. Ibid., 96. This letter comes from the Gibson Papers, vol. viii.f11; fair copy.

39. See P. duBois, *Torture and Truth* (New York: Routledge, 1991).

40. *Works,* ed. Spelling *et al.,* vol. 12, 100.

41. Ibid., vol. 14, 77.

42. Ibid., 79–80.

43. On such practices in France, see Michel Foucault, *Discipline and Punish: The Birth of the Prison,* trans. Alan Sheridan (New York: Pantheon, 1977), Part I, "Torture," 3–69.

44. George Puttenham, *The Arte of Englishe Poesie,* first pub. 1589, ed. Edward Arber (London, 1869), 190–191.

45. Patricia Parker, "Metaphor and Catachresis," in *The Ends of Rhetoric. History, Theory, Practice,* ed. John Bender and David E. Wellbery (Stanford: Stanford University Press, 1990), 60–73.

46. Elizabeth Hanson, "Torture and Truth in Renaissance England," *Representations* 34 (1991), 58.

47. See, for example, the prooemium to Bacon's "The Great Instauration" in *The Works of Francis Bacon.*

48. Hanson, "Torture and Truth," 54.

49. Ibid.

50. John C. Briggs, *Francis Bacon and the Rhetoric of Nature* (Cambridge, Mass.: Harvard University Press, 1989), 25.

51. Kenneth William Cardwell, "Francis Bacon, Inquisitor," in *Francis Bacon's Legacy of Texts,* ed. William A. Sessions (New York: AMS, 1990), 270.

52. Ibid., 285.

53. In Ernst Cassirer, *The Platonic Renaissance in England,* trans. J. P. Pettegrove (Austin: University of Texas Press, 1953), 48.

54. See, for example, Jurgen Habermas, "Modernity—An Incomplete Project," in *Postmodern Culture,* ed. Hal Foster (London: Pluto, 1985), 3–15.

14

Body Memories:
Aide-Memoires and Collective Amnesia
in the Wake of the Argentine Terror

JULIE TAYLOR

If any town in this ... democracy has the right to bad memories, it is Tucuman. ... But are bad memories enough to guard against a return to—even a desire for—military rule?

—*Wall Street Journal*[1]

HOW CAN a democratic Argentina vote back into power a henchman of a repudiated dictatorship? What do Argentines remember and what do they forget about their candidate's military rule when nearly twenty people were killed or disappeared each month? Did he butcher or did he keep the law? Fourteen years ago, as Argentina's ruling junta moved into the period marked by the darkest terror of its decade in power, the dictatorship was represented in the important northern sugar province of Tucuman by *interventor* General Antonio Domingo Bussi. In 1991, Bussi launched his campaign as the candidate for provincial governor favored to win in the August elections. The questions posed by General Bussi's candidacy have arisen all over Latin America in the past decade. In 1991 alone, they were posed specifically not only by the strength of General Bussi's new Republican Force Party throughout all of Argentina, but also by the reemergence of General Antonio Rios Montt in the presidential elections of Guatemala and by the challenge from General Augusto Pinochet to the new civil government of Chile.[2]

These questions concern the memory of terror, a memory offering the guarantee that never again will terror stalk these nations. Argentines—like Brasilians, Uruguayans, Chileans, and others—have actively sought answers. Argentina, attempting to come to terms with a decade of terror and its perpetrators, elected to office a government whose sole political program was the return to the rule of law in the form of the Constitution. The new democracy set as a priority in 1984 the task of recording. One of the first moves by President Raul Alfonsin produced a National Commission on Disappeared People (CONADEP) to document the past decade of terror in a text that proclaimed itself definitive in its title: *Never Again*.[3] A year later, the proclamation echoed in neighboring Brazil—*Never Again Brasil* (1986 [1985]) was to remain on the bestseller list for two years. In 1989, *Never Again: Uruguay* appeared in the wake of the defeat of the referendum on amnesty for violators of human rights.

This essay challenges the conventional wisdom that the *Never Again* projects of official memory were victories at most and good but thwarted efforts at least. What are the relationships between memory, document, law, justice, and truth in Western cultures? How are these related to the guarantee "Never again"? And how does such a guarantee take effect? I want to address these questions through the argument that *Never Again* in Argentina has failed as social memory; that remembering terror is forgetting as well. This essay will end, attempting to avoid closure, with an open question: Can we remember something that does not make sense as dominant cultural forms define it?

Because they saw the crimes that they were protesting as resulting from the suspension of this legal system, the compilers of *Never Again* were adamant that their investigations should be understood within a context of legal concepts and language. But what if, as I will argue, facets of the judicial system itself contained in turn the seeds of the violations that it was being marshaled to remember and denounce? We might discover something profoundly important about the problem of memory and the perpetuation of terror by examining the notion that meticulous recording is a solution to violence.

In Brazil and Uruguay, not one torturer has gone to jail, nor even to court, on the basis of the *Never Again* documents. And in Argentina, after court proceedings and subsequent incarcerations, most spectacularly of the junta members themselves, all the accused had gone free as of January 1991. Others, like Antonio Bussi, ran for public office with solid and widespread support. In the face of such a paradox, it seems far too optimistic and temptingly simple to maintain that the projects behind the reports and the books themselves were a way to bring torturers to account.[4] An article in *Newsweek* commented, "[these documents] … achieved a victory simply by forcing the nation to confront the question. With the vote, 'the interests of truth were served. Facts were established, and the actual history was inscribed in the common memory.'" But could there be something suspect in these famous texts that were thought to seal the fate of the atrocities they recorded with the guarantee "Never again"? It is precisely this meticulous and public recording of atrocity by an official inquiry as a solution to state terror, past and future, that I find so problematic.

The case of Argentina's return to democracy in 1983 is a sobering one. The backdrop, the seven-year rule of the self-denominated Process of Argentine National Reorganization, has become synonymous in the international press with modern reigns of terror. The Proceso, as this dictatorship is often called by Argentines, has the dubious distinction of adding the word *desaparecido* to the world's vocabulary. It represented an important ideological presence on the Latin American scene, the National Security Doctrine as disseminated by the United States, especially through its military assistance from the 1950s onward, based on the idea that the world faced an ultimate war between communist and non-communist forces and that this battle would be waged through nonconventional warfare with subversive forces internal to each nation.

In the wake of the ouster of the military as a result of the Falklands/Malvinas debacle, Argentines now have to their credit seven years of civilian rule, albeit under conditions of continuing severe economic instability. Yet Bussi and other major representatives of the dictatorship's violence are returning to political prominence via the democratic process. This is occurring in the tragic context of aborted efforts to bring to justice those responsible for the disappearances and terror of the infamous "Dirty War" of 1976–1983, waged by the military junta against all "subversion." In spite of attempts at settling accounts with the perpetrators of violence, recent Argentine events continue to confront us with equally dramatic gestures of condoning their actions. General Bussi's strong candidacy in Tucuman could not occur had not large sectors of Argentine society been willing to accept or ignore a violent past.

The *Never Again* volumes were one solution to the problem of remembering terror. The Argentine volume (1986 [1984]) counts 450 pages, derived from more than 50,000 pages of documentation based on 8,960 cases, and organized according to an exhaustively detailed list of subtitles. Activists in Brazil were able to compile their *Never Again* (1986 [1985]) as the military regime was moving gradually toward handing government over to civil authorities in an atmosphere that did not seem to call for the immediate destruction of government records, unlike the atmosphere prevailing during the sudden collapse of the Argentine junta. The Brazilian military government had, as it tortured, kept meticulous records of victim, place, and method, including the name of the victimizer and attending medical help. In an operation kept secret for five years, lawyers were able to smuggle out the complete government files of 707 cases involving 7,000 defendants and occupying 1 million pages.[5]

The gesture of documenting, of recording testimony, in all three cases—Argentina, Brazil, and Uruguay—was to create an official memory of events that were never to be forgotten. This task was carried out in the immediate aftermath of a decade of state terrorism for which no history yet existed. The endeavor, as the title of the resulting document underlines, was an account, but it was also an accounting for—*Never Again* announced that these pages contained a memory with a purpose: to diagnose and prevent. At a still politically potent moment, remembering in the form of creating such a text has political consequences that it would not have at a later time. This record, part of ongoing disputes over a final version of the past and thus preceding any project of writing a history of its era, was to establish juridical truth. In Argentina, on the basis of the information in this record, the perpetrators of crimes not yet denounced when the volume was compiled were to be tried and sentenced.

The rhetoric surrounding the effort that resulted in *Never Again,* both in Latin America and in the international press, is revealing about the nature of the projects. The Brazilian version (1986 [1985]) is bracketed by two quotations. The text is preceded by a biblical citation, "Write this as a memorial in a book." (Exodus 17:14). The volume closes with the word of Kele Maxacali, an Indian from Minas Gerais:

> *My father told me;*
> *I'm going to tell my son.*
> *And when he dies?*
> *He'll tell his son.*
> *That's the way it is; nobody forgets.*

As the Argentine National Commission on Disappeared People (CONADEP) itself stated (1986 [1984]:429), its report emerged from "immediate public response in an incredible process of reconstructing collective memory."

Lawrence Wechsler's excellent book based on his reporting for *The New Yorker* describes this process of remembering as he sees it in the related projects of Argentina, Brazil, and Uruguay:

> Over and over again ... the same two imperatives seem to rise to the fore—the intertwined demands for justice and for truth. The security forces ... will abide neither, but if anything the desire for truth is often more urgently felt by the victims of torture than the desire for justice. People don't necessarily insist that the former torturers go to jail—there's been enough of jail—but they do want to see the truth established. Fragile, tentative democracies ... hurl themselves toward an abyss, struggling over this issue of truth. It's a powerful, almost magical notion, because often everyone already knows the truth. ... Why, then, this need to risk everything to render that knowledge explicit?[6]

Wechsler goes on to say that these were the questions central to discussions at a 1988 Aspen Institute conference on "State Crimes: Punishment or Pardon?" attended by North and South Americans. A participant himself, Wechsler reports how "Thomas Nagel, a professor of philosophy and law at New York University, almost stumbled upon an answer":

> "It's the difference," Nagel said haltingly, "between knowledge and *ac*knowledgment. It's what happens and can only happen to knowledge when it becomes officially sanctioned, when it is made part of the public cognitive scene." Yes, several of the panelists agreed. And that transformation, offered another participant, is sacramental.[7]

This definition of the endeavor that resulted in *Never Again* intimately relates justice to truth as established through the documenting of public memory. Despite CONADEP's explicit purpose of receiving depositions and evidence to pass on to the courts,[8] the desire for truth here is described as being more urgent than the desire for justice. The document becomes an end in itself, an absolute value, a magical notion indeed. What is the magical role assigned here to public memory as a guarantee that what we remember will never again occur? But from another angle, these "*acknowledgments*" of terror can be seen quite differently: Far from sacraments, they may be mere aide-memoires that collude with the deeds they "expose."

Terror can be defined as absolute lack of recourse to the law, lending credibility to the intuitively held view that terror and the law are opposites. Terror may also be seen, in the same vein, as absolute exclusion. Yet the legalistic language used to protest terror in these volumes/documents is itself exclusionary. Attempting to re-member, diagnose, and cure an era of spectacular political violence, *Never Again* resorts to forms—sometimes in contrast with its content—that impede dealing with the exclusionary political nature of the violence and even participates in it.

To explore the reactiviation of the violence of the past through attempts to re-member it accurately and thus conclude it, I want to look at some ethnographic details on the actual trials to which the *Never Again* documents in Argentina led.[9] In an unprecedented move, the new Argentine civil government brought to public trial those responsible for a coup d'etat, the excommanders of the brutal 1976–1983 junta. Together with *Never Again,* the trials were a public and explicit strategy to conclude one historical period and begin another with a decision concerning how to remember.

The form of the trails was also dramatically different from the usual written court proceedings under Napoleonic code. They were oral and attended by any-one from the general public who was able to obtain a pass, for which interminable lines of hopeful people waited overnight. Because of its unusual nature, the struc-ture of the court itself carried particular dramatic impact. The Tribune (*tribuna*) consisted of six judges (*camaristas*) who sat away from all other parties in the trial but in close proximity to symbols of the scales of justice, the Roman Catholic church, and the Constitution. These men made their entrances and exits in a group, unlike all other participants in the trial. As they entered, bearing their col-lective impartial wisdom to illuminate the problem at hand, the courtroom lights went on; as they left, the lights dimmed. Below the judges sat the defense attor-neys representing the accused members of the military, the state prosecutor, and the secretary of the court. Dramatically, the defendants themselves, the recent ab-solute rulers of the nation, occupied a third level with the general public.

In contrast to the social arbiters of the truth in the Tribune, the witnesses en-tered and existed individually, each taking his or her place at a desk facing the president of the Tribune and with his or her back to the public.[10] The witnesses were required to look only at the president of the Tribune, from whom they re-ceived the questions to which they had to respond, such that the prosecution's questions were reformulated by the judge. Politico-ideological questions were considered inappropriate. The Tribune sorted the relevant from the irrelevant and demanded that the trial be carried out in universalist ethical and juridical terms. Testimony could only be taken in the form of direct perception in a descriptive mode based on individual senses. Not only was hearsay thus eliminated, but with it all reference to political beliefs and loyalties. These rules of evidence were applied in ways specific to this trial but in entirely culturally and legally recognizable and acceptable ways with the end of inserting society, events, and behaviors into a strictly legal and depoliticized framework.

All who passed through this process, then, accused and accusors—actors in highly political dramas where they had represented clashing worldviews and collective strategies for implementing them—were refigured as innocent or transgressing individuals with individual rights and obligations. The only collective entities recognized were sums of individuals who constituted juridical societies for ends recognized by law. Collective political motivations were thus not recognized. All social sectors were reconstituted as groups of individuals submitted to the law, which alone was represented collectively, as identified with society itself. Political history became juridical history, recreating a new memory.[11] Collective facts and sociopolitical identities underwent a profound transformation as they were denuded of the political language that had made them accessible to social actors in Argentina. The task of making sense of recent history had been assigned to an expert collectivity representing society. Truth was reached through methods of legal inquiry carried out by members of society other than those who had been the principal actors in the events.

State terrorism had atomized and thrown into crisis Argentine identities through frontal attack on political ties and the crumbling of social bonds in the resulting climate of fear. Now Argentine society reasserted control over the political sphere by demanding the rule of law—only to have this law perpetuate the atomization[12] of collective identities into rights and motivations of the individuals whose testimony the court admitted. The goal of the Repression—la Represion, as the Proceso was also known by many—found its echo in the law.

Outside Argentina, what do we learn from the rendering of the experience of terror into the precise testimony in *Never Again* and from the closely associated trials, with their details of the identities of victimizers and victims and what one did to another and where? To borrow a phrase from Renato Rosaldo, this is "where precision lies." The parallels that the victimizers draw between science and torture, and their emphasis on keeping records of torture along the lines of a scientific endeavor, have been commented on in many contexts, not least in relation to the Holocaust itself and Jacobo Timerman's experience in the Argentine detention centers.[13] But there is the possibility of an equally sinister parallel with torture—the attempt to counter terror with similarly systematic and exhaustive methods and record keeping:

> "It's as if the team members wrung every last piece of information out of the material"—[Wright's] hands squeezed an imaginary sponge—"so that there wouldn't be

any possibility of an original angle for future researchers." … [T]hen something else about the *Brasil: Nunca Mais* project's thoroughness struck me—or, rather, not so much about the thoroughness as about the manner of presentation. It was almost as if through the pristine elegance of the way they marshalled their exhaustive data the team members had imagined they might somehow be able to overmaster the horror."[14]

An examination of the Never Again projects as specific attempts at remembering highlights several important dimensions of their identity: as official voices— their nature as state documents, which opposes the symbolic power of the state to their nature as legal and bureaucratic documents; as encoded in bureaucratic literacy, with consequent implications about subjectivity in the face of the separation of public and private, obligations and rights; and as displaying the inherent problematic nature of human rights discourse and its claims to speak in universal terms when in fact it uses the fragmentary concept of individual rights, just as the voice of bureaucracy erases the subject.[15]

As evinced in the trials of the Argentine junta, in the course of legalistic rendering through recording, official memory is cast into forms that are integral to the judicial process. Such forms, sometimes in contrast with their content, suppress the remembering and the recording of any motivation that is not individual. Only individual motivation, then, is amenable to forms of testimony and evidence related to individual sensorial experience.

The resulting distortion of collective political action and motivation is compounded by another problem of a distortion of memory. This problem arises from the idea or the experience of political violence as the chaotic and intractable opposite of law. The introduction of chaos into experience through terror was an integral part of the political project of the military and as such was part of a highly rational program. (See use of government archives Brasil, referred to above and below, and especially national security doctrine.) The *Never Again* volumes omitted forms of collective action; they do not depict battles between opposing forces or massacres of groups. The opposition of the order of law and the chaos of violence further led to the omission of collective motivation not only of victimizers (national security doctrine as political program) but of victims as well, who were defended as individuals whose human rights had been violated rather than as political activists (a concept that even the prosecution refused to contemplate).

The *Never Again* projects were conceived as part of a reestablishment of the hegemony of law and the wholeness of the subject: "[T]wo nations rediscovered the capacity for acting as the subject rather than the object of history, not by squaring accounts with their tormentors but by setting the record straight."[16] Paradoxically, these two goals are incompatible.

The law is seen in this context as violent itself: constraining, fragmenting, hierarchical, and power-fraught, in contrast with Foucault's distinction between law as universal and discipline as hierarchical, assymmetrical. In light of the disintegration of *Never Again,* the exclusionary nature of universals comes to the fore, as is evident in the experience of women, minorities, and Third World groups traditionally excluded from the norms represented by the law and from the hegemonic separation of the spheres of public and private, rights and obligations.

What is "law and order" when scrutinized in these terms? How do such terms distort, for example, the social memory of military order established at the cost of the violations of human rights denounced by *Never Again?* Was the memory of that order embodied in General Bussi's major campaign symbol, the cleaning broom (*escoba de limpieza*)? Bussi's regime and his broom are recalled by Michael Taussig's reference to the "cleaning or limpieza" of Cali, Colombia, a sugar capital, he noted, like Havana, and—I might note—like another sugar city San Miguel de Tucuman:

> that incredible process in which beggars, prostitutes, homosexuals, transvestites, and all manner of street people supposedly involved in crime and petty cocaine dealing were being wiped out by pistol and machine gun fire from pick-ups and motorbikes. … While there is reason to distinguish this "cleaning" from the more conventionally defined political assassinations, there is also something they have in common: … purifying the public sphere of the polluting powers which the dominant voices of society attribute to the hampa or underworld whose salient political feature lies in its being strategically borderless—invisible yet infiltrating—but decidedly Other; prostitutes, homosexuals, communists, left-wing guerrilleros, beggars …[17]

In Tucuman, when General Bussi ruled, rather than shoot the beggars, he swept them out of the city, transporting them bodily over the border to be stranded in the next province of Catamarca. "Those who are afraid of the return of the military are probably not clean," stated a taxi driver in Buenos Aires in 1990.[18]

The order imposed by a broom has become an order intimately linked with violence in the common conflations of, on the one hand, the military order and the social order in general, and on the other hand, of the religious and moral order and bodily cleanliness and discipline.[19] European culture, in new constructions of hierarchy, rationality, and truth since the late Middle Ages, has granted memory a central role in the establishment of truth and the imposition of law. Memory and the testimony, the evidence, and finally the documentation it is meant to produce, when involved in the imposition of the legal process, are conduits of authority and hierarchy that in the West enable violent domination.[20] In this light, the conceptual opposition of violence and law obfuscates their historical and cultural links. In Europe's religious and juridical traditions, memory is constituted by the process of inquiry with its specific rules, conditions, limits, and techniques. These inquisitorial parameters originated in beliefs about truth, the body, and pain that also gave rise to torture. While actual bodily violence has dropped out of practices central to religion, law, and science—although still deployed in Western education, politics, and the family—their association with violence, when unquestioned, remains at the center of inquiry.

Law is violent and therefore fearful: The idea of refuge in the law becomes absurd, associated as it is with an avoidance of the recognition of the violence of law. This culturally conditioned avoidance[21] is a key to the fact that the guarantee

Never Again has failed. In this role as testimony, evidence, and document, memory does not only salvage, construct, and invent. Memory as constituted is exclusionary: It omits what hierarchy does not recognize. Thus authority admits some narratives and omits others in a process of articulating memory and power. Remembering, then, is also a process of forgetting. It is a process of simultaneously constructing some subjectivities and doing violence to others. It is this dual identity of memory that we need to focus on in Argentina. More than content, memory is an arena. In this arena in Argentina, for example, 70 percent of the population opposed a pardon for the crimes of the junta while more than 40 percent considered Bussi an acceptable political alternative. These numbers do not represent different people, different camps, or different versions. Sides are not clear; there is likely to be no definitive outcome. They represent a struggle not *between* groups and their interpretations but *within* groups, even within persons.

By defining memory in this way, we throw into high relief its nature as a dynamic political category and fact of power. Memory as accessibility of experience, and consequently, recourse to it to make sense of events, is precluded except along lines congruent with facts of power and hierarchy. The province of Tucuman where General Bussi was campaigning for governor is notorious in Argentina for several unique reasons: The junta designated Tucuman the "Cradle of Independence and Tomb of Subversion." Tucuman has seen the advent of independence repeatedly: as the place of the signing of the Argentine declaration of independence and also, 160 years later, as the first area designated a "liberated zone" by guerrilla forces (ERP). Still later, it saw some of the grimmest interventions of the Dirty War, earning the junta's recognition not only as cradle but as tomb. Today the province possesses the nation's only public Museum of the Subversion (against state terrorism in the Dirty War), and its capital has proven to be the only city in the Republic where it has been impossible to establish discussion groups—common elsewhere—of the mothers of the disappeared. Where the junta's official memory of its victims has been enshrined, the startling silence of other memories gives new meaning to the junta's definition of Tucuman as the Tomb of Subversion. The museum itself constitutes another sort of tomb for the battle against the state: the act of remembering as the act of forgetting, of violently excluding, of silencing by fear.

In the trials of the excomandantes, a family of Basque heritage testified against the junta concerning the disappearance of their son. Security forces had taken the young man from their home on the grounds that he and his friends had contacts with another youth who was connected with the guerrilla in Tucuman. The kidnappers invaded the family home and entrenched themselves for days, disappearing the son and his friends as they fell one by one into the trap. The son was never again seen alive. The parents and some of his friends who survived testified.

When cross-examined under oath, the parents remembered that only their son had been abducted. They did not remember that anyone else of his acquaintance had disappeared, except his fiancee. This strange memory, similar to that of other parents testifying about similar circumstances, did not emerge only from this specific confrontation with the courts. It had begun to form within the general parameters of the law in the first frantic days after the loss of their child, when the parents had turned successively to all the representatives of universal, neutral norms: They attempted to file a writ of habeas corpus; they consulted the church; they pled with the U.S. embassy. Their son in their eyes had been disappeared as an individual: His disappearance had been a violation of his rights—a crime that would be recognized and rectified by the institutions that guarantee inviolate individual rights. The dead youth's friends, in contrast, had gone immediately to the military and the police linked with security forces; they knew that these authorities, perceiving their friend as part of an enemy group, had disappeared him. They would have remembered the disappeared as a casualty of a confrontation between different forces and their worldviews. However, the trials forbade questions concerning this memory of war.

Other categories of suffering were not recorded in *Never Again*, nor did they appear in trial. Kidnapping, disappearance, and torture, as in the case of the young Basque Argentine under the Proceso in Argentina, were experiences arguably identified mostly with the middle classes. What of collective massacres, thought to be more representative of the working-class experience? What of whole provinces where mass death came in the guise of open military confrontations that fit the rubric of battles, except for the sinister fact that casualties were never reported or even recognized? What about the memory, significantly almost never voiced, of Tucuman's sugarcane fields in flames when the armed forces set them afire to destroy the hidden guerrilla?

These problems have emerged in other areas of my work concerning exclusionary effects of narrative genres and modes, with particular reference to a specific Argentine literary text and the cultural problems that it raises in making narrative sense out of social nonsense. But in Argentina, two decades of disappearances, torture, war, and economic collapse have thrown into high relief other aspects of parallels as well as causal connections between the absolute exclusion of terror and exclusionary aspects of genres and specific texts defined as culturally central. So, in conclusion, I want to draw a connection between these lines of analysis and Never Again as a new or incipient genre on the world scene: compilations of testimonies—documents, accounts, reports—intended to bring perpetrators of terror to account.

The three horrific reports from Argentina, Brazil, and Uruguay are so widely known and read that we can assume that they share some of the generalizing capacities of genre. Briefly for our purposes here, genre denotes a collectively recognizable shape of accounts of lives and experiences. This recognizable shape is often signaled by being amenable to the label of one of a culture's genres that reproduce dominant modes of discourse. The lack of such shape throws sense into doubt and confounds memory. In this vein, we should ask whether the *Never Again* accounts do not also share capacities to trivialize and exclude experience that does not match textual representation, when this representation purports to be the general and therefore the most significant.

So what I have tried to do in this paper is to reveal what *Never Again* distorts— and possibly allows to recur again and again. The efficacy of the encounter of torturer and victim does not derive from a confrontation of identifiable individuals, nor from an exercise of specific agency. It cannot be located in a locatable place; it does not allow a simple assignation of guilt. The collective nature of the experience, of agency, and of guilt together have remained obscured and forgotten, as incomprehensible and inutterable as the memory of vast sugarcane fields blanketed with the heavy smell of burning human flesh.

NOTES

1. I would like to thank Michael Taussig for his unwavering support for this area of my work in general and, specifically, for having brought to my attention the *Wall Street Journal* article quoted here, *Wall Street Journal,* January 4, 1988: p. 1.

2. General Antonio Domingo Bussi lost the gubernatorial elections of September 8, 1991, to Ramon "Palito" Ortega, a native son and the candidate heavily backed by President Carlos Menem. Ortega's triumph was predicted only days before the election. The relative narrowness of the defeat—Ortega received 51.88 percent of the vote to Bussi's 42.9 percent— and the unexpectedness of this outcome speak to continuing support for General Bussi and the problematic nature of the political phenomenon he represents.

3. CONADEP (Argentina's National Commission on Disappeared People), *Nunca Mas [Never Again]* (London: Faber, 1986 [1984]).

4. L. Wechsler, *A Miracle, A Universe: Settling Accounts with Torturers* (New York: Pantheon, 1990) and M. Jones, "Settling Accounts with Systematic Torturers," *Newsweek,* vol. 4, no. 3, 1990, p. 72.

5. Wechsler, *A Miracle, A Universe,* pp. 50ff.

6. Ibid., pp. 3–4.

7. Ibid., p. 4.

8. CONADEP, *Nunca Mas,* p. 429. Esther Kaufman, *Un Ritual Juridico: El Juicio a Las Huntas Militares* (Master's Thesis, Facultad Latinoamericana de Ciencias Sociales, Buenos Aires, 1987).

9. Kaufman, *Un Ritual Juridico,* p. 24.

10. Ibid.

11. Ibid., p. 37.

12. Ibid., p. 17.

13. See Toni Morrison, *Beloved* (New York: Knopf, 1987); M. Taussig, "Terror as Usual: Walter Benjamin's Theory of History as a State of Siege," *In the Nervous System* (New York: Routledge, 1991); J. Timerman, *Prisoner Without a Name, Cell Without a Number* (New York: Knopf, 1981); E. Scarry, *The Body in Pain: The Making and Unmaking of the World* (New York: Oxford University Press, 1985).

14. Wechsler, *A Miracle, A Universe,* interview with Wright, pp. 54–55.

15. My thanks to Katherine Milun of the Department of Anthropology, Rice University, for her illumination of this area.

16. Jones, "Settling Accounts."

17. Taussig, "Terror as Usual," p. 13.

18. Claudia Briones, personal communication.

19. See T. Asad, "Notes on Body Pain and Truth in Medieval Christian Ritual," *Economy and Society*, vol. 6, pp. 287–327; bell hooks, *Feminist Theory from Margin to Center* (Boston: South End Press, 1984).

20. M. Foucault, *Discipline and Punish: The Birth of the Prison*, trans. Alan Sheridan (New York: Vintage, 1979).

21. See Thomas Dumm, "Fear of Law," *Studies in Law, Politics, and Society*, vol. 10, pp. 29–57.

15

The Official Story:
Response to Julie Taylor

GEORGE E. MARCUS

ONE OF THE MANY striking aspects of Julie Taylor's discussion of the *Nunca Mas* documentation of state terrorism in Latin America is the new ground that it breaks in the current revival of interest in the study of collective memory, not only in anthropology but in cultural studies more broadly. She manages to work around the valuable but somewhat nostalgic agendas that, I think, are motivating much of this renewed interest in social memory. Before commenting on Taylor's essay, I want to outline these mainstream agendas. Memory has become one of those keywords that, merely by its inclusion in the titles of books and articles, signals new hope and possible direction for the nearly exhausted theoretical discussions about culture over the past two decades. In this sense, "memory" in the title of an ethnography or historical study evokes new direction, like similar terms such as "poetics," "narrative," "the self," "the body," and so on, especially when linked to a contrast term such as "politics" or "economy."

While there have been some really stimulating ethnographic and historical works substantively responsible for the renewal of interest in collective memory, especially regarding the art of memory in contemporary, nonliterate, so-called tribal cultures and in largely oral cultures of the classical world, the preponderant effort to make something important of collective memory in the study of modernity follows two broad trends in contemporary anthropology. The study of collective memory is one of the primary forms that the hope for these more general trends currently take. First, the study of collective memory contributes to the attempt in so much recent social theory to frustrate the traditional desire of Western modes of inquiry and knowledge to discover and state objective truths about the social world that were free of context and point of view. The central issue about social memory thus becomes not its accuracy but its multiple constructions.

Second, and relatedly, the study of collective memory has become a means of accessing diverse cultural meanings that—as rites, rituals, and practices of public remembering, for example, festivals, memorials, family histories, and the like— somehow survive homogenization through mass consumer culture, information technologies, and other global, machine-like processes and disciplines. For anthropologists in particular, the study of collective memory has provided a means of discovering and describing indigenous histories against official or professional history and thereby finding historicizing where it was never thought to exist. And further, the study of memory has materialized previously undescribed cultural forms with a vitality that seems to have otherwise dissipated by the late twentieth-century in traditional objects and categories of ethnographic study. In these ways, then, the study of social memory becomes a hope of the now well critiqued "resistance to the state and corporate capitalism" literature in cultural studies.

In the case of either of these left/liberal scholarly agendas for a renewed interest in collective memory—as constructed and contestatory of the oppressive search for objective truth, or as the vital site of salvage for cultural diversity—the process of collective remembering is possessed of virtue and heart against the cold power of state and economic systems. It is the often silent, internal voice of the diverse populace. This interest thrives intellectually on work in the classics on ancient memory and in ethnography. Its promise is the reenchantment in modernity of phenomena that anthropologists, among others, have held dear—ritual, community, symbols. But what is obscured in this trend is the alternative and perhaps main sense of the notion of memory in modernity, and particularly in this age of the computer—memory as the systematic storage of information with its human, bureaucratic analog, the massive time and effort spent in documentation, record keeping, and archive creation. This brute social memory process, conducted often within the formal institutions of states and corporations, through the massive collection and organization of facts, may seem denuded of the richness of cultural meanings embedded in the rituals and narratives of collective memory, out there, so to speak, in everyday social life. But if we leave aside the tendency to view bureaucratic rationality, in the Weberian sense, and administered worlds, in the Frankfurt School sense, simply as monolithic and totalitarian institutional orders, then we may be able to see very important cultural meanings and tendencies in the otherwise seemingly brute processes of official memory that indeed are definitive of the very idea of bureaucratic rationality—the keeping and storing of records, the constitution of the facts and thus of objective truth. As ethnographers attempting to make something cultural of this official process of remembering through archive building, we must strategically locate contexts of historic moment for this otherwise defining activity of bureaucratic rationality.

The great virtues of Taylor's essay are that she has pushed us far in these directions. Memory is not particularly interesting in her discussion as some autonomous object of cultural interpretation, but rather as a metaphor for examining certain quite remarkable and horrible features of political process in several Latin

American societies, especially Argentina. She locates modern collective memory in the state's and society's pervasive engagement with records and documentation and she explores its meanings in a focused period of trauma for Argentines—the accounting by recounting of state terror during the Dirty War. Hers is an extreme case of a whole category of situations through which the study of official memory might be ethnographically pursued. Namely, in the politically volatile period immediately following an event or period of high trauma and rupture in the collective life of a mass, liberal society, there often arises a need to respond to this recent past by examining it, by remembering it in some public way in order to get beyond it. Judicial or parliamentary investigation, a practice that involves the collection of testimonies and records into a massive archive of documents, is the most common mode of such recollection. Often, what needs to be exposed are the abuses, misdeeds, or pathologies in the affairs of state and among the most powerful elites in the society. The situation is often volatile because not only a *re*-counting is wanted but also an *ac*counting, that is, justice. The interest of still powerful or aspiring elites in all this is to maintain "damage control," minimal change. In the end, setting the record straight in full public view is all that substantively comes from such investigations. In U.S. society, one can think of the Warren Commission, the Watergate hearings, and so on, none perhaps as evocative as the *Nunca Mas* recollections, but certainly in the same category of official rememberings.

Only later, much later, usually in another political era, do many more provocative, revelatory rememberings occur as personal memoirs and scholarly histories appear. At the time of the investigation, in the short-term memory of official inquiry, the mode of documentation and evidence in trials controls or represses from public view the multiplicity of experiences and rememberings of the recent past that exist diffusely in society. Indeed, the point is truth-telling as officially remembered, which the disorder of multiple memories, experiences, and narratives of a difficult time would obscure. Indeed, the very possibility of political order and life as usual would be seriously undermined if the space of public discourse was not preempted and monopolized by the very orderly accounting and recounting of official collective memory.

While in the Brazilian *Nunca Mas* case, this documentation of state terror occurred through a remarkable private project inspired within the church, it still took the form of the amassing of the facts of state terror, horrible in their detail, numbing in their volume. The Brazilian case is especially interesting because it involved merely reproducing the detailed records that the torturers kept, thus suggesting a particularly troubling kinship between inquisitorial activity of state terror—the paranoid collection of facts through infliction of pain upon the bodies of victims/subversives—and its exposure through investigation in its aftermath. This is a very perverse set of transformations of the process of official memory.

Talal Asad, in a tentative but ambitious article entitled "Notes on Body Pain and Truth in Medieval Christian Ritual,"[1] provides a way of thinking about these ironic uses of memory functions within official bureaucratic processes of the modern state. He traces the evolution of judicial torture from the ordeal in Western procedural law, not as an advance in rationality, as it is often construed, but as the displacement of the rituals of mortification that had been so much a part of Christian practices of individual confession—of arriving at truth through pain inflicted upon the body. While he does not conceive of it in these terms, the truth that is ensured by self-torture and later judicial torture is actually a result of a mental process of recollection under intense fear and duress. Suggestively extending Asad's Foucaultian genealogy, we could argue that standards for testimony, witnessing, and confession in modern liberal law are traceable in part to medieval judicial evolution. Indeed, liberal rules of law as they apply to testimony, confession, and witnessing are devoted to ensuring that such abuses as judicial and police torture, deep in their historical genealogies, will not reoccur. In the mechanisms of official remembering, in perverse or redemptive circumstances violence is integral to the evolution of even its most liberal practices and is at the heart of acts of collective memory whose purpose is to produce a or the truth. The official remembering of state terror is another side of the coin of the inquisitorial, record-keeping inquiry that stimulated it and provided it with its revelatory documents, most poignantly in Brazil.

Taylor's interpretation is quite different from those that have tried to enhance the social significance of the *Nunca Mas* recollections. For example, as Taylor mentions, Thomas Nagel emphasized the importance of acknowledgment alone in the *Nunca Mas* inquiries, and *The New Yorker* journalist Lawrence Wechsler tried further to elevate these acts of acknowledgment as being somehow sacramental. Yet, other than to preserve political order and normalcy of everyday life after the terror, the official recollections of *Nunca Mas* have apparently had little lasting effect upon the political perceptions of Argentines at least, as is indicated by Taylor's discussion of the considerable support for the return to power in Tucuman of the torturer General Bussi by electoral process. The public truth, arrived at through a process of official recollection, becomes finally the multiple, partial truths in the personal, individual memories of the victims of the terror, their families, and most others who knew it was happening but could consider it none of their business.

The often heroic, well-intentioned effort to expose the terror through massive documentation for all to see thus does establish a truth, but one that becomes reconstructed through its diverse reception in society. Such a mode of liberal collective remembering preserves the state in that it monopolizes the public sphere and limits general access to other kinds of remembering, restricting them to the personal, private anguish of individual memories or deferring their public expression to another later, distant, and politically different, if not less troubled, time. In this way, political order is preserved and saved from the implications of its own darkest episodes of excess. As long as the archive is there, the memory exists as stored information publicly available. A justice of limited proportion has been achieved. Counter-terror, or counter-terrorism, is henceforth not the task of political or public process but left to the dreams and nightmares of those who perpetrated and suffered the remembered events.

NOTES

1. Talal Asad, "Notes on Body Pain and Truth in Medieval Christian Ritual," *Economy and Society* 6 (1983): 287–327.

16

The Electronic Body
at the End of the State:
Ethnicity, National Identity, and
the Japanese Emperor System

TETSUO KOGAWA

IN JAPAN IT IS NOT considered prejudicial to think that a single race can establish a state in a single country. This is not because Japan is an island nation; rather, it is because the basic character of the Japanese state is to integrate people and country into the state.

Many Japanese have official Japanese citizenship, but there is no necessary relationship between their officially registered citizenship and the fact that they are Japanese people. Chinese people or Italian people are always Chinese or Italian wherever in the world they may be living and regardless of their official citizenship status. In the case of the Japanese, although the number of people living abroad is steadily increasing, not many have accepted citizenship in other countries. This difference between affiliation and location is not peculiar to the Japanese people; it is a result of the way the Japanese state has been administered. Sinilarly, non-Japanese living in Japan have rarely been granted Japanese citizenship.

Needless to say, there is no such thing as an ethnic American. Strictly speaking, an American is one who lives in the United States, a country composed of a conglomeration of people from a variety of countries and ethnic backgrounds. Thus, in a sense, to become an American means to abandon one's home country and culture. It also means accepting the notion of a country that is culturally diverse. Even in the film *Stranger than Paradise*, Willy hates to use the Hungarian language when speaking with his aunt and cousin and insists on speaking English. His attitude represents a life-style common among the lower or subsistence classes and less common among intellectuals. By insisting on creating new lives for themselves, working-class immigrants are determined not to remember their former country. In Japan, where we often cultivate romantic images of what it means to be an immigrant, the reasons for this attitude may be difficult to understand. Many of the people who emigrated to America were motivated to abandon their homeland by political upheaval or natural disaster. Their feelings are so strong that they often curse the sort of life they lived in their homeland. In the Italian film *Padre, Padrone,* some young people try to emigrate to Germany from Sardinia. When they board a truck bound for the ship, they spit on their homeland. Even among immigrants to America, there are more than a few who believe they will never speak their native language again.

Since the end of the nineteenth century, America has developed government policies to help integrate people who have left their home countries. These policies are based on the concept of "the melting pot." Melting pot means a smelter in which various metals are melted and combined at high temperatures. Thus, melting pot policies mean that all sorts of people come together from all sorts of countries in the smelter called the United States, and they all become known simply as Americans or American citizens.

However, the reality is that America's recent history is a history of the failure of melting pot policies. Actual American history, as reflected in Michael Cimino's film *Heaven's Gate,* shows that not all ethnic groups have been equally assimilated. Ethnic groups have never been integrated into the American mainstream; rather, there is a process of bloody struggle among ethnic groups in which those who have been in the country longer try to control and repress the new arrivals. In the 1960s there was a violent struggle for the liberation of minority groups, and thus the dominant system had to change its policies. From this point of view, Nathan Glazer and Daniel P. Moynihan, in their book *Beyond the Melting Pot* (1963), argue that it is essential to amend the policy that had been in effect up to that time. In America in the late 1960s, in place of the melting pot policy, a profound appreciation for the role of ethnic diversity developed in national administrative and economic policies.

All this is directly related to basic trends in industries. Power is certainly not monolithic; rather, it is filled with all sorts of unexpected conditions. Incidents that have occurred from time to time have caused the single, monolithic system to begin to *fluctuate.* Today's power system is characterized by such fluctuations. In such a situation, unless the basic power structure deteriorates, nothing "accidental" can occur. Indeed, the civil rights movements and the struggle among ethnic groups in America undermined the monolithic authority that tried to create something like a pan-Americanism; the movement against the Vietnam War and the crimes committed by the state roused people to action against the state, which was urging the people to go to war. In this we saw revealed the limits of the power of the integrating state. We can, however, consider the matter in another way as well. There was no epoch-making revolution as a result of these movements. Neither were there any changes in the national constitution. Rather, the antiestablishment movement can be conceived as having served the purpose of making the United States grow. Although this is a rather Hegelian view of the situation, when we think in terms of changes in industrial structures of production and in dominant technology, this is a very realistic way of viewing the situation.

The system based on heavy industry cannot help but create a state where ethnic and cultural differences are homogenized. A pattern of unification and quantitative ownership is what determines the degree of one's power in such a system. The logic of unification establishes centers, and the logic of quantitative ownership unifies them. Those who oppose this system are driven away from the centers of power, are marginalized, and have virtually no influence over them. However, in a system that emphasizes the information and service sectors, the opposite effect occurs: The older type of system is actually counterproductive. A simple unification will not produce a power base; temporary and speculative ownership is preferable to constant ownership. In such a system, power does not focus on a single center but divides itself into various centers, and factors that used to be antiestablishment are co-opted into one of the decentralized powers. Power will establish itself in a number of small pockets. At this point, the thesis of center/margin is no longer relevant. The state, therefore, moves from a static organization to a more flexible network.

This change does not mean that the state itself has become weak. The state we have known up till now, which is really out-of-date, is advanced and refined as a regulating apparatus—we might also call it an apparatus of "transcendental apperception"—of a capitalist system. Even in an era when the information and service sectors have come to have priority, heavy industry will not entirely disappear. Indeed, the latter will follow the logic of the former and will reemerge in a new, consolidated form. Consequently, in one sense the state is drawn by the logic of consolidation and large ownership. In such a situation, the power of the military and the police forces continues to represent the power of the state. Crimes and conventional-type opposition may also exist, but quite apart from these things, a completely different form of power will also begin to grow. In this new power system, both the pressure and the oppression brought to bear by the police and the military cause a further growth of the system, and to the extent that this can be successfully absorbed, it can benefit the state.

In Japan we have had the modern Emperor system since the Meiji period. This system corresponds to the melting pot policy of the United States: Ethnic differences among people in Japan have been obliterated, and geographically and culturally everything has been homogenized. If we examine the absence of ethnic diversity in the Japanese population carefully, we find that it is because the Ainu, the Koreans, and the Chinese have all been forced to become assimilated and made one with the Japanese people. This Japanese version of the melting pot has clearly succeeded to a far greater extent than what we see in the United States. The Japanese are considered to be a nation of people who have been made into Japanese: a people having a single language and a single way of thinking and using the same body language and gestures.

This pan-Japanism was so efficient for the heavy industry–oriented system that Japan accomplished modernization in a short period of time before and after World War II. After the break in the process of modernization caused by defeat in the war, the economic development of the postwar period has spread this process to the entire society. The system of general mobilization imposed by the military authorities before the war has been adopted into daily life throughout Japanese society, and not only among young people or middle-aged men; rather, from childhood to old age every member of society is driven as though on a battlefield of work. This is true of every aspect of people's lives, whether it be spending money, taking examinations, finding jobs, or working for a living.[1]

Ever since the so-called Nixon Shock of 1971 (when financial exchange was suspended and the Bretton Woods agreement collapsed) and the oil shock of 1973, the Japanese industrial structure has worked for change. These events allowed Japanese industry to make a big ceremony of change. At the same time, the state, in its role as regulating apparatus of the industrial system, also had to adapt.

During the 1980s, the government set out on the road of promoting deregulation. Clearly this is an impossible course under the conventional form of the state that has existed up until now. Consequently, we are heading toward a state that would be unsuitable for an industrial structure focused on the information and service sectors. The Emperor system, which is the basis of the Japanese state, will be a major impediment to making progress in this direction. The constitution of Japan defines the Emperor as "the symbol of the State and of the unity of the people."

There is room for deregulation (multipolarization of national authority) in the industrial fields that have been less related to culture and information. However, the Japanese will experience difficulties if any problems develop in the fields related to culture and information. Insofar as the Emperor system functions within the logic of unity and homogeneity, a state based on that sort of logic does not lend itself to a multipolar regulating apparatus of decentralization.

The dilemma that results involves problems of education, human rights, expression, and ethnicity and gives rise to some uneasiness about what the future holds for informational creativity, which will become increasingly important in Japan. For Japanese nationals living in Japan, whether male or female, it is not enough simply to have official Japanese citizenship. All of them have to accept the Emperor as a symbol that unites them with others. The Japanese national polity submits them not only to the law but also to the cultural and religious feeling that belongs to the Imperial family. Even though people can be united in a legal sense, they cannot in a cultural or religious one.

In order to view the Emperor as a "symbol of the State and of the unity of the people," we must first accept the premise that each and every person is a "child of the Emperor" or that the Japan state is not democratic but dictatorial. Both are impossible. Thus Japan, as it exists today under the Emperor system, in principle, cannot reach the fullest levels of individual freedom made necessary by the new levels of development in culture and information. This explains why at the level of mass media and education, which are directly involved with culture and information, there has been virtually no decentralization and diversity. In comparison to the changes that took place in the mass media and education policies of other advanced industrialized countries during the 1970s, Japan has been radically slow to change. The ultimate conclusion to be derived from all of this will be clear in the decade of the 1990s, when Informational Capitalism[2] will not be the sole possession of the advanced industrialized nations. If the thrust toward Information Capitalism continues and Japan continues to cling to the Emperor system, the prosperity that Japan is currently enjoying will completely dry up by the year 2000.

More important than whether a nation rises or falls is the question of what is the essence of the state. Is the state really just the amount of authority given to individual citizens?

How will the state actually function in a system that leads to the development of Informational Capitalism? If this development inevitably leads to the abolition of the state, then the question is, What has to be changed? All these questions belong to the nature of the state itself.

Asking what is the essential nature of the state is not the same thing as asking what its origin is. Even if we know why the state was born, this does not change the state itself. For example, what purpose is served by the arguments for the origin of the state made by Shu Kishida and Takaaki Yoshimoto, who say that the state was born because communal society dissolved and isolated individuals created the state for their survival? Nothing has been changed by such arguments as that the state was brought into the world through the *kyodo genso* (cooperative illusion). The essence of the state is not the same as the origin of it. Before we can ask what is the essence of a thing, surely we must first ask what is the essence of the origin of it. If the essence of a thing is the same as the origin of it, then we would have to pose the question of the origin of the origin. When we consider the essence of the origin to be the issue, then we realize that our thinking about the origin is historical. Consequently, in asking questions about the essence of a thing, we must deal with nothing less than its entire course of development from beginning to end.

If we see the state as a regulating apparatus of an economic system, or as a machine for the oppression of individuals, or as a "night watchman" sort of state that guarantees a peaceful life for individuals, then Gramsci's argument that the state is defined by "educators" is one aspect of the state that we still have today:

> In reality, the state must be considered as an "educator" to the extent that it tries to create a new type or level of civilization. From the fact that the state has essential in-

fluence over economy, it reorganizes and develops the apparatus of economic production; it innovates the basic structure, one must not conclude that matters of superstructure themselves should be left as they develop spontaneously or germinate by chance and sporadically. The state, also in this field, is an instrument of "rationalization," acceleration, and taylorization.[3]

When Gramsci, in his *Prison Notebooks,* explores this view of the state as an educational apparatus in terms of the superstructure, he knows that the culture industry will soon have greater weight in the economy. Today we cannot make any clear distinction between cultural and economic matters. It is clear that it is hard to distinguish between the production of tangible items and information products. Consequently, we can make an argument regarding the economic system by means of Gramsci's cultural concept of education; it reveals what the issue essentially is.

However, Gramsci's conception of the state as being equivalent to education does not seem to have been developed to its ultimate conclusion. Gramsci sees the essence of the state as the educator and tries to transform the repressive and authoritarian educator to the creative and democratic educator: "The educational and formative task of the state always has as an end the creation of new and higher types of civilization, the adaption of the 'civilization' and the morality of the masses to the necessity of the continuing development of the apparatus of economic production, consequently, to elaborate a new type of humanity even physically."[4] In Gramsci's time, when fascism was rampant, this was a remarkably revolutionary idea, but in today's world in which a sort of diversified network of power is the basis of the state, this way of thinking merely helps to affirm the power of the state.

Of course, even today's advanced state still retains the repressive and authoritarian function of educator, but it is in need of a creative and informationally productive educator. The fact is, however, that although the state has to produce creatively free individuals for the originality of national information production, the state is rarely involved in noninstrumentalized genuinely cultural education. Especially in Japan, it is extremely limited. And if Japan does not strengthen this aspect of the "cultural educator," it is easy to imagine that Japan will come to a deadlock in the future development of a system capable of reaching the level of Informational Capitalism.

That being the case, the problem lies ahead of us. In order to ask about the essential nature of the state, we have to ask, If we have a national state as an 'educator,' where will that lead us in the end? In terms of this, Gramsci's argument about the state places too much emphasis on describing the function of the state. Yet I suppose this is because Gramsci depends on Hegel's view of the state in terms of its finality.

Hegel's argument about the state is too eschatological, and consequently many misunderstandings arise from it. By trying to combine Gramsci's view of the state with Hegel's, however, we would probably avoid misappropriating it for a concrete description of the state. As far as Hegel is concerned, the goal is the Idea (*Idee*) and the "objective spirit" of the state: *the state on the last day of history.* Consequently, Hegel says the following:

> As far as the Idea of the state itself is concerned, it makes no difference what is or was the *historical* origin of the state in general (or rather of any particular state with its rights and determinations)—whether it first arose out of particular conditions, out of fear or trust, out of corporations etc., or how the basis of its rights has been understood and fixed in the consciousness as divine and positive right or contract, habit, etc. In relation to scientific cognition, which is our sole concern here, these are questions of appearance, and consequently a matter [*Sache*] for history.[5]

All will become manifest on the last day of history. Up until that time it functions potentially. The state, according to Hegel, is "the actuality of the ethical Idea, the ethical spirit as substantial will, *manifest* and clear to itself, which thinks and knows itself and implements what it knows in so far as it knows it."[6] Furthermore, Hegel calls the "ultimate self of the will of the state"[7] "the monarch": "the personality the state has actually only as a *person, as the monarch*."[8]

This monarch has a function of "transcendental apperception" (which controls everything from within as if omnipotently from outside) and is the purest form of "I will." This monarch is the ultimate subject in which all sorts of phenomena such as reason, power, energy, monads, and information manifest themselves substantially. Hegel writes, "In a well-ordered monarch, the objective aspect is solely the concern of the law, to which the monarch merely has to add his subjective 'I will.'"[9]

Hegel's monarch exists as an Ideal concept and does not necessarily actually exist. This point sometimes leads to misinterpretations. In order to fully understand Hegel, one must realize the meanings of "transcendental self" which Husserl later explored comprehensively in relation to "life-world" (*Lebenswelt*) and a "living present" (*lebendige Gegewart*). So, when Hegel's monarch actually exists, he will not be limited to the expression of solemn majesty; on some occasions he may very well be like Orwell's Big Brother, or he could be like some sort of artificial intelligent (AI) that gives expression to the state.

Shlomo Avineri has given us a brilliant interpretation of Hegel's monarch that shows that it is not directly related to the Prussian monarchic system. In writing about the state, the first thing Avineri emphasizes is, "It has to be pointed out that on no account can Hegel's theory be so construed as to refer to any existing state; it is the Idea of the state with which Hegel is dealing and any existing state cannot be anything but a mere approximation to the Idea."[10]

As far as Hegel is concerned, the state must be "the hieroglyph of reason": "the rationality which permeates the world of man becomes apparent for the first time in the state"; "only in the sphere of the state does reason become conscious of itself."[11] Since the state is an Idea, real life must be alienated from the Idea or *politicized* toward it. For Hegel, the state has *not yet* actualized itself. The state is not

based on a free contract that individuals or groups could make or cancel; therefore, for Hegel, the abolition of the state would not be a problem. On the contrary,
the state protects the freedom of the individual—"the rational"—and strives to
move in that direction.

That being the case, we can say that Hegel was advocating a constitutional
monarchy, but it is not necessary for us to see if such a constitutional monarchy
ever actually existed in Europe in Hegel's time. As Avineri says, "Since the modern
state is, according to Hegel, based on subjectivity, on self-determination, there
has to be an expression of this subjectivity in the objective institutions of the
state"; a monarch is required to that extent. Avineri goes on to say:

> Herein lies the paradox of Hegel's theory of the monarchy. While keeping the tradi
> tional form of the monarchy, Hegel divests the monarch himself of any real power by
> making the Crown into the symbol of self-determination. Hegel, it seems, thought
> that the only effective way of combating the old absolutist Idea of the monarchy and
> legitimist theories of the Restoration would be to keep the form of the monarchy as a
> symbol for the modern political Idea of subjectivity and self-determination.[12]

This is a trenchant interpretation: Hegel is able to maintain the monarchic system even as he dismantles contemporary monarchy. In the supplement of section
280 of *Elements of the Philosophy of Right,* with regard to cases in which the monarch is "ill-educated or unworthy of holding the highest office," Hegel writes, "In
a fully organized state, it is only a question of the highest instance of formal decision, and what is required in a monarch is someone to say 'yes' and to do 'it'; for
the supreme office should be such that the particular character of its occupant is
of no significance." This is certainly a scathing parody of the actual monarchic
system.

The view of a monarch as "a mere symbol of the unity of the state,"[13] according
to Avineri, "at the time Hegel formulated it, was far from being actualized anywhere in Europe."[14] The interesting thing is that if we interpret Hegel's views of
the state in this way, Japan's Emperor, who is defined as "the symbol of the State
and the unity of the people" in Article 1 of the constitution, is very close to the Hegelian concept of the monarch. This is even in the case of this symbolic Emperor
whose authority has been diminished since the Meiji period to the point where he
is able just "to say 'yes' and to do 'it'" in "matters of state as are provided for in
this constitution" (Article 4). This suggests that the symbolic Emperor system of
Japan is an exiled form of Hegelian modernism. If we see the Hegelian monarch
as something that was created belatedly in order to maintain modernist subjectivity, then the symbolic Emperor is also merely a residue of modernist subjectivity.
But the problem is that while Hegel's monarch was strategically conceptualized in
circumstances in which modernist subjectivity was still relevant, the Japanese version is not. We live in a era, in Heideggerian terms, when "Western Metaphysics is
completed" and electronic technology is rampant, erasing modern subjectivity. In

this situation, the symbolic Emperor is an anachronism that goes against the flow of history.

The various contradictions that are to be found at present in various forms in Japan's symbolic Emperor system result from Hegelianism continuing to live on in exile in Japan. These problems are inherent in the Hegelian concept of the state itself. When a monarch is considered inevitable for the state, the state will fail to separate itself from religion even if, as Hegel thought, "the state is the divine will as present spirit, *unfolding* as the actual shape and *organization of a world*."[15]

In terms of subjectivity, Hegel stood right at the very beginning of the end of the modern period. He considers subjectivity as "transcendental," but he inherited Descartes' *cogito*. It is true that as the first "postmodernist" he went further than Kant and put close limits on the transcendental nature of the *cogito*. However, he, in his radical procedure, dissolved everything physical and objective into the transcendental self and the absolute spirit. In Descartes' *cogito* and Kant's "pure reason," the physical and objective thing is carefully maintained.

This difficulty, however, is not to be found within the narrow confines of Hegel's concept of insight or mental acuity. Philosophical thought is entirely an expression of history. Even if a thinker has wrong ideas, the thinker speaks the language of history. Hegel does nothing more than speak of the end of modern history.

As Husserl confirmed some fifty years later, the transcendental in the history of modern philosophy became so purified that bodily elements and the intersubjective, that is, the "life-world," were forgotten. This forgetting, however, is not a mistake, either for the individual or for the group; it serves as compensation for the development of technology and marks the consequence of modernism. Heidegger called such a basic affair "forgetting of being" (*Seinsvergessenheit*). Therefore, this forgetting is not the sort of thing that, just because it has abandoned the world until now, can now become something we can ignore. Without this, modern history would not have been possible.

Marx's criticism of Hegel is related to the *inconclusiveness* of this forgetting. Marx's insight is that the modern, historical process is, certainly, the generalization of the transcendental. But Marx also had the insight to see that this process of forgetting alone was not the whole of the historical process. This was not merely a theoretical insight; it also applied to things that actually exist.

For Marx, the transcendental belongs not only to the absolute spirit but also to bodily and intersubjective elements. From his perspective, Hegel's description of the essences of modern trends is filled with contradictions. Certainly, in the modern, historical process, the transcendental continues to proliferate, but that which it cannot cover is also proliferating. Even Hegel's description reveals this paradox. We have already seen his argument about the monarch where it does not matter that he might be stupid. It was an idealistic description. And yet, one hundred years later, we find an example of that very thing in Japan's symbolic Emperor. This Emperor, however, is not the realization of the Idea of Hegel's theory of the state; he is really a deformation of the Idea and nothing more than the creature of "one-dimensionalization" (Marcuse) and the "eclipse of reason" (Horkheimer).

The Hegelian Idea is something that will not emerge until the final day of human history. Until that moment, this Idea will function as a technological rationality to one-dimensionalize, abstract, and digitalize our "life-world."

The Japanese constitution has diminished the power of the Emperor, and yet he still has overwhelming authority because, as the second article of the constitution makes clear, "The Imperial Throne shall be dynastic." This dynasty has been passed on and is in the blood and flesh of the Imperial family; it is impossible without physical body. The Emperor system is a premodern system where the physical, bodily aspect becomes very important. In spite of that, this system is idealistic to the extent that the subjectivity of the Emperor is a transcendental symbol. This is a contradiction. In order for the system of a symbolic Emperor to be not a premodern system of rulership, in order for the idealistic aspects of the symbolic Emperor in the first article of the constitution to work, the Emperor must be an android.

In *Critique of Hegel's "Philosophy of Right,"* Marx points out the same contradiction in Hegel's monarch. His monarch has the appearance of being regulated by the essence of reason, and yet in contrast with the essence of reason, Hegel finds the hereditary right of kings and the law of primogeniture to be natural. Marx believes that this in itself is a contradiction. Insofar as we are willing to accept heredity and primogeniture, it is fraudulent to think that either the monarchy or the state is regulated by the essence of reason. Basically, Marx's criticism of Hegel is that the human subject is by no means transcendental and that it is defined by the physical. In short, Hegel partly endorses a kind of "materialism" while he remains in idealism. And this, of course, is contradictory.

From Marx's point of view, the human subject of the Hegelian modern world is not the spirit but landed property. Both the inherited right of kings and the right of primogeniture derive from the permanent possession of landed property and "petrified private property."

When we consider the above arguments in terms of the symbolic Emperor system, we can see that it is a refinement of the Hegelian system of monarchy that is based on "petrified private property." As a result of the new constitution, most of the Emperor's holdings became the possession of the state, and the Imperial family's prewar landholdings were lost. And yet this very fact means both that the Emperor and the state have become more closely connected than before the war and that the function of the Emperor has shifted to exclusively inherit the *diachronic* information of the Japanese people. If this authority and legitimacy over information were lost, then the Emperor could not exist as Emperor.

For Hegel, of course, the right of the monarchy and of the aristocracy to inherit wealth is extremely arbitrary; in the same way, the right to inherit information and the history of a people is also extremely arbitrary. In practical terms, the sovereignty of information resides in each citizen individually. Without a social contract, it would be unjustifiable to put the right to inherit information under the exclusive authority of the Emperor. Furthermore, no matter what sort of contract is established, no one can synthesize and store the memory of each individual citizen in a symbolic subject, to say nothing of a personality.

Hegel's theory of the state requires a monarch because the monarchy guarantees permanence in the form of the dynasty. As modern subjectivity shifts from landed property to ownership of information, it becomes clear that the key issue is not so much what is being inherited but whether it can be inherited permanently. In a dynastic system, the fact that "blood" is so important is due only to the fact that it provides the only way to guarantee permanence. In this sense, if blood or family lines are not necessarily the things that guarantee ownership, then something else has to be established to do that. Permanent ownership of information is not necessarily based on blood or family lines. It might be guaranteed by highly efficient computers. The ownership of information, thus, becomes the central issue today in the theory of the state, and the dilemma of the Japanese Emperor system poses this problem in a radical form.

Today's state still inherits the essence of the Hegelian state. Even without the existence of a monarchy, the essence of the state has not changed. As Gramsci has already said, "The modern prince, the myth-prince cannot be a real person but only an organization. … This organization has been given by the development of history and is the political party."[16] Political parties are "the modern prince." In other words, the modern state has its transcendental subject in the dominant parties that have established continuity. In such a case, this transcendental subject is instructional rather than authoritarian. Gramsci's notion of the state as "educator" is also based on this assumption. Fundamentally, the Hegelian rationality of the state is an "enlightenment of reason."

As Adorno and Horkheimer so trenchantly show in *Dialectic of Enlightenment*, however, the enlightenment of reason clearly led to Nazi propaganda technology and to Auschwitz, and even in Gramsci's notion of the state, where the party becomes the secularized monarch, it still has no real future. Gramsci proposed "the vision that a newspaper (or a group of newspapers) and a magazine (or a group of magazines) are also a 'party' or a 'fraction of party' or a 'function of determinate party.'"[17] The circumstances in which this sort of media or culture functions as a transcendental subject, however, are no longer a surprise in the Japan of the 1990s.

Gramsci, of course, says, "For a party that intends to abolish all class distinctions, the perfection and completion of this intention is that the party's existence comes to an end."[18] Thus, he does not approve of the party becoming permanent as an absolute transcendental subject. Rather, it must continually dismantle itself and continually reshape itself in different forms as "ensembles," to use Félix Guattari's term. This sort of networked party is what Gramsci has in mind. "The party can stop existing by means of its own power."[19] This is the unique feature of the party. Such a party, however, can exist only after the state has ceased to exist.

The abolition of the state certainly cannot proceed in a *digitalized* fashion, that is, through a stage-by-stage discontinuation of a transcendental subject like the party or the monarch. That abolition can emerge only out of a postmodernism that does not hypothesize a transcendental subject. Heidegger once traced the etymology of the word *subject* to the Latin *subjectum* and then to the Greek *hypokeimenon* and found that in premodern times it meant "that which already lies before us," and later meant the consciousness or spirit that defined the world. This historical process is nothing but the process of modernization, where despite the fact that land and money (transferable land) are the basis for property, absolute spirit and reason work as if they are the subject, that which already lies before us. Indeed, the essence of the modern state can be found in the question, Why is there the transcendental rather than nothing?[20]—the question about the tradition in which something that exists each time becomes what is conscious, the transcendental. To the extent that we can not go beyond this tradition, the modern state will certainly not be abolished.

Thus, the various problems regarding the essence of the state are referred to the problem of why ontology becomes metaphysics. Also, as far as the problem of the state is concerned, it is related to the problem of technology that *projects* something that exists toward the transcendental. Electronic technology is different from mechanical technology, which can only put Ideas into virtual form; it is a way of realizing a concept as something tangible and physical (if it is something that has already established a pattern beforehand). The emergence of this sort of technology is peculiar to the situation of the completion = end of metaphysics.

Marx and Engels once said that "'emancipation' is the task of history, not the task of thought." Today's electronic technology, however, simulates theories, and thoughts can instantaneously bring them into reality (virtual reality will eventually not be virtual), and thereby it has been crippling "the task of history." This is not to say, however, that 'emancipation' has become the "task of thought" itself. On the contrary, piling up the various theories that have appeared in history to make a fabricated, comprehensive theory and then trying to put it into "practice" has become obsolete as far as 'emancipation' is concerned. In short, 'emancipation' is now nothing other than the task of history itself. Consequently, what is necessary is to subordinate all Ideas and theories to technology itself and view them as a reflection apparatus on the historical situation that technology brings about.

Today, the state is moving toward becoming an electronically networked state. The electronic technology needed to bring about that sort of state belongs to "the completion of metaphysics." Therefore, because it has reached its finality, this state cannot continue except along a path of "eternal recurrence." For that reason, in the fluctuations of this electronic technology we can get a glimpse of something that goes beyond the state. Will the state remain completely unchanged in form forever? Or will it die out? At this moment we find ourselves at the very brink regarding these questions.

NOTES

This article, translated by Stephen W. Kohl and the author, is revised from Tetsuo Kogawa, "Hegeru-teki Kindai-kokka to Shocho-tennousei" (The Hegelian Modern State and the Symbolic Emperor System) in *Denshi Kokka to Tennousei* (The Electronic State and the Emperor System) (Tokyo: Kawade-shobo Shinsha, 1986).

1. My earlier English articles "Japan as a Manipulated Society," *Telos,* no. 49, Fall 1981, pp. 138–140, and "Beyond Electronic Individualism," *Canadian Journal of Political and Social Theory,* vol. 8, no. 3, 1984, pp. 15–20, will help in understanding these problems. Also, Douglas Lummis and I had a series of critical conversations on them. See: "Japan's National Illusion Machine," *AMPO,* vol. 16, no. 4, 1984, pp. 28 –35; "Japan Takes Leave of 'Asia,'" ibid., vol. 17, no. 1, 1985, pp. 50–55; "The Psychology of 'Travel,'" ibid., vol. 17, no. 2, 1985, pp. 52 –55; "The Political Economy of Marriage," ibid., vol. 17, no. 3, 1985, pp. 48–53; "Japanese Corporatism's Dirty Mind," ibid., vol. 17, no. 4, 1985, pp. 62–66.

2. For more on the concept of Informational Capitalism, see my *Media no Rogoku* (Prison of Media) (Tokyo: Shobunsha, 1982), particularly pp. 177ff., and also *Joho Shihonshugi Hihan* (Critique of Informational Capitalism) (Tokyo: Chikuma-shobo, 1985).

3. Antonio Gramsci, *Quaderni del carcere,* vol. 3 (Torino: Einaudi, 1975), pp. 1,570–1,571.

4. Ibid., pp. 1,565–1,566.

5. G.W.F. Hegel, *Element of the Philosophy of Right,* Trans. H. B. Nisbet (Cambridge/New York/Port Chester/Melbourne/Sydney: Cambridge University Press, 1991), §258, p. 276.

6. Ibid., §257, p. 275.

7. Ibid., §280, p. 321.

8. Ibid., §279, p. 317.

9. Ibid., §280, p. 323.

10. Shlomo Avineri, *Hegel's Theory of the Modern State* (Cambridge, New York, Port Chester, Melbourne, Sydney: Cambridge University Press, 1972), p. 177.

11. Ibid., p. 178.

12. Ibid., p. 187.

13. Ibid., p. 188.

14. Ibid.

15. Hegel, *Element,* §270, p. 292.

16. Gramsci, *Quaderni,* p. 1,558.

17. Ibid., p. 1,939.

18. Ibid., p. 1,732.

19. Ibid., p. 1,735

20. Heidegger's original question is "Warum ist überhaupt Seiendes und nicht Nichts?" (Why is there something rather than nothing?) in *Was ist Metaphysik?* (Frankfurt a.M.: Vittorio Klostermann, 1960), p. 42.

PART FIVE

ALTERNITIES

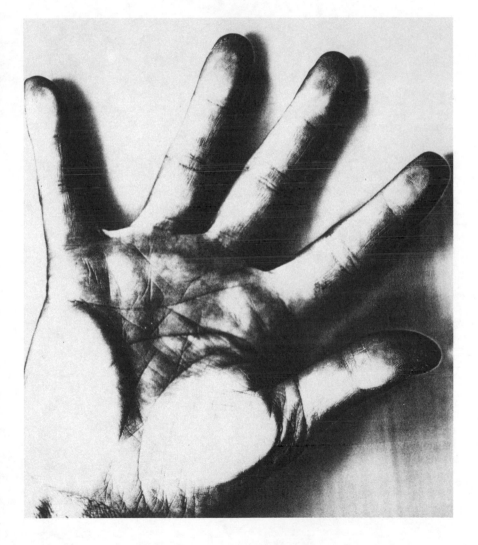

17

Toni Negri's Practical Philosophy

MICHAEL HARDT

TONI NEGRI'S political history reads like a Hollywood movie script: a dazzling roller-coaster ride of spectacular successes and defeats, of subversion, false accusations, intrigue, imprisonment, flight, exile, etc. History can be so much stranger than fiction. Notwithstanding the lure of such drama, understanding the outlines of Negri's history is important for reading his work, principally because it helps us grasp the extent to which his intellectual work is closely tied to the contingencies and immediate needs of practical political movements. Negri is perhaps unique among contemporary political theorists in the depth of his own practical involvement in political militancy and in the effort to recast his theorizing continually to keep step with the innovations and evolutions of social practices.

In the early 1960s Negri became involved in the worker struggles that were flourishing in the factories of northern Italy. The growing wildcat strikes and worker militancy taking place outside of the framework of the Communist party and its unions was the principal inspiration for young scholars such as Negri, a political science professor at the University of Padua, and led to an Italian renaissance of Marxist and Leninist studies that came to be called *Operaismo*, or workerism. This developing practical and theoretical structure provided much of the support for the explosion of militancy that began in 1968. While the revolutionary energies of that year faded somewhat in other countries, such as France, there was a continual rise of worker and student militancy in Italy well into the 1970s. Several new groups formed to the left of the Communist party, outside of the institutional framework of politics, creating a large "extraparliamentary Left." During this period, Negri participated actively in a group called Potere Operaio (Workers' Power) that focused its activity on the large factories in northern Italy, particularly the FIAT plant in Turin. In this politically charged environment, his intellectual and academic work became ever more closely interlaced with the concerns of the organization of workers' movements and the subversion of state authority.

In 1973, there as a "crisis of the movements" that resulted in part from a growing resistance to centralized leadership and to the exclusive focus on factory workers as the political vanguard. Many of the groups formed in 1968 were dissolved. This crisis, however, did not result in a lull in activity, but merely in a reorganization of the movements. The Red Brigades formed to pursue a military strategy with a clandestine and rigidly hierarchical structure. Negri participated in the formation of Autonomia (Autonomy), a network of independent collectives that sought (with a certain success) a nonhierarchical form of organization to link the workers' movements with the other social movements that had recently gained power, particularly the feminist movement. In this context, several different currents of Italian thought began to question and revise traditional Marxist concepts, such as productive labor and working class, redefining and broadening their scope.

The kidnapping and assassination of Aldo Moro by the Red Brigades in 1978 marked a political turning point and was followed by massive government repression of all the groups on the extreme Left in order to regain control of the political situation. Many militants fled the country. Along with thousands of others, Negri was arrested in 1979 under emergency measures that allowed the government to hold suspects without formal charges or a speedy trial. The judges and politicians argued that while there appeared to be several groups on the Left, some of them violent and some peaceful, they were all linked by hidden ties to one large organization: The Red Brigades were merely the tip of the iceberg, the military arm of a vast network of subversion. Furthermore, Negri's accusers claimed that even though he had publicly argued against its terroristic tactics, Toni Negri was secretly the leader of the Red Brigades and the entire clandestine organization. In 1983, when several thousand militants had been held for four years without trial and when a large portion of the public thought the extended detention was unjust, Negri was elected to parliament by the Radical party with the mandate to represent the political prisoners. Despite the anger of many in the government, he was released from prison to pursue his parliamentary duties, but after only a few months the parliament voted to rescind his freedom. Instead of returning to prison, Negri fled to France. The Mitterand government has repeatedly refused extradition requests. In absentia, Negri was condemned to thirty years imprisonment on the basis of his political writings. He continues to live in Paris and recently has begun to teach in the Political Science Department at the University of Paris VIII at Saint-Denis.

What is striking at each turn of events is the extent to which Negri has managed to weave together his practical and theoretical work. However, situating Negri's work historically is not enough: In addition to the historical context we must also recognize Negri's conceptual context. Since his thought evolved in such close connection with the Italian movements and since these movements developed an extended vocabulary all their own, the concepts Negri uses often seem obscure to non-Italian audiences. The most difficult and problematic concept in the following essay is that of "collective entrepreneurship," and I think that we can approach this concept best by situating it in relation to two other concepts common to the Italian tradition: the refusal of work and self-valorization. These two concepts suggest a tendency or a trajectory that can help us place Negri's suggestion of the new function of entrepreneurship.

The "refusal of work," one of the central tenets of Operaismo in the 1960s, functioned not only as an organizing principle but also as a political strategy. This refusal was conceived as the rejection of the *relationship* between capital and the working class, not as the denial of the creative capacity inherent in labor. In other words, in traditional Marxist terms, the refusal of work is intended to negate the capitalist relations of production while if affirms and releases the real productive forces of the working class. This concept, then, can be understood along the lines of the discussion against the "liberation *of* work" and for the "liberation *from* work" that took place in other countries, such as France. On the strategic level, the refusal could take either the form of direct actions against capital, such as organized strikes, slowdowns, riots, direct appropriation, sabotage, and so on, or the form of indirect actions that reject the terms of capitalist relations of production, such as absenteeism, drug use, or mass emigration. In the 1970s, Negri and others developed the concept of "self-valorization," taken from Marx's *Grundrisse*, as a complement to the refusal of work, or rather, as a means of characterizing the affirmation inherent in the refusal. Self-valorization refers to the various economies of value that are created in the realm of nonwork, in the realm not ruled by the capitalist relations of production, by the working class and all the social forces that oppose capital. This concept is meant to characterize the new cultural models of organization that arise independently of the control of capital. The processes of self-valorization, according to Negri, are constructed as a sort of primitive accumulation, not an accumulation of fixed wealth, but of the needs, pleasures, and practices that define the power of the autonomous reproduction of society, separate from the reproductive power of capital.

The power of collective entrepreneurship follows as an extension of self-valorization. In the nineteenth century, Marx saw capital, with its entrepreneurial spirit, as the great orchestrator organizing the cooperation of labor in production. Negri, however, reads the successes of twentieth-century social movements as the gradual appropriation of this organization capacity by the working class. As this new power of the cooperation and innovation of the working class develops and solidifies, the productive function capital once served becomes increasingly obsolete. This new definition Negri gives to entrepreneurship can be seen as a reelaboration of the ideas of self-management in the factory, extending them to cover production across the spectrum of society. In this sense, Negri speaks of entrepreneurship in the context of the "prerequisites of communism" latent in contemporary society. After the negation of capitalist relations of production in the "refusal of work," self-valorization and collective entrepreneurship are conceptual attempts to account for society's capacity to construct a terrain of nonwork, a democratic organization of productive forces outside the domain of capital. These various conceptual propositions should always be brought back to a more concrete project that Negri has pursued through decades of Marxist analysis and revolutionary practice: the project of reading the possibilities of our future immanent to the field of practices in contemporary society.

18

The Physiology of Counter-Power: When Socialism Is Impossible and Communism So Near

TONI NEGRI

Translated by Michael Hardt

Communism as the Minimum Objective

Ever since the *Bernsteindebatte,* both the revolutionary and the reformist traditions have considered socialism as a transitional period between capitalism and
communism (or, in social democratic terms, between capitalism and postcapi-
talism), and therefore they have considered socialism as a concept that is separate
from both the former stage and the latter. That the social democrats later abandoned the terrain of utopia in order to make themselves pure administrators of
capitalist modernization is their business; it becomes our business again, however, when today we find that, through an ideological sleight of hand, the period
that everyone had called socialism is now said to be communism. Responsibility
for this banalization of utopia should certainly go in no small part to the ideologues of Stalinism and the politicians of the "radiant future." That, however,
does not diminish our disrespect for those who today unanimously celebrate the
end of communism, transforming it into an *apologia* of the present state of affairs.

Let us return, then, to our distinction. Neither the Marx of *The Class Struggles
in France, 1848–50* nor the Lenin of *State and Revolution* ever conceived of socialism as a historical epoch. They thought of it, rather, as a brief and powerful state
of transition that would put into motion the abolition of the apparatus of power.
Communism existed already in the transition as its motor, not as an ideal but as
an active and effective subjectivity that confronted the complex of conditions of
capitalist production and reproduction, reappropriating them and, at this point,

229

destroying and going beyond them. Communism was defined as the real movement that destroyed the present state of things—this is the process of liberation. It was only in the 1930s that the Soviet leadership came to consider socialism as a productive activity that could create, at whatever expense, the material bases of a society in step with the rhythm of its own development and that of the capitalist countries. From that moment on, *socialism* did not refer so much to the supersession of the capitalist system and waged labor, but rather it came to mean *a socioeconomic alternative* to capitalism. In socialism, according to this theory, certain elements of capitalism remained: One of these, the state, was subsequently extended in the most extreme authoritarian form; the other element, the market, was suffocated and eliminated even as a microeconomic criterion in the calculation of value. Both the Luxemburgist opposition, which focused on the creative, democratic, antiauthoritarian process of the transition, and the Trotskyist opposition, which extended its critique to the totality of subjugating relationships determined by the world market, were destroyed. Instead, with regard to the first point, they accomplished only the atrophy and then the fatal suffocation of political exchange; with regard to the second point, they strangled socialism within the world market and made it impossible to recuperate the force of the internal lines of development spurred on by the revolutionary and anti-Fascist class struggles that flourished in various countries throughout the world in this epoch. For this reason, many insist—and we ourselves are convinced—that even with the revolutionary spirit of the Gorbachev reforms, the Soviet Union is no longer able to recuperate the hegemonic function over the world class struggle that the October Revolution had given it. Too much time has passed and we have seen many too many tragedies since Red Square has ceased to be the reference point for Communists.

That said, however, *communism* lives. It lives everywhere that exploitation persists. This is the only way to interpret the natural anticapitalism of the masses. Or rather, the more that capitalism reproduces itself, the more it grounds and extends the desire for communism—determining, on one hand, the conditions of collective production, and on the other hand, the irrepressible collective will to reappropriate that production freely. If in today's orgy of anticommunism someone were honestly to believe that exploitation and the will to subversion had disappeared, it would only be proof of an obtuse blindness. Now is the time, then, to begin once again to think of the *Communist transition* as a moment to come—as the classics of Marxism insisted—constructing itself directly within capitalist development. Ever since the 1960s, the critical currents of Western Marxism have worked in this direction, without illusions about Red Square or about a socialism of poverty. Ever since then, communism as the minimum objective has been the only theme of the political science of the transition. An enormous quantity of experiences and knowledge have been accumulated around this point. The method is materialism: Ground the analysis in the present mode of production; reconstruct the contradictions that arise in always new forms between the mode of production, the productive processes, and the productive subjects; critique modernity and its by-products; work toward the recomposition of the collective subjects and their communicative networks; transform knowledge into an effective will. In this way, we find ourselves faced with a series of *prerequisites of communism* that exist in our societies, at a level of maturation that has never been seen before. And if the word "prerequisites" is troubling, making someone suspect that we are comparing reality to some ideal, don't worry. Our only teleology is that which we take from Marx's genealogical method: "Human anatomy contains a key to the anatomy of the ape."

The Irreversibility of the Workers' Gains

What is a prerequisite of communism? It is a collective determination, within the mode of production, on which the results and tendencies of the struggle against work are gathered by those who are exploited in their labor. In the highly developed societies, there are many of these prerequisites, both within the labor processes and within the institutions: If the socialist societies have died from the residues of capitalism, the capitalist societies seem to live only by articulating the elements that anticipate communism. But why should we define this obvious fact as a tendency? Why should we give the name "prerequisites," and furthermore "prerequisites of communism," to these results of the collective struggles that have accumulated within the capitalist mode of production, equally within its juridico-political structure and its socioeconomic structure? Because these determinations seem to be structurally defined by *three attributes:* the collective element, the element of irreversibility, and that of the dynamic of contradiction and crisis. The tendential nature follows from these three characteristics, just as movement follows from a motor—and there is nothing finalistic in this. We speak of *collective determinations* in the sense that a multitude of workers are linked through continually more strict categories of communication and cooperation (of labor, of interest, of language). We call them *irreversible* insofar as they constitute conditions of social life that have become unavoidable, even in the case of catastrophe. In this way, an element of historical collective aggregation becomes a profound institutional moment; a cluster of contradictory and conflictive collective wills becomes ontology. But even though these determinations are ontologically solid, they remain contradictory. The struggle against exploitation continues to cut across them, just as it produced them. It keeps them open and even goes so far as to propose *potential crises* on the horizon of the entire system.

The *institutions of the Welfare State* provide an elementary example of the functioning of a prerequisite. These institutions are the product of struggles that forced the state, through an institutional compromise, to accept at its heart the representation of organized collective interests, which were sometimes antagonistic. This representation, which was put in the service of a tendentially egalitarian redistribution of social income, always under a more comprehensive pressure of collective interests, has become a solid institutional reality. The irreversibility of these institutional phenomena is further reinforced by the griddings of power relations that ran throughout its beginnings, by the repeated conflicts of interest, and paradoxically, by the inertia of the institutions themselves; in short, irreversibility is an effect of the systematic comprehensiveness of the apparatuses. We have witnessed it in the capitalist countries in these twenty years of neoliberal counterrevolution—and I believe we can also posit it in the crisis of "real socialism." Political science and the study of civil law have had to alter their own *scientific statute* in relation to these phenomena, abandoning traditional formalism and subordinating the analytical procedure to the continual permeability of struggles and institutions; the consequent dynamics of control have been forced onto a terrain on which they privilege the interchangeability and indistinguishability of the social and the political. Science is limited to the intersection between the social mobility of subjects and movements and the institutional ontology of the results that derive from them—the processes of government are grounded on this foundation. Comprehensiveness and rigidity are wedded together; every act of governance risks modifying the entire system of social production and reproduction. And it is precisely this game which continually reopens the crisis and defines sequences of growing contradictions. In effect, the determinate contradiction of collective interests, irreversibly grounded on the institutional level, can only be resolved by collective means.

In the terms of classical economics and of its critics, one could say: In this phase of development of the mode of production, every attempt to maneuver or control the proportion of necessary labor comes back in the reproduction costs of socially consolidated fixed capital. This rigidity, then, is irreversible. Now, this claim is certainly *beyond* Marx's analysis (although perhaps recuperable within his conception of the tendency), but it is even further outside contemporary economic thought, either in its neoliberal or its neo-Keynesian form. In these schools, the mobility of all the factors is presumed, in more or less intensive form, as a condition of government. Our claim, however, translated in terms of the critique of political institutions and thus in terms of the analysis of the Welfare State, means that the government of social reproduction is only possible in terms of the collective management of capital. In fact, the conditions of the existence of capital are no longer only implicitly but explicitly collective. They are no longer, that is, simply linked to the abstraction of collective capital, but they are part of the empirical, historical existence of the collective worker.

The Welfare State and its irreversibility (just like, at first sight, the irreversibility of certain fundamental determinations of "real socialism") do not therefore represent deviations in capitalist development—on the contrary, they constitute real *islands of new social cooperation,* new and intense collective conditions of production, recognized as such on the institutional level itself. From this reality follows the crisis that the *mere continued existence* of the Welfare State permanently provokes in the liberal-democratic state. From this follows the dynamics of rupture which that irreversibility continually breaks open in the present state-form, because the determinations of the Welfare State are both necessary for social consensus and required for economic stability. Are these *active* prerequisites of communism? It would be stupid simply to suppose that they were. But nonetheless they are irreducible prerequisites of a permanent destabilization of the systematic axes of the liberal or socialist management of the state. They are prerequisites of a *passive revolution.*

The Collective in the Organization of Labor

Much more important, though, are the prerequisites of communism that, in the contemporary era, can be identified in the evolution of the organization of labor. In the previous period, Taylorism determined an extraordinary process of abstraction of labor-power. Fordism made available to this abstract subjectivity the mechanisms of the collective negotiation of consumption, posing the bases of the attraction of the state (and its public expenditures) within the productive mechanism. Keynesianism proposed a progressive schema of proportions between socially necessary labor and surplus value, and the Keynesian state accomplished the labor of Sisyphus by continually organizing compromises between antagonistic subjects. Today, in the field of organized labor, these relationships have been overthrown. In effect, in the development of struggles in the 1960s and 1970s, the abstraction of labor went beyond its subjective dimensions and spilled over to the terrain of subversion. The subsequent capitalist reaction had to reduce the *quality of the new subject to an objective quality of the labor process* by means of economic restructuration.

Today we are in the midst of this process of restructuration. In the passage from Taylorism to post-Taylorism, from Fordism to post-Fordism, subjectivity and productive cooperation are encouraged as a condition of the labor process. The Fordist relationship between production and consumption has been internalized in order to optimize the logic of production, the logic of circulation and the realization of the value of the product. Certainly, new mass production requires a total flexibility; likewise, the "self making" of the working class has to be reduced to the immediate element of production and circulation: But in this way industrial efficiency is *subordinated* to the autonomy and the self-activation of the working class. The thousands of varieties of "the Japanese model" and its fortunes throughout the world all reduce in the final analysis to the most explicit recognition of the *immediately* valorizing function of workers' subjectivity—in contrast to the period of the hegemony of Taylorism, when subjectivity was only recognized as antagonistic estrangement. It is quite true that this acceptance of the productive function of the subject within the organization of labor does not go without some preemptory conditions: It is possible from the capitalist point of view, that is, only in terms of an industrial integration and a negation of the traditional workers' statute, in its syndicalist and class form. But only those with an incurable fetish for the past (insofar as the past can be seen as glorious) can deny the determinant *positive modification* that is brought about by the transformation of the workers' statute. Even though it is the fruit of a historic defeat, following the cycle of struggles in the 1960s and 1970s, this new workers' figure shows a high degree of the consolidation of collective subjectivity in the labor process.

Without overlooking the passive aspects, it is possible to move up *from* the antagonism of abstract labor-power *to* the concreteness of a collective labor-power—*not yet* antagonistic *but* subjectively *active.* The threshold of the inertial passivity of the revolutionary process that is demonstrated in the Welfare State is here somewhat attenuated. The working class has maintained, in its daily existence, the values of cooperation—experienced in previous phases—on the terrain of abstract antagonism. Today this cooperating and subjective activity is carried, as if in a *latent state,* within the labor process. The contradiction is acute and it cannot but become more powerful to the extent that the process of restructuration is developed. In general terms, we can conclude that living labor is organized within the enterprise *independently* from capitalist command; it is only afterward, and *formally,* that this cooperation becomes systematized in command. Productive cooperation is posed as *prior to* and independent of the entrepreneurial function. Consequently, capital is not presented in the role of organizing labor-power but rather in that of registering and managing the autonomous self-organization of labor-power. The progressive function of capital has come to an end.

In this case, too, we are well beyond the terms of *classical economics* (and even those of its critics) that retain as productive only the labor incorporated within capital. And it is interesting to note how all the schools of economic thought turn impotently around this unheard-of truth of post-Fordism: Living labor is organized independently of the capitalist organization of labor. And even when this new determination seems to be grasped, such as in the *regulation school,* it lacks the capacity to be developed further, to understand the inversion of the theory of industrial integration in the theory of the developed antagonism. Economic science continues, in its blind objectivism, to wait for some miraculous power to transform living labor "in itself" into the working class "in and for itself"—as if this transformation were a mythical event and not instead what it really is, *a process.* Still it is the intelligence of this process that keeps theory out of the only terrain on which we can explain the permanence of the crisis that began in the early 1970s (parallel, therefore, to the restructuration): the terrain on which the process of the political liberation of labor emerges. It is here, and only here, that all the production of value is accumulated. Consequently, the figure of the entrepreneur disappears into always more external and parasitic activities, and thus it is impossible for the collective capitalist to intervene in the crisis. In the final analysis.

The Social Quality of Productive Subjectivity

Analyzing the third prerequisite of communism we move on to the terrain of subjectivity; we touch on, that is, a higher degree of connection between the passive aspects of the process of transformation of the mode of production and the potentialities that come alive within this process. The processes of the creation of value, as we all know, are no longer centered on factory work. The dictatorship of the factory over society, its position at the crossroads of all processes of the formation of value, and therefore the objective centrality of directly productive (manual, waged) labor are all disappearing. Recognizing these obvious facts does not mean renouncing the theory of labor-value; it means, on the contrary, *reexamining its validity* by means of an analysis that grasps the *radical transformation* in its functioning. Moreover, recognizing these obvious facts does not mean mocking the reality of exploitation, pretending that in a so-called postindustrial society it has been removed from our experience—rather, it means locating the new forms in which exploitation is practiced today and therefore identifying the new configurations of class struggle. It means asking ourselves, first of all, if the transformation deals not so much with the nature of exploitation but with its extension and the quality of the terrain on which it is put into play. Only in this dimension can we witness the eventual modification of the nature of exploitation, almost as a passage from quantity to quality.

The fundamental characteristic of the new mode of production seems to consist in the fact that the principle productive force is *technico-scientific labor* insofar as it is a comprehensive and qualitatively superior form of the *synthesis of social labor*. In other words, living labor is manifest above all as abstract and immaterial labor (with regard to quality), as complex and cooperative labor (with regard to quantity), and as labor that is continually more intellectual and scientific (with regard to form). This is not reducible to simple labor—on the contrary, there is a continually greater convergence in technico-scientific labor of artificial languages, complex articulations of cybernetics and systems theory, new epistemological paradigms, immaterial determinations, and communicative machines. This labor is social because *the general conditions of the vital process* (of production and reproduction) pass under its control and are remodeled in conformity with it. The entire society is invested and recomposed in the process of the production of value by this new configuration of living labor: invested to the point that, within this process, exploitation seems to have disappeared—or better, seems to have been restricted to irremediably backward zones of contemporary society.

This appearance, however, is easily swept away. What happens in reality? In fact, capitalist power dramatically controls the new configurations of living labor, but it can only control them *from the outside* because it is not allowed to invade them in a disciplinary way. Thus the contradiction of exploitation is displaced onto a very high level where the subject that is principally exploited (the technico-scientific subject) is recognized in its creative subjectivity but controlled in the management of the power that it expresses. It is from this very high point of command that the contradiction spills over onto the entire society. And it is therefore with respect to this very high point of command that the entire social horizon of exploitation tends to unify, situating within the antagonist relationship all the elements of self-valorization, at whichever level they arise.

The conflict, then, *is social:* And it is social because technico-scientific living labor is a massified quality of the laboring intelligentsia; it is social because all of the efforts of the refusal of work of all the other exploited social strata tend to be identified with and converge toward technico-scientific labor in an antagonistic way. It is within this flux that new cultural models are constituted in the old workers' subjectivities, where emancipation *through* labor is opposed to the liberation *from* waged and manual labor. Finally, the conflict is social because more and more it is situated on the general linguistic terrain, or rather on the terrain of the *production of subjectivity*. Here there is no room left for capitalist command: The space that capital has won is simply that of the control of language, both scientific and common language. This is *not* an *irrelevant* space. It is guaranteed by the monopoly of legitimate force, and it is continually reorganized, in a ceaseless critical acceleration. And yet, the acceleration determined by capitalist development on the subsumption of the past and present forms of workers' subjectivity, and their reduction within a compact and totalitarian horizon of command, do not succeed. Not only do they fail to recompose the disciplinary determinations of the old class strata, which on the contrary reelaborate antagonistic configurations within the new fabric of class relations, they also fail to stabilize the highest level of the subsumption where the opposition between subjugated language and language produced by living labor can be configured clearly more and more as the opposition between dictatorship and freedom.

On the Communist Transition

On the basis of these conditions, then, what is the transition to communism? It is the critique of the existent state of affairs and the constitution of a new society within the transformations of labor; it is the reinvention of politics within the new dimensions of collectivity—of a liberated collectivity, become subject. And we should keep in mind here that the conditions of the liberation of the collectivity are *the very same* conditions that produce the subject. No longer is there a gap imposed between these two determinations, so that the liberation of the collectivity could hypothetically be produced by an external motor, a mythical vanguard or dictatorship; this hypothesis is in fact the *formal condition* for that concept of socialism that we rejected at the beginning, and its *derivation* consists in the degradation of socialism to an alternative within the capitalist mode of production that we have considered as consequent to this hypothesis.

Now, to come back to the issue of the foundation, there are *three points of view* from which to confront this problem: that of the critique of political economy, that of the juridical and constitutional critique of the liberal-democratic state, and that of the constituent power. From the first point of view, we have already emphasized several essential facts. But a point of view that refers only to the objective prerequisites represents a very rudimentary approach, even if that objectivity reveals a new concept of politics, and therefore a new form of democracy. We need to go deeper into the issue. What does it mean, then, to ground a new politics today? It means above all *positively* grasping the *passive collectivities* or, if you wish, the *latent subjectivities* that are directly implied by the institutions of the Welfare State, by the new configuration of the labor process, or by the recent social hegemony of technico-scientific labor. We have to apprehend the site of an absence, the positivity of a latency, the invisible hand of the collectivity. We have to recognize how on this site, confronting a *destabilization* of the enemy power, the motor of the social *destructuration* of domination is established.

On the basis of this continuous crisis and this profound precarity of the capitalist regime, the point of view of the critique of the juridical and political science of the liberal-democratic state (and therefore the point of view of the transition) becomes more explicit. In effect, the political projection of the collective dimensions of labor encounters the constitutional structures of the liberal-democratic state as its *direct impediment*. The concept of *political representation*, as a function of the mediations of private individualities, is in effect an impediment to the representation of a society that is *not* defined by the presence of individualities *but* by the activity of collectivities. The emancipation of the *citizen as individual* and the constitutional guarantee of private economic freedom (that represents its corresponding element) constitute an impediment to the expression of the already consubstantial relationship between society and the state, between production and the determinations of politics. The rules of the *Rechtsstaat*—or rather, the thousands of subterfuges of the privilege that liberalism has lent to constitutional democracy—are established to forcefully negate the insuppressible emergence of the need for collective management of social production. What can still be meant by the general and abstract Jacobin *supremacy of the law* if not the expression of a fundamental limit, a final instance, a function of systemic dictatorship confronted by the uncontainable gestation of autonomous productive and institutional processes, produced by collective subjectivities? The immense amount of nonsense that provides the support for the material constitution of the liberal-democratic state cannot be obscured by the opportunities that are produced by this same practice of power—by, for example, neocontractualist or neocorporativist instruments. In fact, the *contractual* instruments have to reduce the distance between the processes of social manipulation and political emancipation. The *corporativist* instruments have to attenuate the level of empty generality of representation, submitting it to the mechanisms of collective delegation or of the organization of interests. Neither of these propositions, however, seem to be very substantial. Both merely *suggest* partial elements, even though they are collective, of the process of destroying the separateness of the domain of politics, breaking its *tendency toward universality.* The process of destruction is a tendency, instead, toward the abolition of the autonomy of politics, an extremely radical negation of the pretense of the institutional mediation of social processes and conflicts and of Communist self-organization. There is no way to modify the disciplinary character of constitutionalism if not by smashing its line, if not by radically reducing the foundation of democracy to the organization of collective subjectivities. Many factors—representative mediation; the guarantee of constitutional and administrative justice, predisposed to maintain the mediation within the limits of the *material constitution* of capitalism; the consequent bureaucratic structure, conceived as the generalization of the institutional mediation (in other words, the legislative power and the power of political direction, the separation of powers and their functional interdependence, the administrative and constitutional organization of the state)—suppose a foundation and a distribution of power that *excludes* every production from the base, from the masses, every popular determination of the rules and the movements of the collective reappropriation of power. The dogmas of constitutional democracy are nothing other than authoritarian means to *abstract* from the power of the masses, to *crush* the equality of the citizens, to *separate* the citizen from the producer, and to *monopolize* productive capacity. The instruments of constitutional democracy are nothing other than a machine predisposed toward the production of inequality, the destruction of collectivity, and the eternal guarantee of these processes.

Therefore let us invert the standpoint and assume definitively that today the true *entrepreneurial capacity* (which produces wealth by means of a laboring cooperation that is continually more intense and widespread) is constructed independently, that the collectivity is the elementary form in which the productive force of labor is presented, and that the singularities spontaneously seek their realization in the collectivity. Collective entrepreneurship incorporates the independence of the socially organized collective labor that represents the new nature of productive processes; it assumes the autonomy of productive cooperation as a fundamental lever capable of throwing off every external and empty instance of capitalist command, however cogent it may be. How is it possible, on the basis of these premises, to confront the constitutional problem? How is it possible to link the political issue to this new productive power? There is only one response to this question: Unite the exercise of *collective entrepreneurship* and that of *political representation.* Here we find ourselves on the terrain of *constituent power. Communist democracy* is born as the unification of representation and entrepreneurship, insofar as both participate in the new collective subjectivity—they liberate what is latent and activate what is passively present. This democracy excludes, in the name of entrepreneurship, every privilege, and from this perspective, is absolutely egalitarian. This entrepreneurship excludes as well, in the name of democracy, every finality outside the universal values of a free society. Here, production and its determinations constitute politics in the same way that politics is presented as a condition of productivity. The prerequisites of communism are realized not by modifying but by radically transforming a constitutional structure in which democracy is conceived as a cloak masking inequality and in which entrepreneurship is guaranteed as the destruction of collectivity. The transition to communism, then, is realized in a process of the constitution of collective, producing subjects who create a machine for running a society that is predisposed toward their liberation. The government by which the process of the transition must be realized is a *government of systems from below*—a process, therefore, that is radically democratic. It is the process of a constituent power, of a power, therefore, that (radically accepting every material and immaterial productive tension from below, explaining its rationality and expending all its power) configures everything in a dynamic system that is never closed, never limited as a *constituted power*. It is a power within the networks of production, of self-valorization and of self-organization of all that springs up in society, produced by collective subjectivities. It is a constituent power that has a fundamental rule: to be, each and every day, a collective invention of rationality and freedom.

The Present Dynamics of Struggle
as a Constituent Power

What we have been talking about is *not* a utopia. On the contrary, it represents an outline of the *interpretation* and the *physiology* itself of the widely socialized workers' and proletarian struggles that are unfolding in both the West and the East. If the parties and unions of the old workers' movement decline inexorably, tied to the forms of counter-power that Fordism absorbed in the logic of development and subjugated to capitalist command, and if their renewed desire to adopt antagonistic behaviors seems merely pious and unrealistic—if, therefore, the old workers' movement no longer exists as a radically conflictual element, then we have to discover the *autonomous forms* of Communist democracy that are being set into motion wherever the reality of exploitation is crushed.

In the West, a new cycle of struggles began in 1968. In the mid-1980s, after twenty years of counterrevolution and restructurations (which interpreted the innovative elements that the new cycle expressed, and anticipating its intelligence, controlled it and put it to use for the good of capital), this new cycle of struggles began to express itself autonomously. It is characterized by *two* fundamental traits: The first is democratic, and that is the trait of base organization, the transversal coordination of political and protest actions, the radical expression of equality; the second is Communist, and that is the trait of the conscious expression and collective reappropriation of workers' autonomy as the agents of productive processes. It is not by chance that the unification of these two themes has been expressed principally in the struggles initiated by the new productive mass intelligentsia in the sectors most socially relevant to the restructuration: in the productive service sectors, in the schools, and in the advanced tertiary sectors. It is here that the different functions of the workers' struggle—the destabilization of the adversary and the destructuration of power, protest, and reappropriation, the construction of new languages and new values—have found a common denominator. On this terrain the new figure of capitalist command has been identified, and it has been opposed with original elements of strategic and practical intelligence adequate to advancing the struggles. The old workers' struggles always contained the ambiguity of a *dialectical relationship* with capital and with the regulating norms of the organization of labor: They were struggles *within and against* the mode of production. The autonomy of the class was defined in an unresolved antinomy between the aspiration to power and the understanding of the necessity of development. *Today* this dialectic is broken apart. The struggle is *against and outside* the mode of production. Autonomy is a *premise* and not a goal. Each of these struggles expresses a constituent power that unfolds, as a condition of the struggle itself, *from* an immediate economic interest *to* a project for society. From here follow the transversal characteristics of the cycle of struggles and its procedure, which vacillates between acute moments of conflict and long phases of clandestine extension when there is an *ontological sedimentation* of the organizational results that have been achieved. This process results in: (1) the transformation of the inertial elements of antagonistic behavior into the construction of subjectivity; (2) the production of new cultural models that are often socially important; (3) the definition of new networks of the destructuration of power and the launching of new proposals. No two struggles are the same; no struggles are futile; every struggle starts off from the most advanced levels of the previous struggle. Under the blanket of snow a powerful spring prepares its bloom.

In the East, the cycle of struggles initiated in the beginning of the 1980s demonstrates analogous characteristics. In this case too—much to the dismay of the new mystificatory demiurges of terminology—the struggles and their objectives can be grasped under the category of Communist democracy. In this case too, the most important subjects are those of the technico-scientific and productive mass intelligentsia. Here, in the immediately social and political dimension of the movements, the ontological prerequisite of their activity is found in the indissoluble *exchange* between active revolution and passive revolution; it constructs a process that alternates continually between the dissolution of a crumbling structure of power and the search for a new social tie, between the capacity to maintain the consolidated counter-power in the hands of the autonomous social movements and the revolutionary expression of a new constituent power that would configure a government from the base of the social system. It is not pertinent here to make predictions about this enormous rearticulation of the dynamics of class struggle: Still, unfortunately, phenomenology holds the place of strategy. But not for long, if it is true that the destabilization of the systems and the movements of crisis have become so generalized that a new repressive reaction is difficult to foresee and that consequently a further maturation of the movements is necessary. In the East, in any case, constituent power is the order of the day.

19

Possible Worlds:
An Interview with Donna Haraway

AVERY GORDON

DONNA HARAWAY teaches in the History of Consciousness Program and in Women's Studies at the University of California at Santa Cruz. Her teaching and writing in feminist theory and science studies are addressed to the politics, histories, and cultures of modern science and technology. In general, she is consumed by questions about love, knowledge, and power in what gets to count as nature for differently situated twentieth-century people. In her first book, *Crystals, Fabrics, and Fields: Metaphors of Organicism in 20th Century Developmental Biology* (New Haven: Yale University Press, 1976), she asked how metaphor functions to shape experimental work in developmental biology. In *Primate Visions: Gender, Race, and Nature in the World of Modern Science* (New York: Routledge, 1989), she examines popular scientific practices, such as natural history museums and television nature specials, along with technical lab and field primatology, to explore the tangled intersections of colonialism, decolonization, unequal gender and racial arrangements, cultural resources, and national and institutional forces in generating potent narratives about the meanings and lives of monkeys and apes for contending human constituencies. *Simians, Cyborgs, and Women: The Reinvention of Nature* (London: Free Association Books, 1990, and New York: Routledge, 1991) is a collection of essays that range from contentious feminist readings of Anglo-Nigerian women's fiction in a U.S. women's studies classroom to explorations of popular and official immune system discourse, arguments for situated knowledges in feminist epistemology, and the promise and threat of "cyborg" (a hybrid of "cybernetic" and "organisms") images for progressive political practices. She is currently writing on the promises of monsters, in and out of science fiction and the fictions of science, for feminist cultural studies. This interview took place in Santa Cruz on October 18, 1990.

AVERY GORDON: I'd like to begin by asking you to describe your work in general and to tell us about your book *Simians, Cyborgs, and Women,* and how you see it related to your most recent book, *Primate Visions.* I've heard you are writing a triptych, but this could be just a rumor.

DONNA HARAWAY: We'll see. I'm thinking of it as a diptych because the first two parts are finished, but there is a thread that I continue to be really passionate about in both works. It is a thread that I formulated as a question in *Primate Visions:* What gets to count as nature? Why does that continue to matter to people in the last quarter of the second Christian millennium? It is kind of apocalyptic in a sense that I think I've felt for many years. The stakes of what gets to count as nature continue to intrigue me, particularly given the recent understanding of nature as a profoundly constructed object deeply embedded in the histories of colonialism, inextricably related to class, sex and gender repressions, and the deep ties of nature to racialization. This is the kind of work that Michel Foucault made inescapable for us. "Nature" is like what Gayatri Spivak talks about as those impossible things which we cannot not desire, but which we never possess: the kinds of important objects and formations deep in the culture within which we situate ourselves. And I situate myself as having been profoundly formed within those cultures for which nature is extremely important, socially constructed, and right at the heart of the embodiments of systems of domination and of liberatory projects and imaginations. I think that continues to be true and that the discursive constructions of nature have traveled so that they have become global. Whatever you can say about nature as in some way paradigmatically Western in its original constructions, it has traveled such that nature is a global object in a complicated, uneven, heterogeneous order. My work continues to be about how that happened. What is nature? What kind of discursive object is this? What kind of productions are we talking about? Who's engaged? Whose lives are at stake? And, partly as a story line, partly as an enabling device (partly because I think it is a pretty good enabling device), I've paid attention to the construction of the relationships between human beings and other animals. I've paid a lot of attention to situations in which the salient social partners are particular human beings with other animals, and simultaneously, human beings with their own artifacts, in particular, machines. I've been calling both animals and machines social partners, such that neither of them is "object" to ourselves as "subject." That kind of construction (or fiction) of a dual relationship, a simultaneous relationship facing two directions, has informed my work for a long time. I'm using a whole lot of very general categories in doing this: the category of the human, the category of the machine, the category of the animal. All three of those function as unmarked categories in many discourses. So, throughout the work, I try to pay attention to what goes on between specifically located animals, people, artifacts, and machines, and to the way the language games work.

The book that got published last year, *Primate Visions*, took up one whole aspect of this larger concern and developed it at length. The book that is coming out now, *Simians, Cyborgs, and Women: The Reinvention of Nature*, is a series of essays that I had been publishing while I was writing *Primate Visions*. *Simians, Cyborgs, and Women* has a kind of unity of its own that probably started with "A Manifesto for Cyborgs," which *Socialist Review* asked me to write to address what had happened to socialist feminism in the Reagan era, in the mid-1980s. Like the fact that it had disappeared (laughter) … as a collective practice, disappeared as anything but a concept. Socialist feminism had disappeared as a living social movement in the United States. Although it hardly ever existed as a living social movement in the United States, or frankly all too little, it had been a kind of compelling vision, a kind of consensual hallucination anyway … just a little bit like American Marxism outside of the CPUSA [Communist Party, USA]. That kind of consensual hallucination has motivated a lot of people to imagine possible worlds and to engage in practice. So, I wrote "A Manifesto for Cyborgs" in response to the request by *Socialist Review*. They sent a bunch of us letters and said, "Look, you were all socialist feminists. What happened? What does it mean in the Reagan years?" "A Manifesto for Cyborgs" emerged as a kind of dream-space piece. I set out to do one thing, and over a whole summer a lot else happened. That "a lot else" allowed me to articulate the interlocking of several worlds that had been compelling to me as an historian of biology who had watched the organism as a discursive object emerge and mutate. Over an extended period of time—you can give some key dates in the 1940s and 1950s—the organism mutated into a communication system of a particular kind, subject to stress and certain kinds of malfunctions that had to do with communication systems malfunctions. I was watching key concepts within the theory of natural selection and evolution mutate; watching the sciences of animal behavior; watching cell biology and genetics; watching the "discursive object" mutate into a heavily militarized command-communication-control and information system. For people located in first-world techno-science cultures, these were the strong threads in what got to count as knowledge of nature. To put it crudely, all possible objects of knowledge became Cold War objects of knowledge in a deep way.

Marx tells about technology as dead labor—technologies as kinds of frozen embodiments—and the concept is a very useful one. But, it was not good enough for what we needed to be able to think. Dead labor remains an important concept in terms of, literally, reminding oneself of the deadliness of labor built into the kind of arid, material world of exploitative systems of production. But the concept wasn't lively enough. It didn't get at some of the escape from origins, the ways that artifactual productions (the machines) escaped from the intentions of their makers. Or, escaped the kinds of moves of the critical theorists of the Frankfurt School, who could understand domination but couldn't get at the ways techno-science worlds were *also* not reducible to that. They couldn't get at the liveliness and the possible worlds built into the technology. I've always regarded the *critical* project of critical theory as, at its heart, opening up a possible "elsewhere," providing a sense that built into criticism is some sense of possibility. If that's not true, it's not political. It's quite the opposite: a kind of invitation to cynicism. I felt that it was really crucial for feminism, in particular, and for a broadly "progressive" outlook to come to terms with techno-science in ways we had not—certainly not collectively. There are some very interesting things out there, and we didn't have a shared discourse. "Cyborgs" was my first intervention into the imaginative framework, while taking serious account of issues like the international division of labor and the transnational productions of science-based cultures. Who was inducted into which part of techno-science? I was trying to pay attention, paradigmatically, to women's work in science-based industries, and the race, class, and gender issues embedded in them. But that's not the whole terrain: That was a kind of window into it.

The "Manifesto for Cyborgs" also paid attention to the explosion in the 1970s of women's SF writing. Interesting worlds emerged from one of the most unpromising genres imaginable! Also, I was using SF as a way of walking around the invitation into psychoanalysis for theorizing the same issues. I specifically didn't want to accept the use of psychoanalysis as a privileged theoretical window. I constantly tried to work out other languages that can do some of the same work without being quite so constrained by the dominant psychoanalytic family of stories about subjects and collectives. But, like many other theorists in the same zone of conversations, I too wanted to get at some account of an unconscious; some account of the unexpected, the condensations, the irruptions, the structures of stories that are not under any kind of linear control. So I needed a way to do that and I'm still engaged in trying to do it, in oblique relation to psychoanalytic theory.

Simians, Cyborgs, and Women also includes "Situated Knowledges," which is my first effort to try to take seriously what I now think of as a very old move in European traditions: to the move toward reanimating matter. A lot of what's going on in Green politics, in eco-feminism, as well as in a great deal of other feminist politics, is trying to rethink "the body" for writing and cultural activism by refusing the notion of the world as the dead stage on which Man's projects are directed and performed. I see myself—us—embedded in critical liberatory work that requires a refiguring of our partners. Partly, this is a very old move within European traditions. It is also a move made in many other cultural traditions. In too generalizing a way, I borrowed the metaphors of the coyote and of the world as a kind of moody trickster with whom any relationship is always very problematic. Coyote and trickster stories don't hold still. They are not always very nice stories, and the world is definitely not some sort of humanist projection.

Also in the book is a piece on immune system discourse that picks up the heterogeneity of scientific discourse. Part of my work is committed to the proposition that what's going on in the practices of the natural sciences is not reducible to the kind of straw-person characterizations many of us have made, reducing science to positivism, and so on. There's a great deal of very lively cultural work going on in the knowledge-producing practices of the natural sciences and we would be well-advised, as cultural workers on this larger map, to be in deep conversation with what's going on, to be in an open-eared critical conversation.

I've also got a piece in there on gender because I agreed to do something quite impossible for a German project, to translate a French Marxist dictionary into German. The Germans wanted to include all of the new words that had been left out of the Marxisms that had produced the French dictionary, which was already a multivolume book. All of the new social movements, all of the feminisms, all of the critique of colonial discourse, theories of race and raciality—these had produced new "keywords." There was a huge list of new words, assigned to a long list of leftist scholars around the world. I had five pages to write about the sex-gender system. The keywords were to appear in Spanish, German, French, Russian, English, and Chinese. This was daunting. The U.S. term "gender" barely translates into other Anglophone practices. "Geschlecht" is not "gender." God knows, neither "genre" nor "genero" is "gender." This project erupted into a long discussion about nontranslatability and about the question that is euphemized as "difference." The concept of difference as it has emerged in much feminist theory assumes a Eurocentric starting point, which is nuts! How do we refigure a politics and a discourse of articulationism without the normalizing and, usually implicit, Eurocentric starting points? The word "gender" forces these issues to the surface.

Some writing I just finished a couple of weeks ago, called "Promises of Monsters," tries to look at the politics of "articulationism" and "artifactualism." It is a politics of location problem. How do you work out of a situation or location in such a way as to build articulations or connections which remain power- and history-sensitive? These issues pervade the domains of techno-science, which is a heterogeneous global system, and which is where I've situated myself to do my work. How do we think about articulationist politics? *Simians, Cyborgs, and Women* is basically the sum of that work.

There is also a piece in there on Buchi Emecheta's novels. She's a Nigerian, born in Nigeria of Ibo parentage, who emigrated and ended up in London. As a single mother of several children, she puts herself through school, writes through college, and so forth. She gets a degree on sociology and writes several novels: She's a major public writer. One of her books, *The Joys of Motherhood,* is canonized in the African Writers Series that Chinua Achebe edited. Buchi Emecheta has written a number of novels that are read in different contexts. I was interested in the politics of reading her in women's studies classrooms and the ways that U.S. women's studies students have a tendency to read autobiographically, to read fiction as autobiography, as witnessing. I was interested in how to disrupt this kind of appropriation in a reflexive women's studies reading practice that looks at how Buchi Emecheta is read by three differently positioned critics. The first reading is by a Nigerian feminist building Nigerian women's studies partly by ruling

Emecheta *out* of her canon and using various kinds of heterosexual and heterosexist nationalist language to do it. The second reading is by Barbara Christian. Her use of Buchi Emecheta very interestingly figures a certain kind of community of mothers and daughters that centers lesbians. Third, my own use of Emecheta is to figure certain kinds of international travels, local and global mobilities—refusals of stable location—that I resist labeling with a postmodernist agenda, but which has got to heard with those echoes. What are my stakes in reading that way, after all, as a women's studies teacher in this institution? How do the three of us differently intervene in the various kinds of arguments about women's witnessing to their own experience, and to the construction of the "we," the collective political subject? What are the historical and political stakes for each reading?

AG: I'd like you to elaborate on your deliberate use of science fiction as an alternative to psychoanalysis. I find this a very interesting turn and it is partially connected to another question I have. You talk a lot about traveling and the relationship between global and local contexts. And indeed your work travels—between and within Marxism, feminism, and the history of science. Yet it also seems to situate itself in a distinctly American context and political/intellectual tradition. I wonder whether you would articulate the political project, if there is one, of insisting on America as the home base, so to speak.

DH: I don't know how seriously to take an obviously provocative statement! And this is not about science fiction actually, but SF.

AG: I have to interrupt you. It is not as provocative as the statement you made last year to the Harvard History of Science Department, where you introduced your presentation by telling them that you viewed the history of science as a subfield of feminist theory. I found that a provocative statement!

DH: I take *that* totally seriously, especially saying it in the Harvard History of Science Department. It was, of course, very deliberate.

AG: Well, we liked it!

DH: Good. I'm glad you liked it because I feel very strongly about that one. I'm clear about that! I'm less clear-headed about SF as an alternative to or in tension with the very rich, multilayered languages of psychoanalysis and related contemporary theory. And so I say it as a serious joke, wondering how far one could go with it. The serious joke has a structure to it. I use the sign "SF," rather than the words "science fiction" or "sf," because I think of SF as much more than science fiction. I think of science fiction as only one of SF's genre conventions. And SF exploded into a profusion of genre conventions and modes of cultural production that have escaped "genre" over the last twenty years. I am interested in the various kinds of speculative fabulation, science fantasy, speculative feminism, and the particular way that all of these moves—which are about possible worlds—seem to me to step away from the nineteenth-century conception of the imagination—and some of the workings of Freudian discourse up to and including Lacan. Imagination (and its mutant, the imaginary) is not the point: Possibility is. And that maybe is what I see as a U.S. twentieth-century preoccupation. We live in peculiar times. On the one hand, everything seems possible; on the other, nothing does. The utter freezing of the possibility of social change: What are the possible worlds of social change as you watch Bush and crowd? How do we seriously envision social change from North America, particularly from the United States, under the circumstances of such impoverishment of oppositional movements. I think of SF as one tiny little blip—more than a blip—but certainly no solution. SF can be a kind of work that is about possibility, that works at the level of language in much the same way as, or, in a way that is friendly to some psychoanalytic theory. Psychoanalysis gets at certain kinds of linguistic moves really nicely. I think of SF as language practices; language practices that are about cracking open to get at possibility, to get at an unconscious that doesn't relate to the nineteenth-century notion of imagination, to which historically psychoanalysis is deeply related.

SF has been a practice within "unmarked" feminist writing that intrigues me. But, it has not been nearly as much a practice in explicit antiracist writing, or in intercultural, multicultural writings. SF has not, on the whole, been a major writing practice here, although there are compelling exceptions. I think of Jewelle Gomez's work on vampires, of Samuel Delany's rich corpus, Octavia Butler's hybrid worlds, and of the "almost SF" practice (but it isn't) of parts of Toni Cade Bambara's *The Salt Eaters*. Why is it that a Joanna Russ would find SF so serviceable for an interrogation of certain kinds of involvement of gender and multiple identity for "the 4 J's" in *The Female Man,* but Gloria Anzaldúa refigures the multiplicitous character of the *mestiza* with very different resources? Anzaldúa's writing is about an opening up of a sense of possibility, of unexpected alliances, but it works very differently from SF. The project within which I see my own interventions into SF is a project of unexpected alliances: a kind of cracking up of what seemed frozen in the way the sentences in SF work literally. It's odd that in genre conventions that seem so produced to formula, the writing practices can be particularly *not* formulaic, but require that you learn to read for the cracks. Psychoanalysis at its best also teaches those doing cultural analysis to read "differently." The language does something else than it did before.

The body of psychoanalytic work is too easily—I know this is reductive, but still true—limited to a certain story cycle, a certain set of cultural groups. It seems to normalize conversations perversely. For example, we had a meeting here last week, a seminar by bell hooks which included an interesting discussion around psychoanalysis and revolution. One person made an intervention reminding people about Lévi-Strauss's translation of Shamanistic curing as a psychoanalytic, therapeutic intervention. Other parties to the conversation said, "But look, that's a power-charged, directional translation of Shamanistic practice. It normalizes the relationship of a different set of stories and practices to European psychoanalytic practice, and that politics of normalization is not okay." You can show it is an act of translation and that impacts some of the power dimensions, but it is not good enough. You need to develop somehow a practice of in-depth conversation among different families of stories that account for who is in the world and what kind of languages and consciousness are in the world. Psychoanalytic theoretical discourse as political discourse is overdetermined to naturalize the world in terms of European stories. And I often feel that it is too hard to break that normalizing grip. That's a vaguely connected, vaguely coherent response to why I think SF has more interest in practice! Of course, also, SF is inescapably imperialist in the U.S., Japan, the Soviet Union—where does science fiction come from, right?

AG: Or where does it go?

DH: SF is a very culturally specific set of polluted writing practices, and since I like dirty locations, I'm attracted to it.

AG: It also strikes me that science fiction is very much about social movements, about traveling. One needs to really stretch with psychoanalysis.

DH: SF had better be about social worlds because it certainly is not very good in terms of the individual subject!

AG: In talking about SF, you bring us on to the terrain of cultural politics. I wanted to ask you to talk about what you think is at stake for cultural politics in the emerging (at least in the U.S.) field of cultural studies. You might say something about the changes in the journal you are working on.

DH: Cultural studies is now a term that means everything and nothing. But I still think it's useful. It has different histories, and it does talk about certain kinds of interventions. The notion of cultural studies is politically motivated and should be kept that way. I think a lot of people have stakes in keeping cultural studies as a politicized word in and out of the academy. I have been affiliated with a journal that used to be called *Radical Science Journal,* which grew out of the critiques of science and technology by the anti–Vietnam War and related movements. *Radical Science Journal* belonged to the same generation as *Science-for-the-People. Radical Science Journal* was a London-based undertaking, and some very fine scholars and activists in the History of Science were associated with it. It changed its name a few years ago to *Science as Culture* and changed its publishing format. This change was about a political transformation, a transformation of analytical vision, a politicized analytical vision that, on the one hand, took popular culture very seriously. Cultural studies is, in part, about taking popular culture more seriously and not allowing various versions of one-dimensional man to substitute for analysis. Rosa Linda Fregoso, who does film studies, has an interesting take on the word "popular" that I want to borrow for hearing the tones of the cultural studies movement. When she talks about cultural studies, she talks about the popular *not* as, you know, "science for laypeople as opposed to science for physicists. Call one popular, call the other technical." That's not what she means by popular, by *la popular*, in oppositional Chicano/a and Latin American culture. Rather, she is talking about something more similar to what Chela Sandoval means in her use of the notion of oppositional and differential consciousness: variously articulated everyday practices of resistance and productions of other possibilities. In hegemonized situations, there are moments of possibility, forms of resistance, that "the popular" articulates. That is, I think, close to the heart of cultural studies.

And, in that sense, science studies as cultural studies—or science as culture (not quite the same thing, but related)—makes a couple of interventions that I feel part of. On the one hand, "science studies," as that term has emerged in academic, professional sociology, history, philosophy, and anthropology of science, has been evacuated of political meaning. Deliberately, I think. If it wasn't deliberate, then folks are dumber than I think they are! That's not fair. But, there is a way in which what has come to be called science studies—its journals, arguments, and so on—has been eviscerated of possible political meaning. It has been academicized, disciplinized, and turned into strategies to build professional empires. It's really disappointing because so much of the work is very interesting, really important. But, it seems so resistant to politics. For me, cultural studies suggests a way to intervene. A relocating of science studies into cultural studies isn't about the divide between the technical and the lay, the technical and the popular. In that sense, both zones need analysis. But it is a relocation from the professional to the popular in the sense that Rosa Linda Fregoso uses the term. And in that sense, it is not technical and lay, but professional and political. I think of science studies and of cultural studies generally as about attempting to build a politics of articulation. Of course, Laclau and Mouffe are part of this conversation for obvious reasons. But, I want a concept of articulation that refuses some of the relativistic moves in some of Laclau and Mouffe's ways of thinking. I think that feminist and antiracist work, in particular, is getting at a notion of situated knowledges that are not "essentialist" in the way that word is often used. The stakes are otherwise located. It may intersect with that conversation sometimes, but it is not what the whole conversation is about. So, this is a kind of family of issues that I feel associated with when I think of the move from *Radical Science Journal* to *Science as Culture*. In addition, you can't call something *Radical Science Journal* after the kind of Thatcher-Reagan gutting of the language of Marxism, the language of radicalism. I also think we can't *think* it that way anymore. Whether you were in opposition or totally complicitous, Cold War culture provided you with ready-made theoretical issues, really fundamental political issues. We need thoroughly to rethink our political languages. Cultural studies should be part of that project.

AG: Much of your work is about what are incredibly frightening, but also exciting, changes in the sheer nature of social realities. Given the scenario of "Cyborgs," what kinds of new political practices—new ways of doing politics—will emerge out of the new political and social realities confronting the post-1968 social movements?

DH: That's obviously an impossible question. I don't want to make any pronouncements about it. But many promising things *are* happening that give hints for how we might work. For example, look at the work going on in relationship to the tropical rain forest issues and the redwood forest issues, the North and South American rain forests, particularly in the potential for linkage and the ways of refiguring who are the key social actors. I'm thinking of Alexander Cockburn and Suzanna Hecht's new book, *The Fate of the Forest,* and Terence Turner's work with the Kayapó Indians in Brazil around the issues of indigenous peoples in the Americas. There are new collective subjects with whom articulations and alliances can be built in relationship to planetary and local issues. How to do that? What counts as "local" is not determined entirely by geography in the narrow sense. A "situatedness" is to be built: It does not come out of some sort of automatic location on the map. Not everyone can move anywhere freely. You just can't construct yourself into any old thing. Yet, articulations can be world-building.

AG: That kind of mobility is a strategy of capital.

DH: Capital's strategy is precisely to move anywhere it wants, and within its power, it can do just that. An oppositional strategy can't rely on a naive localism: saying simply, for example, that you can't move U.S. jobs offshore. You can get some amazing xenophobic, chauvinist labor politics out of that position. And yet, how do you challenge the capitalist transnational strategy of limitless mobility with savvy situated and mobile articulations? We were talking about rain forest politics as an example. They exemplify the struggles within which modes of promising political work are emerging. I feel some hope in those struggles. But, in general, our lack of coherent analysis of direction in the U.S. is really stunning. I feel some sense of political potential emerging in conservation politics: maps, analyses, practices. I don't feel anything like the same hope in relationship to Persian Gulf issues, which seem paradigmatic of the high-stake politics of the post–Cold War era. Maybe I'm just speaking out of the moment's despair. ... The sense of pervasive irreality is stunning. I think that cultural politics has got to deal with that: We have to face a vast public culture that has no imaginative comprehension of what's going on in the world. What we collectively lack is a kind of comprehensive narrative or a family of narratives. We really don't have a story for what is going on locally or globally. Folks can spin out various stories, but we really don't have shared family histories. We need to learn collectively to inhabit new stories.

How do you move from articulated social conditions and analyses of cultural production to social movements in this world? None of us has a very good idea. What I'm saying is that we're located in a particular field of work, of study, which has political implications. I think cultural studies, at its best, is about learning to contribute to building a critical practice that enhances the possibility of shared survivable worlds.

20

Frankenstein's Dream: Constitutional Revision and Social Design, or How to Build a Body Politic

MICHAEL RYAN

"It's alive! It's alive!" —The Bride of Frankenstein

Preliminary Anecdote

By the middle of the nineteenth century, a monster had been created, and its name was liberalism. It was created to defend the idea that privately held property and individual liberty are the highest ideals of civilization and that the purpose of government and laws is to defend those values and institutions. Earlier ideals of justice—equality in the distribution of property, for example—in thinkers as diverse as Plato, Aquinas, and Winstanley, were thereby placed outside legality. Justice henceforth consisted of legal justice alone, and legal justice consisted of the defense of property.

The first pieces of the monster were put together by a bunch of white guys in western and southern Europe at the beginning of the modern era. With time, more body parts were added, masses of laboring former peasants mostly, as well as slaves from Africa. The wealth they created also created a class of wealthy merchants, but for all their wealth, they constituted a body without a brain, a practice without a theory. Eventually, a brain was found in England, and it was, just as in the movie, the brain of a criminal. He went under many aliases, from Hobbes and Hume, to Locke and Bentham and Mill.

The criminal mind of liberalism supplied a justification for the violence against others upon which liberalism seemed to thrive. It declared that violence rational and established legal systems to make it work more efficiently. Violent responses to liberal violence were enjoined, and they soon ceased altogether as people learned to curtail their desires and to turn them to utility-maximizing uses. They began to act normally and to behave in an orderly fashion. Much good work was obtained from them in this manner, and everything soon was in keeping with the rules of efficiency and the dictates of reason.

But liberalism was still a monster for all that, and if anyone behaved irrationally, which is to say, if they claimed that a different way of doing things was possible or if they argued that it was not right for a few men to own large amounts of social property, they were killed. They could justifiably be killed because liberal law, which was the embodiment of reason, said it was just and right to do so.

If you weren't willing to be a monster, then, you were likely to be in deep hot water. So most people became monstrous. They acceded to the rules of liberalism and behaved as if it was okay to let millions starve while a few lived in luxury. Still, some people complained, and some suggested alternatives. The utopian Socialists came first, offering visions of egalitarian communities, but as it was an era of hard-nosed facts, they were scorned into oblivion. Then, Marxists and Communists argued for state-imposed equality, but that idea didn't work out so well either. Then, communitarians were heard from, as well as some less than thoroughly monstrous liberals. But they didn't sound all that different from the essential monster. And they spoke in graphs, which is always a bad sign.

Then postmodernism came along. And it was more dangerous because it was a virus that got inside the monster himself. It made his bowels ache and turned his guts inside out. It drove him to make flatulent complaints against it in the intellectual journals he controlled, and eventually, it drove him to the bathroom, where he sits still, like Elvis on that fateful night in Memphis, feeling a driving necessity that threatens to tear him apart, but still unable to let go, still unable to save, to pursue the analogy, his body politic.

This essay is dedicated to the death of the monster, as well as to his bride, who got it right when, upon seeing him for the first time, exclaimed: "Aaaakk-kkkkkkkkkkkk!"

Introduction: The Postmodern Alternative to Liberalism

In the postmodern era, grounds are trembling, and the tremors have reached such essential institutions of liberalism as property and personhood. The systems of legal, political, and epistemological authority that hold those institutions in place have begun to lose their legitimacy, and it is possible now to imagine alternative ways of doing things—more egalitarian distributions of property, more relational, less individualistic styles of personhood, more directly democratic political institutions, more therapeutic, less punitive legal systems, and forms of knowledge more alert to the social contexts and the worldly consequences of particular styles of knowing.

The authorities—epistemological, political, legal, economic—that held the modern world in place served as anchors against contingency, the possibility that the institutions of liberalism might prove groundless and revisable. The common term of those authorities was liberal rationalism, the theory according to which our notions of the true and the good derive from the reasoning mind of the rational man. That mind served as an authority because it could transcend the contingencies of historical existence and attain access to a meta-empirical formality. Where the rational man lived, how much property he possessed, what kind of sexuality he practiced, and similar "contingencies" or "externalities" were irrelevant to (his) reason.

All of the grounding authorities, from the epistemological to the economic, that his mind discovered were noteworthy for expelling such contingencies. The ground of cognitive authority was a logic conceived as immune to the disabling effects of its own necessarily historical and nonformal examples. The ground of political authority was a set of formal procedures that did not favor any particular group unfairly, especially those in power. The ground of economic authority was a neutral market that objectively registered the outcomes of free choices on the part of rationally motivated economic agents. The ground of legal authority consisted of principles that applied equally to all, regardless of worldly differences of power and wealth. The principles of reason were true and authoritative so long as they transcended the specificities of the world and remained aloof from the particularities of existence.

Postmodern philosophy has proven such transcendence illusory; it is impossible in the purely formal sense of which liberal philosophy dreamed. For one thing, the rational principles of liberalism always worked in favor of the rational man, the one who benefited most from political sovereignty, economic rationality, legal authority, and epistemological clarity and rigor. These liberal ideals favored two things that the rational man was particularly avid in promoting—his own liberty and his own property—even though the principles of rational universality could just as reasonably be seen as promoting more communal ideals such as a relational sense of responsibility for the care of others or a reciprocal equality of position and power or an equitable distribution of wealth. Disinterested reason always seemed guided by an internal gyroscope oriented toward the attainment of certain very interested social ends whose necessary derivation from the first principles was debatable. The ideal of a reason that transcended the world was betrayed by its own very substantive agenda. The rational man was still a man, for all that.

Postmodernism displaces reason from the realm of formal transcendence and resituates it within the world. Circumstance, contingency, difference, context, relationality, and the like must now be accorded a larger role in shaping our political, economic, and legal values and ideals. The true and the good can no longer be defined in strictly formal terms because the objects governed by rational formality are matters of substance—the concrete issues of daily life and the particularities of need and desire in highly specific, nonformalizable historical contexts.

Economic optimality can no longer be conceived as individual rational choices leading to augmented interests because that picture ignores the relational character of the self, its historicity, constructedness, and inherent sociality. Legal rules cannot promise due process or equal protection when substantive differences of social power mock the formal ideal. Political sovereignty can no longer claim formal neutrality when its representational system allows one race, gender, and class to substitute its interests for those of the multiple others left—proportionally— out of the picture. True and authoritative conceptualizations of society cannot claim allegiance if they allow such contingencies as the howling pain of inequality to be silenced by the violent call to order embedded in formal conceptuality.

The picture of the world assumed by liberal reason has been inverted in the postmodern age. According to that picture, human nature possessed certain internal traits or powers, such as liberty, that found external expression in the legal, political, and economic forms of liberal social life. Those forms embodied or represented an already constituted human nature, and they had no determining effect on its essential being. In the light of postmodernism, that picture is no longer convincing. It is no longer possible to imagine that liberalism merely embodies internal capacities and powers that are not shaped and constructed by the very rules and procedures liberalism has established. Instead, we have come to see that the liberal system of social, economic, political, and legal rules and procedures does not so much embody the human nature assumed by liberalism as it creates it. People are not born to be natural economic predators; the imperatives of survival in a system that permits no other means of survival itself constructs them as such. Nor are people born feeling strong urges to lay claim to an absolute, presocial right to free speech; the reality of political or legal threats to the capacity for speech transforms it into a right to be defended. The identity of the thing inheres in its context and in the relational situation in which it is embedded.

Postmodernism thus abandons the myth of supposedly internal psychological or existential powers and realities ("the individual," "freedom," etc.) and moves instead toward an understanding of the determining role of contextual relations. From this perspective, the legal, political, and economic forms of liberal society can no longer claim legitimacy by referring to a noncontextual interiority or to a presocial nature that they embody—from the predatory and self-interested individual assumed by capitalist economic life to the mythic rational man, exempt from circumstantial differences of income and status, assumed by the liberal legal system. Instead, focus shifts to the role of situation, context, circumstance, cultural representation, and social norms and rules in the creation of such supposedly nonrelational and acontextual realities. "Liberty" is not an internal quality of human existence; it is assigned, subtracted, enlarged, and diminished by already accumulated economic, political, and social powers, by social contexts that include more or less likelihood of being shot by the police, and by external relations to an alternately antagonistic or supportive social environment that shapes one's psychological capacities for the actions named by "liberty." The European-American businessman is far more free than the African-American welfare mother, not because of a difference in internal qualities but because of a difference in context.

This shift in focus entails a different attitude toward the project of social reconstruction. It puts in question those projects of revision that place their faith in either subjective forces or supposedly natural energies, from libidinal desire to labor power, that seem to exist independently of and prior to relational networks or determining contexts. Instead, emphasis shifts to the way contexts, representations, laws, signifying systems, differential relations, and the like create effects that appear to have the independence of subjective forces or supposedly natural energies. "Liberation" becomes as much a matter of reconfiguring all of those things as of releasing people from oppression. A postmodern revision of liberalism would thus concentrate on changing those constructive mechanisms that shape human "nature" and define the contours of human "liberty." In such an undertaking, the mechanisms of economic, legal, political, social, and cultural representation would be conceived not as embodying already constituted human powers but as artificially creating human natures whose depth, breadth, and variety depend on how such mechanisms are designed.

I refer to such an effort as "social design" because it would require adopting an architectural posture toward a social world that under liberalism has located all efforts at reconstructing the basic framework of society in a state whose power must be resisted in the name of individual freedom and private property right. Yet one could argue that the ideal of social design is already embedded in the nonstatist mechanisms of liberalism itself, as a necessary condition of their existence. For example, liberalism considers individual freedom and property right to be natural, true, and good because they are unconstructed, nonartificial, and self-identical. The state, in contrast, is unnatural, false, and evil, an artificial construct that interferes with the quasi-natural process of property acquisition in the market and shatters the identity of self and property that sees property as a direct expression of selfhood. But property and freedom are themselves sustained by state artifice, most obviously by legal rules that construct and protect them, while the state is itself no more and no less under liberalism than a reflexive loop in the "natural" system of property. The artificial design of which the state is accused is already an essential feature of liberalism.

Moreover, the liberal ideal of individual freedom already presupposes social design in several ways. Free action constitutes a structure of behavior that is oriented in a predictable way toward achievable ends. It has design and is "free" only to the degree that it is deliberate. Irrational, uncontrolled, nondeliberate behavior is not free precisely because it is not freely chosen, which is to say, not freely designed. Free action can only occur with the kinds of expectations of control and rationality that guarantee its deliberateness, its orientation toward achievable ends attained through conscious design, and when the context in which it occurs is itself designed, which is to say, when it is structured in such a way as to not render free actions irrational. A designed or structured context allows ends to be achieved and one's own free designs to be rational and predictable. Without such a contextual guarantee, free action might go astray and become altogether unfree and undeliberate.

Liberalism itself, therefore, presupposes a certain social design that rationalizes contexts in such a way that deliberate actions can achieve predictable ends without contextual interference—can, in other words, be free. Although liberalism teaches us to ignore them, we inhabit social designs. We see apparently spontaneous acts of freedom where we should see highly over-designed contexts and environments. An entrepreneur in the desert will find that his individual freedom and creative energy will be of little use, but in a well-financed company with skilled workers and a cutting-edge product, he'll find that the context in which he operates, with its well-established market, educational system, banking network, and protective legal system, will allow him to thrive. To propose the adoption of a posture of social design toward liberal society, then, is not to suggest the appending of something external to a self-sufficient or nondesigned system. It is to suggest a more conscious, deliberate way of going about what is already the case, which is to say, to use liberalism's own vocabulary, to suggest a more "free" way of doing it.

Because the alternative to liberalism already inhabits its system, as the very thing that makes that system possible, an alternative social design need not situate itself outside or in opposition to liberalism. That position usually inverts the premises of liberalism into ideals of state ownership and administered allocation. But the oppositional structure that allowed liberalism to seem the superior term in a debate between reason and free action, on the one hand, and the irrational dream of utopia achievable through state control, on the other, is no longer credible. Statist solutions themselves constitute a false other constructed by liberalism's own pretense to free, nondesigned spontaneity. A different strategy is therefore required.

One possibility is for an alternative social design to locate itself on the margin between the private and the public, the individual and the social, the internal and the contextual—neither entirely statist nor entirely market-driven, neither rooted entirely in the spontaneous actions of individuals nor lodged solely in the state-dictated commands of law. The concept of social design assumes the necessity of artificial mechanisms and legal instruments that build new social contexts and economic relations, but it need not eschew economic interaction that is independent of legal or political determination. Contextual mechanisms can provide new possibilities for human activity, but that activity—the human power to imagine, to work, and to create—would seem to be as essential to a redesigned society that seeks to expand the powers and rights of its participants. The liberal ideal of freedom of action was not in itself repugnant; it was simply wrongly limited to those who already possessed property or economic power. In between the naturalist ideology of the liberal marketplace and the artificial-command ideology of the socialist state, then, one might find the alternative of an undertaking that is both deliberately constructed and seemingly self-moving, consciously designed and "free."

I will in this essay offer an example of one exercise in social design that follows these strategic imperatives. I will sketch out a revision of the U.S. Constitution that takes postmodernism into account by expanding and converting certain crucial premises of liberalism. It will not be assumed, for example, that everyone already is in possession of an internal quality called "liberty" that is best preserved through the nonaction of the state. Rather, the revised constitution aims at the construction of contexts and relations that guarantee that all will have access to the range of behaviors named by "liberty."

In this revision I also convert liberalism's system of formal rights into a system of substantive guarantees. If all have a right to property, all should possess property, with property meaning both the goods of everyday life and the productive assets of society as a whole. I assume that liberalism was mistaken when it claimed that individual freedom precedes property and is its cause; this experiment in constitutional revision suggests that it is possession of property and of the power that goes with it that is the cause and condition of freedom. A certain equality of sustenance is therefore necessary for liberalism's commitment to the ideal of universal freedom to be fulfilled.

Finally, liberalism claimed that liberal society constituted a self-sufficient system that with minimal regulation from artificial state rules could sustain itself. But liberalism was always more rule-bound than it claimed. Certain basic rules, like property right, allowed liberal society to appear to be an unregimented civil society by effacing themselves as rules. My proposed revision follows liberalism's unstated premise by taking for granted the necessity of basic rules or structuring premises in generating an apparently rule-free civil society. In this instance, equity and equality are the basic principles.

I do not pretend that the mere sketching of an alternative constitutional picture will help bring an end to the monstrosities of liberalism—inequality, poverty, homelessness, unemployment, etc.—or bring about a more just alternative. An altogether more difficult labor of creation is required. As part of that endeavor, however, our powers of imagination can at least provide debatable proposals, models, and suggestions that can aid us in formulating desirable alternatives to statism and liberalism. And if this effort seems altogether too artificial, that need not necessarily be seen as a drawback. Liberal capitalism maintains its undemocratic power in part by claiming to embody natural processes that are immune to artificial attempts at reconstruction. To acknowledge the necessary artificiality of our own undertaking is in part to underscore its democratic availability to design and redesign.

Postmodernism licenses us to think that we might live in a world that is of our own making, the product of our best labors together, rather than in a world consisting of a piece of nature staked out for protection by civil law, as liberalism claimed. It is perhaps time to see the virtue of such artifice and to begin fabricating new—in the very best sense of the word—"monsters," ones whose monstrosity inverts liberalism's monstrous normality and helps bring into being new forms of social life.

Rewriting the Constitution

Writing in an era of liberal rationalism, the framers of the U.S. Constitution chose the route of a formalism that left unaddressed the shape and substance of the society they were constituting. State power would be attenuated, and social power would be allowed free rein—unless it abridged the liberal principles of individual liberty and property ownership. The violence of the war of all against all in capitalist society would be tolerated so long as certain legal boundaries were respected. With time, that violence has exacerbated substantive inequality, and the Constitution, shaped as it is by the liberal ideal of a restrained state removed from the field of individual economic liberty particularly, offers no remedy.

In proposing one possible revision of the Constitution, I have kept before me this problem of liberal formalism particularly. Therefore, rather than construct a government that at best responds to and only mildly regulates an autonomous social and economic arena in which the aggressive antagonisms of liberty are permitted to have violent consequences (economic inequality, sexual predation and abuse, etc.), I have instead proposed a constitutional system that includes those social institutions and practices left autonomous in the current Constitution. Thus, for example, economic liberty is preserved, but it is tempered by standards of equity, rules that guarantee ownership and economic participation by all, and stipulations for the distribution of work and rewards that assure that violence to others will not be a normal consequence of economic life.

I begin with a shorthand list of the major "articles." The list is followed by an expanded restatement of each article and a gloss that explains some of the reasoning behind each one.

The New Constitution

Preamble

We the multiple and varied people of America, in order to come together both in commonality and diversity, to create a society both of equality and of difference, where all shall be protected from political, economic, social, and personal harm, and where all shall be assured the means of developing themselves fully, do hereby establish the following principles and institutions for our lives together:

Articles

One. All shall begin life in a state of material equality.

Two. All members of society shall be guaranteed a share in the productive assets of society, and economic production shall be governed by the principles of equity and democracy.

Three. Society shall be devoted to protecting and assuring the well-being of each of its members.

Four. Social relations shall be governed by a principle of respect of person and protection from harm.

Five. Political institutions shall be instruments of the will of the electorate and shall only exercise those powers as are granted expressly by the electorate.

Six. All members of society shall have a right of access to instruments of public expression.

Seven. Society shall use other means than punitive harm to remedy harmful behavior.

Eight. All rights, powers, prohibitions, and rules of procedure enumerated in the current Constitution shall be preserved with the exception of those, such as the right to bear arms, that threaten harm against others or that are superseded or annulled by this document.

Nine. No statement in this document may be interpreted in such a way as to contradict the principles articulated above.

Ten. This document may be revised at any time with the support of 60 percent of the electorate, unless such revision results in harm to a social or political minority.

Preamble Gloss

The federal system of states united under a national government whose powers are limited in regard to those states is unnecessary—hence "America" instead of "the United States of America." A first step in any revision of a political system that permits inequalities of rights and services between states is the abolition of the source of inequality, which is to say, the federal state system itself. The federal state system doubles government and doubles the labor necessary to carry out government functions, and it results in an unequal distribution of basic services while allowing citizens to be victimized by localist prejudices.

ARTICLE ONE. All shall begin life in a state of material equality.

1. To assure this end, all shall be guaranteed an initial basic income, a free education, and an equality of supporting material conditions.

2. To assure that all may begin life with at least the same basic resources, each person shall receive an initial income, beginning when he or she finishes education and starts a career and lasting for ten years or until such time as the person's income from her/his own activities make the subsidy unnecessary, whichever comes first. The size of the subsidy shall not fall below the average income of the self-sustaining members of the society. Those not attaining economic independence over and above the initial subsidy after ten years shall be guaranteed an occupation sufficient to sustain them in a healthy and fulfilled life. To assure that those born into wealthy families do not have an unfair advantage, wealth shall not be inheritable and must revert to society at death.

3. All shall receive the same quality and level of free education, and to that end, all schools shall be provided with equal funding by society. It shall be a primary

duty of society to its members to provide such an education to all that no one shall be prevented for external reasons, such as differences in cultural context or geographic location, from having a fair chance of attaining the same material rewards and achieving the same personal success as others. Because of the importance of education to an equalization of chances of success, a complete education (including professional training) will be considered a right of all members of the society.

4. Society shall guarantee an initial equality of material conditions for all of its members. These shall include reasonable housing, healthy food, pleasing surroundings, means of transportation, free time to pursue cultural activities, access to capital, and the like. Society is obliged to rectify disparities of material conditions that might give one person or group an unfair advantage over others in living their lives. To this end, environments that would negatively affect the chances of success or full personal development of those who live there will be reconstructed.

Gloss

This constitution accords equality as much importance as liberty. The most important equality is of initial position. While results are determined by differences of capacity, starting points can be made at least roughly equal by providing everyone with the same basic material conditions, such as housing and free time, quality of education, and basic income until independence is achieved.

The idea of equal guarantees is often associated with a loss of freedom, but in fact, such guarantees as a basic income for the initial precarious stage of life introduce more freedom into the social system. Guarantees would allow more people to take both personal and economic risks, to discover what they are capable of and what they can create or produce. Now, only the wealthy can afford to treat themselves as a seedbed of possibilities, of potentials that require nurturance in order to grow. With such a subsidy, more people could afford to develop themselves into productive and creative contributors to society. They could be more inventive because they could experiment without fear of losing everything—the downside of freedom untempered by equality. And if they did lose, they would still be guaranteed an occupation and an income. The rules of participation in enterprises (see Article Two) would be such that these compensatory occupations would not be demeaning or menial and would be accompanied by assurances of ownership rights, a power of democratic participation in one's firm, guarantees of respect, and the like. By making it possible through an initial subsidy and a guarantee of access to capital for more people to be economic experimenters, many more enterprises would be created than now is possible, and with that multiplication would come a multiplication of positions that would more than adequately absorb those who would require a guaranteed occupation.

Funds for the equalization of initial positions would come from a wealth reversion procedure whereby wealth at death was rechanneled back into society and not permitted to be inheritable. Only then would all children begin in a state of near equality. Some would still benefit from growing up with wealthier parents, but because of the requirement that material environments be equalized as much as possible, their worlds would not be substantially different from others in regard to education, services, cultural opportunities, and the like. And those children would not inherit wealth and thereby unfairly preserve advantages. Society would constantly readjust to a state of equality. What this means as well is that everyone could reap the benefits of their work and accomplishments, but no one could get a free ride by being given the wealth someone else had accumulated. The justification for the reversion of wealth is that it would constitute repayment to society for the supports and services provided during one's lifetime.

It is important that all begin with the same high quality of education because inequalities in this arena unfairly weigh down the chances of many people. Moreover, differences in the funding of educational systems—either on the beginning level, where such differences can result in serious differences in life chances, or on the more advanced level, where "elite" schools, because of superior funding, can create a sense of privilege for some and exclusion for others that translates into differences of station—are less the result of differences of capacity than they are the mechanisms for creating such differences. Conservative ideals of meritocracy are usually aligned with the current educational imbalances and inequalities for good reason. They assure that people born into different places in society—white well-to-do or black and poor   will remain in those places. The only way to assure that differences of individual capacity will manifest themselves fairly is to make certain that all begin with the same support system, educationally, culturally, and materially. This means leveling the radical differences between educational and cultural contexts. Otherwise, the meritocratic race will be won—as it is won now—by making the guaranteed losers run with leaden shoes.

It is not enough that differences in funding for education be eliminated or that cultural environments be improved by a more equitable distribution of funding. No one studies well on an empty stomach or in a dilapidated environment. It is important as well that everyone have access to the same material advantages, from healthy food and good housing to free time, pleasant surroundings, and the instruments of economic participation. This goal can be accomplished by equalizing material environments so that some can no longer learn and thrive in comfort while others contend with deprivation and blight. Social wealth would be applied to the reconstruction of living conditions, the rehabilitation of housing and cities, the provision of community services such as care centers and libraries, and the creation of the necessary conditions of material security and comfort that allow minds to grow.

In addition, society would make capital funding available to everyone. Private control over investment capital now limits access to economic creation to those in empowered positions. Personal growth is predicated on the availability of economic instruments that permit one to develop one's capacities and interests. By guaranteeing access to such investment funding, for everything from new enterprises to more creative personal endeavors, society would expand the available possibilities of success while assuring a broader range of successful results.

One of the most obvious obscenities of modern American life is the callous misallocation of such basic necessities as housing between the rich and the poor. Many people own several private dwellings as well as thousands of property units that they rent for income. Such secondary ownership (beyond the immediate necessities of shelter) should be limited so that all may have access to the basic necessities of life. Ideally, one would be allowed by law to own only a certain number of dwellings, and one would not be allowed to profit from so basic a need as housing by renting dwellings in one's possession on a full-time basis. All shelter would be primarily for one's own use.

ARTICLE TWO. All members of society shall be guaranteed a share in the productive assets of society and economic production shall be governed by the principles of equity and democracy.

1. All members of society shall receive shares in the society's trust funds. Those funds shall be maintained by taxes, the wealth reversion requirement, payments for retirement, disability, and health insurance, and a rule that 25 percent of the stock in all firms over a certain size (say, fifty participants) must be sold to the trust funds.

2. All participants in an enterprise shall receive an ownership share in that enterprise (not to fall below 25 percent for everyone other than the initiator(s) of the enterprise). This rule shall apply to small as well as large firms. The distribution of ownership rights shall change between small and large companies. While one person may own most of a small company, once a company achieves a certain size determined by number of participants (say, fifty), it must sell 25 percent of its stock to the society's trust funds. Departure from a firm implies the sacrifice of one's ownership share.

3. Ownership rights shall not constitute a claim on more than an equitable share of a company's income, nor shall ownership grant a right of power over others. All decisions as to the well-being of a firm as well as to the distribution of work and rewards must be made by a democratic decision-making process involving all participants in the firm. Economic and professional institutions shall as much as possible be organized in such a way as to equalize power between people, but where unavoidable inequalities of power resulting from inequalities of capacity or role exist, compensation shall be made to those accepting less empowered positions. No one may exercise authority over another without that person's consent, and no institution or organization may presume a permanent and nonconsensual inequality of authority between participants. People may not be allocated positions that place them at a permanent disadvantage in relation to other participants.

4. No profit margin may exceed 10 percent of costs unless this requirement does not guarantee all participants an income sufficient to their well-being. Prices for goods and services shall be allowed to move within a set range determined by whether accumulated prices permit a person earning the sufficient income subsidy to lead a full life. All prices shall be maintained at a level that assures the healthy functioning of enterprises.

5. Economic life shall be regulated by the standard of just interaction. No one may gain at another's expense or exploit another's weakness for personal profit. The survival of firms or the need for profit shall not take precedence over either the principles of respect of person, protection from harm, equality of material circumstances, or the imperative of protecting the natural environment.

Gloss

The purpose of this article is to democratize ownership and economic power by guaranteeing everyone a share in the assets of society. The United States is now a political democracy rather than an economic one. In the supposedly "private" economic realm, power is unrestrained by any kind of popular, democratic governance, and ownership contains the right to shape people's lives and career possibilities by determining what kind of work they do, how much they pay for goods, and the like. Society is thus victimized by private powers that claim to act under the banner of freedom. Moreover, the principles that govern business culture and business organizations themselves are more feudal than modern. People live in hierarchies of authority and command that are linked to highly unequal patterns of distribution of tasks and rewards. The principles that govern the workplace and the business institution must be transformed to make them more in keeping with the general principle of civility that necessarily governs interaction in a society predicated on equality.

Thus, in this economy, property ownership would be universal. Everyone would own shares of society's productive assets by owning shares in the society's trust funds. Those funds would be financed by payments for the various kinds of insurance, by the wealth reversion procedure, and by the purchase of 25 percent of the shares of all large enterprises. The trust funds would thus function in the same way as mutual funds now operate, only their capitalization would be much more substantial, since they would combine the funding that now goes to inheritance, retirement, health insurance, social security, and a sizable share of the productive assets of the economy. They would also, by purchasing shares in all firms of a certain size, guarantee that all enterprises would benefit from investment funding.

Moreover, all participants in an enterprise would be entitled to an ownership share in that enterprise, the sum total of which would not fall below 25 percent. Conjoined with the 25 percent that in large firms would have to be sold to society's trust funds, this means that no person would be allowed to own more than 50 percent of an enterprise. All decisions regarding investment and the like would therefore be made in partnership with all other participants as well as representatives of the social trusts. This deconcentration of ownership would democratize the economy while increasing the psychological investment of all participants. The current system of minoritarian decision making has a demoralizing effect on workers, whose lives are affected by the decisions but who have no right of participation in making them. Their motivation to be creative and productive is diminished. It would be augmented if they themselves owned a share of the world in which they worked and if they genuinely participated in the decisions that shaped that world.

All decisions regarding investment, work allocation, and reward distribution within a firm would be made democratically. The democratic input of all participants would replace relations based on assumptions of authority and of the right to command. In addition, the internal workings of all enterprises and professional organizations would have to conform to the principle of equity. Income would be distributed fairly among participants. Thus, while a larger ownership share by the initiator of an enterprise might result in greater income, it could not lead to an inequitably greater share, nor could it be the basis to a claim to power over other participants. The old hierarchy between managers or owners and workers would give way to a principle of equal participation. In a practical sense, what this means is that tasks would be distributed consensually rather than by coercion. Given the difference between tasks, additional compensations should be given to those accepting more difficult work or work that entails less status. All distributions of work would be democratically revisable, and none could result in the permanent disadvantage of any participant. Participants in an enterprise could not be "let go" without just cause, a vote by the other participants, and a review by an appropriate judicial body.

Finally, interaction between economic entities would need to be governed by a principle of justice. The strong would no longer be allowed to prey on the weak, nor could economic efficiency be offered as a justification for harm done to society or to the environment. Companies could not be "taken over" unless they wished to merge. Scarcity would not be permitted to give rise to inflated prices and exorbitant profits. Economic interaction would be governed by such principles of ethics as reciprocity of responsibility and duty of care for others. To this end, prices should be regulated in relation to costs and an ideal of just profits, and efficiency should be redefined to include a measure of the gain or loss to society and the environment of whatever economic activity is undertaken.

ARTICLE THREE. Society shall be devoted to protecting and assuring the well-being of each of its members.

1. To this end, the protection of potential victims of abuse (children, women, sexual and racial minorities, etc.) shall be a priority of the community.

2. To prevent harm to children, all prospective parents must either prove their capacities for healthy childrearing or undergo training in that regard. Community care centers shall be available for children from birth, and each center shall be

staffed with professional caregivers and counselors to meet the needs both of children and of parents. Potentially abusive parents shall be required to undergo training in nonabusive parenting. All adults diagnosed as being potentially abusive (sexually, psychologically, physically) must also agree to receive therapeutic assistance, and community care centers shall be established to assure that all women in abusive relationships can receive protection.

3. Every member of society is guaranteed access to supportive social relationships conducive to psychological well-being and emotional health. Care shall be provided by society to those unable to establish such relationships.

4. Society is responsible for the physical health of its members and shall guarantee health care to all.

Gloss

Everyone's actions contribute in some way to "society," that is, to the whole community in which she or he lives. It should follow that society owes a debt of provision and of protection, a guarantee of well-being, to all of its members. That guarantee must apply equally to all.

Initial equality is not only a matter of education, housing, assets, income, and other material factors. It is also a quality of experience that can vary depending on what situation one is born into. Depression, fear, and anxiety may characterize one person's inherited emotional situation; anger, aggression, and shame another's; and joy, self-assurance, and spontaneity another's. People's life chances are largely shaped by such experiential differences. The more self-assured proceed more easily on life's course, while the fearful and angry either fare less well or fail altogether. While emotional strength probably cannot be guaranteed, emotional wounding at least can be targeted for prevention. In addition, efforts can be made to assure that all have access to social contexts that are conducive to personal strength, to relations that provide a sense of well-being, and to the emotional resources that enable one to achieve self-fulfillment and success in one's endeavors.

The reconstruction and equalization of material settings would contribute enormously to the amelioration of negative emotional settings. Food, shelter, health, fulfilling employment, security—all would no doubt remove some of the major causes of the emotional wounds inflicted by deprivation and inequality. But emotional health is also a matter of one's relations to others, one's access to care and affection as well as to social stimulation and confirmation. Initially, such things are provided by parents in a family setting, but family settings are too often sites of violence, against women and children particularly. We assume marriage and parenting come naturally, but both are skills as well as matters of disposition, which are shaped by material and emotional contexts. If we were to guarantee that families were not sources of emotional wounding—which impedes personal growth and life success while giving rise to temperaments likely to harm others— we must conceive of marriage and parenting as difficult undertakings requiring either proven capacities or appropriate professional help.

Psychology is inseparable from culture, from the representational setting in which one grows up. Men, in particular, are prone to internalize representations of interpersonal violence and sexual abuse from their cultural environment and to translate them into harmful actions such as physical abuse and rape. Such interpersonal imagery is usually connected to established public patterns of political, economic, and military violence in the larger society, and until such patterns are entirely remade, it will be necessary to address their psychological effects on a more individuated and interpersonally therapeutic basis. To this end, people who are violent or sexually abusive, especially men, should be obliged to accept assistance in remedying their harmful behavior.

Related to this endeavor is the need for society to aid those who cannot establish fulfilling emotional relationships on their own, either within or outside of the family environment. There are many ways to be a victim, and one of them is to be stigmatized and excluded by a society that privileges the survivors who satisfy its norms. Society owes a duty of provision to those who are in need of care, be that physical or emotional. Fulfilling human relationships are as much a social right as shelter. The soul also needs housing. The means of carrying out such a duty could range from guaranteed psychotherapy to the creation of institutions that bring people in need together.

One of the crimes of economic liberalism is the denial of health care to large numbers of people in the name of private profit. Like so many other harmful effects of "freedom," this one could be remedied through guaranteed protection provided by society as part of its responsibility to its members.

ARTICLE FOUR. Social relations shall be governed by a principle of respect of person and protection from harm.

1. It shall be a study of all members of society to treat each other fairly and equitably, and it shall be considered a harm both to the person and to society as a whole for anyone to violate another in word or action.

2. Groups that have been previously discriminated against (ethnic or racial minorities, practitioners of alternative sexual life-styles, women, etc.) shall be guaranteed proportional representation in all areas of social life. All large enterprises must include members of such groups in proportions equal to their membership in the community. No one may exclude or in any way discriminate against members of these groups

Gloss

As principles, respect of person and protection from harm in civil interaction are as important as the rights to expression and association. Rather than rights of action, they are more appropriately understood as rights of protection and probably should come under a broad duty of care that all people owe each other as members of a social system in which one's well-being cannot be dissociated from the actions of others and in which one's own actions cannot be separated from their consequences.

Rights need to be expanded to include the contexts and relations in which they are situated. This expansion involves more than merely noting that a right entails or imposes privileges, duties, obligations, and the like. It also means taking into account the necessary inherence of contextual situation in action and the necessary indissociability of acts from effects.

Rights mythically separate actions from contexts and thus leave intact the situations of potential harm that give rise to the need for rights in the first place. Even as they describe internal qualities of individuals or of actions (freedom of speech, for example), rights point to the contexts that bear harm within them, the situational threats that make rights necessary as responses to them. The right to free speech or to assembly, for example, would not need to be guaranteed if the context that threatened speech and that made protection necessary did not exist. Yet rights themselves do not address these contextual causes. Assuring freedom of speech by assuring that its exercise is protected from harm does not in itself remove or alleviate the context out of which the threat of harm emerges.

To assure the protection of rights, it is necessary, then, to assure that converse principles are in place that call for behavior that does not threaten rights and that seek to eliminate those behaviors that make rights claims necessary at all. To assure the protection from harm and respect of person inherent in a rights claim like the right to freedom of speech, it is necessary to establish as principles the nonharmful attitudes that such a protected action as free speech implicitly requires as part of its context. Now, we in a very limited way attempt to accomplish this end by punishing harmful behavior after the fact of occurrence. A standard of nonharmful interaction conjoined with a principle of respect of person would instead target the psychology that gives rise to such behaviors—well before the fact. While such things can hardly be policed (a $50 fine for an insult?), the very existence of standards could influence behavior away from acts that harmed others or abused their rights.

The discourse of rights conceals the interconnectedness of social agents by making rights seem to be properties of individual persons or separate groups, yet the actions protected by rights are embedded in relationships with other people. No one engages in speech, for example, without the implied desire to be heard. A rightful act invariably occurs in a context of reception in which others are implied. Still, while no right is ever singular, the system of rights only addresses singular claims (to the freedom to speak, not to a guarantee of not being spoken to in a certain way), and the right to speak is thus separated from the relational context in which it is inextricably embedded. Given that certain rights—to racist speech, for example—necessarily result in harm to others to whom that speech is addressed, the discourse of rights must be expanded to include the full relational equation of the actions in question. Such a relational focus would necessitate a different system of rights, one that included a guarantee of protection from harm as well as a duty of respect of person. A relational system that focused on reception as much as action would necessarily take into account the addressee or receiver of such things as racist speech. It would judge a speech act by the harm it causes, and the method of judging harm would necessarily take into account the historical situation and the context of reception for such speech. An act of racist speech against African Americans, for example, when measured historically and contextually, would be seen as evoking a history of harm while being directed against justified sensitivities to injury. In this instance, the principle of protection from harm would outweigh the right of free speech.

In a similar fashion, the principle of nondiscrimination can only be made effective through affirmative guides that direct institutions toward a standard of proportional participation by groups previously discriminated against. Now, such an ideal of representation is made difficult by the enforced scarcity of modern liberal economic life, which distributes resources and rewards in so inegalitarian a fashion that many oppose the ideals of nondiscriminatory fairness because they seem to result in further inequalities. As with so many liberal formalist remedies, this one can only be made truly practicable by so reforming the determining contexts that scarcity is eliminated. Scarcity is the result of a maldistribution that allots excess to some and deficiency to others. Once such maldistribution is remedied, perhaps in the manner suggested above, the formal rules of proportional representation and participation could be realized without giving rise to "reverse" discrimination. In the short term, however, such rules would still be needed, if only because attitudes linger long after their motivating cause has been alleviated.

ARTICLE FIVE. Political institutions shall be instruments of the will of the electorate and shall only exercise those powers as are granted expressly by the electorate.

1. The government shall have three branches—the administrative, the legislative, and the judicial. The sole purpose of the administrative branch shall be to oversee the implementation of this document. It shall manage the society's trust funds. Its membership shall consist of a nonpolitical civil service. The administrative branch is directly answerable to the legislative and shall have no independent powers of its own beyond those necessary to carry out the regulations and rules or implement the principles and standards set forth in this document.

2. The legislature shall research and generate proposed legislation to be placed before the electorate for approval. It shall also oversee the operations of the administrative branch. The legislature shall not constitute a "state" with an existence apart from the full, direct participation of the members of society. All decisions regarding the operations of the society, its laws and procedures, the allocation of its resources on an annual basis and its future direction shall be made by the direct vote of the members of the society. No agent of the government has the power to make any decision pertaining to society without consulting the electorate or without receiving a grant of delegated power from the elec-

torate. The legislature may be granted limited powers for a set period of time to decide matters not requiring the participation of the entire electorate.

3. The elected members of the legislature shall be chosen according to demographic proportions, with each constituency in the community, from men and women to the different ethnic and sexual-preference groups and any other group that constitutes a minimum of 3 percent of the population, electing a number of representatives proportional to their numbers. No one may participate in more than one such group at a time, although all may change groups at any time. Upon petition to an appropriate legislative body, votes by society may be broken down according to constituency affected so that only women vote on women's issues, for example. Such petitions shall only be denied in exceptional circumstances and may not be denied for reasons of electoral efficiency. The legislature will sit for a term of three years, and no one may serve more than two terms. All elected representatives may be recalled and replaced at any time.

4. On a rotating basis, one member of the legislative body shall assume the office of chair for a period not to exceed six months. The rotation shall be across all the constituent groups. The chair shall fill the executive function of the society and shall oversee the operations of the political institutions. Her power shall be limited to assuring that their actions are in keeping with this document. She shall have no other powers.

5. The judiciary will review all conflicts and have the power to make decisions in keeping with the principles set forth in this document as well as with those principles of the legal tradition that are not superseded by this document. Any judicial decision may be rescinded by a majority vote of the electorate. The judicial bodies shall all be elected on a four-year basis. Anyone may run for a judgeship. Judges may sit two consecutive terms in office. Before matters come before the judiciary, they must pass before a board of mediation that shall seek to resolve the conflict. In judging conflicts between the rights of citizens and the powers of government, the judiciary shall assume that the rights of citizens, unless they contradict the principles of this document, are superior.

6. Anyone of any age may become a member of the electorate by declaring themselves members.

7. The society shall not tolerate a standing army and shall respect and promote the principle of universal disarmament.

Gloss

An era that has witnessed the use of such slogans as "executive privilege," "national security," and the like to subvert the will of the electorate and to augment and protect the "implied powers" of public officials is also one that can recognize the need to limit the power of officeholders and of political institutions to direct expressions of the will of the electorate.

The present Constitution places the institutions of political representation first, but in this constitution, such matters would come after substantive rules and principles for the arrangement of society were established in such a manner that all could participate equally and fully in political life. Material and psychological well-being is a precondition of political participation.

The most important new political principle in this constitution is the idea that the state has no autonomy from the electorate and has no powers to act independently of the directly expressed will of the electorate. Wars may not be fought, money may not be spent, programs may not be initiated, and no actions of any kind may be taken without the directly registered consent of the electorate. There would no longer be any implicit powers assumable by those who held office. For the most part, decisions would be made not by a group of "representatives," but by direct voting. The communicational media would permit the direct participation of the population in the regulation of its own affairs without having to adopt a part-for-whole method of representation that excludes many people from access to political decision making. The purpose of the legislature would thus change. It would function to research issues and to present them in such a way as to allow the population at large to judge wisely when directly voting. For this reason, it would be important that the legislature be made up not of representatives of minoritarian economic factions or of ideological interest groups, who are less likely to be able to present issues neutrally, but of as many representatives as possible of the various social groups that made up the entire society. This procedure would help assure that the presentation of issues for popular voting would be shaped by the participation of all those who would vote on the issues and would therefore strike a balance between perspectives.

Political representation as it exists is unrepresentative. Large constituencies (women, ethnic minorities, lower income groups, sexual-preference groups, etc.) go unrepresented in the sense that members of these groups do not sit in the legislature. Under the new constitution, all such groups, as well as any others that constitute at least 3 percent of the population, would be guaranteed a place in the legislature. Those groups would elect their own representatives. In addition, voting on issues before society could also be broken down according to constituency affected, so that women, for example, would be the only ones empowered to vote on issues pertaining to their lives.

The executive is abolished in this constitution. No single individual should have the power to make a society over in his image. This form of democratic dictatorship is inappropriate for a society devoted to the full development, including political development, of all of its members. In place of an executive, a chair would be selected on a rotating basis from the various constituencies represented in the legislature; the chair would oversee the running of government for a short period of time, but her role would be limited to that function.

The judiciary would exist as it does now with the exception of the requirement that all conflicts undergo mediation before coming to the bench or to trial. To correct the tendency of conservative jurists to favor state power over the rights of citizens, a clause is added here to establish as a rule that judges should always favor citizens' rights over the claims of the government, unless those claims legitimately seek to fulfill the principles of this document.

Finally, there would be no standing army, and the society would be devoted to the elimination of violent conflict between nations. Just as economic and political violence is quelled by removing the weapons of state power and the inequality of property, so in regard to war, the remedy is the elimination of weaponry.

ARTICLE SIX. All members of society shall have a right of access to instruments of public expression.

1. In order to further this end, all privately owned media shall be required to set aside a portion of their programming for such access; society shall itself operate its own media access to which is guaranteed to all, and funding shall be made available to make it practically possible for all to become media participants.

2. Socially owned media shall be regulated by independent, elected commissions, which shall allocate the management of such media to any group or individual wishing to engage in broadcasting. The distribution of such programs and channels shall respect the diversity of the population and seek as much as possible to promote such diversity. Operation rights must be renewed every five years.

3. Privately owned media specializing in minority perspectives or in points of view that fall outside the mainstream shall be funded by society.

Gloss

A universal right of access to instruments of public expression is important because inequalities of power are created by the current system of institutionalized speech. The right to speech is meaningless so long as access to the means of distributing such speech is implicitly denied by the powers that now control the means of public expression. Under this system, only sanctioned speech is heard. In order to guarantee the right of speech, it is important to guarantee access to the instruments of expression.

The media constitute a power over minds; it shapes beliefs and attitudes and permits or disallows perspectives. This power should not be left entirely in "private" hands or be allowed to serve as a vehicle for only the views of a closed elite. By assuring a right of participation in the media, society would assure that a full diversity of perspectives would be felt in public discussion. To further this end, private media would be required to set aside some of their programming for public access, and social funding would be used to assure that such access matched the quality of the privately funded programming. In addition, society would itself own and operate media devoted to public access and the ideals of diversity of representation.

ARTICLE SEVEN. Society shall use other means than punitive harm to remedy harmful behavior.

1. In all instances, therapeutic remediation shall first be attempted before a punitive restriction of freedom is imposed. Such therapy shall include whatever changes in the life conditions of the harm-doer are needed to alleviate the needs or the feelings that provoked the act of harm—change of dwelling, supply of satisfactory occupation, provision of monies, satisfaction of physical needs, restoration of community, access to emotional and psychological well-being, creation of a sense of dignity and self-worth, etc.

2. In cases where therapy is ineffective or where reentry into even a reconstructed social environment might result in harm to others, doers of harm may have their freedom restricted to their own dwelling and environs and will be obliged to undergo training in nonharmful social interaction. Restricted harm-doers shall be released whenever they can prove to an appropriate judicial body that they are capable of nonharmful behavior.

3. Society may not criminalize any activity that is not harmful to others.

4. The police function of society shall as much as possible be replaced by a provision and care function. Those police that are necessary shall be governed by a standard of nonviolent intervention in social problems. Force may only be used in situations that threaten life, and such force may only be nonlethal. All police must hold doctoral degrees that include training in nonviolent interaction, social ethics, the principles of this constitution, and law.

Gloss

Nonpunitive remedies must be found for those who break the basic rules of society. This is so because many "criminals" are as much victims as perpetrators. Harmed by the context in which they are condemned to live, they translate the harm done to them into harm done to others. The predatory nature of economic life under liberal capitalism conspires to teach these victims how to act toward their own prey. Rape is an extension of the normality of the male occupation of all positions of power in society and of their demeaning treatment of others. Robbery is simply a violent version of normal business operations. Fraud and the normal business practice of extracting as much as possible for as little as possible are indistinguishable except for the criminalization of the one and the sanctification of the other. Battery is merely a repetition of other batteries that went unpunished because they constituted a normal disciplining of the weak by the strong, the young by the old, the suborned by the privileged.

To punish those who learn violence from the existing system of sanctioned violence is merely to compound the wrong. It assures the legitimacy of institutional violence by punishing those who were given "bad natures" or harmful behavior patterns by the context in which they were unfortunate enough to be born. They thereby learn that the legitimacy or illegitimacy of violence is a matter of power, not right, and that the system of legitimate violence will respond to threats to its power with a further abuse of the dignity and welfare of its victims. The punitive infliction of violence in the penal system is not an appropriate response to this larger problem of violence. Other remediative means are required and available.

For example, the response to crimes based on reasonable needs should be the filling of those needs. The response to crimes based on deprived living conditions or contexts should be the reconstruction of those contexts. The response to crimes that replicate learned patterns of violation should be to provide other patterns for emulation, ones based on the principles of respect, protection from harm, and equality. Anyone found deserving of a restriction of freedom for the purpose of preparation for reentry into society must themselves be treated in accordance with those same principles.

In addition, for too long, society has policed activities that are harmless to others and that should be left to everyone's discretion. Too much social energy is wasted on the attempt—inevitably unsuccessful—to control such moral offenses as prostitution and drug use. Such things are usually symptoms of other deficits in society, deficits that this constitution is designed to address.

Finally, in situations of inequality, the police are now instruments of repressive order. Their violence is as criminal as that against which they are meant to defend. To recast the function of the police, it is necessary first to establish a superior principle of provision and care. Within that framework, the character of the police would change. It would no longer be a punitive force that exercised a violent power. Rather, the police, as disarmed as possible, would work through nonviolent means to maintain the principles of this constitution. Those principles would reshape police purposes and actions, but all police would also be required to undergo training to assure they did not abuse their powers. That training would include ethics and law because a knowledge of the rights and duties of all in a constitutional legal world would work to restrain potentially abusive members of the police. Finally, a rule of nonlethal force should apply to the police; such a rule would be made realistic by the banning of the possession of arms throughout society.

ARTICLE EIGHT. All rights, powers, prohibitions, and rules of procedure enumerated in the current Constitution shall be preserved with the exception of those, such as the right to bear arms, that threaten harm against others or that are superseded or annulled by this document.

1. All existing civil rights—to privacy, expression, religious autonomy, political participation, and the like—shall be preserved. Freedoms of expression, association, and assembly are limited by the following exceptions—so long as the well-being of hitherto discriminated against groups or any other stigmatized group or minority is not abused, so long as the purpose of assembly or association is not to impugn others for religious, ethnic, or other social or nonpolitical causes, and so long as the principles of respect of person and protection from harm are not contravened. Such limitations shall not apply to the criticism or satire of people for actions conducted as part of public life.

2. All existing legal rights—to jury trial, against self-incrimination, to due process and equal protection, etc., as well as any rules and principles of the common law not superseded by this document, shall be preserved.

3. Rights that shall not continue include the right to bear arms, to engage in commerce without consideration for harm done either to others or to the environment, to just compensation for property taken for the purpose of realizing the stipulations of this document, such as those regarding the noninheritability of wealth, the equalization of material conditions, or the mandatory sale of stock to the social trusts, and any other rights not enumerated that contradict or are superseded by the principles and stipulations of this document. No right may be denied without a hearing, to which the law of due process shall apply.

4. All powers of government that are not abolished or superseded by this document, such as the minting of money and the levying of taxes, shall be preserved. All powers that might be construed as discretionary, such as the power to wage war or to ratify treaties, shall be reserved to the electorate.

5. All current prohibitions, such as those against unreasonable searches or bills of attainder, shall be preserved, with the exception of those, such as that against governmental interference with contracts for the sake of assuring fairness, equity, and equality, that are superseded by the principles of this document.

6. All rules of procedure listed in the current Constitution are preserved if they are not abolished or replaced by this document. Where a rule of procedure that would apply to institutions or rules peculiar to this document is absent, it shall be assumed that the decision regarding such procedure shall rest with the electorate.

7. Any new rights created by this document, such as the rights to well-being, respect of person, protection from harm, equality of material conditions, and the like, shall be considered superior to any existing rights with which they may come into conflict.

Gloss

It is important to preserve those rights and rules of the current Constitution that are part of a settled legal culture. The best way to deal with the issue of preservation is simply to assume that anything not superseded by this constitution should be continued or else given limits dictated by the principles of this constitution.

All existing rights, for example, are preserved, with the exception of those that harm others. No society devoted to the well-being of its members can tolerate arms or weapons of violence. The justification for holding arms—the possible need to bear arms against a tyrannical state—is removed through the creation of a fully accountable political structure. Civil and political rights, including the protections of speech and assembly, are qualified by the principles of respect of person and protection from harm.

Not all of the governmental powers and prohibitions described in the first Constitution can carry over, given that some—the right to just compensation for property taken, for example—are superseded by the necessities of the social design put in place by this constitution. Those that are preserved—against unreasonable searches, for example—need if anything to be strengthened against potential conservative counterattacks.

Finally, few of the current rules of procedure—regarding impeachment, for example, or presidential succession—would be necessary in the new constitutional world created by this document. As a safeguard, however, since this document avoids detailing such rules, it should be assumed that if rules of procedure applicable to the new institutions and principles are not listed, they will be determined by the electorate, with the aid of the legislature.

ARTICLE NINE. No statement in this document may be interpreted in such a way as to contradict the principles articulated above.

1. That is, by furthering material inequality, preserving existing power structures, condoning harm to ethnic, gender, or political minorities, promoting hierarchical differences among people, assuring the continuation of invidious forms of status and privilege that demean others, marginalizing or victimizing anyone except those whose current power must be refigured in order for this constitution to be realized, maintaining an unequal distribution of property, contravening the fundamental principle that all shall begin with the same educational, cultural, and socio-environmental advantages, disestablishing the ideals of the democratic limitation of political power, the consensual determination of work and reward distribution, and the mandatory democratization of ownership, or in any other way undermining or limiting the principles of equality, democracy, respect of the personal, equitability of interaction, and other principles propounded above.

Gloss

It is necessary to restrain potential counterinterpretations of this document that undermine or depart from its principles because those principles constitute such a threat to entrenched power. Those deprived of power by its provisions would quite naturally try to find ways to attenuate or neutralize those provisions. Much like Article Nine of the current Bill of Rights, which reserves to the people and the states any rights not described in the Constitution, this default clause is meant to cover any "silences" in this constitution that might be interpreted "flexibly" in a manner counter to its principles.

ARTICLE TEN. This document may be revised at any time with the support of 60 percent of the electorate, unless such revision results in harm to a social or a political minority.

Gloss

All documents of this kind must be revisable, and such revision should be as easy as possible—though not so easy as to allow harm to result to disadvantaged minorities.

The present system of power is held in place by rules that prevent or at least make nearly impossible significant changes in the original Constitution. This system must be modified to allow for the fact that the society the constitution orders has changed and will again change. The one limitation on revision is a clause that protects social and political minorities (i.e., those based on ethnicity, gender, lifestyle preference, ideology, etc.).

Conclusion

At the end of *The Bride of Frankenstein,* the monster, upset that his bride-to-be treats him with repulsion and horror, destroys her, Dr. Frankenstein's laboratory, and himself. He allows Dr. Frankenstein himself to get away, probably less out of a sense of justice than out of a sense of the possibility of sequels. Still, this story might serve as an allegory for liberalism. Whenever it is threatened, it resorts to the same kind of frenzied destruction and violence that its victims engage in when they are driven to the wall by an oppression that has become too heavy-handed. During the Los Angeles riot of 1992, numerous African Americans were murdered by Asian-American merchants whose property was in jeopardy. The action was monstrous, a trading of lives for things that is all too characteristic of a liberal capitalist morality. One could, I suppose, claim that the killers' actions were motivated by fear of not being able to support their families if their shops were burned. Yet that graph of fear merely intersects with the line of anger drawn by the African-American community, for both emotions originate in deprivation, in an absence of provision and security, of guaranteed well-being sufficient for a healthy life not characterized by deadly competition, murderous resentment, and violent prejudice. And the fact that the rent revealed in liberalism's seeming coherence as an ideological and social system by the rebellion will be repaired by wealthy white male businessmen, anxious to restore their own security, only reinforces the sense that the imbalances in place can never be anything but reinforced as such by liberalism. It cannot recognize its monstrous legacy for what it is—the mirror image of its own monstrous normality.

But in Los Angeles, liberalism also demonstrated its capacity to give birth to another, very different kind of being. That new creation threatens liberalism by pointing to a world in which security is so guaranteed that both the sanctioned violence of liberalism and the violent effects it generates come to an end. Not surprisingly, the provisional outline of that creation was drawn most vividly by the victims of the current regime, the dispossessed ethnic minorities. When they directly seized property, they placed their needs above the rules of enforced scarcity and unequal abundance that define liberalism. In their taking could be glimpsed an appetite as much for an entirely other world as for the goods of this one, an appetite whose yearnings cannot be quelled by a return to the violent pacification that is the daily life of the dispossessed in liberal society. Those yearnings designate an irreparable faultline in liberalism's social design, an inability to supply certain needs that must go unmet, certain demands that must go unanswered. The demand spelled out on the streets of Los Angeles was particularly unanswerable because it was for a different principle of distribution altogether. Taking without exchange, fulfilling needs from the available abundance—between the pools of blood, new constitutional principles were chalked on the streets of Los Angeles.

Supply-on-demand—that new being, that other social design, is also the progeny of liberalism—of its flesh but of another body politic altogether. A monster in the eyes of liberalism because it inverts inequality, it is so new that it hardly breathes and its heart scarcely sounds, but rather than despair at its inaudibility, we might instead heed the good Dr. Frankenstein who, upon hearing the first murmurings of his own creation, took heart and exclaimed: "It's alive!"

About the Book and Editors

This remarkable book looks at the physical and metaphorical attributes of the human body as a site of contention, politics, and cultural protest. Essayists from the social sciences and the humanities discuss a range of issues, from torture and moral panics to the "AIDS plague" and the homosocial subtexts of George Bush's political speeches. Sometimes written in shocking and graphic language, these essays embrace the notion that there is a viable place in scholarly writing for anger, sadness, joy, despair, grief, and celebration—an infusion of passion. The tradition of emotional involvement in the issues was lost in late twentieth-century academia but is revisited here through the theories of postmodernism.

Trading upon the theory that good cultural studies can affect politics, the contributors to this book take on current political and social issues of consequence. Pierre Bourdieu, Nancy Armstrong, Stephen Pfohl, Donna Haraway, Toni Negri, George Marcus, and others tackle such subjects as the politics of pharmacology; women, war, and AIDS; ethnicity, national identity, and the Japanese Emperor system; the meaning of property; and the "death and sinister afterlife" of the American family.

These dynamic essays go beyond examination and point to ways in which the societies they identify can be improved, rebuilt, or redirected toward ends other than power, social discipline, inequality, and violence. The intent of the volume is transformative—assuming that politics is culture, the essayists attempt through cultural analysis to offer a means of remaking politics. A compendium of innovative scholarship, *Body Politics* bristles with interesting information and creative energy.

Michael Ryan is professor of English at Northeastern University. **Avery Gordon** is assistant professor of sociology at the University of California–Santa Barbara.

Index